MW01027609

Ivan Panin's
Numerics
in Scripture

*How Mathematics Proves
Holy Scriptures*

by
Mark Vedder
and
Jim Thompson

Copyright 2014
ISBN 978-1-941776-10-0
New England Bible Sales
262 Quaker Road
Sidney, ME 04330

jptbooks@gmail.com
www.NewEnglandBibleSales.com

Index

I
Who Was Ivan Panin?

Ivan Nikolayevitsh Panin was born in Russia, December 12, 1855. As a young man he participated in a movement to educate the under-classes, which movement was labeled 'nihilist' by outsiders (primarily German), though the they merely called themselves revolutionaries. These were the times in Russia when many of the upper classes would leave their luxurious homes to go to the factories and teach the less fortunate, for which efforts they were tortured, often to the point of insanity or death. In short, the newly freed serfs (1856 and 1861) were seen by these 'nihilists' as not actually free, but merely being sold into wage slavery, and one solution settled upon was to educate them. The government, led by the Czar, did not look kindly upon this.

Finding himself exiled at the early age of 18, he emigrated to Germany, where he held citizenship from 1874 to 1877. He always had a voracious appetite for knowledge, especially in literature and linguistics; and had already learned a variety languages. At the age of 22 he emigrated to the United States and entered Harvard University, where he spent four years, incidentally picking up Greek and Hebrew, and graduating with a Master of Literary Criticism.

Having already written *The Revolutionary Movement in Russia* in 1881, he traveled around giving lectures on Russian Literature (especially Pushkin, Gogol, Turgenet, and Tolstoy, authors who had contributed to the social upheaval that forced changes in Russia's during the mid 1800's) which kept his audiences spellbound. These were the days when a five-hour lecture was normal and appreciated. His wit and range of thought were legendary ...as was his firm Agnostic stance. He was the editor of two newspapers and a master of quirky little quips that makes one stop and think, such as:

To be a good root, feeling must be passionate; to be a good fruit, its expression must be dispassionate.

To quote Karl Sabiers, who wrote *Russian Scientist Proves Divine Inspiration of Bible*[1] during Panin's last year,

> "After his college days he became an outstanding lecturer on the subject of literary criticism. He lectured on Carlyle, Emerson, Tolstoy, and on Russian literature, etc, being paid as high as $200.00 for each address. His lectures were delivered in colleges and before exclusive literary clubs in many cities of the United States and Canada. During this time Mr. Panin became well known as a firm agnostic— so well known that when he discarded his agnosticism, and accepted the Christian faith the newspapers carried headlines telling of his conversion."

Then in 1890, his attention was caught by the first chapter of John, in which the article ("the") is used before "God" in one instance, and left out in the next: *...and the Word was with the God, and the Word was God.* His keen literary and mathematical mind was aroused, and he began to examine the text to see if there was an underlying pattern contributing to this peculiarity. Making parallel lists of verses with and without the article, he discovered that there was an entire system of mathematical relationships underlying the text. This lead to his conversion to Christianity, as attested to by his publication in 1891 *The Structure of the Bible: A Proof of the Verbal Inspiration of Scripture.*

Until his death in 1942, Panin labored continuously, discovering complex numerical patterns throughout the Hebrew of the Old Testament and especially the Greek New Testament—often to the detriment of his health. He worked tirelessly and consistently,

---

1 First published 1941, currently available as *Mathematics Proves Holy Scriptures* from New England Bible Sales; see the title page of this publication for contact information.

refusing lucrative career positions so that he might continue his work. The overwhelming conclusion drawn from his studies is simple: Were this done intentionally by man, it would have demanded the collaboration of all writers of the Bible—stretched over many disparate years—in addition to the condition that each of them be a mathematician of the highest order.

Among his writings, there are two great works that he has handed down to us: his *New Testament in the Original Greek* published in 1934, and *The New Testament from the Greek Text as Established by Bible Numerics* published in 1914.[2] The latter is one of the finest English translation available, and has the additional advantage of making available to the reader the 50 years of study by Mr. Panin in which he felt confident that he had the correct reading of all disputed or uncertain variations in the original manuscripts.

It is to be noted that Panin's discoveries are *raw material*. While he searched out and transcribed thousands of seemingly impossible mathematical patterns, he did not, like most of those who take up this subject today, attempt to find mystical meanings or prophecies in them. He simply did his work, and did it thoroughly. His was a true noble mind whose treasures have even yet to be fully searched out.

Published works:
- 1881: The Revolutionary Movement in Russia
- 1889: Lectures on Russian Literature
- 1891: The Structure of the Bible: A Proof of the Verbal Inspiration of Scripture
- 1899: (Letter to the *New York Sun*) Inspiration of the

---

2 This English translation from Panin's discovery of the original Greek Text is available from New England Bible Sales both in the exact form Panin published it in 1914, and in a carefully revised form with contemporary vocabulary (thee/thou changed to you). See the title page for contact information.

Scriptures Scientifically Demonstrated
- 1899: Thoughts
- 1903: Aphorisms
- 1914: The New Testament from the Greek Text as Established by Bible Numerics
- 1918: The Writings of Ivan Panin
- 1923: Bible Chronology[3]
- 1928: Verbal Inspiration of the Bible Scientifically Demonstrated
- 1934: The Shorter Works of Ivan Panin
- 1934: New Testament in the Original Greek
- 1943: Power of the Name
- Bible Numerics
- The Last Twelve Verses of Mark
- A Holy Challenge for Today—On Revision of the New Testament Text
- The Inspiration of the Scriptures Scientifically Demonstrated
- The Inspiration of the Hebrew Scriptures Scientifically Demonstrated

See *The Life and Times of Panin's Labors* by J. S. Bentley, section one on page 119 for more details of Ivan Panin's life.

John Heading of Aberystwyth, Wales was employed at the University College of Wales, having written and edited many mathematical books and commentaries on Chronicles, Daniel, Luke, Acts, 1 & 2 Corinthians, Hebrews, and Revelation. In his commentary on John he writes re chapter 8, "In cases of MS uncertainty, the author is always attracted to the work of Ivan Panin, *The New Testament in the Original Greek. The Text Established by Means of Bible Numerics.* Ivan Panin discovered a numerical pattern that pervades every paragraph, sentence and

---

3   Also available from New England Bible Sales. This is a most excellent and thorough work.

word in the NT. Even if so much as one word is displaced, altered or omitted, the pattern is obliterated. By this means Panin was able to demonstrate the status of every disputed paragraph, phrase and word, caused by variations in the hundreds of Greek MSS. As a result of this all-pervading numerical pattern, Panin concluded that **the passage John 7:53 to 8:11 actually should be present in the NT**, otherwise the whole pattern, evidently the result of divine inspiration, would be destroyed." —quote from What The Bible Teaches: Volume 6 (John) by J. Heading, page 142 hardback, or page 141 paperback, Ritchie Christian Media, Glasgow UK.

II
The Issues

Here we look at the deeper value of Panin's work. While most of us are attracted to the fact that God's word is being thoroughly vindicated, there is another more important issue which bears on all of us from the casual reader to the accomplished scholar.

This issue was the very reason that Panin was motivated to spend the entirety of his life working on Numerics; it is the subject of *manuscript variations.*

Now bear in mind that we are not talking here of translations. There are great debates regarding which English translation of the Bible is best, and those debates are necessary and fine in their place. But when translating one needs a Greek (or Hebrew) text to translate *from*. The phrase used for the establishing what was most likely the original 'autograph' is **critical text**.

There are, at last count, 5,366 different manuscripts of the Bible ranging from nearly complete volumes to scraps the size of your palm. Of the nearly 3,000 from the New Testament, we have 34 complete copies and about 50 nearly complete copies, dating from the 9th to the 15th centuries. Two of the oldest of these 'codices' (meaning a number of books bound together) are the Sinaiticus, purchased by Britain from Russia in 1933 which dates to 340, and the Codex Vaticanus which dates to between 325-350. Also among the oldest is the Codex Alexandrinus which dates from the late 4th century to the early 5th century.

The trouble is that all these copies have slight variations from each other. And in some cases, major differences, such as the entire last section of Mark being left out.

Ironically, it is not the codices, but the fragments that give us the most accurate information. The oldest known fragment is the John Rylands Papyri, discovered in Egypt, which dates from 117-138. It shows John 18:31-33 and would fit in the palm of your hand. But its antiquity shows that John's writings were circulated as far away as Egypt within a mere 30 years of his writing them. The Bodmer Papyri II contains the first fourteen and last seven chapters of John, and dates from before 200. These older fragments allow us to check and recheck the accuracy of the later codices.

Now lest we get ourselves all in a bind over the variations of the texts, let us note that of the 300,000 individual variations, most of them are simply spelling differences or inverted phrases (such as *Jesus Christ* rather than *Christ Jesus*), affecting the meaning of the passage not all. The codices and fragments agree with each other 98% of the time. Simple textual criticism solves most of the remaining differences. Only about 400 words are in doubt, and none of them change the meaning of the scripture one way or the other. **The Bible has been shown to be the most remarkably preserved book of all human literature**.

Yet the 'scholars' love to pick away and dissect God's word. They had Isaiah all divided up into pieces by different authors and supposed they had done a fine job analyzing it properly. Then the Dead Sea Scrolls were found, and there was a copy of Isaiah, word for word exactly as we have it. The book of Enoch, though not part of our Old Testament, has clear teaching regarding the Trinity, so the scholars had relegated it to the first or second century after Christ. Once again, there it was in the Dead Sea Scrolls, which dates it to *at least* 200 B.C.

So we need not be concerned when someone with a chip on their shoulder claims that the Bible has been handed down so many times that we have no idea how it was originally written. We know *exactly* how it was originally written; the evidence is simply overwhelming.

However. . . there are many of us to whom the 400 or so variant readings *are* important. We wish to know *precisely* what each passage says, and know it with confidence. Textual criticism, the study of how to determine which reading is accurate, can only go so far. . . though to be sure, today it has reached a point of refinement that is little short of breathtaking. Tens of thousands of scholars have worked on this issue for centuries, and their efforts have yielded an impressive measure of success.

Enter Panin.

Suppose you were handed two photographs of a wagon wheel: one is the true photograph, and one has been doctored. You are asked which one is the real picture. Suppose further that you counted the spokes on each wheel, and noticed that one photo had an extra—or missing—spoke. It would be obvious to you which one was the doctored picture.

The Bible is made up of words, and it is difficult to tell if a word is missing or added. But the Bible is *also* made up of numbers, and it is patently obvious if a number is missing. If we are counting to ten and leave out the number six, any child could spot the error. Appendix I shows one of the ways that the Greek and Hebrew letters were used for numbers, and that is only the beginning; every kind of numbering in scripture has perfect patterns. The number of syllables, the number of times a name is used (Moses is mentioned 847 time in scripture, which is 121 sevens, or 7×11^2), the number of words in a paragraph. . . in short, *any* way of counting in scripture yields a perfect pattern. Like a well-balanced wagon wheel with the perfect number of spokes.

The question is, What are these patterns, and how do we find them? Where do we start? Before we grab our calculators and attempt to come up with patterns and proofs, the following is good to bear in mind: It has been said that every successful human endeavor is the result of three necessary elements: deep research (understanding), hard work, and endurance. In other words, if you pick up a calculator and a Bible one afternoon and play around with patterns, yes you may find *something*, but you have no idea of its context, value, or application. Panin spent 50 years methodically working out the patterns he discovered, and this without a calculator.

To again quote Karl Sabiers:

> "It was necessary for Mr. Panin to prepare and construct special "tools" before he could begin the actual work of discovering the thousands of numerical facts in the structure of the Bible. He has had to construct concordances, vocabularies and other analyses [sic] of the Bible which require the utmost accuracy to the slightest detail.

> "His specially prepared concordance of the Greek New Testament words consists of a thousand pages and contains every one of the 137,903 occurrences of the New Testament Greek words. The words are arranged in alphabetical order and all the references of the chapters and verses are neatly listed directly under each word. Of course certain words occur hundreds of times throughout the New Testament, yet each occurrence is listed in the concordance. The best Greek concordances in print were not complete enough or accurate enough for Mr. Panin's work, therefore it was necessary for him to construct a concordance of his own.

> "Mr. Panin's specially prepared concordance for the forms of the New Testament Greek words is a manuscript which contains more than 2,000 pages. It is constructed on the same plan as the first concordance, and contains about

twice as much material.

"The construction of these two manuscripts, needless to say, was no small task. More than six years of tedious and continuous labor were required to complete them. But this is not all—Mr. Panin has prepared special books for the vocabulary words of the Greek New Testament. It is strictly a scientific vocabulary. Each New Testament word is listed and there are sixteen columns of numeric data for each word. Four columns containing the order number, place value, numeric value, value, precede each word. Behind each word there are twelve columns containing the number of occurrences, number of forms, syllables, letters, writers, books, diphthongs, etc. The completion of the vocabulary required more than two years of strenuous labor. In some of his work Mr. Panin has marked certain words in green, red, blue, and purple ink. Each color bears some particular significance.

"All this work was merely the preparation of some "tools" which were necessary before Mr. Panin could begin the actual work of discovering countless thousands of numerical facts. Since the work was begun, Mr. Panin has accumulated some 40,000 pages of material on which he has made calculations, worked out mathematical problems, and recorded numerical facts. Upon these pages he has thoughtfully and prayerfully written millions of small and neat appearing figures. His work constitutes volumes and his discoveries are seemingly without end. Throughout the past fifty years Mr. Panin has been earnestly devoting from twelve to eighteen hours daily exploring the vast numerical structure of the Bible. The mental and physical toil involved has been tremendous."

This is what is meant by deep research, hard work, and endurance. The good news is that we do not have to attempt to duplicate his efforts; he has done the work for us. He is like Eleazar, one of David's might men, of whom it says:

> *"And after him, Eleazar the son of Dodo the son of an Ahohite: he was one of the three mighty men with David, when they had defied the Philistines that were there gathered together to battle, and the men of Israel were gone up. He arose and smote the Philistines until his hand was weary, and his hand clave to the sword; and Jehovah wrought a great deliverance that day; and the people returned after him only to spoil."*

In the same way Ivan Panin has carved out an enormous door to the scriptures and defeated the hosts of ignorance who would put down God's word. He has produced a Greek text of which he was fully confident <u>precisely</u> <u>represents</u> <u>the</u> <u>original</u> <u>autographs</u>. This is quite a claim, yet it is backed up by more than 40,000 pages of study over 50 years that has never been refuted. And as time has progressed and scholarship has increased, the universally accepted version of the original has been nudging itself closer and closer to what he transcribed in 1934. His work is constantly being vindicated. . . Today Nestle-Aland's *Novum Testamentum Graece*, Edition 28 (NA28) is the latest in contemporary scholarship regarding a critical text. In Panin's day it was Westcott & Hort's critical text. <u>Appendix V has a complete list of improvements made by Nestle-Aland on Westcott & Hort, and how Panin treated the same passage.</u>

And since this is the onset of the book, it may be helpful to address the main claim of Panin's detractors. In their ignorance, they claim that Panin simply manipulated the text to suit his numerics.

They cannot have read the material, or they would realize what an enormous compliment they are giving him. The numerics he presents are so interwoven, layered and complex, that it would take *centuries* to produce even a small part of them.

In order for him to manipulate the text to produce what he discovered, he would have had to have been a genius of a caliber greater even than Solomon. Look at the material. It simply cannot be done. A person could add a word to a passage with 76 words, to make 77, but that would throw off the number of letters. Which in turn would throw off the numeric value of the passage, which in turn would throw off the forms, number of letters, number of verbs, nouns, place values, order, etc. The scripture is so wonderfully balanced that it is utterly impossible to fake or manipulate the phenomena.

Thus the main complaint of those unfamiliar with his work is actually an enormous compliment.

So here we have the two main issues—there are many others— that are addressed by Bible Numerics. *First is the proof that the Bible is God's word,* and second is the establishing of how *even the minor variations of God's word as we have it today can be simply resolved.* The Lord never promised that he would miraculously keep every one copying the Sacred Text from making a mistake, otherwise we would have no differing copies, and there would be no need of the warning of Revelation 22. Honest attempts to ascertain which manuscripts were most likely accurate copies of the original autographs do not run afoul of Scripture's most solemn warning: "I warn everyone who hears the words of the prophecy of this book: if anyone adds to them God will add to him the plagues described in this book, and if anyone takes away from the words of the book of this prophecy, God will take away his share in the tree of life and in the holy city, which are described in this book." Revelation 22:18-19 ESV.

To give some examples of Panin's changes consider:

In many places in the gospels when referring to things the Lord did some manuscripts would state "Jesus did" and other manuscripts "He did". Someone changed the text. What would the enemy gain by changing "Jesus" to "He"? The context is abundantly clear it is speaking of the Lord Jesus. Could some well meaning scribe think he is making the text a bit more clear by changing "He" to "Jesus"? Panin suggests "He" is most likely the accurate copy.

Or could some scribe who had memorized much of Scripture and had just copied Ephesians 1:7 "In him we have redemption **through his blood**, the forgiveness of our trespasses", and then when copying Colossians 1:17 "In whom we have redemption, the forgiveness of sins", by mistake from memory (or to add emphasis) have added "**through his blood**"? So we are faced with some manuscripts of Colossians that have the phrase "through his blood" and some without. Which most likely is an accurate copy? Panin suggests the phrase belongs in Ephesians, not Colossians. Textual scholars agree.

Those who believe in soul sleep like to put a comma after "today" in Luke 23:43 implying that "today" refers when the statement was made, not the time of arrival of the thief into Paradise. Panin points out that this misplaced comma does damage to otherwise neat numeric patterns.

In Mark 14:68 after Peter denied the Lord the first time some manuscripts have the phrase "and the rooster crowed" at the end of the verse, and other manuscripts do not. (It is clear after Peter denied the Lord three times the rooster did crow the second time.) Could some scribe have inserted this reference to the first crowing? Luke 22:61 clearly states "Before the rooster crows today, you will deny me three times". So the copy that omitted "the rooster crowed" in verse 68 is most likely the accurate copy. Panin's numerics confirms this and ESV also has so noted.

In Acts 12:4 Panin and textual scholars agree that "Easter" should rather be "the Passover".

In the authorized text the reading of First John 2:20, "But ye have an unction from the Holy one and ye know all things," has puzzled many for years. Does not omniscience belong uniquely to God? The ESV has "But you have been anointed by the Holy One, and you all have knowledge" with a footnote "some manuscripts *you know everything*". Panin's numerics suggest the correct text is "And you have an anointing from the Holy *One* and you all know—I have not written unto you because you know not...".

In Revelation 22 verse 14 "Blessed are **those that do his commandments**, that they may have right to the tree of life" is perhaps more accurately "Blessed are those who **wash their robes**" (salvation is by cleansing of the blood of the Lamb, not by works). And in verse 19 the taking away is from the **tree of life** rather than the **book of life** (a person can lose reward, but not salvation). Panin and textual scholars agree on these two verses.

In the next chapter we will take a brief look at numerics in God's creation, then move on, after a warning against making idols out of numbers, to some of Panin's discoveries.

III
A Peek at Creation

If you were to slice an apple horizontally and look at the core, you would see a five-pointed star. This might remind you of your hand with five fingers, or possibly a starfish. That perhaps would be the end of the musing for most of us, but what if we kept thinking and researching like Panin did? What *does* five mean? Is there a way to understand numbers and the way God uses them in both creation and his word? The answer to this question would help us greatly in understanding the roles of numbers like **37** and **73** that played so prominent a part in the last part of the example given in chapter five.

First of all, we have to discard the idea that some numbers are more important than others. By definition, no one number can be taken out of the matrix of all numbers without the whole system collapsing. Yet we also find that every number has its own *character*, its own personality. And we find groupings of personalities, such as all even numbers, or all perfect squares. And further, we find that scripture uses particular *kinds* of numbers; some for **landmarks**, and other kinds for **content**.

Panin became an expert at finding the landmarks, because in traversing the landscape of scripture, these could inform him in a unique manner where he was heading, where he was coming from, and most of all, where he *was*. The landmarks give the structure so that the content can fill in. And interestingly enough the landmarks almost always tend to be *prime* numbers.

Now as we consider the *meanings* of numbers, we find that they are related one to another in the same way that the numbers themselves are. For example, our apple with its five-pointed star at the core is a *fruit*. Our hand with its five fingers represents our *ability*. It doesn't take too much thinking to realize that these two ideas are intimately connected; something or someone with *ability* can produce *fruit*, often called *the fruit of his labors.* And thus we begin to get a sense of what the number five means.

So we keep thinking. We have *two* hands; one responds to the other. This brings us up to *ten* fingers; five for ability and five more for response to that ability. Then we realize what we have just said: ten is the number of <u>response</u>-<u>ability</u> or quite simply responsibility.

Do all numbers and their meanings work this way? Yes they do. Does scripture clearly use every number in conjunction with its true meaning? Yes it does.

Would we go to 25, we would find that it means *satisfaction.* Why? Because it is 5^2, meaning the ability to use ability. Many people have great abilities, but do not know how to use them. Thus the simple meaning of 25 teaches us that having the ability to use our ability leads to great satisfaction. In Appendix II, we sketch out the meanings of the first 50 numbers; this could be taken as far as we have time to search out; for now the first 50 are a good start.

At this point in our discussion we are getting a sneaking suspicion regarding the numbers Panin keeps finding as landmarks. As we have said, *they are almost always prime numbers.* 5, 7, 13, 23, 31, 37, 43, and 73 are all prime. This means that they cannot be split up any further into smaller numbers that multiply into them. Let us examine why this striking phenomena would be so.

As we mentioned with 10, both its numerical value and its meaning are derived from 5 and 2. Responsibility is both the *nature* (2) of *ability* (5) and the *fruit* (5) of *substantiation* (2). All numbers which have factors work this way. This is one reason that 12 means a full organizational system; it has 2, 3, 4, and 6 all as factors, and the combined meanings of all those numbers make

16

up the universally large meaning of 12. But let us go one more to 13; it has no factors at all. Thus its meaning, *accountability*, is a new and unique idea whose parts have not yet arisen in the matrix of the meanings of numbers. A prime number is always a brand new idea.

And that is how scripture bookmarks itself. Again and again, Panin finds that navigation through the complexities of scriptural numerics is dependent entirely on prime numbers. Scripture is using unique ideas to organize itself, and *filling in* with the ideas that hold many relationships... the non-primes. An analogy can be made with how our skeletal system keeps the structure of our body, and the flesh and organs provide the systems to make it operate.

Now was Ivan Panin aware of this? we do not know; he does not mention it anywhere that we are aware of, but it is best not to second-guess someone whose work we have barely begun to understand. If he was *not* aware of it, it is somewhat remarkable that he consistently in every work dealt primarily with prime numbers. For all the writing about *proofs* that he does, this is a glaring one that he never mentions. Thus is God's Word, and thus is God's creation; no matter where we look, the stamp of the Divine is looking back. We have 33 vertebra just as the combined ages of the ten patriarchs before the flood and the ten patriarchs after the flood give us exactly 33 years of 360 days each. Adam through Abraham were the backbone of Humanity.

An insect has six legs, which is what is to be expected from the *mechanics* (3) of *nature* (2), just as a snowflake has six points. The number six means *freedom*, or *that which God allows*. Thus the number 666 represents the full extent to which God will allow something; how far he will allow evil in its use in Revelation, and how far he will allow riches in the case of the amount of gold that came to Solomon each year (Second Chronicles 9:13). If you place a penny on the table, precisely six pennies fit around it. If you count the middle penny, you come to seven, which means *perfection*. Thus a beehive with all its six-sided chambers has a *perfect* spot in the center of each cell in which to make the honey, or grow a new larva. Seven is always in the center of six, just as God completed everything on the sixth day so that he could rest the seventh.

Seven, then, is the primary key to both creation and scripture alike. There are seven notes in a musical scale, the eighth makes an *octave*, as seven means *perfection* and eight means *that which is perfected*. So we have seven perfect notes to which we add one for *that which is completed*.

There are seven colors which distinguish themselves in the rainbow. Cyclic processes also occur in sevens; all animals' gestation periods occur in multiples of seven days. Furthermore, the lifespan of animals is always seven times the age of their sexual maturity. Interestingly, man is the exception here; according to this pattern we should be living to 120, as says Genesis 6:3.

There are seven gland centers that control the body, seven main organs, and we have five holes in our head (two nostrils, two ears, and a mouth) which gives us the *ability* to sense, but with two eyes we have seven, which *perfects* that ability. Add to this the seven seas and seven continents, and we could go on ad infinitum. The number seven has rightly been considered the number of perfection in every culture on earth, as the universality of the 'week' attests.

Looking at the number nine in creation, we find that it means both *a full system* and *judgment*, the reason being that when a system is finally full, it is assessed, or 'judged'. The universe is made up of Space, Time, and Energy. Space is composed of height, width, and depth. Time is composed of past, present, and future. Energy is composed of modulation, volume, and intensity (or if you're talking of its manifestation in matter: proton, neutron, and electron). These add up to nine, which makes up the full system of the universe. Likewise there are nine planets and a woman's pregnancy lasts nine months, each required for a full system.

Eleven means *response*, as musical notes demonstrate: the number of vibrations per second for each musical note is in multiples of eleven. And as the sun responds to the earth, its sunspots occur in eleven-year cycles.

Everywhere we look in nature, we see it carefully arranged according to very specific numbers. There are thirteen bumps in the counterclockwise spiral of a pineapple. Never twelve, never fourteen; always thirteen.

And it is not just simple numbers by which nature (and scripture) arrange themselves. There is a series of numbers called the Fibonacci Series, which is replete throughout nature. The Fibonacci Series is simply what you get when you add the last two numbers in sequence. So it turns out to be 0, 1, 1, 2, 3, 5, 8, 13, 21, 34, 55, 89, etc.; each number being the sum of the two previous.

This number describes all growth processes, the spirals of seashells, leaf arrangements, pine cones, seed heads, and petals on flowers. Let's look at this last one.

3 petals: Lily, Iris
(4 petals Very few plants show 4 petals but some, such as the Fuchsia do.)
5 petals: Buttercup, Wild Rose, Larkspur, Columbine, Pinks
8 petals: Delphiniums
13 petals: Ragwort, Corn Marigold, Cineraria, some daisies
21 petals: Aster, Black-eyed Susan, Chicory
34 petals: Plantain, Pyrethrum
55, 89 petals: Michaelmas Daisies, the Asteraceae family.

Some species like buttercups are very precise about the number of petals they have, and the others have petals that are very near those above, with the average being a Fibonacci number.

Now. Has anyone yet searched the scriptures to see where the Fibonacci Series occurs? Not as far as I know, which is somewhat of a shame. The treasures of scripture are sitting there waiting for us to explore. We see that nature is organized numerically, and we are just beginning to understand that scripture is similarly organized. God's stamp is on both.

But before we go into Bible numerics, let us do a sanity check.

IV
A Question of Sanity, Wisdom, and Faith: Approaching the Scriptures

We will be looking at mathematical phenomena in the scriptures in a variety of applications. While a fascinating pursuit, this can lead to fanaticism if not firmly grounded in *what the scripture actually says about itself.* This is forever our Standard, and when so often we find ourselves out in no-man's-land looking at mathematical patterns that can make our minds spin, we must always return to the straightforward simplicity of *what the words say.* When we cease to approach the Scriptures as children, our arrogance will lead us to places that our pride is reluctant to abandon. For this reason we introduce this subject most tentatively. The phenomena are there; the numbers are astounding; the patterns are universal. **But if for a moment they distract us from reading and understanding the plain sense of Truth found on every page of the Bible, we have allowed Numerics to become an Idol.** It would be a pity to be so taken up with the numerics behind the text and miss the message.

We do not wish to belabor this point, as moralizing is not the object of scripture. If a warning is necessary, it is given once, then the writer moves on to the better things; our relationship to our God and Father and his Christ. This is where our hearts expand and our souls can feed. Yet even in allowing the Spirit to encourage and nurture our souls, knowledge as well as wisdom is useful. Peter ends his epistle by saying "But grow in grace and knowledge of our Lord and Savior Jesus Christ..." Both are needed... the grace to expand our hearts so that there is a place for the knowledge, and the knowledge to structure our heart in its new expanded state, that it does not shrink when so often we lose the sense of grace in the storms of life.

So let us look—once again as children—at the place of **Wisdom**

21

and the place of **Faith**; for we will need both of these if we are to navigate what may seem to be labyrinths of numbers and mathematics throughout scripture.

We tend to be attracted to miraculous signs and magic pills that will solve all our problems. In health, periodically something such as 'eat more fiber' sweeps through and everyone grabs on to this latest fad as if somehow the one difference will turn their health around. Of course, it never does; health must be approached as holistically as anything else in life; there is no 'magic pill' either to our health or our understanding of the scriptures. Thus, 'numerics'—a subject which many have loved and have spent decades investigating—if treated as if it by itself could solve anything in scripture, will result in the same disappointment as someone who adds fiber to their diet but doesn't stop indulging in Twinky Ho-Ho's that have caused a compromised condition to begin with.

What we require is **Wisdom**. I highly recommend taking the next available opportunity to read Proverbs chapters 8 and 9. It only takes a few minutes, and is always a delightful read. There are two things in research that will prevent us from using wisdom: mysticism and legalism. Wisdom must be freshly accessed in every new situation; there is no such thing as having it all prepared. Wisdom is always new, always fresh, and requires an open—yet knowledgeable—approach to life in fellowship with God. Let us look briefly at '**mysticism**' and '**legalism**' as pertains to Numerics; and perhaps through this fascinating subject we can delineate a course that will keep our hearts and minds alive and aware so as to appreciate Numerics rather than falling prey to idolatry or pedantic insistence on dubious 'proofs'.

Mysticism will tell us that there is something so deep, so intricate, so... well, 'magical' about the numbers in scripture, that they reveal higher truths which are inaccessible without numerics. This, of course, is baloney. While the numerics enhance and compliment the scriptures, there is nothing—nothing whatsoever —that equals the plain meaning of the words and what they communicate. Are the numbers significant? Very. But without the larger significance of the plain meaning of the words, the numbers are meaningless. Wisdom requires that we are grounded and in context, not attempting to prove things which at best, are mere guesses. That is mysticism.

Legalism works in a similar vein, though it appeals to an entirely different attitude. Legalism *demands* that things be in such-and-such an order, and *insists* that this order is God's order. The trouble is that God does not work like that; he is easily entreated, full of mercy, interested in what we do: like bringing the animals before Adam *to see what he would call them.* And most of all, God desires fellowship with us. Jonah would like to insist that God judge Nineveh like he said he would; God does not work like that. Some who delve into Numerics would like to insist that they work (or cannot possibly work) a certain way, and that this way *proves* something about scripture. God does not work that way either. The numbers are there in the text just as beauty is there in creation. We may know everything there is to know about the geometry of how an Oak tree's leaves grow, but this does not allow us to predict the exact shape of a single one of the thousands of leaves that a tree will produce in the spring. That is God's way. There is perfect order, yet it is still unpredictable and brand new every single time. So how does one recognize an Oak leaf when presented with one? Once again, wisdom, knowledge, and experience.

Thus as we go through various examples of the amazing numerics in scripture, it can be easy to get overwhelmed. This is okay. It is the beauty, the consistency, and the depth that is meant to attract our hearts to appreciate yet another element of the infinite scriptures, that our present walk by faith is enhanced by some bit of appreciation that no matter what we look at, the Author's hand is evident. This brings us to the last subject of this introductory chapter: **Faith**.

It is remarkable to see that regardless of a person's intellect or education, there is one and only one element that will determine how much they discover in scripture: and this is whether they **believe** that it is possible that there is something significant there *or not*, and willingness to find it. It seems to be the personal vendetta of so many seminary professors to deliberately erode the idea that God's Word is, in fact, God's Word. And it's easy to do; all one needs is to be sufficiently educated, put on a persona of being 'open', and one may proceed to overthrow the faith of the young Christian. To be sure, much of the fault lies in failing to ground young Christians in true faith to begin with; when we merely feed our children with happy-Jesus sound bites and fail to present the true Person, they are ill prepared to defend their faith against the vultures that crowd the halls of 'higher' learning.

Yet the problem is no small one. So few well-meaning Christians actually believe that the first chapter of Genesis means precisely what it says and is perfect truth. Is this not remarkable? If we *begin* our journey through the Bible by mythologizing it, what is to be said for the rest of it? At what point do we begin to believe that it is speaking truth? At the flood? With the judges? The Kings? Do we even take Jesus' signs and miracles seriously? When pretending to know more than the scriptures, where do we draw the line?

Every word of God's Word is **truth**. It does not need us to defend it or even believe it to be truth. Second Corinthians 13:8 says *"For we can do nothing against the truth, but for the truth."* The Scripture stands on its own as the most powerful element that has ever existed among men. The fact that we can pick up a Bible and physically hold it in our hands is astounding. The fact that we would rather sit around watching the telly than read it astounds the angels.

Now faith comes of hearing, and hearing by the word of God. So the faith of mysticism is to be avoided; it is necessary for us to understand what it is that we believe. To do this, we must educate ourselves in the Word. This requires a process, and as long as we are living, this process is never over. What is needed to make this process work is *motivation* to continue on; something that John in his epistle calls **joy**. Without enjoying the scriptures, without having fellowship with the Father and the Son, we become empty clanging bells, merely going through the motions for personal gain or from a sense of duty. That is not living.

One element of motivation that God has put into both his creation and his Word is **beauty**. If there were nothing but dead trees and dry ashes outside, we would hardly be motivated to venture outdoors. But there is cool moist earth swarming with a thousand organisms seen and unseen; plants of every description competing to show God's glory; breezes of subtle and invigorating flavors; in short, there is *beauty* everywhere we look and in every breath and sound. And when we turn to the scriptures, we likewise find stories subtle and powerful enough to bring us to tears; psalms that comfort when no other words work; epistles that teach when all other empty moralizing fails... again, we are looking at *beauty*.

And that is how we want to approach mathematics and numbers in scripture. Yes, they can be used to 'prove' the validity of the scriptures, but if we did not **start with faith** in validity of God's word, all the proof in the world is not going to change our minds. There is a danger in wishing to 'bonk' people over the head with the Word rather than letting them be attracted by it, yet it is the *goodness* of God that leads us to repentance, not the *proof* of God. The fact that our dear friend Ivan Panin was enraptured with the numerics he discovered in scripture—as proofs—indicates that his heart had already been touched by its beauty; and what he spent 50 years searching out was in fact, the **beauty of numerics**; whether that beauty could also be used as undeniable proof or not.

With this in mind it is time to investigate some of the depths of what he discovered, and what the implications are to those of us who are standing by the sidelines watching this most disciplined athlete run the good race.

V
An Introduction to Ivan Panin's Methodology

Before we go on in our exploration of the amazing world of Numbers in scripture, let us pique our interest with an actual example of one of Panin's discoveries, taken from *The Shorter Works of Ivan Panin* from 1938 and *Ivan Panin's Astounding New Discoveries* from 1941. These are his observations regarding the first verse of the Bible. Then we will examine it and see if we can find what exactly Ivan Panin is discovering.

Genesis 1:1
"In the beginning God created the heavens and the earth."

בראשית	In the beginning
ברא	Created
אלהים	God
את	(Indefinite article emphasizing the next word)
השמים	The heavens
ואת	'And', with emphatic indefinite article
הארץ	The earth

Note that Hebrew is read from left to right.

Panin's comments:

I
This verse has seven words (feature 1), with 28 letters, or 4 sevens (feature 2): of which the first three words, the subject and predicate of the sentence, have 14, with a Place Value of 140, or 20 sevens (feature 3); the last four, the two objects of the sentence, have also 14, or 2 sevens (feature 4). Of the two objects each has seven letters (feature 5). Another division of

seven into three and four produces the following: The three leading words: God, the heavens, the earth, have 14; the remaining four have also 14 or 2 sevens (feature 6): with 924 for the value, or 132 sevens (feature 7) divided thus: The Place Value has 147, or 3 sevens of sevens (feature 8); and the Numeric Value has 777, itself 111 sevens (feature 9); of which the units have seven (feature 10); the tens, seven (feature 11), and the hundreds have seven (feature 12). The middle word, the shortest, has seven letters with its right hand neighbor (feature 13); and seven with its left hand neighbor (feature 14).

This enumeration is in no wise exhaustive; but the chance for these 2 sevens of features of seven being accidental, undesigned is already only one in seven multiplied by itself 14 times, or, 678,623,072,849 one in nearly SEVEN HUNDRED THOUSAND MILLIONS. An elaborate design of sevens thus runs through the seven words of the first verse of the Bible.

II

The number of letters 28, is 4 x 7, a multiple of FOUR as well as of seven (feature 1); divided thus: the first four (feature 2) words have 16 or four fours (feature 3); the last three have 12 or 3 fours (feature 4); the same division into 16 and 12 is formed thus: the first two and last two words, the outer four (feature 5) have 16 or 4 fours (feature 6). The three between have 12, or 3 fours (feature 7). The same division is for the third time formed thus: The first, last, and middle words have 12, or 3 fours; the remaining four (feature 8) have 16 or four (feature 9) fours (feature 10). The numbers for the letters in the seven words are 2, 3, 3, 4, 5, 5, 6. Four are duplicates; 3, 3, 5, 5, (feature 11); their sum is 16 or four fours (feature 12); leaving 12 for the others, or 3 fours (feature 13). The duplicates are the ODD numbers. Those in the odd places, 2, 3, 5, 6, have also 16 or four fours (feature 14); the even places have 12, or 3 fours (feature 15). The largest and smallest numbers have 8, or 2 fours; the others have 20 or 5 fours (feature 16).

The chance for these 15 features of 4 to be here UNdesigned is less than one in 3,600,000,000 or three thousand, six hundred millions. An elaborate design of FOURS as well as of sevens runs through the seven words of Genesis 1: 1.

III

The NUMERIC VALUE of Genesis 1: 1 is 2,701, or 37 x 73, the combination of THIRTY-SEVEN (feature 1) with its reverse 73; divided thus:

Words 1-5 have	1998	or	37 x 18 x 3
Words 6-7 have	703	or	37 x 19

This division is by 37 (feature 2); and the sum of the figures of 1998 x 703 is 37 (feature 3). The number 703 is in its turn divided thus:

Word 6 has	407	or	37 x 11
Word 7 has	296	or	37 x 2 x 2 x 2 (feature 4)

Of the last division it is to be noted that the sum of the figures of the factors is 28 or 4 sevens; and that of the figures of 407 x 296 is also 28 or 4 sevens.

The leading nouns, GOD, THE HEAVENS, and THE EARTH have 777 or 21 thirty-sevens, the other words have 1924, or 52 thirty-sevens (feature 5); and the sum of the figures of 777 and 1924 is 37 (feature 6). Of the 777 GOD, THE HEAVENS have 481 or 37 x 13; and THE EARTH has 296 or 37 x 8 (feature 7). The words with the largest and smallest Numeric values 913 and 86 have 999, or 37 x 3 x 3 x 3; the others have 1702, or 37 x 2 x 23 (feature 8), with the sum of the figures of 999 and 1702 also 37 (feature 9). The sum of the figures of their factors is 36, itself 6 x 6, but neighbor of both 37 and 35 or 5 sevens (feature 10).

Again: Words 5—6 have for their Numeric Value 802, neighbor of 803, or 11 SEVENTY-THREES, the reverse of 37; leaving for the other 1899, neighbor of 1898 or 73 x 2 x 13. This division is by

73. But the sum of the figures of 802 and 1899 is 37 (feature 11). Again: the seven Numeric Values of the words of Genesis 1: 1 arranged in their actual order 86, 203, 296, 395, 401, 407, 913, their numbers 1—3 have 585, or (73 x 2 x 2 x 2) + 1; and 4—7 have 2116, or (73 x 29) - 1. This division is also by 73, but the sum of the figures of the factors of 585 and 2116 is 37 (feature 12).

If now the four figures of 2701 be multiplied by their order numbers 1, 2, 3, 4, we have

$$
\begin{array}{rcccr}
2000 & x & 1 & \text{is} & 2000 \\
700 & x & 2 & \text{is} & 1400 \\
0 & x & 3 & \text{is} & 0 \\
1 & x & 4 & \text{is} & \underline{4} \\
\end{array}
$$

3404 or 37 x 4 x 23 (feature 13)

The same multiplication inverted gives

$$
\begin{array}{rcccr}
2000 & x & 4 & \text{is} & 8000 \\
700 & x & 3 & \text{is} & 2100 \\
0 & x & 2 & \text{is} & 0 \\
1 & x & 1 & \text{is} & \underline{1} \\
\end{array}
$$

10,101 or 37 x 3 x 7 x 13 (feature 14)

The chance for these 14 features of 37 being UNdesigned is one in 37 multiplied by itself 14 times; 352,275,361 multiplied by itself THRICE taken 1369 times, a number of some TWENTY-EIGHT FIGURES.

An elaborate design of 37 as well as of 4 and 7 thus runs through the 7 words of Genesis 1: 1.

IV

The Numeric Value 2701 is the combination of 37 with SEVENTY-THREE (feature 1) its reverse. At feature 11 of the 37 it was already seen that the division is by 73 (feature 2). The Numeric Values of the 7 words of Genesis 1: 1 are 913, 203, 86,

401, 395, 407, and 296, which in their natural order are 86, 203, 296, 395, 401, 407, and 913, as seen above at feature 12 of the thirty-seven. It has already been seen that the division at feature 11 above is by 73 (feature 3); likewise the one at feature 12 above (feature 4). Now the first and middle words in the text have for their Numeric Values 913 and 401, or 1314 which is 73 x 18; the others have 1387, or 73 x 19 (feature 5). This division is moreover by the nearest two halves 18 x 19 into which the uneven 37 can at all be divided (1314 + 1387 = 37 x 73).

If now the seven Numeric Values be multiplied by their order numbers 1, 2, 3, . . . 7 we have:

$$
\begin{array}{rcccr}
86 & x & 1 & is & 86 \\
203 & x & 2 & is & 406 \\
296 & x & 3 & is & 888 \\
395 & x & 4 & is & 1580 \\
401 & x & 5 & is & 2005 \\
407 & x & 6 & is & 2442 \\
913 & x & 7 & is & \underline{6391}
\end{array}
$$

13,798 or (73 x 7 x 3 x 3 x 3 x 3) - 1

The combination of SEVENTY-THREE (feature 6) with SEVEN, divided thus:

Words 5, 7 have   8396 or (73 x 5 x 23) + 1.

The others have   5402 or 73 x 37 x 2 (feature 7).

The chance for these seven seventy-threes to occur here undesigned is one in 73^7 or 10,640,000,000,000.

A most elaborate design of sevens, fours, 37's and 73's runs through the seven words of the first verse of the Bible in Hebrew. As no mere man could by his own attainments perform the feat of SUCH four different schemes here, this verse alone thus demonstrates its Inspiration by the Master Mathematician of Creation, who duly weighs and counts all that comes from His hand.

Wow. If that didn't make our heads spin, what will? Let's take that apart a bit and see if we can find out what is going on.

In his terminology, he talks of the **Numerical Value** of a word. This is derived from the fact that each letter in both Hebrew and Greek also represents a number. There is a chart in Appendix I that shows what these are, as well as **Place Value**, which is simply where in the alphabet the letter appears, as in the 11th or 22nd or whichever letter of the alphabet.

However, we note that Panin does not limit himself to any one particular way of counting. He advantages himself of any and all phenomena which bears fruit. This can be quite confusing if we are looking for a regular consistent method. This did not bother Panin one whit; he found quite simply that the more he looked, the more he found. There appears to be no upper limit on what one will find in Scripture if one searches. However, this brings up a very important warning; there is a serious pitfall that Panin avoided, but almost every other Numerics author I know has fallen into. And that is: *What does it mean?*

If you search the internet for Numerics sites, you will find one that attempts to prove that humans turn into angels—using numbers. I have a book beside me with a dizzying array of Numerics very well ordered . . . but it had attempted to prove that Jesus was returning in 1984. And so on. Note that Panin did *not* ever attempt to prove anything with Numerics. What he provides us is **raw data**—and he very nicely leaves it at that. He makes no predictions, no doctrinal declarations, no hidden secrets or mysteries; this is the character of a man with a noble spirit. The closest he came to actually *using* the treasures he searched out for 50 years was to **determine what exactly was the proper reading of a scriptural passage when there was doubt as to which manuscript was correct.** And the critical text he arranged a century ago has, since then, been validated over and over. Even places where he went completely against the opinion of the crowd at the time have subsequently been shown to be the preferred choice of scholars, such as the proper spelling of *David* in the New Testament, which can be found in Paper III in the back of his *Numeric English New Testament.*

It is important to realize that Ivan Panin is not attempting to draw conclusions from his work. Certainly conclusions *can* be drawn, but that was not his calling. His job was to dig out the raw gold ore, and set it before us. It is another's job to refine it into pure gold, and yet another's to take that pure gold and make beautiful art.

There are three manners of treating numbers that Panin uses: **Cardinal**, **Ordinal**, and **Cyclic**. . . and, of course, the relationships between the three, which relationships bring up a veritable infinity of possibilities. By cardinal we mean simply the amount of a number. By ordinal we mean what order is it found in; first, second, third, etc. Cyclic is somewhat trickier; he would search out how the same number would appear over and over just like a certain spot on a tire ending up on top at regular intervals. Think of a clock.

In this chapter we have introduced Panin and his methods. In the next we will look at some of the questions that quite frankly have a tendency to become the 'elephant in the room'; and that is, why the particular numbers that he is finding? What is so special about, say, 37 or 13? And why do these strange numbers keep cropping up with such regularity? Fortunately, we have someone who has already done the work for us; we need only to examine it in light of Creation and God's Word to find the answers. Let us move on.

VI
A Closer Look at Panin's Numbers

In the example we quoted from Panin's examination of Genesis 1:1 in the previous chapter, he ends by noting that there is a pattern of **37**'s and **73**'s embedded in the verse. Now if we were to do our homework and search the scriptures for the significance and use of **37** by scripture, what might we find?

We have noted that each letter of both Hebrew and Greek also represents a number, as listed in Appendix I. Thus we find that "Christ" is numerically represented as follows:

$$X \quad \rho \quad \iota \quad \sigma \quad \tau \quad o \quad \varsigma$$
$$600 + 100 + 10 + 200 + 300 + 70 + 200$$

The total of "Christ" in Greek is 1,480 which is 40 x **37**.

How strange to find this large prime number in "Christ". Where else might we find it if we search?

1. The total value of all the letters of the Greek alphabet is 4,995 which is **37** x 5 x 3^3.
2. The value of "Jesus" in Greek is 888 which is <u>24</u> (the number of letters in the Greek alphabet) x **37**.
3. The value of "Cross" in Greek is 777 which is <u>21</u> x **37**.
4. The number of the beast, 666 is <u>18</u> x **37**.
5. Note that in the last three examples there, <u>18</u> is 6 + 6 + 6, <u>21</u> is 7 + 7 + 7, and <u>24</u> is 8 + 8 + 8. Where else do we find 37 lurking?
6. II Corinthians 4:4 says *"...Christ, who is God's Image..."* The words *God's Image* have a value of 1,369 which is **37** x **37**, or **37²**.
7. *"The holy of holies"* has a value of 2,368 which is **37** x 8^2. 2,368 is also the the value of *"Jesus Christ"*.
8. *"Godhead"* (from KJV Romans 1:20, other translations

say *"divinity"*) has a value of 592, which is **37** x 2^4. Notably, when 592 is added to the value of *"Jesus"* (888), it equals 1,480 which is the exact value of *"Christ"*.

9. *"The Son of Man"* from Matthew 13:37 has the value of **37** x 80. This value of 2,960 is the total of the three figures in the previous example: *Godhead* 592 + *Jesus* 888 + *Christ* 1,480 = *the Son of Man* 2,960.

10. *"The Lord Christ"* from Colossians 3:24 has the value of **37** x 120.

11. *"The Son of God"* from Galatians 2:20 has the value of **37** x 66.

12. *"Of the Seed of David"* from John 7:42 has the value of **37** x 70.

13. *"Christ is the son of David"* from Luke 20:41 has the value of **37** x 75.

Let us pause for a moment and catch our breath. It is apparent that God has woven the number 37 into both the old and new testaments in a very specific manner. The question for the intelligent seeker is *What is that manner?*

We see in example **4** above that 666 is **37** x <u>18</u>. So the multiplier (18) would be the key to how to treat **37** in that case, just as the multiplier in *Jesus* (example **2**) is <u>24</u>. The number **37** is established in both examples as the **core**, and the multiplier is in each case the **descriptor**.

So looking at the two descriptors here, <u>18</u> and <u>24</u>, what do we find? One way (there are many) of considering them is that <u>18</u> is **3** x **6**, while <u>24</u> is **4** x **6**. So there is something about taking three sixes that lands us on **666**, and something about four sixes that lands us on **888**.

Looking at Appendix II in the back, we see that three is *mechanics*, four is *universality*, and six is *freedom*. It would be possible to conclude then that to merely be interested in the *mechanics* (**3**) of freedom (**6**) leads to **666**, while being interested in the *universality* (**4**) of freedom (**6**) leads to **888**. In other words, the *mechanics* of freedom leads to self-interest, while the *universality* of freedom leads to freedom for everyone. This would be the message of the numbers here, why one descriptor (**18**) is the number of the beast, while the other descriptor (**24**) is the number of Jesus . . .when multiplying both by **37**.

The above paragraph is a *suggestion* only. We must be careful not to make rules in an arena in which we are merely children picking up interesting shells on the beach.

But what about when the descriptor and the core are the same? In example **6** above, *God's Image* equals **37** x **37**. Most remarkable. Where else might we find **37** x **37**?

And the Spirit of God moved over the face of the waters.

ת	פ	ח	ר	מ		ם	י	ה	ל	א		ח	ו	ר	ו
400	80	8	200	40		40	10	5	30	1		8	6	200	6

ם	י	מ	ה		י	נ	פ	ל	ע
40	10	40	5		10	50	80	30	70

And there it is in the very second verse of the Bible. Adding those letters up equals 1,369, which is **37** x **37** again.

Now if we recall, the first verse of Genesis adds up to **37** x **73**. When we get to the third verse, it begins to branch out into the other significant numbers in scripture, such as the 153 fishes of John 21:11. "*And God said Let there be light, and there was light*" adds up to **813** (as does the phrase "*And God divided between the light and the darkness*" as well as the words *resurrection* and *trust* in Greek). This peculiar number is 3 x (**37 + 37 + 73 + 73 + (**3 x 17**)**). I have underlined 3 x 17 because it equals the strange 51, which is one-third of the 153 fishes of John. But more simply, **813** = (20 x **37**) + **73**. Look at the next verse,

verse 4: its value is 1776, which is 48 x **37**. It is also 2 x **888** (Jesus). It isn't until we get to the fifth verse before we find a value (2141) that isn't divisible by 37 or anything else; it's prime. However, if we subtract the previous verse's value (2141-1776) we get the number of days in a year (**365**) as well as the age of Enoch when he was translated. . . which oddly enough is 5 x **73**. And we get the same thing with the 6th verse whose value is **1660**; subtract from that **2141**, and we get **481** which is 13 x **37**. And the 7th verse? Well it's **4541**, so if you subtract verses 6 (**1660**) and 4 (**2141**) from it you get **740**; 20 x **37** again. And if you like 20 x **37**, go to the next verse, the 8th, **2255**, which is **37²** + (20 x **37**) + **73** + **73**. And so on throughout all the scriptures as far as we wish to explore.

Now it is somewhat valuable to know what we are doing besides playing with numbers. The section of verse two that is **37²** is only half of it; the part that says the Spirit was hovering over the face of the waters. The other half adds up to the seemingly useless **2177**. But if we look at the *content* of the verses, things begin to make sense. **2177** is the section that says the earth was waste and empty and darkness was on the face of the deep.

Thus the first three verses of chapter 2 where God rests has a value of **10,502**, which gets us nowhere. But if we *subtract* the **2177** of "waste and void", we get **8325**, which is **15²** x **37**. The idea is that in order for God to rest, the original problem of waste and void has to be taken away. 15 means "possession", and **15²** is a very emphatic way of showing that God it taking possession of the earth again. Watch this theme continue to crop up.

In verse 31, God looks over everything and sees that it is "very good". This verse has a value of **3065** which once again gets us nowhere with 37 or 73. But if we again subtract the "waste and void" (**2177**) we get **888** which is both the numerical value of "**Jesus**" and 24 x **37**. This tells us who is going to fix the "waste and void" and make things very good.

Again, verses 26 through 30 deal with the creation of Man. The value of these verses is **23,942**, which once again gets us nowhere. If we add God's rest (**10,502**) from the first three verses of chapter two, we still get nowhere *until we subtract the 2,177 waste and void*, at which point we arrive at **35,332** which is **22²** x **73**. Twenty-two means "answering" and it is Jesus as Son of Man who "answers" God's interrupted rest and restores it.

Looking at Man's relationship with creation, the entirety of the sixth day adds up to **34,150**. Adding in again the creation of the land animals (**7143**) and the whole 5ᵗʰ day of fish and birds (**13,689**), we arrive at **54,982** which is **37** x 2 x 743. Seven hundred forty-three is a prime number meaning *"Finishing the full application of universal wisdom"*

But all is not rosy with the creatures over which Man has been placed. If we read carefully in Genesis, we will notice that the fish were not named by Adam; just the birds and beasts. And in Revelation when describing the new earth, it says "the sea exists no more" (21:1). So if we take verses 26-30 that talk of Man's creation (**23,942**), _add_ the creation of the beasts in verses 24 & 25 (**7143**), _add_ the entire verse having the Spirit hovering over the waters in verse two (**3546**), and then _subtract_ verses 20 through 23 that deal with the fish (**13,689**), we end up with **20,942** which turns out to be **37** x 566.

Take verses 3 through 5 regarding the whole First Day ("Let there be light"); the value is **4730**. Subtracting the entire **3546** of the "waste and void" verse gives us **1184**, which is **2⁵** x **37**.

Take verses 6 through 8, the second day (**8456**) and subtract the **2177** section of the "waste and void" verse, we end up with **2553**, which is **69** x **37**. Sixty-nine means judgment being meted out willy-nilly any way the judge wants; it's probably no coincidence that the second day is the only one that was not declared good.

Take verses 9 through 13 regarding the dry land and the plants; we find that it *already* has a value divisible by **37** like the first verse; they add up to **15,984** which is 3^2 x 2^4 x **37**. This and the fifth days are the only ones that needs no adjustment. Perhaps God considers the plants and birds to be just fine the way they are. The fifth day (20 through 22) except for the last verse (23) adds up to **12,629** which is **73 x 173**.

The fourth day regarding the "light bearers" from verse 14 to 19 is somewhat strange. The value of that section is **16,843**, and the first and second days (**4730** and **8456** respectively) must be *subtracted*, as well as the entire verse regarding "waste and empty" (**3546**). We are left with **111**, which is **3 x 37**.

Note that for many of our discoveries here, we are constantly subtracting the section that says "*And the earth was waste and empty, and darkness was on the face of the deep*" which has a value of **2177**. In Psalm 139:22 we have a verse with the same value of **2177**: "*I hate them with perfect hatred: I count them mine enemies.*" There is something very significant about that phrase, which is open for exploration.

In Isaiah 5:15 (also **2177**) we get a hint as to what needs done: "*And the mean man shall be brought down, and the mighty man shall be humbled, and the eyes of the lofty shall be humbled*". Yet there is hope given in Job 4:4 with yet another verse whose value is **2177**: "*Your words have upheld him that was falling, and you have strengthened the feeble knees.*" So there is a story woven throughout scripture that can be identified by these numerics.

We have covered the last three days already, and as you can see, this quickly becomes complex, so let us touch on a few more facts and return to our subject.

14. "*The fish*" + "*Alpha and Omega*" = **2701** which value is

73 x **37**, and the same value as the first verse.

15. "*My wrath*" from Hebrews 3:11 has a value of **999**, which is **3³ x 37**.

16. **3** x **888** (*Jesus*) = **2,664**. Adding **37** to this gives us once again the value of Genesis 1:1, which is **2701**.

17. Likewise, **3** x **2701** = **8103**, which when we add **888** (*Jesus*) equals **8991**, which is **3⁵ x 37**. It is also **9** x **999**; this is somewhat significant when we look at number 15 above.

18. It is said that the end of Deuteronomy relates to the beginning of Genesis. The last two verses in the Pentateuch (first five books of Moses) add up to **7373** which is **101** x **73**.

Is there a place we can find 37 geometrically? As we've mentioned before, any number which relates to a cube is highly significant. The numbers 8, 27, 64, 125, and 216 all make perfect cubes. Where does **37** come in?

(Note that in chapter 8 we will go into detail on a geometric square in which the number **37** is prominent.)

Let us take a perfect cube of 64 blocks. That is 4 x 4 x 4, or **4³**. It looks like this:

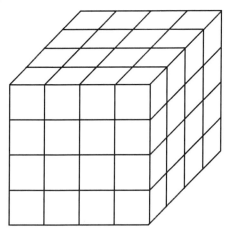

This cube is a good visual for the "*Truth*", whose value is also **64**, or **4³**, as there are **64** blocks in the cube. Of these **64**, there are **37** blocks that can be seen at any one time, and **27** (**3³**) that are hidden from sight at any one time. That is one was of visualizing how scripture uses this strange number.

The phenomena we have seen in Genesis 1:1 of a reversed number (**37** x **73**) is actually found throughout scripture. For example, if we take the well known John 1:1, "*In the beginning was the Word, and the Word was with God, and the Word was God*", we find that it's value is 3,627 or 3^2 x **13** x **31**. Or if we take Matthew 1:1 we find a strange way of using 13: "*Genealogy of Jesus Christ, David's son, Abraham's son*"; the value is 2^2 x **113** x **13**.

Yet there is far more than we even imagine involved in the sacred text and its numbers. Let us take a brief look at 'Triangle Numbers'. These are what we get when we stack pennies. Here are the first three Triangle Numbers, **1**, **3**, and **6**:

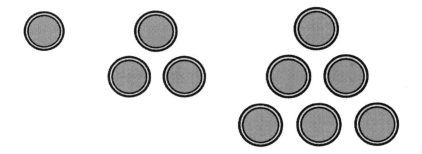

What we are looking for here here are are the numbers **73** and **37** that make up Genesis 1:1 when multiplied together. . . and how they unfold from **Creation** into the rest of the Scriptures.

It so happens that the **73rd** Triangle Number is **2701**, the very value of the first verse. If we were to explore that, we would find some very interesting connections to **John 1:1**. But let us start with the **7th** Triangle Number, **28**, as Genesis 1:1 has **28** letters. Here it is:

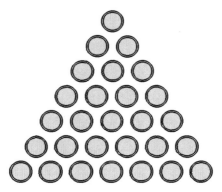

Now there are not only <u>Triangle</u> <u>Numbers</u>, but <u>Hexagon</u> <u>Numbers</u> and <u>Star</u> <u>Numbers</u>, as follows:

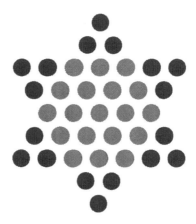

Here we have a <u>star</u> of **37** pennies nesting a <u>hexagon</u> of **19** pennies by putting an inverted **28** star upon itself. The Hebrew word for *the heart* is "הלב". The <u>ordinal</u> value of these letters (they are the 5th, 12th, and 2nd letters respectively) equals **19**. Their <u>cardinal</u> value (5, 30, and 2) equals **37**. And our star above has **19** pennies in the center hexagon, and **37** pennies altogether. Does this relate to Genesis 1:1? The phrase *"and the earth"* has a value of **703**, which is **19** x **37**. And **703** is also the **37th** <u>triangle</u> <u>number</u>.

Now counting from **1** to **1,000,000,000,000,000** (one quadrillion) there are only **12** numbers that can make both a star and a hexagon, and there is only **one** under **1,000**. If you guessed **37** you were right. Here is the **37**-hexagon embedded in a star:

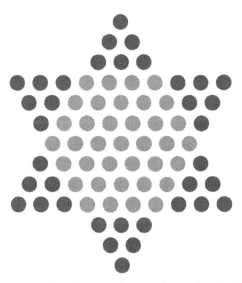

And how many pennies do we have altogether? **73**. This shape gives us a **visual map of Genesis 1:1**. And we use a map to *find* something, so what are we to find with this? Let us consider for a moment who was there with God *in the beginning.*

"Jehovah possessed me in the beginning of his way, before his works of old. I was set up from eternity, from the beginning, before the earth was. When there were no depths, I was brought forth, when there were no fountains abounding with water. Before the mountains were settled, before the hills was I brought forth; while as yet he had not made the earth, nor the fields, nor the beginning of the dust of the world. When he prepared the heavens I was there; when he ordained the circle upon the face of the deep; when he established the skies above, when the fountains of the deep became strong; when he imposed on the sea his decree

that the waters should not pass his commandment, when he appointed the foundations of the earth: then I was by him his nursling, and I was daily his delight, rejoicing always before him; rejoicing in the habitable part of his earth, and my delights were with the sons of men."

Let us look at Wisdom here. Specifically, let us look at ‎ח כ מ ה, which is "Wisdom" in Hebrew. *Ordinally* the four letters are the **8ᵗʰ**, **11ᵗʰ**, **13ᵗʰ**, and **5ᵗʰ**. *Cardinally* (their value) the letters are **8, 20, 40,** and **5**. The first adds up to **37**, the second to **73**. Thus we see that one of the great secrets hidden in the first verse of the Bible, whose value is **37 x 73**, is pointing us directly at Wisdom.

Now before we started looking at the triangles, we noted that John 1:1, *"In the beginning was the Word, and the Word was with God, and the Word was God"* has a value of **3627** or 3^2 x **13** x **31**. Let us rewrite that by spreading the **3**'s over the **13** and **31** by multiplying **(3 x 13) x (3 x 31) = 39 x 93 = 3627**. Once again we have two reversed numbers describing a seminal verse.

And if we combine **Genesis 1:1 (2701)** and **John 1:1 (3627)**? We get **6368** which turns out to be the **112th Triangle Number**. And what is **112**? It happens to be the value of

‎יהוה אלהים

...which we know as "Jehovah Elohim". It is also the value of "pure" and "think". . . something to think about.

And while we are in John 1:1, let us finish this chapter with a look at "Logos", whose value is **373**. . .

Λ	o	γ	o	ς
30	70	3	70	200

373 is **(7 x 37)** + **(6 x 19)**. Here we have **7** <u>stars</u> of **37** pennies each, and **6** <u>hexagons</u> of **19** pennies each, to equal **373**: **Logos**, made up of the very elements that were hidden in **Genesis 1:1**.

And so far we have been getting out visual clues through flat **2-dimensional** pictures. Imagine how much further ahead we would be if we were using three dimensions. . .

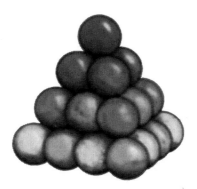

Thus we find that when carefully examined, every verse in the Bible has treasures. Some are hidden, some are glaringly obvious. What we have done in this chapter is take just one of Panin's discoveries and apply it like a spotlight on other scriptures. We have found bright reflections in many places, and if we were to continue to search we would find so much more. But for now the demonstration has been fruitful, so let us move on in the next chapter to more of this servant's discoveries.

VII
Letter to the *New York Sun*

This chapter will be devoted to the famous letter that Ivan Panin wrote to the *New York Sun* in November of 1899. The paper had been devoting a large section of its Sunday edition to a discussion of the truth of Christianity. On November 19th, a certain W.R.L. denounced Christianity using many of the old, tired, and often refuted arguments of his camp. He made the challenge for "...some champion of orthodoxy to come into the arena of the *Sun*..." and give the readers some "facts" in defense of the Christian religion. Ivan Panin had not read the *Sun* for some years; he was taking the train from South Framingham to Grafton, Massachusetts and found a copy left behind on a seat. Reading the challenge by W.R.L., the following letter, which was published, was his reply.

In addition to the letter to the *Sun*, he published a fifty-page pamphlet which included the Greek text of Matthew 1:1-17 along with the vocabularies so that his statements could be verified.

Here is the famous letter along with the after-comments published by Panin in his pamphlet.

Sir:—In to-day's *Sun* Mr. W.R.L. calls for a "champion of orthodoxy" to "step into the arena of the *Sun*"; and give him some "facts." Here are some facts:

1.   The first 17 verses of the New Testament contain the genealogy of the Christ. It consists of two main parts: Verses 1-11 cover the period from Abraham, the father of the chosen people, to the Captivity, when they ceased as an independent people. Verses 12-17 cover the period from the Captivity to the promised Deliverer, the Christ.

Let us examine the first part of this genealogy.

Its vocabulary has 49 words, or 7 x 7. This number is itself seven (Feature 1) sevens (Feature 2), and the sum of its factors is 2 sevens (Feature 3). Of these 49 words 28, or 4 sevens, begin with a vowel; and 21, or 3 sevens, begin with a consonant (Feature 4).

Again: these 49 words of the vocabulary have 266 letters, or 7 x 2 x 19; this number is itself 38 sevens (Feature 5), and the sum of its factors is 28, or 4 sevens (Feature 6), while the sum of its figures is 14, or 2 sevens (Feature 7). Of these 266 letters, moreover, 140, or 20 sevens, are vowels, and 126, or 18 sevens, are consonants (Feature 8).

That is to say: Just as the number of words in the vocabulary is a multiple of seven, so is the number of its letters a multiple of seven; just as the sum of the factors of the number of the words is a multiple of seven, so is the sum of the factors of the number of their letters a multiple of seven. And just as the number of words is divided between vowel words and consonant words by sevens, so is their number of letters divided between vowels and consonants by sevens.

Again: Of these 49 words 35, or 5 sevens, occur more than once in the passage; and 14, or 2 sevens, occur but once (Feature 9); seven occur in more than one form, and 42, or 6 sevens, occur in only one form (Feature 10). And among the parts of speech the 49 words are thus divided: 42, or 6 sevens, are nouns, seven are not nouns (Feature 12). Of the nouns 35 or 5 sevens, are Proper names, seven are common nouns (Feature 12). Of the Proper names 28 are male ancestors of the Christ, and seven are not (Feature 13).

Moreover, these 49 words are distributed alphabetically thus: Words under α-ε are 21 in number, or 3 sevens; ζ-κ 14, or 2 severs; μ-χ also 14. No other groups of sevens stopping at the end of a letter are made by these 49 words, the groups of sevens stop with these letters and no others. But the letters α, ε, ζ, κ, μ, χ, are letters 1, 5, 6, 10, 12, 22, of the Greek alphabet, and the sum of these numbers (called their Place Values) is 56, or 8 sevens (Feature 14).

This enumeration of the numeric phenomena of these 11 verses does not begin to be exhaustive, but enough has been shown to make it clear that this part of the genealogy is constructed on an elaborate design of sevens.

Let us now turn to the genealogy as a whole. I will not weary your readers with recounting all the numeric phenomena thereof: pages alone would exhaust them. I will point out only one feature: The New Testament is written in Greek. The Greeks had no separate symbols for expressing numbers, corresponding to our Arabic figures, but used instead the letters of their alphabet: just as the Hebrews, in whose language the Old Testament is written, made use for the same purpose of theirs. Accordingly, the 24 Greek letters stand for the following numbers: 1, 2, 3, 4, 5, 7, 8, 9, 10, 20, 30, 40, 50, 60, 70, 80, 100, 200, 300, 400, 500, 600, 700, 800. Every Greek word is thus a sum in arithmetic obtained by adding the numbers for which its letters stand, or their numeric values. Now the vocabulary to the entire genealogy has 72 words. If we write its numeric value over each of these 72 words, and add them, we get for their sum 42,364, or 6,052 sevens, distributed into the following alphabetical groups only: α-β, have 9.821, or 1,403 sevens: γ-δ, 1904, or 272 sevens; ε-ζ 3,703, or 529 sevens; θ-ρ, 19,264, or 2,752 sevens; σ-χ 7,672, or 1,096 sevens. But the numeric value of the 10 letters used for making these groups is 931, or 7 x 7 x 19, a multiple not only of seven but of seven sevens.

Let Mr. W.R.L. try to write some 300 words intelligently like this genealogy, and reproduce some numeric phenomena of like designs. If he does it in 6 months, he will indeed do a wonder. Let us assume that Matthew accomplished this feat in one month.

2. The second part of this chapter, verses 18-25, relates the birth of Christ. It consists of 161 words, or 23 sevens; occurring in 105 forms, or 15 sevens, with a vocabulary of 77 words or 11 sevens. Joseph is spoken to here by the angel. Accordingly, of the 77 words the angel uses 28, or 4 sevens; of the 105 forms he uses 35, or 5 sevens; the numeric value of the vocabulary is 52,605, or 7,515 sevens; of the forms, 65,429, or 9,347 sevens.

This enumeration only begins as it were to barely scratch the surface of the numerics of this passage. But what is specially noteworthy here is the fact that the angel's speech has also a scheme of sevens making it a kind of ring within a ring, a wheel within a wheel. If Mr. L. can write a similar passage of 161 words with the same scheme of sevens alone (though there are several others here) in some three years, he would accomplish a still greater wonder. Let us assume Matthew accomplished this feat in only 6 months.

3. The second chapter of Matthew tells of the childhood of the Christ. Its vocabulary has 161 words, or 23 sevens, with 896 letters, or 128 sevens, and 238 forms, or 34 sevens; the numeric value of the vocabulary is 123,529, or 17,647 sevens; of the forms, 166,985, or 23,855 sevens; and so on through pages of enumeration. This chapter has at least four logical divisions, and each division shows alone the same phenomena found in the chapter as a whole. Thus the first six verses have a vocabulary of 56 words, or 8 sevens, etc. There are some speeches here: Herod speaks, the Magi speak, the angel speaks. But so pronounced are the numeric phenomena here, that though there are as it were numerous rings within rings, and wheels within wheels, each is perfect in itself, though forming all the while only part of the rest.

If Mr. L. can write a chapter like this as naturally as Matthew writes, but containing in some 500 words so many intertwined yet harmonious numeric features, in say the rest of his days—whatever his age now, or the one to which he is to attain: if he thus accomplish it at all, it will indeed be marvel of marvels. Let us assume that Matthew accomplished this feat in only 3 years.

4. There is not, however, a single paragraph of the scores in Matthew that is not constructed in exactly the same manner. Only with each additional paragraph the difficulty of constructing it increases not in arithmetical but in geometrical progression. For he contrives to write numeric relations to what goes before and after. Thus in his last chapter he contrives to use just 7 words not used by him before. It would thus be easy to show that Mr. L. would require some centuries to write a book like Matthew's. How long it took Matthew the writer does not know. But how he contrived to do it between the Crucifixion, A.D. 30 (and his Gospel could not have been written earlier), and the destruction of Jerusalem, A.D. 70 (and the Gospel could not have been written later), let Mr. L. and his like-minded explain.

Anyhow Matthew did it, and we thus have a miracle—an unheard-of literary, mathematical artist, unequaled, hardly even conceivable. This is the first *fact* for Mr. L. to contemplate.

A second fact is yet more important: In his very first section, the genealogy discussed above, the words found *nowhere else in the New Testament*, occur 42 times, 7 x 6; and have 126 letters, 7 x 6 x 3, each number a multiple not only of seven, but of 6 sevens, to name only two of the many numeric features of these words. But how did Matthew know, when designing this scheme for these words (whose sole characteristic is that they are found nowhere else in the New Testament) that they would *not* be found in the other 26 books? that they would not be used by the other 7 New Testament writers? Unless we assume the impossible hypothesis that he had an agreement with them to that effect, he must have had the rest of the New Testament before him when he wrote his book. *The Gospel of Matthew, then, was written last.*

5. It so happens, however, that the Gospel of Mark shows the very same phenomena. Thus the very passage called so triumphantly in today's *Sun* a "forgery," the Last Twelve Verses of Mark, presents among some *sixty* features of sevens the following phenomena: It has 175 words, or 25 sevens; a vocabulary of 98 words, or 2 sevens of sevens with 553 letters, or 79 sevens; 133 forms, or 19 sevens, and so on to the minutest detail.

Mark, then, is another miracle, another unparalleled literary genius. And in the same way in which it was shown that Matthew wrote last it is also shown that Mark, too, wrote last. Thus to take an example from this very passage: It has just one word found nowhere else in the New Testament, θανασιμος, *'deadly'*. This fact is signaled by no less than seven features of sevens thus: Its numeric value is 581, or 83 sevens, with the sum of its figures 14, or 2 sevens, of which the letters 3, 5, 7, *from both the* BEGINNING *and* END *of the word* have 490, or 7 x 7 x 5 x 2: a multiple of seven sevens, with the sum of its factors 21, or 3 sevens. In the vocabulary it is preceded by 42 words, 7 x 6; in the passage itself by 126 words, or 7 x 6 x 3, both numbers multiples not only of seven, but of 6 sevens. We have thus established before us this third fact for Mr. L. to contemplate: *Matthew surely wrote after Mark, and Mark just as surely wrote after Matthew.*

6. It happens, however, to be a fourth fact, that Luke presents the same phenomena as Matthew and Mark; and so does John, and James, and Peter, and Jude, and Paul. And we have thus no longer two great unheard-of mathematical literati, but eight of them *and each wrote after the other.*

7. And not only this: As Luke and Peter wrote each 2 books, John 5, and Paul 14, it can in the same way be shown that each of the 27 New Testament books was written last. In fact, not a page of the over 500 in Westcott and Hort's Greek edition (which the

writer has used throughout) but it can be demonstrated thus to have been written last.

The phenomena are there and there is no human way of explaining them. Eight men cannot each write last, 27 books, some 500 pages cannot each be written first. But once assume that one Mind directed the whole, and the problem is solved simply enough; but this is Verbal Inspiration—of every jot and tittle of the New Testament.

There remains only to be added that by precisely the same kind of evidence the Hebrew Old Testament is proved to be equally inspired. Thus the very first verse of Genesis has seven words, 28 letters, or 4 sevens: to name only two out of the dozens of numeric features of this one verse of only seven words. —*N.Y. Sun*, Nov. 21, 1899—*Corrected.*

To this letter several replies appeared in the *Sun*, but not a single answer. For in only three ways can it be refuted.
(a) By showing that the facts are not as here given.

(b) By showing that it is possible for 8 men to write each after the other 7; for 27 books, for some 500 pages to be each in its turn written last.

(c) By showing that even if the facts be true, the arithmetic faultless, and the collocation of the numerics honest, it does not follow that mere men could not have written this without Inspiration from above.

Accordingly, as many as nine noted rationalists (of whom Drs. Lyman Abbot and Charles W. Eliot are still living) [now in 1927 also gone to where they may know] **[sic]** were respectfully but publicly invited to refute the writer. One was not "interested" in the writer's "arithmetical" doings; two "regretted" that they "had no time" to give heed thereto. Another "did not mean to be unkind," but . . . . The rest were silent. For the special benefit of these the writer printed the original data with numerous details, enabling them in the easiest manner to verify every statement made by him, *if they wished*. And to the best of his ability he has for years seen to it that no scholar whom surely these things specially concern remain in ignorance of the facts here recounted and of like cogency.

A notable exception to the above is a lawyer of standing [now also dead], whose books on Law are deemed as of authority. *He* had intelligence enough and candor withal to confess that the case for the Bible as made out by the writer is impregnable, that the Bible *is* thus proved to be an "absolutely unique book." This much the case itself exhorts from the but too well equipped writer on—EVIDENCE; and accordingly he henceforth reads the writer's Numerics with intense appreciation. And then, fresh from this confession, he betakes himself once more to the circulation of his anti-Christian books in the writing of which, he joys to spend his leisure hours.

In the second letter to the *N. Y. Sun* the author, in discussing some irrelevant "answers" to his first letter, recited the three ways of refuting him and then continued:

No sane man will try to refute me by the second method. To refute me by the first method I herewith respectfully invite any or all of the following to prove that my facts are not facts: namely Messrs: Lyman Abbott, Washington Gladden, Heber Newton, Minot J. Savage, Presidents Eliot of Harvard, White of Cornell, and Harper, the University of Chicago, Professors J. Henry Thayer of Harvard, and Dr. Briggs, and any other prominent higher critic so called. They may associate with themselves, if they choose, all the contributors of the ninth edition of the Encyclopedia Britannica who wrote its articles on Biblical subjects together with a dozen mathematicians of the calibre of Professor Simon Newcomb. The heavier the calibre of either scholar or mathematician, the more satisfactory to me.

They will find that my facts are facts. And since they are facts, I am ready to take them to any three prominent lawyers, or, better

54

still, to any judge of a superior or supreme court, and abide by his decision as to whether the conclusion is not necessary that Inspiration alone can account for the facts, if they are facts.

All I should ask would be that the judge treat the case as he would any other case that comes before him: declining to admit matters for discussion as irrelevant when they are irrelevant; and listening patiently to both sides, as he does in any trial.

Note the multitude of phenomena Panin utilizes in his work. He does not limit himself to any one particular *method*, but freely makes use of any and all numerical symmetries and coincidences. This is one of the elements that has stumbled many a reader . . . we would like to have a quantifiable method; something we can do over and over to get our results. That attitude is somewhat like the ELS camp. 'ELS' stands for Equidistant Letter Sequencing, and has been popularized by Michael Drosnin's book *The Bible Code*. In Appendix III we look at this phenomena, as well as several others that share the realm of Bible Numerics.

Next, let us look at what Panin said about his efforts in translating . . .in his own words. The following chapter will be from a lecture he gave at Caxton Hall, Westminster, England on February 19th, 1934. This was the same year that he published his Greek version of the New Testament, and twenty years after publishing his English translation.

VIII
Panin's Approach to Translating in His Own Words
Extracted from "*Bible Numerics*", 1934

This is the second half of an address given by Panin at Caxton Hall, Westminster, England on February 19th, 1934. This was the same year that he published his Greek version of the New Testament, and twenty years after publishing his English translation. The lecture was very well received; this second half began at 8:00 p.m. and was introduced by Mr. Herbert Garrison, who took the time to mention that Ivan Panin had been "offered a very tempting post as president of a College, and they were astonished because he would not accept it. But he chose to follow a course of his own, on account of the conversion he had experienced in the great old-fashioned Wesley and Whitfield way." This transcription will make for a long chapter, and it is thoroughly worth reading to get a sense of the man and his ways.

*   *   *

There were two things I had not time to bring before you this afternoon in connection with the subject about which I spoke, namely the impossibility of men constructing the Bible, every portion thereof, in the manner I pointed out to you this afternoon; and the first thing is this: When you and I wish to say "1", we do not spell "one" but we write the figure "1" and the same for "2" and all the other figures. In other words we have distinct symbols for numbers. But the Greeks in whose language the New Testament was written, and the Hebrews, in whose language the Old Testament was written, had no special symbols for numbers. When they wished to say "1" they wrote the first letter of the alphabet. They had a definite system where every letter of the Greek language stood for a special number. The first nine letters stood for 1-10 then from 20-100, and from 100-400. The Hebrews had the same system. They had 22 letters instead of 24, but each letter stood for a number, and each word is simply a sum in arithmetic, by adding the numeric values of the special letters.

The numeric value of the Name of our Lord—"Jesus"—in Greek is 888. I have chosen that Name because it is a good illustration. We are living in times when the anti-Christ is to be revealed, and the Scriptures warn us—"Who hath wisdom let him count, for his name is the name of a man." And the number is "666" and our Lord's number is "888". Anyone a little familiar with spiritual things would know at once that this collocation of 666 and 888 is not accidental; so we will just rapidly run over the meaning of the first eight numbers.

"1" we all know is "unity", "Divinity", and "God"; there is only one God. But God wants a witness, and the second Person of the Trinity is the Witness to the Father, so 2 is the number of Testimony, Witness, and the Lord Jesus Christ is the "Faithful Witness". The Holy Spirit, the third Person of the Trinity, witnesses to the Son, and thus at the mouth of two or THREE witnesses is every matter established" Two are enough, but the third clinches it, establishes beyond possible question. Three is thus divine completeness. Where one point suffices for the start, and two points suffice for the direction, thus making a line, three points are necessary for the geometrical figure.

There was a time in Creation when we could, so to speak, hear the Blessed Trinity saying—"Suppose we create something outside of ourselves,"—and so the world is created. The world was not eternal, it was created by God, the Father and the Son, and the Holy Spirit; so '4'—one added to the Trinity, is the number of the world—there are 4 winds, 4 corners of the earth, 4 rivers of Paradise, 4 world Empires, and so on. Then God said, "We have created the world, let us create one to be head of the world," so man was created. Man was to be ruler of this world. Man is marked all over with fives: 5 fingers, 5 toes, 5 openings into his head, etc. So we have "4" the world, plus "1", something over the world—man.

Unfortunately, man did not keep his sovereignty over creation. In his folly he sinned against God, and empowered someone else to take his place, and this someone else is Satan, one superior to man; that is the reason his number is "6".

Now "7" is the addition of 3 and 4—Divinity plus the world, in other words, completeness. God plus creation completes everything you can possibly think of, so "7" is the number of completion, perfection if you like, but not Divine perfection, because Satan also can do a something perfect, but it is not perfect in God's sight, it is Satanic work. So 7 is something ahead of 6: Satan coming short of perfection.

But in the Lord Jesus Christ there is a new creation, an entirely new order, a new octave, as it were, started in creation with the Resurrection, which is on the eighth day, the first of the new week. In music it is the same: the octave note is the beginning of the new seven. That is the reason why the number of the Lord Jesus Christ is 888, exactly as the number of the Satanic creature is 666. For our purpose tonight I need go no further.

Every Greek and every Hebrew letter being a number, suppose you put the number over each letter and over each word, and count up its numeric value. I told you this afternoon that there are a certain number of words in the vocabulary to a certain passage, say, of the birth of our Lord. When you add the numeric value of all those words you find it is a multiple of 7. The number of forms in the account of the Birth of our Lord has a numeric value of sevens and the entire passage has a numeric value of a multiple of seven. In other words every single letter of that passage, which runs into hundreds, is simply a contribution to the general scheme of seven, and it can be demonstrated that men could not possibly write a whole Book, the letters of which run into hundreds of thousands, and agree among themselves that each letter should be a special number. No one realized, until the Gracious God permitted me to discover Bible numerics, this scheme of numeric values in the Scriptures.

Every letter in the Greek alphabet has two values, a place value and a numeric value, and if you take the passage I analysed you will find it will have two distinct systems of values running through it. Imagine any single letter being so adjusted to a scheme like that, and it is simply impossible that even a smaller number of letters could be adjusted in that manner. That is one of the points I wanted to bring out this afternoon.

The second point I wish to remind you of is this. That there are a number of sentences in the Word of God that, even if we had today the best MSS. in the world, fresh as they came from the hands of the Apostles, we would not be sure, after all, that we were translating the true text. For instance, in the oldest MSS. the text of the Bible has the words together; there are no spaces between the words nor punctuation marks, so that the first verse in Genesis would read something like this to you: "inthebeginning. ."etc. The daughter of a godly family was once approached by an infidel who came to visit them. And he wrote down on paper—"Godisnowhere," and showed it to the child and said:—"My child, I make out this to mean "God is nowhere". But she quietly looked at it and said,—"Oh, no! divide it here, then it will read—"God is now here". Well, logically, who is going to decide which is correct? I would not feel at liberty to become a martyr at the stake because I read a passage one way, and someone else reads it another. The Bible has many such possibilities, therefore you see, even if we had today the inspired text fresh from the hands of the Apostles and Prophets, we would still need some real test by which those who press one reading over against another can be sure that they are right. Now numerics do that.

Suppose we are absolutely sure that the Sinai MS is one of the original MSS. of the Apostles themselves. There would be many questions about it; we should have to decide how it should be printed, and numerics alone do that. I will explain that particular point a little later. But let me repeat that the Bible is full of that kind of difficulty. Now, the Holy Spirit comes and gives you the means to bring irresistible evidence that this is how it should be read and not otherwise.

Very early in my numeric career I came in contact with Professor Griffiths Thomas. Probably he is pretty well known in England; he came from Wycliffe Hall, and from there he was called to Toronto to be Professor of Hebrew, and eventually, probably Principal. He heard about my work and one day I received a postcard from him—"Please send me all your writings, with bill". Now, it so happens that I do not send any bills, my work is not for sale. I print it only when I have funds; when it is paid for I don't want any special reward for what the Lord has given me, so anyone can have it. I sent him my works, and when he was established in his Professorship of Hebrew he wrote me a letter something like this:

> "Dear Mr. Panin: I am Professor of Hebrew in Wycliffe College, Toronto. Will you kindly tell me which is the true reading of Isaiah 9:3? I read from the American Revised Version—'Thou has multiplied the nations; thou has increased their joy'; and the Authorized Version reads: 'Thou has multiplied the nation, thou HAST NOT increased their joy'. A difference between 'Yes' and 'No'. Will you kindly tell me which is the true reading?"

In the Hebrew the difference is only a difference of one letter. Well, I read this passage, and I found that the Revised Version gives beautiful numerics, whereas if you read it the way the Authorized Version gives it, it forms no numerics, so —I could tell the Professor—"Numerics prove Revised Version is right".

You will naturally think it does not make much difference anyway, but suppose the question had been about—"Who believeth and is baptized shall be saved"; or "Who believeth and is baptized shall not be saved". How would you like that? There is often a very important question in the Word of God which hinges on one letter; here is a case:

If you turn to the 13th chapter of I Corinthians, the Revised Version reads:—"If I speak with the tongues of men and of angels, but have not love I am become sounding brass or a clanging cymbal. . .and if I give my body to be burned. . ." The Authorized Version and the best authorities also thus read it except Westcott and Hort, the best Editors who read: "If I give my body so that I may glory," or rejoice, or boast. Well, what kind of sense is that? It does not seem to make any sense. That is exactly what the scribe of the MSS. felt. He perhaps said—"I think it is a mistake from one letter to another". That is the trouble with scribes: when they come to a passage that they do not quite understand, they think they can improve on the author. That is the case with a great many readings—until the critical Editors arrived. When they find a hard reading against an easy one, they hold to the hard one, because no sensible man would change an easy reading into a hard one; so Wescott and Hort say—"so that I may glory" and they are right, numerics prove that. If you change one letter to the other, the whole numeric scheme fails. Now you see how important it is becoming.

Then in the same way I Timothy 3:16, reads thus:—"And without controversy great is the mystery of the godliness. He who was manifested in the flesh, justified in the spirit, seen of angels, preached among the nations" but the Authorized Version reads: —"God was manifest in the flesh, justified in the spirit, seen of angels, preached among nations. . .". Then came the godly critical Editors, who were bound to revise the text and give us the pure Word of God, and they said that it did not read "God was manifest in the flesh". The the dear orthodox folk were shocked and called

61

the Editors heretics, and some of them were weakened, and against their better judgment kept to the old reading. But the abbreviation for "God" in the old MSS. is the first and last letters of the word, simply two letters, with a little mark dividing the Th. into two halves, and the word for "Who" is exactly the same, except that there is no little sign in the middle. So Editors have been fighting for two centuries over that. Some insist that it is terrible to exchange the word "God" for the word "Who", but the difference is only a little mark. The Vatican MS. is defective in this particular passage, but the Alexandrian MS gives "He Who" only in such a manner that a mark from the other side of the leaf happens to show in that very place, so that you can make it look like "God" or "who". Thus, the battle has been going on as to whether the sign is from the other side of the page, or the same side. The in come numerics and enable us to say—"Gentlemen, we are very sorry; we believe in the Divinity of our Lord just as much as you do, but we believe in truth, and the passage should read just as the Revised Version makes it read—"He who was manifested. . .".

There are dozens of such cases; one of them is rather serious. In the second Gospel—Mark—the Authorized and Revised Versions make the first verse read: "The beginning of the Gospel of Jesus Christ the Son of God. . ."; but the two great MSS. are divided. The Vatican leaves the words "Son of God" out; the Sinai keeps them. Westcott and Hort, like honest men, whenever there is an uncertainty, left what is called alternative readings. The left 3,000 readings in the New Testament alone. I have gone over every one of these 3,000 readings, testing them by numerics. Numerics favour the primary reading of this particular passage by omitting the words "Son of God".

It is established as a definite point of teaching among all the scholars and theologians of the New Testament that the four Gospels were written on a definite plan. . Matthew represents our Lord Jesus Christ as the King. The genealogy of the King need not go any further back than Abraham, therefore Matthew's genealogy begins with Abraham. Luke, on the other hand, being the Gospel of the Son of man, puts its genealogy back to Adam. John, being the Gospel of the Son of God, goes back beyond Adam—"In the BEGINNING was the Word, and the Word was God. . .". Now Mark, it is well understood, is the Gospel of the Servant.

The key-word of the Gospel of Matthew is the "Kingdom of the Heavens". That phrase is not found in any other Book in the New Testament. It is the ringing of the bell, as if the Holy Spirit were saying—"I want you to study the Lord Jesus as the King," and the key-word, the word found nowhere else in the New Testament, is the "Kingdom of the Heavens". Other Gospels refer to this as the "Kingdom of God", but never as the "Kingdom of Heaven".

The key-word in Mark is "immediately". In the Authorized Version this word is also give as "straightway". It occurs 37 times, more in Mark than in the rest of the New Testament. The business of the servant is to do everything with dispatch, immediately, straightway. Now, if Mark begins by saying "Son of God" then the whole becomes topsy-turvy. You see how dangerous it is to put in the words "Son of God". If we are going to be servants of the Lord Jesus we must first of all own Him as our King, we must first of all learn to obey Him. We are all babes in Christ, wishing to become servants; and the Lord says—"Don't you get into Mark until you have gone through Matthew. Have you learned to obey Me first?" When we have gone through Matthew and Mark and have learned to know our Blessed Lord as King and Servant, then we are fit to see the Blessed Son of God as He is in Luke represented as the Son of man, the gentle, loving Saviour. But it is not enough to know the Lord merely as King, or Servant or Son of man, we need to know Him also as the eternal Son of God. Now we are fit to enter into John. You see, there is a definite order of theology, providing you do not mix it up and put the words "Son of God" in Mark. There are not a few of this kind of theological questions that can be settled apparently in no other way than numerics.

The first thing to learn, then, is that the New Testament is not only made sure with regard to its inspiration, by numerics but also that it enables us to settle the text and its meaning.

Westcott and Hort, as I have mentioned before, are, perhaps by far the best Editors of the Greek New Testament. The were godly men; they loved the Book. Bishop Westcott wrote me, some ten years before he died, "Holy Writ is as precious to me as ever". They were both godly men as far as the love of the Book was concerned. Dr. Hort wrote me something very similar. After twenty-eight years Westcott and Hort came to this honest conclusion: That the last twelve verses of Mark are not part of the Word of God, because the two oldest MSS. do not contain it; and they had a definite reason for assuming that wherever the two oldest MSS.—the Vatican and the Sinai—agree, it is dangerous to disregard their verdict. So they marked the verses, in double brackets, designating that in their honest judgment the verses did not belong to the Testament. Westcott and Hort were equally satisfied without any doubt in their mind whatever, that the story of the woman taken in adultery in John's Gospel is not the Word of God, that when we read it we are adding to the Word of God. And Tregelles, who was a strictly orthodox Editor of the New Testament, who also held strongly to the inspiration of the Scriptures as much as any of us on this platform do today, had to confess honestly, that the story of the woman taken in adultery, though good tradition and instruction, is not part of the Word of God.

Well, you and I wish to be rather particular. We do not wish to have a passage expunged, for instance, which tells us "these signs shall follow them that believe. . ." or "he that believeth. . .shall be saved," etc. Personally, I feel that I could not eat my breakfast in peace until I knew whether these things are real, or whether there is something in my Bible which ought to be torn out.

Let us suppose that there is someone else who has something to say about the Bible besides you and me. Suppose there is a devil who says—"Can I let these passages stand in the Bible, which say —"they shall cast out demons in my name, etc? No, I will do all in my power to have them out". And then he comes to the passage concerning the woman taken in adultery and says—"Can I have that passage in, when it says to a woman caught in the act —"Neither do I condemn thee, go and sin no more"? You can see that Satan would do all he could, with his might power to expunge these passages. Probably that is the true origin of the way those two passages disappeared from the two oldest MSS. By the grace of God, Westcott and Hort are the most correct Editors in other respects, except in those dozen passages which they double bracket as "interpolations". They are wrong in every one of those passages which they expunge as not being truly part of the New Testament. With regard to the Prayer of our Lord from the Cross—"Father, forgive them, for they know not what they do" you and I wish to know did the Lord offer that prayer or not? We wish to know did the Lord Jesus have that Agony in the Garden so that drops of blood were pouring from Him. Westcott and Hort mark these passages as interpolations. There are twelve passages of that kind, about which, according to their honest judgment, though they were the very best equipped Editors of the New Testament, they had to say—"We are sorry, but the evidence is all against it". **Now come numerics and establish every one, with one exception, and the curious thing is that every one of these strong passages which the adversary was anxious to expunge, the Holy Spirit has marked in a very peculiar way.[4]** There is one word in the last twelve verses of Mark which is found nowhere else in the New Testament. It is the word "deadly". Its numeric value is 581; the sum of its figures is 14— twice seven. Its numeric value is 7 x 83. There are six features of seven in that little word alone.

---

4   Emphasis added. —*Ed.*

Now, every passage on which aspersion is cast shows numerics. The first passage expunged is Matthew 16: 2,3. That passage has three words which occur nowhere else in the New Testament. Take those three words out and the wonderful numeric design is destroyed. So the Holy Spirit has definitely protected these passages in His own way.

But if Matthew knew that those three words are not found anywhere else in the New Testament, that would be a proof that he wrote his book last. But you can prove the same with Luke; and you can equally show that Paul wrote last. You can show that every part of the New Testament was written last, in the same manner. So you see how impossible it was for eight men to have each written their books last; eight men cannot all write last. A very injudicious man came into a house once, where there were a happy father and mother and a dear child of about six, and the dear man had the injudiciousness to ask the child—"Well, my dear, which do you love best, Papa or Mama?", and the little girl said—"I love both best!" You can love both best as the little girl, who was embarrassed by the question, but you cannot write two books each last. So it makes it absolutely impossible for men to have written a book thus.

Any number of details of this kind can be brought out, so as actually to establish every questionable point in the Word of God. Take, for instance, the saying of our Lord to the thief in the Cross —"Today, thou shalt be with me in Paradise". The dear Seventh Day Adventists, who hold the dead to be asleep, say that cannot be true, it is only the question of a comma—"I say unto you to-day, thou shalt be with me in Paradise".

Well, there is no way of refuting them, there is no proof. But then come numerics, and we analyse that sentence and find that if we read it one way we get no numerics at all, but if we read it the right way—"To-day thou shalt be with me in Paradise" there is an elaborate double scheme of numerics. So you see what a commentary on the Bible numerics are. In the case of any doubtful interpretations, numerics always give a definite and clear answer; the true one shows numerics, the false one fails to show them.

Without the aid of Westcott and Hort I could not have really done my work, because the text of the Authorized Version from my point of view—not from the point of view of salvation or doctrine even, but from the textual point of view, the text of the Authorized Version was useless to me, and for this reason: it has too many inaccuracies for my special purpose. Erasmus, for example, who was the Editor of the first Greek text in print was very anxious to get ahead of the Roman Catholic scholars who were issuing a Bible of their own; and he was in such a hurry that he used one MS. for the Book of Revelation and the last page of Revelation was missing in that MS. So what do you suppose Erasmus did? He simply concocted his own Greek for that page; he took the Latin Vulgate and translated it into his own Greek! So that the last page of the Authorized Version is a translation of Erasmus into Greek of a Latin inaccurate translation itself! Now, you and I wish to have an inspired page of the Bible, not one man's mere guessage. The Received Text has a great many suspicious readings of that kind. They do not affect doctrine or conduct seriously, because the great blessing of the Word of God is like the Lord himself —if you only touch the hem of His garment, you can be made whole. God has seen to it that His blessed Book, no matter how distorted it is in any language—sometimes the missionaries are at their wits' end to know how to translate the word "God"— nevertheless, the Word of God is so full of spiritual power, that if we only get the fringe of it to them, those dear heathen can be converted by it. But you and I wish to have the last page of Revelation as it was truly the inspired Word of God. Westcott and Hort based all their work largely on the Vatican and Sinai MSS., and decided that wherever the two MSS. agreed, that should generally settle the reading. Well, you know, there has been some doubt cast upon the Sinai MSS., because a very shrewd Greek copied a great many MSS. and tried to foist his own MSS. on the folk, so that has left a cloud on the Sinai MSS., and some people see fit to cast doubt on it even now, when there is the question as to whether the British Government did wisely to take part in its acquisition. But first of all, it is certain that if Westcott and Hort's work stands the test of numerics, it would have been impossible that the Vatican should be found to agree with a FORGED MS., it would be wholly out of the question. This would be what I would call the indirect evidence of numerics. But, —fortunately, this is not all. I have analysed the Greek words for the Sinai and Vatican Codexes. I have here page after page of the numerics of these words in Greek. Whenever we wish to study numerics relating to our own affairs of life or anything else, we must always remember that the language in which God wishes us to count is Greek, because He left that name of the anti-Christ in Greek. You and I will have to stand the test when anti-Christ comes. The Holy Spirit has given us warning—"Be sure not to receive this mark of the beast upon you," because it will be the number of the beast upon ourselves. The Holy Spirit warns us that he is 666, that is, in Greek. You and I have to go to numerics in Greek when we wish to prove the correctness of a passage. The three words show striking numerics. There is a system there of sevens and nines at once on the blackboard. I have here page after page of the numerics of those three words.

That is how God has set His seal on His Book: so that by the aid of the text presented to us by Westcott and Hort, I was able to verify everything they stated, and verify all the doubtful readings, so that those two great MSS. can be established in such a way that no one can attack their authenticity. This is the testimony of numerics as to any aspersion on the Sinai Codex.

My prayer is simply this. That God may make that blessed Book of His as precious to you as He has made it to me. It has been an inexpressible joy in my life to work these things out, simply because of the testimony of the majesty and the marvel of the loving-kindness of God vouchsafed in this Book unto our charge. Pray for me, and may the Lord bless you.

*   *   *

Thus ends Panin's speech, and there we see some bit of his spirit and his work. His confidence is complete; but it is a confidence in the One who gave him his work and guided him through it; not, as so often is the case with us, mere self-confidence. A noble mind will say what he knows and stop there; a wise man knows that he does not yet know everything, and can freely admit it. In the next chapter we will look at a distinction that Panin saw—and did not know what it signified, only that it signified something important. We will build on that distinction, and show how even the hints of a master builder can produce fruit in his apprentices.

IX
Panin's Hints: Building on the Master's Foundations

Let us now quote from Panin's excellent work ***Bible Chronology*** (1923)[5] In it he solves many a knotty problem that has puzzled scholars for centuries. But here we are going to look at a distinction that Panin freely admitted he did not yet understand, though he is careful to emphasize its importance. This first quote is from part **VI**, Canon III, paragraph 12:

> "Three peculiar but usual idioms of the Hebrew are to be noted here: (1) the numbers are given not in the letters of the alphabet (corresponding somewhat to the modern Arabic figures), but in their own names, words in full: **eighty** and **four hundreds**, not 480, nor even 80 and 400. (2) The word **year** is repeated: not 480 years, but 80 years and 400 years. (3) The word **year**, though plural with numbers up to ten, is singular with numbers above ten. Hence it is not 80 years and 400 years, but 80 year and 400 year, necessitating a transposition of the number in the English, which perhaps varies somewhat the sense of the phrase in the original."

And this quote is from part **VIII**, Canon V, paragraph 32:

> "In Ex. 6: 16, 18, 20, the years of the lives of Levi, Kohath, and Amram are given respectively as "seven and thirty and hundred years," "three and thirty and hundred years," and "seven and thirty and hundred years." Years is given only once; and the order is: units, tens, hundreds. But the lives of Sarah, Abraham and Ishmael are given thus: "And Sarah's life was hundred years and twenty years and seven years—years

---

5   Also available from New England Bible Sales. See title page for contact information.

of Sarah's life." "And these [are the] days of Abraham's life which he lived: hundred years and seventy years and five years." "And these [the] years of Ishmael's life: hundred years, thirty years and seven years" (Gen. 23: 1; 25: 7, 17). Here **year** is repeated thrice, which each denomination: and the denominations, moreover, are reversed from the order of Levi, Kohath and Amram. Here the order is: hundreds, tens, units. Of Isaac it is: "And Isaac's days were hundred years and eighty years" (Genesis 35: 28), which in the absence of units still holds to the manner and order of his father, mother, and brother. But with Jacob it is: "And Jacob's days were, the years of his life, seven years and forty and hundred years" (Gen. 47:28). Here the order is the same with Levi, Kohath, and Amram; units first, hundreds last. The repetition of **year** is kept, but only once instead of twice; so that the case of Jacob is mid-way between Abraham, Sarah and Ishmael, with their **year** thrice, and Levi, Kohath and Amram with their one.

The reason for these changes in the notation of the length of life, and other like them, are unknown to the writer. But a dull reader indeed would he be of **God's** book, if he were to take all this as mattering naught, unimportant, meaningless . . .

This matter of **year** and **years**, as well as the order of how they are listed, will be sketched out for examination. Panin has pointed out that it is significant, and has freely admitted that he has not yet searched out that significance. So let us begin by listing the patriarchs, and paying close attention to the exact language used by Scripture.

We have ten patriarchs before the flood, and ten after. Let's set them up parallel to each other. And when the text says, for example, "900 year and 30 year", we will list 900 separately from 30. Anytime the text says **"years"** instead of **"year"** we will put a plus sign ("+") in front of that number. Let's see what we get:

	List 1 Pre-flood	First Son	Lived After	Total Age	List 2 Post-flood	First Son	Lived After	List 1 & 2 Total
1	Adam	130	800	900 and 30	Shem	100	500	1,530
2	Seth	100 + 5	800 + 7	900 and 12	Arphaxad	35	400 + 3	1,350
3	Enosh	90	800 and 15	900 + 5	Shelach	30	400 + 3	1,338
4	Cainan	70	800 and 40	900 +10	Eber	34	400 and 30	1,374
5	Mahalaleel	60 + 5	800 and 30	800 and 95	Peleg	30	200 + 9	1,134
6	Jared	100 and 62	800	900 and 62	Reu	32	200 + 7	1,201
7	Enoch	65	300	300 and 65	Serug	30	200	595
8	Methuselah	100 and 87	700 and 82	900 and 69	Nahor	29	100 and 19	1,117
9	Lemech	100 and 82	500 and 95	700 and 77	Terah	70	200 + 5	1,052
10	Noah	500		900 and 50	Abraham	100 and 70 + 5		1,125[6]
Totals using the same formats:		1,315 and 231 + 10	6,300 and 262 + 7	8,100 and 460 + 15		490	2,700 and 119 + 32	11,816

All our information from the text is there, laid out according to the **grammar** of the text.

- Where the word "and" is used, it means that "Year" was used twice. For example, number 6, Jared is "100 and 62" because the text says *"And he is living—Jared—two and sixty **Year** and hundred of **Year**."*
- Where the "+" sign is used in the chart, the text says "years" instead of "Year", for example number 5, Mahalaleel is "60 + 5" because the text says *"And he is living—Mahalaleel—five **years** and sixty **Year**."*
- Totals of each paired set of pre- and post-flood patriarchs are on the right, and the grand total is in the lower right.

God's day is 1000 years, and each person lived a proportion of

---

6 Ironically, Abraham added to Noah here equals 1,125 which is 3 times the number of days Noah was on the ark.

that. The flood occurred in year 1,656, and after the flood, there were 713 years until the death of Joseph, giving us 2,369 total years in Genesis. So we have the following raw figures:

- The ages of the patriarchs as worded in the text, including when their first son was born,
- The 360 day 'perfect' year,
- The 1,656 years before the flood,
- The 713 years after the flood,
- The relationship between pre-flood and post-flood patriarchs.

Now let's take each person's age and see how evenly 360 divides into it[7], and what is left over. This shows how many *cyclic* years are involved. Each 360 is of a circle, so the remainders are *degrees of a 360° circle*. Our object here is to have the ages to evenly add up to a multiple of 360.

		Age		Age	Total	/360	Remainder
1	Adam	930	Shem	600	→1,530	4	90°
2	Seth	912	Arphaxad	438	→1,350	3	270°
3	Enosh	905	Shelach	433	→1,338	3	258°
4	Cainan	910	Eber	464	→1,374	3	294°
5	Mahalaleel	895	Peleg	239	→1,134	3	54°
6	Jared	962	Reu	239	→1,201	3	121°
7	Enoch	365	Serug	230	→595	1	235°
8	Methuselah	969	Nahor	148	→1,117	3	37°
9	Lemech	777	Terah	275	→1,052	2	332°
10	Noah	950	Abraham	175	→1,125	3	45°
				Totals	11,816	28	1,736°

---

7 Note that 460, one of the figures at the bottom of the "Total Age" column in the first chart, when multiplied by 3.6 (360/100), comes to exactly 1,656, the date of the flood. The number 460 and its multiples (230, 23 especially) keep popping up as we will see.

1,736° has four more 360°'s that can be subtracted from it, leaving us with:

11,816	**32**	296°

Here 32 is the total number of 360° cycles so far. The remainder of 296° cannot come out even until we return to our first chart and add up <u>every</u> <u>single</u> "<u>+</u>" <u>figure</u>, which is every time in the text that the word "**years**" instead of "**Year**" is used. They add up to +64. We add that to 296° and get 360°, and since you are probably just looking at the charts and not reading these words, here`s your visual:

11,880	**33**	0°

And here we have our first clue. There are 33[8] cycles of 360° in the combined ages of the twenty patriarchs, which are not apparent until we take the nuances of grammar seriously, meaning we double up the word "**years**" when adding to the word "**Year**".

Using this cyclic method, let's look at the other figures at the bottom of the first chart. We have the **initial** figures (meaning the word "and" is not in front of them, nor is a "+" sign) of:

- 1,315 which is   3 x 360° with a remainder of 235°[9]

---

8 The 33 cycles refer to both the 33 days of a woman's being unclean upon bearing a male, and the 33 paired chambers in Ezekiel 41:6 (almost always translated "30" because the translators do not realize that a *circular* structure is being described). We have then the dual ideas of what it takes to establish mankind as recovering from the 'uncleanness' of eating the fruit, finally producing an Abraham who can establish faith, and God's establishing of those who take part in that process as permanent fixtures in his temple. This theme of 33 and the dual Establish/Maintain relationship is the thematic backbone of the book of Hebrews, as seen in Apostle/High Priest.

9   Note that Enoch and Serug, row 7 in the chart, also have a remainder of 235°.

- 6,300 which is 17.5 x 360°
- 8,100 which is 22.5 x 360°
-   490 which is   1 x 360° with a remainder of 130°
- 2,700 which is   7.5 x 360°

So we see that there are definitely clear-cut patterns emerging. The task is to find out what they mean. All we have done so far is to establish that the patriarchs' ages are correlated to the 360 day year.

What we need to do next is find out how the 360° year (and thus the ages of the patriarchs) are correlated with the year of the flood (1,656) and the years after the flood (713) until Joseph's death which ends Genesis.

The first clue we get is by adding up all the pre-son ages of the patriarchs from Adam to Seth. This gives us precisely the number of years to the flood: 1,656. This is a bit remarkable because it appears that Seth was the second-born after Japheth, and was 98 when he left the ark; Noah would have had him at 602. In other words, there is no obvious reason why this should come out even, but it does.

The second clue we get is by adding up all the patriarchs in Genesis to find out what kind of figures we are working with. If there were 9 patriarchs, we would expect everything to be in multiples of 9. As it is, we have 10 (pre-flood), + 10 (post-flood) + 3 (Isaac, Jacob, and Joseph) = **23**.

23 is a prime number, and if it is the 'prime' number to be used, we can expect to find it virtually every time we do a calculation. Let's look at a few of the places it appears:
- 1,656 years before the flood   = 72 x **23**
- 713 years after the flood   = 31 x **23**
- 1,656 / 3.60 (360°/100)   = 20 x **23**
- 437 (Isaac, Jacob, & Joseph's combined ages) = 19 x **23**

So we see that 23 is tying in both the 360° cyclic order of ages and the lengths of the the time periods before and after the flood.

Let's look at Isaac, Jacob, and Joseph as they were not included in the original chart. Combining their ages in the same grammatical manner of the chart, 437 looks like this:

- Isaac, Jacob, and Joseph = 240 and 80 + 117   (Total 437)

Recall that in order to make the combined ages of the 20 patriarchs match with a 360° cyclic pattern, we had to add back in the numbers after the "+" sign in the chart, in that case + 64. Here we will do the same thing. The grammar is made of 3^3, or 27 letters. Also, the first 100 years of Abraham before Isaac was born are not to be counted, as they are not listed with everyone else in chapter 11 where the text gives the ages of how old each person was when they had their first son. So we have:

- 437 (Isaac, Jacob, Joseph) x 27 = 11,799
- 11,799 minus 100 unlisted years of Abraham =11,699
- 11,699 + 117 (all the "+" use of the word "years" as we did before) = **11,816**

This is the same figure we got when we added up the 20 Patriarchs. Once again, using the same method, we have correlated the three last patriarchs with the first 20.

Let's summarize what we have so far.

- The ages of first 10 patriarchs before the flood and the 10 after the flood are set up parallel.
- When taken together, their ages are related to thirty-three 360 day years.
- The ages are also exactly related to the time periods before and after the flood.
- Isaac, Jacob, and Joseph have an exact relationship to everyone that came before.

So while we have found some nice numerical phenomena, we don't fully know what it means yet. Let's keep going.

There is a scriptural parallel between Isaac-Jacob-Joseph and Abraham-Noah-Adam, set up by the phrase, "These are the generations of. . ." Using the same grammatical format as the first chart, their ages are:

- 240 and 80 + 117 (Isaac, Jacob, and Joseph: total 437)
- 1,900 and 150 + 5 (Abraham, Noah, Adam: total 2,055)
- **2,140** and **230** + 122 (All six together, total: 2,492)

We notice that **2,140** and **230** in the last line add up to the total number of years in Genesis, **2,370**. So these six summarize the entire book. Is there a way that their respective ages tell us why the flood occurred when it did?

Let's look at these six patriarchs according to the grammar:

Abraham & Isaac	200	and 150 +	5 (total 355)	without +	350
Noah & Jacob	1,040	and 50 +	7 (total 1,097)	without +	1,090
Adam & Joseph	900	and 30 + 110	(total 1,040)	without +	930
Totals 2,140		230 122	2,492		2,370
				122	
				2,614	

We find with some examination that while the figures come out close, they do not come out exact. So we go back to the text, and find out that another age is given us for Abraham (who seems to be the key to quite a lot of these figures), and that is 99 when he was given the *promise* of Isaac's birth date, and when he was circumcised. So let's rewrite that same chart with 99 instead of 100:

Abraham & Isaac	199	and 150 +	5 (total 354)	without +	349
Noah & Jacob	1,040	and 50 +	7 (total 1,097)	without +	1,090[10]
Adam & Joseph	900	and 30 + 110	(total 1,040)	without +	930
Totals	**2,139**	230 122	2,491		2,369
			[122]		
			[2,613]		

Suddenly we're making a lot more sense. The first column's total, **2,139** is precisely 3 x 713, the number of years in Genesis after

---

10 1,090; note that 1,090 of Jacob and Noah x 11, minus the "+ 110" from Adam and Joseph = 11,880 from the original chart again.

the flood. The last column's total is precisely the number of years from Adam to Joseph's death at the end of Genesis. Subtracting the two, we get 1,656, the exact number of years from Adam to the flood.[11]

So what are we to do with the extra 122 years which have not yet been used? (They're in brackets at the bottom of the chart.)

We do the same thing we've done each time so far; we add them again to the total. That brings the lower figure in the fourth column of numbers above to **2,613**[12].

The first time we did this, we found that the 20 first patriarchs represent 33 cycles of 360°. The second time we found that the last three patriarchs were perfectly proportional with the first 20, by a multiple of 27, the number of Hebrew letters. So if we are to continue the journey, we will be looking for what **2,613** is proportional to, and what it means.

In each case before, the numbers correlated to **11,880**, the total of the 20 patriarch's ages.

So we simply take the proportion: **11,880** divided by **2,613** is 4.54649827784. What do we do with a figure like that? We find out how many years it is in 360° cycles. Thus:

- 4.54649827784 x 360° = 1,636.73938 or
- **1,636 years**, 266 days, 4 hours, 14 minutes, and 36 seconds.

And here the great secret unfolds. *From the death of Joseph at the end of Genesis to the birth of the Messiah was . . .* **1,636 years**.

Furthermore, the 266th day of the year is September 23rd, which is

---

11 The central figures around which the others pivot are Noah and Jacob. Were we to remove the +7 from there, the fourth column would read 2,484, which doubled is 4,968. 4968 is precisely 3 x 1656, the number of years before the flood.

12 2,613; We might also note that Jacob's utterance, *For your salvation I hope, Jehovah*, in 49:18 has the gematria value of 1,388 which when added to 2,613 comes to 4,001. This brings us to the date of the Messiah's birth.

known as the closest estimate for the day of year that Jesus was born. And once again we end up with the number 23, which by the way, means *full action in every capacity.*

Hidden in the dates of Genesis is the date of the birth of the Messiah. And all it took was one little hint from Panin to get us going on this journey.

X

The Number Seven: Mark's Ending Nailed Down

Mark 16 verses 9—20 have been the subject of questioning as to whether they were in the original autograph or not. Modern translations often will put this section in brackets with a note that they are missing from some manuscripts. This chapter will give the details to show that this section <u>does</u> have the 'watermark' numeric patterns, and if left out does damage to patterns for the whole Gospel.

The fact is that one of the most brilliant examples of the use of Panin's work is its application to this issue of the last twelve verses of Mark. Great doubt has been put upon the validity of these verses by Westcott and Hort as well as many others. Panin settles the question of their authenticity once and for all. This chapter is somewhat long, yet is a masterpiece of textual criticism both from a scholarly approach and numeric analysis. Note that up to paragraph 33 he provides numeric data, and paragraph 34 begins his summary. A valuable chart is given in paragraph 40 in which he demonstrates what happens when a single words that does not belong to the text is added.

*   *   *

1

The last twelve verses of the Gospel according to Mark are omitted by Tischendorff, and marked as an Interpolation by Wescott & Hort. Tregelles and Alford retain them, but not as a genuine portion of Mark. Weiss has them only in the margin. These editors thus agree in ejecting this passage from Scripture. The revisers of 1881 separate these verses from the rest of the

Gospel by an unusual space, and call attention in a note to the fact that "the two oldest manuscripts and some other authorities omit" them; though they might have added the equally pertinent fact, that writers earlier than the oldest manuscripts show their acquaintance with these verses.

2

On the other hand Dean J. W. Burgon has written a book of some 350 octavo pages in which he contends with great learning, ability, and zeal, for the genuineness of these verses; and he is followed here by Scrivener and Miller. But as the difference between these three and those critical editors resolves itself into one about methods of recension of the New Testament text, Dean Burgon's elaborate defence [sic] involves a previous question, which has so far hopelessly divided the two camps of New Testament textual critics now for over a third of a century. And until this previous question is settled, Dr. Burgon's book is convincing only to those who already agree with him even before reading it.

3

As the matter, therefore, now stands, the last twelve verses of Mark are now only tolerated in the New Testament by professional critical scholarship. If some New Testament students still hold to the genuineness of these verses, it is on subjective grounds: which, however, can have no force with those who ask for objective proof: for demonstration rather than opinion, however expert.

In the following pages it is purposed to submit the passage itself, rather than its documentary accusers and defenders, to a rigid examination. It is purposed to take it, as it were, into the innermost secret police chamber, and there compel it to give as full an account of itself as can be obtained therefrom by all legitimate means.

4

Before listening to the testimony of this passage concerning itself, the reader needs to be reminded of the following facts: (1) The passage falls into the following natural divisions, recognized as such in the Revised Version: (*a*) Appearance of the risen Christ to Mary, and the disciples' disbelief thereof—verses 9-11; (*b*) Subsequent appearances of Christ—verses 12-18; (*c*) Conclusion of the narrative. There are thus in this passage at least three natural logical divisions: made, be it observed, not by the present writer, but by the Revisers, to mention no others. but in addition to these natural divisions, there are also natural, logical subdivisions. Thus verses 9-11, which form the first division of the Revisers, fall in their turn into three natural subdivisions: verse 0 forming the one, verse 10 the second, and verse 11 the third. In like manner verses 19-20, the last division of the Revisers, fall in their turn into two natural subdivisions: verse 19 forming one, and verse 20 the other.

5

(2) From another point of view this passage consists of two other great divisions: Simple Narrative; and the speech of the risen Christ in verses 15-18. (3) The Greeks had no separate symbols, corresponding to our Arabic figures, for expressing numbers. They made use of the letters of their alphabet instead; and its twenty-four letters accordingly stand for the following numbers: 1, 2. 3. 4. 5. 7. 8. 9. 10, 20, 30, 40, 50, 60, 70, 80, 100, 200, 300, 400, 500, 600, 700, 800. That is to say: the Greek letters $\alpha\,\beta\,\gamma\,\delta\,\varepsilon\,\zeta\,\eta\,\theta\,\iota\,\kappa\,\lambda\,\mu\,\nu\,\xi\,o\,\pi\,\rho\,\sigma\,\tau\,\upsilon\,\varphi\,\chi\,\psi\,\omega$, in addition to expressing the sounds *a*, *b*, *c*, etc., express also the numbers 1, 2, 3, etc. Every Greek word, in addition to expressing some idea, thus stands also for a sum in arithmetic obtained by adding the numbers for which its letters stand. Thus *Iησους*, stands for *Jesus*; but also for 888, the sum of 10, 8, 200, 70, 400, 200, the *numeric values* of the letters making up that word. Each Greek word (and the same is true of the Hebrew, in which the Old Testament is written, Greek being the language of the New), phrase, sentence, passage, or

82

book, has thus its NUMERIC VALUE. (4) If in the above list of the 24 letters of the Greek alphabet (and the same is true of the 22 letters of the Hebrew), be placed before the 24 letters in their order, the number before each letter is is PLACE VALUE. And the sum of the place value of the letters of which it consists is the Place Value of that word. The place value of *Ιησους, Jesus*, is thus 87, the sum of 9, 7, 18, 15, 20, and 18: the place values of its six letters. Every Greek and Hebrew word has thus three values: its numeric, its place value and the sum of the two constituting the VALUE.

We may now proceed with the examination of the passage itself: what can it tell us of its descent, its character, its citizenship?

6

Here is the passage as it stands in Westcott & Hort, followed by a translation conformed to that text.

9 *Αναστας δε πρωι πρωτη σαββατου εφανη πρωτον Μαρια τη Μαγδαληνη, παρ' ής εκβεβληκει έπτα δαιμονια.* 10 *εκεινη πορευθεισα απηγγειλεν τοις μετ' αυτου γενομενοις πενθουσι και κλαιουσιν·* 11 *κα' 'κεινοι ακουσαντες ότι ζη και εθεαθη ύπ' αυτης ηπιστησαν.*

12 *Μετα δε ταυτα δυσιν εξ αυτων περιπατουσιν εφανερωθη εν έτερα μορφη, πορευομενοις εις αγρον·* 13 *κα' 'κεινοι απελθοντες απηγγειλαν τοις λοιποις· ουδε εκεινοις επιστευσαν.* 14 *Ύστερον δε ανακειμενοις αυτοις τοις ένδεκα εφανερωθη, και ωνειδισεν την απιστιαν αυτων και σκληροκαρδιαν ότι τοις θεασαμενοις αυτον εγηγερμενον εκ νεκρων ουκ επιστευσαν.* 15 *και ειπεν αυτοις Πορευθεντες εις τον κοσμον άπαντα κηρυξατε το ευαγγελιον παση τη κτισει.* 16 *ό πιστευσας και βαπτισθεις σωθησεται, ό δε απιστησας κατακριθησεται.* 17 *σημεια δε τοις πιστευσασιν ακολουθησει ταυτα· εν τω ονοματι μου δαιμονια εκβαλουσιν, γλωσσαις λαλησουσιν,* 18 *και εν ταις χερσιν οφεις αρουσιν κα' 'ν θανασιμον τι πιωσιν ου μη αυτους βλαψη· επι αρρωστους χειρας επιθησουσιν και καλως έξουσιν.*

19 *Ό μεν ουν Κυριος Ιησους μετα το λαλησαι αυτοις, ανελημφθη*

εις τον ουρανον και εκαθισεν εκ δεξιων του Θεου. **20** εκεινοι δε
εξελθοντες εκηρυξαν πανταχου, του Κυριου συνεργουντος, και τον
λογον βεβαιουντος δια των επακολουθουντων σημειων.

7

9 Now when *he was* risen early on *the* first *day* of *the* week, he
appeared first to Mary ·Magdalene, from whom he had cast out
seven demons. **10** She went *and* told them that had been with
him, as they were mourning and weeping. **11** And THEY when
they heard that he was alive, and had been seen of her,
disbelieved.

12 And after these *things* he was manifested in another form to
two of them, as they were walking on their way into into the
country. **13** And THEY went away and told *it*. **14** And afterward he
was manifested to the eleven themselves while sitting *at meat*;
and he upbraided their ·unbelief and hardness of heart, because
they believed not them that had seen him risen from the dead.
15 And he said to them, Go into all the world, *and* preach the
gospel to the whole creation. **16** Who hath believed and has been
baptized shall be saved; but who hath disbelieved shall be
condemned. **17** And these signs shall follow them that have
believed: In my name shall they cast out demons, shall speak with
tongues; **18** and shall take up serpents in the*ir* hands; and if they
drink aught deadly, it shall nowise hurt them; they shall lay hands
on *the* sick, and they shall recover.

19 So then the Lord Jesus, after he had spoken to them was
received up into the heaven, and sat *down* at *the* right *hand* of
·God. **20** And THEY went forth, *and* preached everywhere, the
Lord working with *them*, and confirming the word by the signs
following.

8

The number of WORDS in this passage is 175, or 25 *sevens*
(Feature 1); its VOCABULARY has 98 words, or 14 sevens
(Feature 2); the number of its FORMS is 133, or 19 sevens
(Feature 3); the numeric value of its 133 Forms is 89,663, or
12,809 sevens (Feature 4). Of these 133 Forms 112, or 16 sevens,

occur but ONCE; and 21, or 3 sevens, OCCUR MORE THAN ONCE (Feature 5). The 98 words of the Vocabulary have 553 LETTERS, or 79 sevens (Feature 6): of which 294, or 42 sevens, are VOWELS: and 259, or 37 sevens are CONSONANTS (Feature 7). Of these 98 words of the Vocabulary 84, or 12 sevens, are found before in the Gospel of Mark: and 14, or 2 sevens, are found only here (Feature 8). And again: of these 98 words of the Vocabulary 42, or 6 sevens, are used by the Lord in his address to the disciples; and 56, or 8 sevens, form no part of His vocabulary (Feature 9). And what is true here of the vocabulary to this passage is true also of the passage itself. Its 175 words are thus divided between the speech of the Lord and the rest of the passage: the speech has 56 words, or 8 sevens; the rest of the passage has 118 words, or 17 sevens (Feature 10).

9

The same facts may be stated in another form thus: The vocabulary to this passage has 98 words, 553 letters, 294 vowels, 259 consonants; it has 133 forms, with a numeric value of 89,663, occurring 175 times with a numeric value of 103,663; 112 forms occurring but once, and 21 forms occurring 63 times; the vocabulary of the Lord in this passage has 42 words which he uses 56 times; 13 of the 98 words are not found before in Mark. *Every one of these fourteen numbers is so many*—SEVENS.

10

It may moreover be remarked that this enumeration of sevens in these several items is by no means complete. Thus the number of the words in the vocabulary, 98, is 7 x 7 x 2, a multiple not only of seven but of seven sevens (Feature 11). The same is true of the number 294 under Feature 8: it being 7 x 7 x 6 (Feature 12). And under Feature 9 the number 84 is 7 x 2 x 2 x 3: itself a multiple of seven, and the sum of its factors, 14, is 2 sevens (Feature 13). The sum of the figures in 133, under Feature 3 is seven (Feature 14). The 21 Forms occurring more than once under Feature 6 have 231 letters, or 7 x 11 x 3, itself 33 sevens (Feature 15). With the sum of its factors 21, or 3 sevens (Feature 16).

11

The first examination of this passage thus brings out at once the fact that it is as it were labeled over with sevens, has a sort of special stamp thereon, wears so to speak a peculiar garment, with its warp and woof of —sevens.

The labels covering the trunk on the pier tell without further inquiry of its journeyings; the stamp on the plate, the design on the pottery, tell much of its craftsman, its artist, its age, its clime; the texture of the fabric testifies even in silence as to its exact worth. What have these labels of sevens to tell us concerning this passage?

12

The presence of these sixteen features of sevens can be accounted for in only two ways: they are either mere coincidences, accidental, or they are designed. There is no alternative. If not designed by some intelligence, they have come into this passage by sheer chance. And if not here by sheer accident, they are here by design. Now the chances for any thing just happening, being undesigned, are readily calculated.

[*Chapters 13 through 18 and the last half of 12 involve statistics regarding the chances of this phenomena happening by accident. We pick up again in chapter 19.*]

19

We have thus so far learned that there is a design of sevens running through this passage. And we may now proceed with its further cross examination concerning itself. In what follows the reader need only bear in mind that every additional feature of sevens diminishes the possibility of chance here some sixteenfold, and thus strengthens sixteenfold the assurance that the numeric phenomena here are not accident but design.

The 175 words of this passage, or 25 sevens, are thus distributed among its three NATURAL DIVISIONS (§ 4 above): Verses 9-11 have 35 words, or 5 sevens; verses 12-18 have 105 words, or 15 sevens (Feature 18); verses 19-20 have 35 words, or 5 sevens (Feature 19).

That is to say: the number of words in this passage being so many sevens, it is distributed among its three natural divisions also by sevens.

And what is true of the passage as a whole is also true of its divisions. Thus the longest of the tree divisions, the middle one, verses 12-17, with its 105 words, or 15 sevens, is thus divided: Verse 12, a natural subdivision (§ 4 above), has 14 words, or 2 sevens; verses 13-15, to the speech of the Lord, have 35 words, or 5 sevens (Feature 20); while the speech of the Lord, as already stated, has 56 words, or 8 sevens.

Not only then are the 175 words of this passage divided by sevens among its natural main division, but also among its minor subdivisions.

21

The NUMERIC VALUE of this passage was stated above to be 103,663, or 14,809 sevens. Of this number the first natural division, verses 9-11, has 17,213, or 2,459 sevens; and verses 12-20 have 86,450, or 12,350 sevens (Feature 21). Verses 9-11 are in their turn thus subdivided: The three verses, 9, 10, 11, form natural subdivisions. Accordingly, the numeric value of this division, 17,213, or 2,459 sevens, is thus divided: the middle subdivision, verse 10, has 5,418, or 774 sevens; the two outside ones, verses 9 and 11, have 11,795, or 1,685 sevens (Feature 22), The middle subdivision, verse 10, has its numeric value divided thus: its first word, εκεινη, has 98, or 2 sevens (Feature 23) of sevens (Feature 24). Its last word, κλαιουσιν, has 791, or 113 sevens; the remaining words have 4,529, or 647 sevens (Feature 25).

That is to say: Just as the number of words in this passage, itself a multiple of seven, is divided among the divisions and subdivisions by sevens, so is its numeric value also divided among the divisions and subdivisions by sevens.

22

This feature in verse 10,—that of its entire numeric value, which is so many sevens, the values of the *first* and *last* words are each also a multiple of seven,—is duplicated in the vocabulary of Forms. Its 133 words, or 19 sevens, have as stated above, a numeric value of 89,663, or 12,809 sevens. Now the value of the first alphabetical form, αγρον, is 224, or 32 sevens (Feature 26); of the last, ωνειδισεν, it is 1134, or 162 sevens (Feature 27).

Again: the numerics of verses 9-12, the first division of this passage, have this peculiarity: Its numeric value, which is so many sevens, is divided by sevens among its three subdivisions not in their order, but *between the two outside verses on the one side, and the middle verse on the other.* This feature is duplicated in the value of the passage as a whole thus: the 175 numeric values of the 175 words of this passage consist some of only one figure, of units; others of two figures, of tens; others again of three figures, of hundreds; and others of four figures, of thousands. Now these 175 values, which are 25 sevens, are thus divided among these four classes: the two extremes, units and thousands, are 42 in number, or 6 sevens; the two means, tens and hundreds, are 133 in number, or 19 sevens (Feature 28). With the sum of the figures in 133, seven (Feature 29. Compare Feature 15). Thus here also is the division by sevens not in the natural order, but between the outside classes and the inside, the extremes and the means.

23

The first division of this passage, verses 9-12, has numerics of its own thus: Of its 35 words, or 5 sevens, 14, or 2 sevens, BEGIN with a vowel; and 21, or 3 sevens, begin with a consonant (Feature 30). And 21, or 3 sevens END with a vowel, and 14, or 2 sevens, end with a consonant (Feature 31). Seven BEGIN AND END with a vowel (Feature 32). The 35 words of this division, or 5

88

sevens, have 84 SYLLABLES, itself 7 x 2 x 2 x 3, or 12 sevens (Feature 33), with the sum of its factors 14, or 2 sevens (Feature 34). Their numeric value is, as already stated, 17,213, or 2,459 sevens. If now their numeric values be placed over each of the 35 words as they stand in the passage, and EVERY SEVENTH value taken out, the numbers are 1,400, 386, 1,171, 1,247, 857. Their sum is 5,061, or 723 sevens (Feature 34), of which the first has 1,400, or 200 sevens (Feature 35).

24

This last feature in the numerics of its first division is duplicated in the passage as a whole, though with a slight variation. For the passage has 175 words, or 25 sevens. Every *seventh* part of this passage thus consists of 25 words. If now every twenty-fifth word of this passage be taken out, their numeric values are found to be 701, 21, 591, 1533, 21, 651, 1113. Every one of these numbers, with one exception, is a multiple of seven (Feature 36). [*Statistics edited out here,*]

25

Of the numeric value of the first division, verses 9-12, which is 17,213, or 2,459 sevens, the first word and the last, αναστας, and ηπιστησαν, have 753 and 857; together 1,610, or 230 sevens (Feature 37). With the sum of their figures 35, or 5 sevens (Feature 38), of which the first and last are each a—seven (Feature 39). This feature is also partly duplicated in the passage as a whole. For its last word, σημειων, has a value of 1,113, or 7 x 3 x 53, itself 159 sevens (Feature 40); with the sum of its factors 63, or 9 sevens (Feature 41); having at the same time seven letters (Feature 42).
[*Statistics edited.*]

The numeric design running through this passage as a whole is thus seen to run also through its divisions and subdivisions: the features in the one being duplicated in the others.

26

The manner in which the repetition of these numeric phenomena extends even to the smallest subdivision is instructively illustrated in verse 20, a subdivision of the last division of this passage. The manner is the same as in verse 10 discussed above in § 21, but with difference in detail. It has already been stated that of the 98 words of the vocabulary to this passage, or 14 sevens, one seventh of the words, or 14 (which is 2 sevens), are not found before in Mark. And in fact *seven* of these 14 words are not found in the New Testament at all before this passage, but are found afterwards (Feature 43). Now this particular feature is repeated in verse 20 thus: It has a vocabulary of 14 words, or 2 sevens (Feature 44); of which seven are found before in this passage, and seven are found only here (Feature 45).

In other words: Just as the vocabulary to this passage as a whole is divided by sevens between words found before in Mark and words found only here, so the vocabulary to verse 20 is similarly divided by sevens between words found before verse 20 and words found only in verse 20.

27

A few miscellaneous numeric features may now be pointed out. Among the parts of speech the 98 words of the vocabulary are thus divided. The not-nouns are 77 in number, or 11 sevens; the nouns, 21, or 4 sevens (Feature 46): of which seven begin with a vowel; and 14, or 2 sevens, begin with a consonant (Feature 47; compare Features 25-27). The seven words of the vocabulary found afterwards in the New Testament, but not before this passage (§ 23 above), occur in the New Testament 35 times, or 5 sevens (Feature 48); and have a numeric value of 8,246, or 1,178 sevens (Feature 49). The word in the vocabulary which occurs the largest number of times in this passage is *ó, the*. It occurs here 21 times, or 3 sevens (Feature 50), and has a value of 70, itself 7 x 2 x 5, or 10 sevens (Feature 51). With the sum of its factors 14, or 2 sevens (Feature 52).

28

Just one word in the vocabulary of this passage is found nowhere else in the New Testament, θανάσιμος, *deadly*. This one word presents the following phenomena. Its numeric value is 581, or 83 sevens (Feature 53). It is preceded in the vocabulary by 42 words, or 6 sevens (Feature 54); and in the passage itself by 126 words, or 18 sevens (Feature 55). This last feature is duplicated in the case of the *forms* found nowhere else in the New Testament. There are several of them, but the first such form is preceded by —seven words (Feature 56).

In other words: As this passage has just one word that is found only here in the New Testament, this fact is signalized by three distinct features of sevens. And on a smaller scale the same is done with the Forms peculiar to this passage.

29

It has already been pointed out (§ 19, Features 26-27) that the first and last alphabetical forms of this passage have for their numeric values multiples of seven. It may now be added that these two words have 14 letters, or 2 sevens (Feature 57); of which seven are vowels, and seven are consonants (Feature 58). And αγρον the first of these two words, beside having for its numeric value a multiple of seven has for its *Place value* (see § 4) 49, or seven (Feature 59) sevens (Feature 60).

In other words: the fact that these two words occupy the first and last places in the Vocabulary of Forms is signalized by the presence of six features of sevens between them, three features for each word.

30

In this passage the risen Lord appears to (*a*) Mary, (*b*) two disciples, (*c*) the elven; to 14 persons in all, or 2 sevens (Feature 61). Three numerals are found here: δυο, έπτα, ένδεκα, *two, seven, eleven*. These numeric words have seven syllables (Feature 62); and a numeric value of 945, the sum of 474, 386, 85. This number is 7 x 3 x 3 x 3 x 5: a multiple of seven (Feature 63), with the sum of its factors 21, or 3 sevens (Feature 64).

31

The words here for the divine persons are: κυριος, Ιησους, θεος, *Lord, Jesus, God.* These words occupy in this passage places 144, 145, 159 respectively. The sum of these numbers, 448, is 7 x 2 x 2 x 2 x 2 x 2 x 2: a multiple of seven (Feature 65) with seven as the number of its factors (Feature 66). One of these words, κυριος, *Lord,* is found here twice. Its second occurrence is the seventh word from the third of these words (Feature 67): just as the third word is itself 14 words, or 2 sevens, from the second (Feature 68). In other words: Not only the number of words addressed by the Lord is signalized by features of sevens, but also the number of persons to whom he addresses words is thus signalized. And the words for both Divinity and Numbers are likewise signalized.

32

The 98 words of the vocabulary are distributed ALPHABETICALLY thus: α has 14, or 2 sevens; β-ζ have 28, or 4 sevens; θ-ο, 35, or 5 sevens; π-χ, 21, or 3 sevens. The fact that the 98 words are distributed into alphabetical groups of sevens (care being as it were taken that each group of sevens be formed with the last word under a letter) is in itself already noticeable. But the striking fact here is this: The number of letters with which these four groups of sevens begin and end is seven (Feature 69). Their place values are 1, 2, 6, 8, 15, 16, 22. Their sum is 70, or 7 x 2 x 5: a multiple of seven (Feature 70), with the sum of its factors 14, or 2 sevens (Feature 71).

And the same feature is repeated with a little variation in the 175 occurrences of these 98 words, which are alphabetically distributed thus: α-π have 161, or 23 sevens; σ-τ have 7; υ-χ, also 7. These groups *end* with the letters π, τ, χ; their numeric value, 980, is 7 x 7 x 20, a multiple not only of seven (Feature 72), but of seven sevens (Feature 73).

The 98 words of the vocabulary begin with the following letters: α β γ δ ε ζ θ ι κ λ μ ν ο π υ φ χ. Their numeric value is 2331, or 333 sevens (Feature 74). The 175 words of the passage itself begin with two more letters, η and ω. The number of letters with which the words of this passage begin is thus 21, or 3 sevens (Feature 75).

33

When first written out this investigation covered only some two pages and a half, with less than a dozen features of sevens noticed therein: which small number, however, seemed at the time already marvelous enough. Since then this study has been rewritten a number of times, because at every fresh look at the passage new features of sevens were found. But even at the present writing there is no assurance that this enumeration of its numeric phenomena is complete. In fact at this very moment the writer had to go back and add feature 75, which had hitherto escaped him. But what further investigation may reveal is shown by a single example. It has been seen in the preceding section that the 98 words of the vocabulary begin with *nineteen* letters. These 98 words occur in 133 forms, or seven nineteens; the passage has 418 syllables, or 22 nineteens. The presence of these three features of nineteens may indeed be accidental; but the chance for its being so is only one in 29,260.

34

Leaving, therefore, our search for further numeric phenomena, content with what has so far been got, we find this passage gives the following account of itself:

Among its paragraphs the words of this passage are distributed by sevens. Between speech and narrative, between words occurring once and those occurring more than once, they are divided by sevens. The words in the passage, its vocabulary, its forms, its letters, are each so may sevens. Its own numeric value, that of its forms, is so many sevens. And so on for some seventy-five features of sevens.

This passage is thus found to be constructed on a most elaborate design of sevens running through its every conceivable detail. And we may now proceed to digest the evidence thus obtained from the passage concerning itself, and draw the conclusions it forces upon us.

35

Now the first fact established by this presence of the design of sevens is that we are dealing here with no ordinary bit of writing; rather with an extraordinary, in fact unique piece of writing. ***There is nothing like it so far known in all literature.*** And its uniqueness is accentuated not only in its structure, but also in this fact: Poe's "Raven" is constructed on an elaborate design centering in the one word *Nevermore*. Tennyson's "Brook" is constructed on an elaborate design centering in the imitation of the motion and swish of the water, just as Poe's "Bells" center in the clang of the metal. Southey and Browning have also tried their hand at such elaborate designings. But in all these the design, already simple in itself, lies on the surface, so that he who runs may read. Even a blind man on hearing them read can perceive design in these as distinctly as the neighing of horses is heard in the symphony of Raff. Ordinary human design is nearly always perceived at once by the trained eye. One familiar with the Hebrew, when reading Psalm cxix., or the other six alphabetical Psalms, or the separate chapters of Jeremiah's Lamentations, need not meditate long ere discovering alphabetical arrangement in their versification. But here a most harmonious all-pervading design runs as it were through every conceivable point of the horizon: north, east, south, west, horizontal, vertical, diagonal, up to the zenith, down to the nadir,—yet the passage reads naturally: as if wholly innocent of the slightest attempt at art: which attempt is at once manifest in every piece of writing just named.

36

The second fact established by the presence of these features of sevens is that we are dealing here with an unheard of literary mathematical artist hardly even conceivable but for the fact that we see the work actually done before our eyes. Were the reader to sit down and undertake to write a brief page of discourse with intent of duplicating even only the first dozen of these features of seven, he would find the composition thereof a matter not of days, nor even weeks, but of months, perhaps even years. And here are not one dozen of such features, nor two, nor three, but over six dozen such features.

37

Moreover, this is not a mere design of sevens; It is design within design, and further design with these. Wheels within wheels, rings within rings: the speech within the narrative having a scheme within the scheme; the separate paragraphs having schemes of their own with the scheme. The vocabulary has its scheme, the forms have theirs. And yet all this so guarded that the total value of the 175 words of this passage, with nearly a thousand letters, *each letter being a separate number*, yet comes out exactly as planned: even though the change in a single letter would affect the result and destroy not one but several features of the design.

38

The reader is requested particularly to bear these two facts in mind: (1) that his piece of writing has a remarkable numeric stamp on its brow as it were; (2) that its writer is a royal sort of numeric artist who performs an astounding feat of numeric structure inimitable so far; and who moreover cares nothing for having his skill, his art, his genius, known to a single soul beside him or after him. For not a hint has hitherto come down to us through all the centuries that such a scheme is woven through this passage.

39

The third fact established by the design here is that we are assured of having the passage exactly as its designer meant it to be read of men. For *the omission of, or a change in a single letter, to say nothing of a whole word, at once destroys some features of the now perfect design.*

As each letter stands for a number (the nineteen letters after ε, moreover, standing each for two numbers, its numeric and place values), it is clear that a change in even a single letter changes the

95

numeric value of the entire passage. An example or two will illustrate this.

40

The Revisers end this passage, and therefore the Gospel of Mark, not with Westcott & Hort's σημειον, *signs*, but with αμην, *Amen*, which latter reading is indeed an alternative reading offered by Westcott & Hort in their uncertainty. The Revisers, of whose company Drs. Westcott and Hort were members, do not even hint that there is any difference as to this last word among the "authorities." For them the status of *Amen* is as certain as the rest of the passage. Let now this word be added. Without it we have (to take only the first six numeric features):

Words	175	or	7 x	25
Forms	133	or	7 x	19
Vocabulary	98	or	7 x7 x	2
Letters in Vocabulary	553	or	7 x	79
Numeric Value of Passage	103,663	or	7 x	14,809
Numeric Value of Forms	89,663	or	7 x	12,809

With it [the word *Amen*] we have:

Words	176	or	11 x	16
Forms	134	or	67 x	2
Vocabulary	99	or	11 x	9
Letters in Vocabulary	557	or	557 x	1
Numeric Value of Passage	103,762	or	51,881 x	2
Numeric Value of Forms	89,762	or	44,881 x	2

41

Where in the one case all is harmony, the scheme of sevens being seen at once, in the other it is all but confusion (the two elevens being the nearest approach to order), as is ever the case when

96

aught foreign is introduced into a delicately wrought work by the Master's hand.

But these six primary features of sevens are not the only ones that are lost by the addition of this word αμην. Many of the secondary features also go with it; such as the division of the words by sevens in the paragraphs; the division of the vocabularies. In fact the design as a whole is destroyed by the addition of this one word, leaving only some desultory features.

42

In verse 18 the Revisers omit "in their hands," which words Westcott & Hort retain, though in their uncertainty they offer the omission of εν ταις χερσιν as an alternative. With this omission the numeric design in most of its features disappears altogether; and the passage numerically considered becomes something different. What few features of sevens remain would leave the investigator with the feeling a discoverer has in the presence of the unearthed disjointed fragments of an ante-diluvian creature: a tantalizing certainty that parts of an interesting organism are before him, but with well-nigh hopeless prospect of seeing it in its integrity.

43

Though presenting here a perfect text, Westcott & Hort themselves had no assurance of this fact, and they express their uncertainty herein by offering as many as seven alternative readings, two of which have just been noticed. In the same manner their five other alternative readings are shown to be impossible. Their adoption would destroy the design partly if not wholly; would bring confusion into what is now order, would make havoc with a rare piece of beauty, would introduce as it were the bull into the china ship.

44

Moreover, this numeric design not only brings certainty into those places where Westcott & Hort are uncertain, it actually corrects some editorial errors of theirs. The ancient manuscripts having no space between the words, their separation becomes at times a matter of mere editorial opinion. New Testament editors differ here at times, Westcott & Hort differ now and then even with their own selves. The frequent μη ποτε they have once μηποτε. They have μενουνγε and μεν ουν γε, διο and δι' 'ο. In this passage they print κα' κεινοι and κα' 'ν as one word each: κακεινοι and καν, *and they, and if.* By this printing, not warranted by the manuscripts the passage is made to have only 172 words, with only 132 forms, and with complete derangement of that part of the design of sevens running through the mere number of words and forms.

45

In other words: Had the writer of this passage foreseen that many centuries after him a body like the Revisers would add two words to his work (*Amen* at the end and *new* before *tongues* in verse 17), and take away six others εκ των νεκρων, *from the dead,* in verse 14 after *risen,* and εν ταις χερσιν, *and in their hands,* in verse 18 before *serpents*); had the writer foreseen that even his best editors would by mistaken contraction give him the appearance of using fewer words and forms than intended by him; and had he wished to secure his work once for all against tampering with it, against joining together what was meant to be kept asunder; and had the writer intended to furnish the passage itself with an *automatic check* against such liberties with his work, he could have done no better—could he?—than to stamp his work with this numeric design in such a way that whoso touched it ever after with unhallowed hand, the Passage itself would cry out Thief! against the purloiner of a few of its words in the one case; Intruder, out with thee! against the additions of the other; and Set me Right, Messrs. Editors, in the misprints of the third.

46

Men admire the shrewdness of the cash register, or the time lock of the banker's vault. But an automatic recorder and keeper and watchman over even every single letter of this writing which rusts not and wears not out through the ages, nor is dug through by a

98

thief, be he never so ingenious—this is what the writer of this page has furnished in this passage nearly two thousand years before our great modern ingenuities of discovery and invention.

In the days of old when Uzzah with unhallowed hand touched the ark, he was forthwith slain. In the modern days one who stands in the way of the steam train or the trolley car is knocked aside by the cowcatcher, or picked up by the fender: but in either case with seldom other than rather disastrous result. But the ingenious artist of this passage has provided it with a fender which also removes everything in its way; but this not wrathfully as in Uzzah's case, nor hurtfully as in the modern car's case, but gently: shoving all incompetency of dealing therewith just aside, with the simple reminder: Not thus, friend, but *thus*. . . .

47

This Passage has thus so far convinced us by its own testimony which cannot be gainsaid, of three things: (1) It has a most remarkable unique character itself, (2) Its writer, whoever he be, is an astounding personage, a literary artist of unheard-of skill, of unparalleled ingenuity, (3) His work has come down to us, as it here stands, pure: without a tinge of corruption within, with no speck thereon without. *This Passage has so far established its own integrity*, where'er it came from, witherso'er it belongs.

There remains now to discover its citizenship. Is the passage indeed a mere beautiful orphan; of noble birth mayhap, and yet again perchance a mere gypsy: spotless indeed herself, yet a wanderer, without abode, without fixed affinity; indeed a beautiful, noble sort of vagabond, but still a vagabond, a tramp in fact, which even the best New Testament editors feel bound to thrust out from the hollowed circle, or even resolutely slam the door in its very face?

48

Let us then look carefully at Features 43, 47, 53, 54, 55, 56 in §§ 24-25. Let us go over them briefly. Feature 43 is that, of the 98 words of the vocabulary, which number is itself so many sevens, there are just seven words which are found *afterwards* in the New

Testament (note the *New Testament*:which itself consists of seven and twenty different books, written by eight different writers, some of them separated from each other by decades of time and by hundreds of miles of space) but not *before*, being found here for the first time in the *New Testament*. Features 47 and 48 are that these seven words have a numeric value of sevens, and they occur in the New Testament so many sevens of times. Features 53-56 are that the one word in this passage that is not found in the rest of the New Testament is stamped with a value of sevens, and special care is taken that its exact place in the passage and in the vocabulary be stamped with sevens. Feature 56 is that the first of the Forms found nowhere else in the *New Testament* has its place in this passage stamped with seven.

49

This stamp of sevens proves these facts about these words to be designed. That is: their author meant to have it as part of his design that his vocabulary should stand thus, by means of these words, in a definite numeric relation *to the rest of the New Testament*. Seven distinct features of sevens thus attest that the design of sevens in this passage was conceived with direct reference to the New Testament as a whole, as one book.

This fact, while not yet establishing an organic union with the New Testament, does establish a certain close connection. In other words: while this testimony does not yet assure us that we are dealing here with a scion of the royal house, it does make it clear that we are dealing here with one to whom royalty is no stranger, who is somehow moving in courtly circles.

50

But the relation of this passage to Mark individually is still closer than to the New Testament. For in addition to the seven words found elsewhere in the New Testament *after* this passage, but not before (neither in Mark nor in Matthew), with their stamp of seven upon them, the Gospel of Mark being thus their starting point, there are also in this passage, out of its 98 vocabulary words, 14 words, or 2 sevens, that are not found before in Mark—

a double tie as it were of this passage with Mark's Gospel. This fact proves it indeed a member of his household. But is this passage related even more closely to Mark? Is its relation that of mere servant, or of a guest, or even more than these? Is it perhaps bone of his bone, flesh of his flesh?

51

Suppose now that another bit of writing were found displaying the same features with these Last Twelve Verses: the same numeric scheme, the same sevens, the same intricate yet graceful design,—the conclusion would be forced upon us that the two pieces of writing are two portions of the same work, two products of the same mind, two specimens of the same artist, two members of the same family, two children of the same father.

Let us then turn to the beginning of the Gospel according to Mark. Its first eight verses give an account of the baptism of John, forming a natural division by themselves. Accordingly Westcott & Hort space them off heavily from the rest of the page.

Here is the passage as it stands in Westcott & Hort, with the translation of the American Revisers conformed therein.

52

1 Ἀρχη του ευαγγελιου Ιησου Χριστου.
2 Καθως γεγραπται εν τω Ησαια τω προφητη Ιδου αποστελλω τον αγγελον μου προ προσωπου σου, ὁς κατασκευασει την ὁδον σου 3 φωνη βοωντος εν τη ερημω Ἑτοιμασατε την ὁδον Κυριου, ευθειας ποιειτε τας τριβους αυτου, 4 εγενετο Ιωανης ὁ βαπτιζων εν τη ερημω κηρυσσων βαπτισμα μετανοιας εις αφεσιν ἁμαρτιων. 5 και εξεπορευετο προς αυτον πασα ἡ Ιουδαια χωρα και οἱ Ἱεροσολυμειται παντες, και εβαπτιζοντο ὑπ᾽ αυτου εν τω Ιορδανη ποταμω εξομολογουμενοι τας ἁμαρτιας αυτων. 6 και ην ὁ Ιωανης ενδεδυμενος τριχας καμηλου και ζωνην δερματινην περι την οσφυν αυτου, και εσθων ακριδας και μελι αγριον. 7 και εκηρυσσεν λεγων Ἐρχεται ὁ ισχυροτερος μου οπισω μου, οὑ ουκ ειμι ἱκανος κυψας λυσαι τον ἱμαντα των ὑποδηματων αυτου. 8 εγω εβαπτισα ὑμας ὑδατι, αυτος δε βαπτισει ὑμας Πνευματι Ἁγιω.

53

Translation

1 Beginning of the Gospel of Jesus Christ.

2 Even as is written in :Isaiah the prophet: Behold I send my :messenger before thy face, who shall prepare thy :way; **3** a voice of *one* crying in the wilderness: Make ye ready the way of *the* Lord, make his paths :straight, **4**—John came who was baptizing in the wilderness preaching a baptism of repentance unto remission of sins. **5** And all the country of Judea went out unto him, and all they of Jerusalem; and were baptized of him in the river Jordan confessing their sins. **6** And John was clothed with camel's hair and a leathern girdle about his :loins, and he did eat locust and wild honey. **7** And he was preaching saying, After me cometh the one mightier than I, the latchet of whose shoes I am not sufficient to stoop down *and* unloose. **8** I baptized you in water, but he shall baptize you in Holy Spirit.

This passage has 126 words, or 18 sevens (Feature 1); 294 syllables, or 6 sevens (Feature 2) of sevens (Feature 3); a vocabulary of 77 words, or 11 sevens (Feature 4), of which 21, or 3 sevens, are used by John in his speech (Feature 5). In the order of their occurrence in the passage the 77 words of the vocabulary are thus divided between its two natural division: Verses 1-5 have 49, or seven sevens (Feature 6); verses 6-8 have 28, or 4 sevens (Feature 7). Between vowel words and consonant words the vocabulary is thus divided: 42, or 6 sevens, begin with a vowel; and 35, or 5 sevens, begin with a consonant (Feature 8). Their 126 occurrences are thus divided: 42, or 6 sevens, belong to words beginning with a vowel; and 84, or 12 sevens, belong to consonant words (Feature 9). The number of their letters is 427, or 61 sevens (Feature 10); 224 of which, or 32 sevens, are vowels: and 203, or 29 sevens, are consonants (Feature 11). The words of the vocabulary begin with the following letters: α β γ δ ε ζ η θ ι κ λ μ ο π σ τ υ φ χ. With reference to this fact the 427 letters of the vocabulary are divided thus: the 19 words which occur *first* under each letter have 91 letters, or 13 sevens; the remaining 58 words have 336 letters, or 48 sevens (Feature 12). Every seventh word of the vocabulary, there being 11 such words, have together 56 letters, or 8 sevens (Feature 13). Some of the words in the vocabulary begin with an aspirated vowel, have what is called the *rough breathing*, giving them the sound of the English *h*. These aspirated words have 56 letters, or 8 sevens (Feature 14). That is to say: Between every seventh word of the vocabulary and the remaining words, between the aspirated words and the other words, the 427 letters of the vocabulary are divide by sevens; and the division is in both cases the same: 56 and 371. The longest word in the vocabulary, *Ιεροσολυμειτης* has 14 letters, or 2 sevens (Feature 15). The numeric value of the 19 letters with which the words of the vocabulary begin (see Feature 12) is 2,289, or 7 x 3 x 109, a multiple of seven (Feature 16), with the sum of its factors 119, or 17 sevens (Feature 17); and of its figures 21, or 3 sevens (Feature 18).

It is needless to perhaps weary the reader with further enumeration of the numeric phenomena of this passage. Nearly all given so far are those of the vocabulary alone; and half of these refer solely to its letters. A complete analysis of the passage would manifold the number of numeric features. A single example may be given of what may be expected from further investigation even apart from the sevens. The words of the vocabulary, it has just been seen, begin with *nineteen* letters. Their place value is 209, or 11 nineteens. If this is a mere coincidence, the chance for it is only one in 703. But this number nineteen is the same number of letters with which the words of the vocabulary of Mark 16: 9-20 begin. That is to say: this particular feature of nineteens is common to the first and last passages in Mark. This may also be accidental, but the chance for it is now only one in 29,260. But this is not all. The number 209 is 19 elevens (Feature 1): of which the first, last, and middle letters have 33, or 3 elevens (Feature 2); and of these in turn the last has 22, or 2 elevens (Feature 3); and the eleventh letter of the 19 has—eleven (Feature 4). As the number of words in the vocabulary is 77, or seven elevens (Feature 5), the presence of the elevens in this one single item of the place values of those 19 letters, even apart from the sevens and nineteens (the chance for which is less than one in a million of billions) cannot be ascribed to chance, but must be accepted as part of a most elaborate design.

56

The very first page of the Gospel of Mark is thus found to be constructed on exactly the same kind of numeric design as its last page; and both passages prove themselves to be the work of the same artist, the same unparalleled literary mathematician.

One familiar with Raphael's, Veasquez's, or Rembrandt's paintings, with Beethoven's, or Chopin's music, with Thorwaldsen's sculptures, with Carlyle's, Macaulay's, or Matthew Arnold's prose, readily recognizes a portrait not seen before, a symphony or nocturne not heard before, and essay not read before, as the work of the same painter, musician, sculptor, writer. A certain family resemblance in the works of these readily betrays them to their respective connoisseurs. But here it requires no special training or tact to see that what we are dealing with here is not so much with two close relatives, but with the same personage, in the same dress, only in slightly varying postures. If, therefore, the first eight verses of this Gospel are the work of Mark, then the last twelve are also his.

57

Before leaving this passage, it may be pointed out that its numeric structure settles its two readings left in doubt by Westcott & Hort. In their uncertainty they offer as alternatives the omission of the second μου, me, in verse 6; and the insertion of υιος θεου, son of God, at the end of verse 1. The adoption of one or both of these alternatives destroys the numeric design. The Revised Version, which retains the rejected son of God in verse 1, has here, therefore, added to Scripture. But even apart from numerics and manuscript authority, it is shown in a Note at the end of this volume that even on exegetical ground it is impossible that Mark's Gospel should be that of the *Son of God*.

58

There remains only to show that this numeric structure is not peculiar to these two portions of Mark, but is the property of every paragraph in the Gospel so far examined, and therefore presumably also in all the others. At the mouth of two or three witnesses shall every word be established. Two witnesses have been listened to. For a third we may take the brief paragraph that follows verses 1-8. It consists of only three verses, but it presents the following phenomena;

59

It has a vocabulary of 35 words, or 5 sevens (Feature 1); of which it has 14, or 2 sevens, in common with the next paragraph, verses 12-15 (Feature 2). The numeric value of the Forms in which these 35 words are found is 26,887, or 3,841 sevens (Feature 3); while the numeric value of the passage is 27,783, or 7 x 7 x 7 x 3 x 3 x 3 x 3, a multiple of seven (Feature 4) sevens (Feature 5) of sevens (Feature 6); and the number of its factors is seven (Feature 7). The longest word here, σχιζομενους, has a numeric value of 1,652 or 236 sevens (Feature 8); the shortest, ὁ, has 70, or 10 sevens (Feature 9).

60

Thus in about six lines there are nine features of sevens, three for every two lines. But there is in addition this feature: The value of the forms, 26,887, is 7 x 23 x 167, a multiple of *twenty-three* as well as of seven. The number of these Forms is 44, or 4 elevens. Accordingly the number of letters in this small paragraph is 253, or 23 x 11, a multiple of both *twenty-three and eleven*.

That is to say: Supposing that the reader might be left to think that there is no numeric design in the number of forms because it is not a multiple of seven, nor in the number of letters for the same reason, the artist-numberer left as it were his visiting card in this little item, to show that there is design here just the same though not of sevens. The presence here of the double eleven and the double twenty-three (the chance for the one being only one in 231, and the chance for the other only one in 1,035, the chance for both together being only one in 239,085), is thus the same kind of a reminder of the presence here of the great Artist as Michel Angelo is reported to have left of himself when calling on a friend. Not finding him at home, Michel Angelo, instead of leaving a card, drew at the entry of the house a perfect circle. The returning friend recognized the call of the master by the circle which he knew no other could draw thus.

61

The same what may be called visiting card design is found in the next paragraph, verses 12-15. The vocabulary to this passage has also 35 words, or 5 sevens: of which, as stated in § 55, it has 14 in common with verses 9-11, or 2 sevens. Its numeric value is 23,540, which is a multiple not of seven, but of eleven, it being 11 x 2,140. Neither is the number of words in the passage, 65, a multiple of seven; but of thirteen, it being 13 x 5. Accordingly the number of syllables in the *Vocabulary* is 99, or 9 elevens (its numeric value being a multiple of eleven) and the number of syllables in the *Passage* is 312, or 24 thirteens; they forming, as just stated, 65 words, or 5 thirteens, with a numeric value of 31,798, or 2,446 thirteens.

62

It is to be noted, moreover, that in each of these first three passages of Mark examined, in addition to the clear design of sevens the number eleven is also made to play a part. In verses 1-8 the vocabulary has 77 words, or 11 x 7; in 9-11 it is the numbers of Forms and letters in the passage that are multiples of eleven. In 12-15 it is the numeric value of the vocabulary and the number of its syllables that are multiples of eleven.

In other words, these three passages have in addition to the usual stamp of sevens upon them also the bond of elevens between them.

63

As a final example of this visiting card method of numerics in Mark may be given the speech of the Lord in 13:5-37. At the writing of the preceding section, there was occasion to refer to it. Its vocabulary was found to have 203 words, or 7 x 29, a multiple of seven and *twenty-nine*. The number of words in this speech was found to be 522, or 18 twenty-nines. Apart from the fact that the chance for this particular combination of seven an twenty-nines is only one in 11,571, the fact that this kind of numerics has already been repeatedly found in Mark assures us without further search that 522 is the true number of words in this speech.

64

Every paragraph so far examined in Mark by the writer, however large or small, displays the same kind of numeric design. Thus Mark 1:21-31 has vocabulary of 77 words, or *seven elevens* (this is the fourth paragraph in this chapter to show elevens as well as sevens, see § 57); of which verses 21-22 have 21, or 3 sevens; and verses 23-31 have 56, or 8 sevens. Alphabetically the 77 words are thus distributed: $α$-$μ$ have 49, seven sevens; $ν$-$ω$ 28, or 4 sevens. And again: $α$-$ε$ have 33, or 3 elevens; $η$-o 22, or 2 elevens; and $π$-$ω$ also 22. This division is into groups of both sevens and elevens. And *the letters with which the groups end have in both cases numeric values whose sums are multiples of seven*. Thus the value of $μ$ and $ω$ is 840, or 120 sevens; of $ε$, o, $ω$, 875, or 125 sevens.

65

In Mark 2:13-17 the Lord says a few words, and the scribes say a few words. This passage of only five verses has a vocabulary of 49 words, or 7 x 7: of which the Lord uses 14, or 7 x 2; and the scribes use seven.
In 4:3-20 is given the parable of the sower by the Lord with a vocabulary of 49, or 7 x 7.

66

As a last example of particular passages being constructed on an elaborate numeric design 3:13-19 may be cited. Here is given the appointment of the twelve by the Lore; whose names are here: Simon, James, John, Andrew, Philip, Bartholomew, Matthew, Thomas, James, Thadeus, Simon, Judas. As Θαδδαιος, *Thaddeus*, is only a form of Ιουδας, *Judas*, and not a separate vocabulary word, the vocabulary to these twelve names consists of only nine words: Σῖμσυν, Ιακω, βΙωανης, Ανδρεας, Φιλιππος, Βαρθολομαιος, Μαθθαιος, Θομας, Ιοδας: Simon, James, and Judas, being the names for more than one apostle each.

67

Now these nine names have 28 syllables, or 7 x 4, with a numeric value of 7,021, or 7 x 17 x 59; of which the three names that stand for more than one apostle have 2,618, or 7 x 17 x 11. The first and the last in the list have 1,785, or 7 x 17 x 15. The middle one, Φιλιππος, has 980, or 7 x 7 x 20. The value of all the twelve names is 9,639, or 7 x 17 x 9. Of these six numbers, every one of which is a multiple of seven, four are also multiples of seventeen. Accordingly, the value of the nine names, 7,021, or 17 x 7 x 59, is thus divide: the nine initial letters have 782, or 17 x 46; the rest have 6,329, or 17 x 367. And as the vocabulary to these twelve names has *nine* words, the numeric value of all the twelve names is a multiple of seven, seventeen, and *nine nines*.
That is to say: in the mere item of the apostles' names in this paragraph of seven verses there are three distinct schemes of sevens and nines and seventeens.

68

The whole Gospel of Mark then is constructed on the same plan as its last twelve verses. The Gospel as a whole, then, and this its suspected portion are from the same artistic hand; the author of the Gospel according to Mark is also the author of its last twelve verses.
But though the work of the same mind, of Mark, are the Last Twelve Verses an integral part of his *Gospel*? May they not after

all be a separate bit of work by Mark?

To this Numerics give a clear answer in several ways: one or two may suffice.

69

Three words are used in Mark 16:9-20 for the divine persons: θεος, Ιησους, κυριος; *God, Jesus, Lord.* These three words occur in the Gospel of Mark *including this passage*, 48, 81, and 18 times respectively, 147 in all, or 7 x 7 x 3, a multiple not only of 7 but of 7 x 7; and the numeric value of these 147 occurrences is 103,635, or 7 x 7 x 2,115, again a multiple of 7 x 7. This clearly designed result is possible only with the four occurrences of these words *in this passage*. In other words: with the removal of this passage a design of sevens now running through these three words in the whole Gospel is destroyed. This passage is thus at once proved to be a necessary integral part of the Gospel as a whole.

70

Four words in 16:9-20 are found in the rest of the New Testament, and in the preceding portion of Mark; but not in Matthew. Their sole characteristic is thus the fact that they are found in Mark for the first time in the New Testament; they are: γλωσσα, κτισις, πανταχον, φανεροω; *tongue, creation, everywhere, to manifest.* They are found in the New Testament in 7 forms which have 21 syllables, or 7 x 3. The 7 forms are words of 2, 3, 4, and 5 syllables; the sum of these numbers is 14, or 7 x 2: of which the first and the last have 7, and the two middle numbers have 7. As this design of sevens runs through the words found in the passage, whose sole characteristic is that they occur in the New Testament first in the undisputed portion of Mark, this design is impossible unless 16:9-20 is taken as part of the Gospel.

71

But the neatest proof that the Last Twelve Verses are as integral a portion of the Gospel of Mark as any other , is furnished by the two words with which the Gospel of Mark begins and ends. It begins with αρχή, *beginning*, and ends with σημειων, *of signs*. The two words αρχή and σημειων have a place value of 47 and 79, or 126 in all: which is 7 x 18. Their numeric values 709 and 383, give 1092, or 7 x 13 x 12, a multiple of 7 and 13. They occur in Mark 65 times, or 13 x 5, with a total numeric value of 6,409, or 13 x 493; while the five forms of these two words have 13 syllables.

A scheme of sevens and thirteens thus runs through the two words with which the Gospel begins and ends. (Compare for the *thirteens* the analysis of Mark 1:12-15 §58). But this is not all. Their total numeric value, 6,409, or 13 x 29 x 17, is a multiple of 29 as well as of 13. Accordingly, the number of letters in the forms of these two words is 29.

Three distinct schemes of 7, 13, and 29 (the sum of these three numbers being moreover 49, or 7 x7), thus run through these two words. The Gospel of Mark, therefore, as it begins with αρχή, *beginning*, so it ends with σημειων, *signs*. And it ends therefore not at verse 8 of Chapter 16, but at verse 20.

72

In the above investigation only the passage itself has been listened to; the other passages being only incidentally brought into court to testify as to its being in nowise a kind of Tichborne claimant, but a regular member of the household of Mark in the best of standing. The case for the defendant may indeed thus well be left here, leaving its accusers without even the hypothetical geometrical point to stand on. Nevertheless, it may be well to listen also to what the New Testament as a whole has to say here apart from Mark himself. In other words: having already obtained its excellent character in its own town, so to speak, let us consider also, if only briefly, its standing in the whole land.

73
Words with which the New Testament Books
begin and end.

The New Testament consists of twenty-seven books. It therefore has twice 27, or 54 words, with which its books begin and end. some of these words are repetitions. Thus the word *Paul* begins as many as thirteen books; the word ὑμων, *of you*, ends as many as ten books. Now these 54 words have a vocabulary of 28 words, or 4 sevens (Feature 1): of which seven are used only in the Gospels (Feature 2), with a place value of 392, or 7 x 7 x 8, a multiple of seven (Feature 3) sevens (Feature 4). The numeric values of the first, middle, and last words of the vocabulary, 'αγιος, επειδηπερ, θεός, Χριστος, 284, 297, 284, 1480, have for their sum 2345, or 335 sevens (Feature 5): of which the first and the last have 1764, or 7 x 7 x 6 x 6, a multiple of seven sevens (Feature 6); and the middle ones have 581, or 83 sevens (Feature 7). The place values of these first, last and middle words, 46, 84, 46, 118, have for their sum 294, or 7 x 7 x 6, a multiple of seven (Feature 8) sevens (Feature 9). The longest word in the vocabulary, αποκαλυψις, has a numeric value of 1512, or 6 x 6 x 6 sevens (Feature 10). The shortest, ὁ, has 70, or 10 sevens (Feature 11). The two titles of the divine personages, θεος, Χριστος, *God*, *Christ*, with numeric values of 284 and 1480, have for their sum 1764, or 7 x 7 x 6 x 6, a multiple of seven (Feature 12) sevens (Feature 13). The sum of the numeric and place values of the Vocabulary, 19,890 and 1,950, is 21,840, or 3,120 sevens (Feature 14), or 7 x 6 x 13 x 40. An elaborate design of sevens thus runs through the vocabulary of these 54 (or 9 *sixes*) words with which the New Testament books begin and end with *ten* features of SIXES in addition.

74

The Forms in which the 28 words of the vocabulary actually occur have just seven words with numeric values that are multiples of seven (Feature 15). And these seven words: αμαρτιων, αποκαλυψις, εκλεκτῆς, 'ο, ονομα, σημειων, τον, have 42 letters, or 6 sevens (Feature 16), with a place value of 511, or 73 sevens (Feature 17). The total numeric value of the 54 occurrences of the 28 Forms is 46,949, or 6,707 sevens (Feature 18): of which the Gospels have 3,808, or 544 sevens (Feature 19).

The seventh New Testament book, 1 Peter, has 2,765, or 395 sevens (Feature 20); the seventh New Testament author, Jude, has 784, or 7 x 7 x 16, a multiple of seven (Feature 21) sevens (Feature 22); Luke, the first New Testament author of more than one book, has 3,402, or 486 sevens (Feature 23).

A design of sevens thus runs also through the Forms of these words as well as through their vocabulary.

75

The number of words with which the New Testament books begin and end, 54, is six *nines* (Feature 1). The numeric value of the 28 words of their vocabulary, 19,890, is 2,210 nines (Feature 2): of which the letters used as initials, *α, β, ε, θ, ι, ο, π, σ, υ, χ*, have 1,377, or 9 x 9 x 17, a multiple of nine (Feature 3) nines (Feature 4). And of this number in turn the vowels have 486, or 9 x 9 x 6, a multiple of nine nines (feature 5); and the consonants have 891, or 9 x 9 x 11, again a multiple of nine (Feature 6) nines (Feature 7). The numeric value of their 28 Forms, 24,498, is 2,722 nines (Feature 8), of which those beginning with a vowel have 15,696, or 1,744 nines; and those beginning with a consonant have 8,802, or 978 nines (Feature 9).

A scheme of nines as well as of sevens thus runs through these 54 words.

76

The numeric value of the 38 words of the vocabulary, 19,890, is 9 x 13 x 170, a multiple of *thirteen* as well as nine (Feature 1). Of this number the nouns have 13,234, or 1,018 thirteens (Feature 2). The numeric values of every seventh word, there being four of them, 709, 297, 781, 2,010, have for their sum 2,756, or 212 thirteens (Feature 3); while in turn the numeric values of every thirteenth word, there being two of them, 55 and 1,100, have for their sum 1,155, or 165 sevens (Feature 4). The place value of the vocabulary is 1,950, or 150 thirteens (Feature 5). The 28 Forms have 78 syllables, or 6 thirteens (Feature 6); while the number of words in the vocabulary of forms with which the books begin is thirteen (Feature 7). On the other hand, the words in the

112

vocabulary of forms with which the books end have 91 letters, or seven thirteens (Feature 8).

A design of thirteens as well as of sevens and nines thus runs through the words with which the New Testament books begin and end.

77

But the numeric value 19,890, is 17 x 9 x 13 x 10, a multiple of *seventeen* as well as of nine and thirteen (Feature 1). Accordingly, this number is thus divided: the three words in the vocabulary which are found nowhere else in the New Testament, ακολυτως, επειδηπερ, πολυμερως, have 4,573, or 269 seventeens; the remaining words have 15,317, or 53 seventeens (Feature 2), of seventeen (Feature 3). The numeric value of the initial letters α, β, ε, θ, ι, ο, π, σ, υ, χ, 1,377, already seen in § 71 to be a multiple of nine nines, is also a multiple of seventeen, it being 17 x 9 x 9 (Feature 4). The numeric value of all the initial letters of the vocabulary is 1,921, or 113 seventeens (Feature 5). The numeric value of the six forms found nowhere else in the New Testament: ακολυτως, αποκαλυψις, βιβλος, εκλεκτῆς, επειδήπερ, πολυμερως, is 6,987, or 411 seventeens (Feature 6). Lastly: the seven words in the vocabulary of forms, each of which has a numerical value of so many sevens, have for their combined value 5,236, or 308 seventeens (Feature 7).

In other words: the numeric value of the vocabulary to these words being a multiple of nine, thirteen, and seventeen, there are in addition to the scheme of sevens three distinct schemes of nines, thirteens, and seventeens, running through these words.

78

That this enumeration of the numeric phenomena is not exhaustive may be seen from the following fact: The total numeric value of the 54 words with which the New Testament books begin and end, 46,949, or 19 x 7 x 353, is a multiple of nineteen as well as of seven. Of this number the two words with which the New Testament begins and ends: *βιβλος*, *book*, and

113

αγιων, *of saints* (Westcott & Hort), have 314 and 864 respectively; together 1,178, or 62 nineteens. Enough, however, has been given to show that a most elaborate numeric design pervades the 54 words with which the New Testament books begin and end. But this design is possible only with σημειων, *signs*, as the word *with which the Gospel of Mark ends*. Apart then from Mark himself, some one else, the designer of this numeric scheme for the whole New Testament, saw to it that these disputed verses be thus amply attested as a genuine portion not only of Mark but also of the New Testament as a whole, unless indeed it should turn out that the Numerics in Mark and those of the New Testament are designed by one and the same mind.

79

The word αγρος, *field*, has for its occurrences in the New Testament a numeric value of 22,764, or 3,252 sevens (Feature 1); of which the Gospels have 22,190, or 3,170 sevens; and Acts has 574, or 82 sevens (Feature 2), the only two New Testament divisions where it occurs. Only the following letters are used in all their occurrences: α, γ, ν, ο, ρ, σ, υ, ω: their numeric value is 1,624, or 232 sevens (Feature 3): of which the letters with a value of 100 and under have 224, or 32 sevens; and those with a value above 100 have 1,400, or 200 sevens (Feature 4). Lastly, the factors of this number 1,624, are 2 x 2 x 2 x 7 x 29; their sum is 42, or 6 sevens (Feature 5). The Place value of the six forms of αγρος is 336, or 48 sevens (Feature 6): of which those occurring in only one book have 112, or 16 sevens, and those in more than one book have 224, or 32 sevens (Feature 7). The first form, αγρον, has 49, or seven (Feature 8) sevens (Feature 9), of which the first and last letters have 14, or 2 sevens; the others have 35, or 5 sevens (Feature 10)
A design of sevens thus runs through this word in the New Testament.

80

This word αγρος occurs in the New Testament 36 times or six (Feature 1) sixes (Feature 2), in six forms (Feature 3), which have

114

30 letters, or 5 sixes (Feature 4); and the total number of letters in all the 36 occurrences is 180, or 5 sixes (Feature 5) of sixes (Feature 6).

The place value of the six forms of αγρος is 336, or 6 x 7 x 8, a multiple of six as well as of seven (Feature 7): of which number the Singular forms have 132, or 22 sixes, and the Plural have 204, or 34 sixes (Feature 8).

The numeric value of the six forms is 3,804, or 634 sixes (Feature 9): of which the singular forms have 1,728, or 6 x 6 x 6 x 2 x 2 x 2, a multiple of six (Feature 10) sixes (Feature 11) of sixes (Feature 12), with the sum of its factors 24, or 4 sixes (Feature 13); and the plural forms have 2,076, or 346 sixes. The total number value of the word in all its occurrences , 22,764, or 6 x 7 x 542, is a multiple of six as well as of seven (Feature 14). And of this in turn the Singular has 14,844, or 2,474 sixes; and the Plural has 7,920, 6 x 6 x 220, a multiple of six (Feature 15) sixes (Feature 16).

Again: of the six forms of αγρος some occur in only one book, and others in more than one. Accordingly the total value, 22,764, is divided thus: the forms found in only one book have 2,076, or 346 sixes; those found in more than one have 20,688 or 3,448 sixes (Feature 17).

81

The unchangeable stem αγρ- is followed in the occurrences of this word only by the letters ω and ο. Their numeric value, 870, is 145 sixes (Feature 18).

Lastly: the numeric value of the letters used in this word has been shown above (§ 69, Feature 5) to be 1,624, of which the factors are 2,, 2, 2, 7, 29. Their sum, 42, is a multiple of six as well as of seven (Feature 19).

A most elaborate design of sixes as well as of sevens thus runs through this word of five letters in the New Testament.

That this enumeration however, of its numeric phenomena is in nowise exhaustive may be seen from this: the last two numbers analyzed, 870 and 1,624, are multiples of *twenty-nine* as well as of six and (in one case) seven. Apart from the 29 features of sixes and sevens, the chance for these two features of twenty-nines is only one in 1,653.

This highly elaborate design is only possible with the αγρον in Mark 16:12. As the values of this word are 224 and 49, both multiples of seven, the design of sevens in αγρος would be destroyed only partly with the omission of the Last Twelve Verses of Mark. But the design of sixes would be wholly destroyed. As, therefore, the phenomena of the words with which the New Testament books begin and end demand the presence of these verses in the New Testament, so it is also demanded by the phenomena of αγρος,

The searchlight, withersoever turned on, thus always only adds new lustre to the native purity of this Passage. The Last Twelve Verses of Mark are not only a genuine portion of the New Testament, they are among its brightest ornaments.

[Epilogue extracted from his Notes follows.]

The numeric phenomena enumerate for the various passages in the preceding pages do not begin to be exhaustive. Every fresh examination brings to light some additional feature in the items already examined, or a wholly new item. Thus not until this Note was being set up was it discovered that the Vocabulary of the Last Twelve Verses of Mark has its shortest words (in the matter of syllables) consist of one syllable; its longest, of six. The sum of these numbers is—seven. This feature might well be allowed to pass unnoticed but for this fact: These longest and shortest words (fifteen one-syllable words and one six-syllable) have thus together 21 syllables, or 3 sevens; and 49 letters, or seven sevens. This is a wholly new item hitherto unobserved in all the twenty years of the writer's labour in this field.

Again: the number of words in this Vocabulary, 98, is 7 x 7 x 2, or twice forty-nine. Usually in such cases it is every seventh word that is scanned here for numerics. It occurred, however, to the writer to try also every forty-ninth word; their numeric values 321 and 715, have for their sum 1,036, or 148 sevens.

And once more: These 98 words have 553 letters, or seventy-nine sevens. It occurred to the writer to look up the seventy-ninth word. It is παρά with a numeric value of 182, or 26 sevens; and a place value of 35, or 5 sevens.

The reader is now prepared to be told that the genuineness of John 7:53—8:11, which twelve verses are rejected by modern critical editors with even greater assurance than the passage in Mark, is established in exactly the same way, since it is permeated with the same numeric design. So that either Mark was the writer of both passages, or John, or there are after all two such unparalleled mathematical artists. But in his numerous papers the writer has demonstrated in a hundred different ways that not a paragraph in every one of the six and sixty books of the Bible so far examined but is constructed on the same lightly elaborate numeric design. So that there are thus three and thirty mathematical miracles, limited, however, only to *Bible* writers.

But in the same pages it is also amply shown that mere men could not thus write, that those numeric phenomena can be explained only as the work of One Master Designer.

*   *   *

Thus ends a masterpiece of research and reason. To round out our picture of Panin, we have yet only to review the process, patience, and perseverance of his fifty years of work. The next chapter will go into the details of how this servant of God went about providing us with these riches, and what he encountered.

Have ye understood all these things? They say to him, Yes. And he said to them, Therefore every scribe discipled to the kingdom of the heavens is like a man, a householder, who brings forth out of his treasure things *new and old.* Matthew 13:51-52

XI

The Life and Times of Panin's Labors

This chapter is taken from *A Holy Challenge for Today*, the first section of which is by J. S. Bentley.

*   *   *

ON THE REVISION
OF THE NEW TESTAMENT GREEK TEXT
By means of BIBLE NUMERICS

What led Ivan Panin to become impressed with the importance and urgency of restoring the texts of the Scriptures to their original purity? Why did it matter that no question about the text should be unresolved? He found the Old Testament text has been well preserved. And, the New Testament editors in modern times has already done a valiant work in edition the Greek Text, so that now for a century no one has been able to improve on their work to any noticeable degree.

Except—
But wait... Why did Ivan Panin—a promising young man in the field of letters—lay his future on the line to devote his life to settling every question that remained unresolved in the New Testament text?

Why did he perceive that a perfect text is essential as the basis of *verbal inspiration* of the Scriptures—and that verbally inspired Scriptures is the foundation of the Christian Faith?

Let us look back with him, as he looked back from long years of following this unlikely commitment. It was the grace of God that enabled him to labour for and achieve a perfectly restored "Word of God", he acknowledged. But he now recalled visible happenings that were evidence of this grace at work years before this dramatic decision to make this commitment to the One who was now his Lord, and to what was now the *precious* Word of God.

There was the unknown friend who met him on the street of the German city and led him into a tiny prayer meeting—"all Greek to me then", he recalled—and he heard them praying "God bless our brother". Then he was soon gone on his teen-aged lonely way.

There was the day when he as Harvard student, went to hear an English artist speak. This stranger, at the close shook his hand and invited "Come up to where I am staying". And—the artist began praying for blessing on this young man.

There was the day when the maturing agnostic was invited to give an address on literature to a church audience. Afterward, the eminent clergyman host said as he greeted him, "You are my brother. If you ever wish to be baptized, it would be the joy of my life to baptize you . . ."

There was the day when he chose his study schedule at college, when he found he already knew several languages offered—so he compromised for the unlikely, for him, by choosing Hebrew and Greek.

Yes, such unexplained diversion from the natural course of his life he later acknowledged had been God preparing him for his personal encounter with God and the task that came to him. They were all incidental in his banishment from his homeland, his casting about in the wider world, his finding a new life on a new continent.

But the desire to know the Truth about life was growing. It

120

became a passion so that he searched among the philosophers' writings of history and of his day. He cultivated the personal friendship of leading American thinkers within his reach.

He questioned—exactly what were each of these men thinking? Why were their thoughts expressed the way he found them? What were the results of their thinking? He developed in his own thinking, so that many of his aphoristic writings reflected the fast maturity of his own thoughts.

But all this did not answer honestly for him: What is Truth? Where is Truth?
Then, it was the time—his family's old friend, Leo Tolstoy, was being noticed in the news—Tolstoy in *his* search for Truth had turned to the Bible where he read the words of Jesus in his Sermon on the Mount. And he had been impressed enough to decide to obey the words of Jesus Christ as a great Teacher. And he *did* have a profound experience.

As Ivan Panin "thought on these things," he decided also to search in the life and words of Jesus. He analyzed them as he had the writings of the philosophers whose works he had already combed.

He also determined to obey whatever words he found that could be applied to him. One of these was when he read that a man needed to be baptized. So he went back to his clergyman friend in Minneapolis who happily baptized him. When his old society friends heard, they shook their heads.

But he returned as he said "To make the Scriptures his meat and drink day and night, to learn if it was all really so." Studying and going through the same analyzing process of his literary training, he turned to the New Testament in the original Greek, using his "by chance" knowledge of Greek from college.

It was while reading in the Gospel of John that he noticed something puzzling—Why was the article used before the word "God" in one case and not in another? While he was pondering this he noticed other unusual things about the form of the language. he became aware of a mathematical factor in the text. As he checked it out, the number seven stood out as a feature.

A mind that had to have an answer—a reason—was challenged. One of these days, he stood up from the desk—he wanted to call out with the ancient "Eureka"—"I have found it!"

Not for naught had he sat up into the night with his philosopher friends searching out reason and reasoning.

He saw the import of this phenomena, unique among all the writings he had searched and analyzed, and continued to do. he had become aware of the questions still existing about the text of the New Testament. Here could be the means of settling these questions and of achieving a perfected text. This mathematical design coming to light appeared to bind the text—indeed—the whole Bible—into a tight mathematical unit. As he tested it, the law of chances told him that it was impossible for man to produce a book like this.

As he called the mathematical design Bible Numerics, the challenge was to find out the laws that govern this design Henceforth, though he tried to give Bible Numerics eminence, the name Ivan Panin and Bible Numerics were inseparable.

Now, as he delved into all aspects of Bible Scholarship, he found one of the questions was about *Verbal Inspiration*. He accepted the words of 2 Timothy 3:16 "Every Scripture is *God-breathed...*" (NNT). He saw that Verbal Inspiration is crucial to the Christian Faith. And now Bible Numerics provided the means of proving unquestionably that this is a fact.

122

In these days, when, as he often said "when I was a babe in Christ", his spiritual insight was growing. He truly realized that he was a sinner, and surrendered completely to Christ as his Lord and Saviour. "I determined to follow (by the grace of God) the Lord Jesus Christ even if it meant walking on my head," he later said.

And "walking on his head" he did appear to his old friends, and even to some of his new Christian friends—although—one of his old society friends had to confess when he met him on the street one day—"Well, Panin, your eyes are still bright!"

At this point, in Grafton, Mass., in 1891, he made the two resolves about which he writes in this paper, to accomplish during the rest of his life: To supply unquestionable proof that the Bible is written of God, and to restore the still "rather corrupted" text as it originally was in the autographs.

Ivan Panin tells in his writings of how even to get this task off the ground, he had to become practically a recluse, to search day and night for those laws governing the numerical design. He had the endless statistical job of creating vocabularies, concordances, and so on for the purpose, as well as investigating the whole field—all without the present-day electronic helps.

Some suggest he was a kind of "numbers nut." Actually, while numbers were involved in the case of the work God gave him to do, they were to him the means to the end. Numbers he continually unearthed brought to light the creative design of the Scriptures which was a constant amazement and thrill to him about the Great God of heaven. Here—while he was having to search and toil to bring together God's creative design in the Scriptures, God simply "said the Word and it was done"—perfect.

At heart, Ivan Panin was a literary man, but with a mind that gave him mastery in whatever sphere he applied himself. He undertook the work of science and technology with a deep sense of responsibility and fear of God. He was now dealing with the Word of Almighty God. He could be a critic of the works of men, but when he touched the Scriptures he was on Holy Ground. He often spoke with awe as he plied his task, with the warnings of Scripture always before him of the dire consequences of any tampering with the texts.

At the same time he was now labouring on the New Testament Text, he was searching the literature and scholarship of the Bible to amass the knowledge for every area challenging the Bible scholar and editor.

When he presented his discovery with the results he was accumulating to his intellectual friends, he was amazed that the evidence he had, did not change their rejection of God—at least, the God of the Bible. But what really eventually quite broke his heart towards the end of his life, was when Christian leaders generally waved it away as of no significance to the Christian Faith. Some even made attempts to disclaim it.

Only a comparative few caught his foresight that the time would come when, if Christendom could not offer *objective* proof that the Bible was unquestionably a unique revelation of God to man, the Christian Faith was in trouble. The subjective proofs that seemed convincing in other times, such as changed lives, prophecies fulfilled, archaeological evidences, no longer were convincing in a world of "Scientific" thinking and proof. The Christian Church would be faced with an apostasy which could lead to complete rejection of the Bible. What would there be left to convincingly defend "the Faith once for all delivered to the saints?" The Lord Jesus Christ Himself warned "Nevertheless, when the Son of Man cometh, shall he find the Faith on the earth?"

Ivan Panin believed he had discovered God's provision to step into this possible tragedy for men, and send them back to the Bible for wisdom. He presented Bible Numerics as evidence unquestionable that the Bible is what it claims to be: God's written revelation to man; and laid his own life on the line to do so.

He did all he could in one lifetime to demonstrate and leave this evidence for the extreme time of need. It is now challenging Christian leaders' eyes to be opened to see, and for "Science" to thoroughly investigate.

A great prayerful research project could provide authoritative verification that science could not ignore, of the claims that Ivan Panin made. A supporting proof by competent scientists could enable Science to offer, in the mercy of God, the remedy for many present troubles in the world.

Though he does not refer to Bible Numerics and the Numeric Greek Testament in his excellent work *"The Text of the New Testament"*, Dr. Vincent Taylor concludes his review of New Testament textual scholarship up to the present day with a profound statement: "Textual Criticism is an *objective scientific* study."

Ivan Panin saw that a century ago.

The challenge has been there.

When is the Christian Church going to investigate it conclusively for the world?

*   *   *

Part two of *A Holy Challenge for Today* follows.

INTRODUCTION
TO THE REVISION
OF THE NEW TESTAMENT
GREEK TEXT

By
Ivan Panin

(A hitherto unpublished manuscript
Written shortly prior to his death in 1942)

(Abridged by Dr. Allan Vincent)

The purity of the New Testament text in the autographs was lost already as early as the beginning of the third century of the Christian Era, if not earlier.

During the centuries following, continuous copying by hand could only add to the impurity. The invention of printing put an end to this process of growing corruption, but not to the corruption itself. And the printed so-called Received Text has for centuries been holding, and with negligible exceptions, still holds the field not only in the original, but also in nearly all the modern versions.

But not for ever was it thus to be with the Book of God. With Johann Jacob Greisbach (1775-1807) began a new era for the New Testament text. His was its first Critical edition according to certain canons of now established worth. But Griesbach was only a pioneer: he had all the disqualifications of the pioneer for a text of final worth. The axe and the pick are indispensable for the pioneer; but the settler must finish with hammer and saw, plumb-line and square.

Karl Lachmann, the second great critical New Testament editor (1831-50), brought its text nearer to its pristine purity than Griesbach; but his main achievement was rather dispelling the clouds than bringing in the sunshine; shutting the gate against the intruders rather than opening it to admit the king. Lachmann broke the spell of the Received Text under which Christendom had for centuries been held. By turning to the ancient sources only, and ignoring the Received Text altogether, he could at last present a text with the millstone off its neck. But his primary purpose being not so much purity (which was to come later) as antiquity, his text fared like Lazarus at the hands of the Lord: From the tomb he came indeed forth, but bound; the loosing and letting go was left to others.

To this loosening and letting go, the four great successors of Lachmann applied themselves with praiseworthy vigour. Tischendorf laid hold of this matter with the usual hopefulness and self-assurance of youth, Tregelles and Alford joined herein zealously.

But the efforts of these three did not appeal to the sixth great editorship of the Greek New Testament, Westcott and Hort (a two-in-one most effective combine), as on the whole meeting fully with the success deemed by them needful here or even possible, however great their appreciation of at least two of them. Accordingly without renouncing their portion in Lachmann, they reverted to Griesbach's domain, which meanwhile had fallen into rather unaccountable neglect. How vastly this domain had been improved by them and enriched, how profitably this self=imposed stewardship thereof had been held by them, will appear below.
Of the labours of Lachmann's three immediate successors, Tischendorf, Tregelles, and Alford: their indefatiguableness, faithfulness, zeal and devotion, only the best is to be said. But in the matter of achievement their deservedly high rank is usually assigned them in the order as above, with Alford a quite respectable distance from the other two.

The utmost that can be said here is that if Tischendorf was much the superior of Tregelles it was only in worldly fortune; and the world which ever loves its own, and has a fondness even for those of the Kingdom if only they abide in its outskirts, in debatable Borderland, has indeed done well by him. The plain Herr Tischendorf became Von Tischendorf, and was duly adorned in time with its highly prized New Year's Decorations.

Tischendorf, Tregelles and Alford were contemporaries nearly the whole of their lives: born within five years, they died within four; all at an early age: Tischendorf one year under sixty, Alford one year over. Tregelles attained to sixty-two, though a paralytic years before. The two Englishmen were, with Wescott and Hort, members of the Company of Revisers of 1881; but it was Tregellcs' first to be absent therefrom wholly (though present therein by his own Revision); and it was Alford's lot to be called thence within a few months of the beginning of the Revisers' labours. To Tischendorf and Tregelles, moreover, it fell to have to leave the final touches of their life-work to other hands.

Tregelles was thus finished by Hort and Steane four years after his death; Tischendorf's was finished by Casper Rene Gregory and Ezra Abbot some ten years after his death.

Samuel Prideaux Tregelles (1844-1879) after labouring on his Text as his life-work, produced only one edition thereof against Tischendorf's eight. Herzog's Encyclopedae says: "Tischendorf's peculiarity was to publish in rapid succession the swiftly ripened fruits of his restless activity, and to permit his last result to come into existence, so to speak before the eyes of the public.

"Tregelles loved to fix his full energy undisturbed upon the attainment of his one great aim, and to come into publicity only with the completest he had to offer ..... Tregelles did not believe that he could venture on the publication of the only edition of the New Testament which we possess from him until after twenty years' preparation."

The one edition could give for itself the same reason given by Aesop's lioness when chided for bringing forth her offspring without the numerosity of the mouse—"One," said she, "but a *lion!*"

Even Tischendorf himself was not always certain as to which of his first seven editions was most satisfactory; so with praise-worthy candour Tischendorf № 1 quotes now and then Tischendorf № 2 against Tischendorf № 3. But it is not by amiabilities that Truth is established. Not thus is established the Word of God which is settled in the heavens. And this numeric difference between Tischendorf's and Tregelles' One fixes their true relation as to minus and plus here.

To Tregelles it was not given to have the resources of his friend and (within certain limits) fellow-labourer. The Sinai manuscript came rather too late for him. Of the Vatican he got what knowledge there was to be got. But with all his handicap of poverty, ill-health and neglect, had he lived to enjoy the full advantage of his friendly German Competitor, he would have produced a text superior to Alford's certainly, and to Tischendorf's most likely.

It has become the fashion to deal lightly with Alford as a New Testament Editor. Wescott and Hort pass him by altogether as one of their predecessors. Philip Schaff only mentions him. If Tischendorf's noble equipment gets itself scattered to the danger point by defects of temper and poise, Alford's is diffused by choice. He was a poet, painter, Cathedral dean, New Testament commentator, with Textual Criticism thus verging almost to an aside. And as an aside he is thus decreed here by Fashion.

But his New Testament criticism is in no way a mere Aside. It has proved on the whole, next to Westcott and Hort, a most helpful piece of human labour. Tischendorf was a German, with all their virtues and some contraries in no wise peculiarly German.

129

Tregelles was a combination of the Frank with the Briton, with all their merits and none of the demerits. But Alford was an English-man, and a singularly noble specimen of the Englishman's glory, the praise of which has encircled the earth—British Justice.

And as a New Testament textual critic he is the inferior only of Westcott and Hort, the peer of Tregelles, and not a little the superior of Tischendorf in judgment, which is ever what gives to learning its final value.

He, too, has with Tischendorf some of that "Subjectivity", which even Schaff's whitewash had to leave exposed. But where with Tischendorf it was a matter of temper, it became in Alford purely a matter of discretion: seldom failing to put claims therefore which did not require the proverbial Philadelphia lawyer to make good. With all due appreciation of Tischendorf, he distrusts him much; with all justice to Tregelles he differs from him not a little.

It has fallen to the lot of Brooks Fess Wescott and Fenton John Anthony Hort (1853-81) to produce a New Testament text which is herein the last word in so far as this can at all be spoken by mere man. And for about a hundred years now it has indeed remained the last word, without even a respectable attempt to challenge this supremacy, held almost from the first of its appearance. As it stands their revision is the nearest hitherto attained approach to the very words given by the Spirit to the spokesmen of the Most High Through his Son.

Nor could it be otherwise,—the toil at the restoring of the broken walls from Origen to Bentley had consisted only in bringing together the scattered stones into a heap. Bentley and his successors laboured at the blue-prints, and got the stones eve into the cellar walls.

Westcott and Hort's five predecessors had indeed erected the walls: but the roof was left leaky, and the inside ungarnished, with much left that in a recently finished building needs carting away. And the task left to them Westcott and Hort have done beyond all praise. Even their hard-headed, most prosy Introduction, of over 500 pages with strong reminder of the entertainment offered by the pages of Intergral Calculus and Logarithm Tables, for the enjoyable reading of which one needs the mental nimbleness of a rhinoceros, (in nowise through their fault, but because of its subject matter), is a piece of architecture, a veritable poem in stone.

The work of at least three of Westcott & Hort's predecessors ever remind one of a bust by Rodin, which however like its original, looks as if its owner had been freshly guillotined. However good the workmanship, ragged edges are ever in sight. Not so with Westcott and Hort. Minutiae are not for them. To every detail they give the same faithful minute attention, reflecting here indeed the mind of Him in whose sight, as there is naught too great, neither is there aught too small.

Even accentuation which is no business at all of the text, and punctuation which is only that of the Commentator, testify of the master hands that have toiled thereon even to the dashlet, and its degree below the already lowly comma. And the writer could go on at some length with giving himself the pleasure of further praise.

Westcott and Hort were highly favoured in several respects. The already no mean advantage of being Englishmen was enhanced in their case by their being sober Englishmen. And as already in the days before Adam's spouse it had been declared that it is not good for Man to be alone, these two were endowed with the not so frequent gift for yoke-fellowship. And in New Testament Editorship two are indeed ever better than one.

To this was added their happy method of carrying on the partnership. Accounts were here most watchfully kept for peace's sake. And if final agreement was after all not to be had, recourse was had neither to diplomacy, nor to the method of Abraham and Lot before those Sodom days. They agreed instead to disagree with alternative readings as due record thereof. Altogether Westcott and Hort as New Testament Revisers are an ideal combination.

Of the two pillars of the noble edifice thus erected by them, the one its Jachin, was the Genealogical Method of Manuscript Interpretation. Toiled at by Bengel of blessed memory, it waxed strong under Griesbach. But after Lachmann it fell into a kind of decay, and in Tischendorf's seventh edition became even moribund.

But to its final re-establishment Westcott and Hort gave their whole strength. The possible reproach that, like Alford, they were mere gleaners after Tischendorf and Tregelles, with liberal enjoyment of the fruit of their toil, becomes thus a thing of naught.

The well-meant but Vesuvian onslaught of Dean Burgon only resulted in enhancing their worth; and the equally well-meant not so volcanic attempt of the Dean Miller partnership to construct a text against Westcott and Hort was only the obscuration of the light of the sun by Mercury's transit across its face; which becomes known only by its mention in the Almanac, or by the casual newspaper report.

And thus for half a century Westcott & Hort have been holding here not only their own, but their supremacy in the judgment of whatever is worthwhile in this realm; beginning with the successor of Tischendorf himself in Germany and ending with the Roman Catholic Hunshausen, who assigns them 'unstreitig die Palme' (the undisputed Palm) among New Testament editors. This 'Palm' might well be given 'without dispute' by Protestants, for whom Verbal Inspiration has, alas! now become impossible even in the original Greek; but to receive it at the hands of one to whom the Latin (in no wise best done) Translation is the veritable Heaven-descended Infallibility Itself—this tribute could only be extorted here by the work of Westcott and Hort.....

For be it noted that as star differeth from star in glory, the advent of Westcott and Hort into the New Testament sky was in no wise aught like what had come before. The Received Text, after many erratics from Erasmus[13] down, flared forth at last over men with 'Hic habes textum ab omnibus receptum': 'Behold the Text Received by All!' (except by those who did otherwise). Rose indeed rockety enough: colour, hiss, thud, all there, nothing wanting; but with return to earth mournful enough. Then came the diverse magnitudes from the still visible sixth to the Arideds[14] and Dippers of the second. Griesbach and Lachmann, already of magnitude the first, but only of Aldebaran[15] and Farmelhaut[16] light, are obscured for a while by the bursting forth between of meteoric Schelz[17] with gauzy tail of sweep enough to pass muster before the most exacting Hefmarschall[18] for the Etiquette of the heavens, but with head of mustard-seed dimensions. Clearly not

---

13 Erasmus: Catholic priest (1466-1536) who worked on the first New Testament printed in Greek, primarily to allow scholars to verify his Latin version. He printed it with the Greek facing the Latin.

14 Arided—Today known as *Deneb*, it is the brightest star in the constellation *Cygnus* and the 19th brightest star in the night sky. Panin is using wry humor to point out the 'lesser luminaries' in textual criticism, in this case Griesbach.

15 Aldebaran—one of the brighter stars of the night sky in the constellation Taurus. It can be found (in the Northern hemisphere) by following Orion's belt from left to right and continuing on that line.

16 Farmalhaut—today called "Fomalhuat", it is the brightest star in the constellation Piscis Austinus (not to be confused with the larger Pisces).

17 A reference to Scholz who is quoted extensively by Tregelles in his wordy 1854 publication *"The Printed Text of the New Testament with Remarks on its Revision upon Critical Principles together with a Collation of the Critical Texts of Griesbach, Scholz, Lachmann, and Tischendorf, with that in Common Use."*

18 Hefmarschall—today "hofmascall", in Germany an administrative official in charge of courtly affairs. It is wry humor pointed at Tischendorf.

among these came Westcott and Hort to take their place.

Tischendorf broke forth with starhood enough; but with binary companionship. Abundant illumination here, much obscuration there, with periodicity rarely calculable. Alford shines forth as a Sirius, and Tregelles even as Jupiter, if not indeed Venus herself. But Westcott and Hort came note even as the moon, Queen of what is after all still night. The advent of Westcott and Hort into the New Testament horizon was neither as meteor, star, or planet —rather was it as the Sun into the Day.

And with this tribute to their High Estate the writer would fain pause and go his way. The pleasure, the holy pleasure of bearing fitting witness to abiding worth is ever a most satisfying, joyful memory to be borne away at the otherwise sad hour of parting. But alas! it is only the moon the ruleth by night that has been afforded the smiling mien of man. The sun given to rule the Day may indeed shine on in its glory but not without Spots. And Westcott and Hort with all their solar splendour are likewise not without spots, and these moreover of solar dimensions.

So great indeed is this spotfulness that when the Profit and Loss balance is finally struck between the disreputably corrupt Received Text and the meticulously scrubbed and washed and trimmed and groomed text of Westcott and Hort, the godly Bible-loving soul might well find itself in a strait betwixt the two, and say with the Apostle of old, What to choose I wot not.

Even of the Chief Corner Stone laid in Zion, elect, precious, on whom believing one shall not be shamed (on the great and dreadful day of the Lord) it is writ that He can yet become a Rock of Offense. And the very corner stone of Westcott and Hort's wise and loving toil of eight and twenty years brought already at its advent the like offensiveness.

For nothing had become so needful for the right appraisal of New

Testament documents as the Genealogical Doctrine of Manuscripts, which in its essence is: That a thousand descendants of one parent are in no wise 1,000 additional texts, however wise their extent in space and time: but rather the same one text of the one parent: that the witnesses thus present are not a thousand and one, but just the same—one. All that follows in the 250 pages of Westcott and Hort's Introduction to their text is only an amplification, exposition and application of this fundamental fact.

But with this last word of human wisdom, however rightly spoken, there is no help for the here required two stern, though wholly conscientious, major operations performed by them on the New Testament text, joined herein by Tischendorf and Alford rather bluntly, by Tregelles somewhat reluctantly, but by all relentlessly. The guillotining of the Last Twelve Verses of Mark, and of the Incident of the Woman Taken in the Act of John VII. 53, VIII. 11, was accordingly accomplished by Westcott and Hort with Parisian dispatch.

And after such two major operations, minor ones readily follow. So Matthew XVI. 2-3 becomes a kind of vermiform appendix with prompt disposal thereof behind double brackets. The Bloody Sweat of the Lord in Luke XXII. 43-4, with its Gethsemane surroundings, is rejected..... The prayer on the cross 'Father forgive them for they know not what they do' is disposed of in the same manner..... and a whole verse of Luke XXIV. 12, is dispatched to the same—'dumphead'.

But if Christians' Faith must ever be aught more than the erection of metaphysics into a granite cube solid and firm but equally hard, Christians' Book must ever be aught more than the wax-nosed clinical subject it was like to remain in editors' hands. To Christians, contrary to the wise and understanding of this age, the Book must ever remain what it claims of itself on many a page thereof that 'Living is the Word of God, and active and sharper than any two-edged sword; and piercing even to the dividing of soul and spirit, of both joints and marrow, and discerner of thoughts and intents of hearts. And there is no creature not manifest in His sight.' To Christians the Book is not aught to be cut but to—cut! And in presence of these surgics, howe'r well meant, he can only wonder and ponder: 'I am in a strait betwixt two: what to do I wot not.....'

To Christians such dispatch of two pages (and of what pages!) and of two sayings (and of what sayings!) of the Eternal Son of God Himself to the mundane rubbish heap by the highest textual wisdom of man as represented by Westcott and Hort, be the 'operation never so skilful, never so beautiful' is passing grievous. When once he faces his book once more, his God's Book, with such mutilation... For Christians, meant to delight in the law of the Lord and to meditate therein day and night, the cry here is no longer Which two? but What two next?

Of Dean Burgon, whatever his doings otherwise, the writer in common with others can only regret that as a New Testament textual craftsman he is worth successor of Don Quixote, equally lovable but equally fighter of—Windmills. But among his voluminous sayings, one well deserves heed here. Lachmann, Tischendorf, and Tregelles, and specially Wescott and Hort (the last with appropriate Red-Rag-Bull effect on him) are all his windmills; and these he duly charges on his Resinante fleet with zeal goodly enough, but not according to knowledge. But in the midst of these, his doughty doings, there is dropped a veritable literary gem.

Says he: 'Though it is impossible to deny that the published texts of Drs. Tischendorf and Tregelles as texts are wholly inadmissable, yet is it equally certain that by the conscientious diligence with which those distinguished scholars have respectively laboured, they have erected monuments of their learning and ability which will endure forever. Their editions of the New Testament will not be superseded by any new discoveries, by any future advances in the science of textual criticism. The manuscripts which they have edited will remain among the most precious materials for future study.

'Lachman's leading fallacy has perforce proved fatal to the value of the text put forth by Dr. Tregelles. Of the scrupulous accuracy the indefatiguable industry, the pious zeal of that estimable and devoted scholar, we speak not. All honour to his memory, As a specimen of conscientious labour his edition of the New Testament (1857-72) passes praise, and will never lose its value. If in the warmth of controversy I shall appear to have spoken of them sometimes without becoming deference, let me here once for all confess that I am to blame, and express my regret. When they have begged Mark's pardon for the grievous wrong they have done him, I will very humbly beg their pardon also.'

Well said, nobly said, and for once effectively said. Only this demand for apology to Mark (and how likewise to John) is needless, since it is not theirs to accept it, but the Holy Spirit's whose they are. But the Holy Spirit is not given to the witnessing of Himself but to One Other; His witness is; 'The times of ignorance God overlooked; but now He declareth unto men that they should all everywhere repent; inasmuch as He hath appointed a day in which He shall judge the inhabited earth in righteousness by a Man whom He hath ordained whereof He hath given assurance unto all in that He hath raised Him from the dead' For "apologies" it will then be too late; for repentance there, thank God, is yet time even for the truncatings of His Book, His Word.

The Second Pillar of Westcott and Hort's noble edifice, its Boaz in fact, is its unique apparatus of alternative reading with its effective simple notation. It has already been noted how Tischendorf's several editions diverge from one another. Human wisdom even at its highest is never a safe dependence as a finality............

If Westcott and Hort ever wore the badge of citizenship of Cocksuredomland, they did not bring it to their New Testament task. With meekness not often paralleled in editorial regions they undertook to confess systematic uncertainty in the but too many cases where certainty was not to be had. Accordingly their scheme of alternative readings is in itself a piece of the highest wisdom attainable here. When the two-in-one editorship cannot see eye to eye, Alternative Reading bears witness thereof. Where the balance between two or even more readings is zero or nigh thereto, and in more items of the like, Alternative Reading rings its bell.

When on trial for his life Socrates told his judges that the great difference between him and other teachers was: They knew not their ignorance; he knew his. Westcott and Hort knew well what they did know; they knew equally well what they did not know. If the greatest New Testament sin is Evil Speaking against the Holy Spirit, the next greatest is: "If ye were blind, ye would have no sin; but now ye say 'We see', your sin remaineth." Into the sin of saying "We see" when they do not see, Westcott and Hort, rare exception here among men of their like, took good care not to fall.

And thus, as the Genealogical Doctrine of Documents is the glory of their Introduction, their method of Alternative Readings, with its classic notation, is the glory of their Text. The one is the glory of Preparation, the other the glory of Execution.

But this Pillar Boaz brought alas! with itself the fate shared by Jachin. Here likewise the highest wisdom of man made naught by its own Viper. Hardly a page of their text, on the whole the purest yet brought forth by mere man, but has one alternative reading: frequently more, even several; thousands in all for the 539 pages of their honest toil of twenty-eight years.

These thousands of Alternatives affect indeed the sense of the

138

words seldom vitally; but the syllables and letters are oft much affected: and with what import the reader will in the Numeric Greek New Testament now in print see for himself. Here, it need only be observed that in His last appearance toward the end of the Book that is from the beginning to end the Testimony of Jesus, His Name is the Word of God. And it is He that hath said not only: 'The Heaven and the Earth shall pass away, but my words shall not pass away,' but also 'till the heaven and the earth pass away not one jot or tittle of the law shall pass away.' And as with the Great God there is naught too great or too small in His Creation, neither is there with Him aught too great or too small in His Book............

To the question first put nineteen centuries ago at Caesarea Philippi, with its answer awaited afresh from every generation since, mere flesh and blood could give only halting reply with opinings natural enough. 'Who do men say that the Son of Man is?'—'Some say John the Baptist; others Elijah; diverse again, Jeremiah or one of the prophets.' But 'Thou art the Christ, the Son of the Living God,' was for flesh and blood to know only when revealed by His Father Who is in the Heavens; thus enforcing once more the ever-needed reminder that nothing in the affairs of men is really settled until the Great God has had His own say therein.

If the law was given that every mouth be stopped, the Gospel is given that no flesh should glory before God. If 'Be not wise in thine own eyes, and lean not to thine own understanding' must begin already in the kindergarten, 'In all thy ways acknowledge Him' must endure even beyond the University. And the Great God's ways are not as Man's ways, neither doth He see as man seeth.

Now of the New Testament editors passed in review before us the best that flesh and blood could say herein has been abundantly said. But what Heaven has to say here, though plainly enough writ in the Book so that he may run that reads, remains yet to be told: Said the One Who is to judge the quick and dead to... the Twelve: "Who heareth you heareth Me and who rejecteth you rejecteth Me; but who rejecteth Me rejecteth Him that sent Me." "Thy Word I have given to them."

The Book left of these accordingly claims (and if the claim is not made good it only arrogates) for itself that it is not man's book but God's Book, that it proceeds not from flesh and blood, but from the Eternal Spirit; yes, the Eternal Son Himself hath commanded His disciples not to premeditate their words; these were to be given them in the hour of need; what to say, yea, what to write.

But of the six before us, the imperfect number, despite their loving toil, five (the number of sinful man) have failed to give the Book its due.....Greisbach, Lachmann, Tischendorf, Alford, Westcott and Hort, were here ready enough to clasp hands, and even feast with the Book; but as to surrender—Griesbach was a pupil and resident in the house of Semler[19], the head of vociferous foes of the Faith, thriving even in these latter days, though it Anakim[20], David Fiedrich Straus[21] and Ernest Renan[22], flourished some threescore years ago. The one undertook to drum out the Lord of Glory as a mere fiction of His disciples; the other undertook to fiddle him back as a nice boulevard parisian. Greisbach indeed endeavoured to remain at least a Unitarian, but with the fate of the crew that had unlearned to walk and had forgotten how to fly.

---

19 Johann Salomo Semlar—Lutheran theologian appointed as professor at Halle (1752) was an extremely liberal thinker who willy-nilly changed doctrine around as an intellectual pastime, as it were.
20 Anakim—giants in the land of Canaan who were enemies to Israel.
21 Straus—Rationalist and author of *The Life of Jesus Critically Examined* in 1835 that argued against all miracles and mythologized Jesus.
22 Renan—Rationalist and author of *The Life of Jesus* in 1864 that, like Straus, attempted to strip the historical Jesus of any miracles or divinity.

Neither Lachmann nor Tischendorf could hold to the infallibility of the Book. It had become out of fashion in their day. Alford did not hesitate to describe Verbal Inspiration as an 'incubus' on the Book. Westcott was content to oppose it with a calmer chapter in one of his books. But the possibility of settling the thousands of uncertainties in his text by means of Numerics that demonstrated its Verbal Inspiration met with the polite but firm: 'Holy Writ is as precious to me as ever, but your mechanical theory of Inspiration does not commend itself to me as the dynamical' (whatever that may mean).

Tregelles alone was bold enough to nail his flag to the mast and articulately declare that to him the Bible was the Infallible Inspired Word of the Most High, but with result mundane enough. Griesbach ended his days, Lachmann his, Tischendorf his . . .all laden with honours; Tischendorf most, Lachmann least, but all exalted by their fellowmen. Alford ended as Dean of Canterbury, Westcott as Bishop of Durham, Hort as Professor Hulsean at Cambridge. Tregelles, the utmost the World had for him was after years of hardship a pension of one hundred pounds when with one foot in the grave; raised to two hundred when the other was about to follow.

Tregelles had only the promise 'Them that honour me I will honour' though not necessarily here. But for them who 'In their lifetime have received their good things' it is, alas! spoken from on High: "What is highly exalted in men's sight" is in God's sight something far otherwise....

And from these two verities: What is highly exalted in sight of men is an abomination in sight of God; and The wisdom of man is Foolishness with God, there is no escape, whatever faces men may make thereat. 'Thy Word is settled in the heavens': Settled as beyond dispute with words, books, cyclopedias, libraries: And settled in the heavens, not to be dragged about henceforth hither and thither by puny folk with ropes of sand...

The Christian Bible is constructed on a marvelous numeric design running through its every conceivable detail; that this design could not have been carried out by man; that the numeric system on which it is built is similar to the mathematical schemes observed in Nature in the heavens above, or the earth around man. And that this numeric design insures its text against errors and interpolations in much the same way in which the designs on the banknote are guarded against conterfeits. And as the cash register automatically counts the nickles and dimes, so this numeric system automatically checks its own accounts.

But even in the case of God-fearing Bible loving evangelical—faith champion Tregelles, who shall say that he also might not have fared differently even in temporal matters at the hands of a Gracious God (but no respector of persons), if his New Testament Revision had not likewise been weighted down with a millstone of its own. Alford and Westcott wrote against *any* Verbal Inspiration. Tregelles, for reasons best known to His Maker, was permitted to yield to the highest wisdom of mere man (but still foolishness in the sight of God) for at least one page of the Great God's Book, which is now demonstrated to be as much an integral part thereof as every other page. Says poor dear Tregelles of the Passage concerning the Woman in the Act, John VII. 53- VIII. 11: "Though I am fully satisfied that this narrative is not a genuine part of John's Gospel, and though I regard the endeavours to make the evidence appear satisfactory to be such as would involve all Holy Scriptures in a mist of uncertainty, I see no reason for doubting that it contains a true narration . . . And thus I accept the narrative as true, although its form and phraseology are wholly uncertain, and although I do not believe it to be a Divine record".

And this as part of his comment on Horn's decision for this passage in his Introduction to the New Testament, of which Tregelles was one of the three editors . . .Puny man of course, can only sympathize with dear Tregelles' plight therein; but the Great God the Judge, whose eyes are as of fire, seeth not as man seeth...

If differences such as changes of order (e.g. "Christ Jesus" or "Jesus Christ"), the insertion or omission of the article with proper names, and the like are set aside, the words left still doubtful by Westcott and Hort can hardly amount to more than ONE THOUSANDTH part of the whole New Testament. I do not believe that any ancient work has survived with anything like this degree in accuracy.

*   *   *

We will quote one more section from *A Holy Challenge for Today* to finish this chapter. It is section V, and entitled:

BIBLE NUMERICS METHOD
WITH TEXTUAL PROBLEMS

The following section accompanied Ivan Panin's paper *On the Revision of the Greek New Testament Text*, giving examples of problems with words about which there was still question in the Text. He says:

Accordingly, I have recently been permitted to discover that God has left embedded in its own pages the very means needed for not only the detecting, but also the correcting of any corruption that may have been allowed to creep into the text of the Book. Let me give you a single example:

Verses 18-25 of the first chapter of Matthew have no less than five readings concerning which the best scholarship of the age, as embodied in *Westcott & Hort*, has to confess uncertainty and be offering alternative readings, after eight and twenty years of faithful toil on the Text. In *verse 18* they are uncertain whether Μαριαν should not be replaced with Μαριάμ. In *verse 24* they offer as an alternative the omission of the *ὁ, the,* before *Joseph.* In *verse 25* the same is the case with *οὐ.*

These verses tell of the birth of Jesus Christ; the passage forms a division of the narrative by itself, and is accordingly so spaced off by *Wescott & Hort.*

The number of words in this passage is 161, of 23 sevens, with a vocabulary of 77 words, or 11 sevens (Feature 1), which occur in 105 forms, or 15 sevens (Feature 2). The numeric value of the 77 words of the vocabulary is 51,247, or 7321 sevens (Feature 3). As an angel addresses Joseph in this passage, the 77 words of the vocabulary are divided thus by sevens: he uses 28 words, or 4 sevens; he does not use 49, or 7 sevens (Feature 4); and the same is true of the 105 forms: the angel uses 35, or 5 sevens (Feature 5); he does not use 70, or 10 sevens (Feature 6).

The numeric value of the 77 words, 51,247, is divided thus: the six words found nowhere else in Matthew have 5005, or 715 sevens (Feature 7), of which the one word found nowhere else in the New Testament, *Emmanuel,* has 644, or 92 sevens. These six words have, moreover, 56 letters, or 8 sevens (Feature 8). The words found elsewhere in Matthew have 46,242, or 6606 sevens (Feature 9).

Of the 105 forms 77, or 11 sevens, occur but once; and 28, or 4 sevens, occur more than once (Feature 10); 35, or 5 sevens, are verbs; and 70, not-verbs; seven are Proper verbs; and 70, or 10 sevens, are not verbs (Feature 11). Of the 70 not-verbs seven are Proper names (Feature 12), and these have 42 letters, or 6 sevens (Feature 13). Just seven forms have the *Iota subscriptum* (Feature 14). Lastly, the numeric value of the 105 forms is 65,429, or 9347 sevens.

Again: the simple vocabulary and the vocabulary of forms have 20 words in common; these occur 56 times, or 8 sevens (Feature

144

15), and have a numeric value of 10,255, or 1465 sevens (Feature 16). The forms not found elsewhere in Matthew, though found elsewhere in the New Testament, are 14, or 2 sevens (Feature 17), with a numeric value of 8715, or 1245 sevens (Feature 18). And the total numerical value of the entire passage is 93,394, or 1906 sevens (Feature 19) of seven (Feature 20).

An elaborate scheme of sevens thus runs through this passage.

But 77, the number of words in the vocabulary to this passage, is a multiple of eleven as well as seven, it being 11 x 7 (Feature 1). There is accordingly also a scheme of elevens running through this passage thus:

Of the 77 words, 33, or 3 elevens, begin with a vowel; and 44, or 4 elevens, begin with a consonant (Feature 2). Of the 33 vowel words *α-ι* have 22, or 2 elevens; and *o-ω* have eleven.

No other division among the letters of the alphabet produces elevens; that this division, however, is part of the Numeric scheme is shown by the *place* value of these four letters being 49, or *seven sevens*.

The number of letters in these 77 words is 396, or 36 elevens (Feature 3); of which the words beginning with a vowel have 143, or 13 elevens; and those beginning with a consonant have 253, or 23 elevens (Feature 4).

Of the 24 letters of the Greek alphabet, *ζ* and *ψ* are not used in this passage; leaving in use 22, or 2 elevens (Feature 5); while the first word in this passage, *τοῦ*, has for its numerical value 770, a multiple of both seven and eleven: it being 7 x 11 x 10 (Feature 6).

A scheme of elevens as well as of sevens thus runs through this passage.

This in nowise exhausts the numeric phenomena of this passage. Enough, however, has been given to show that not a letter could be taken from the passage, or changed in it, without destroying its numeric design.

Take, for example, the first of the five cases about which *Westcott & Hort* are now uncertain: the case of *Jesus* in *verse 18*. The so-called internal evidence is all against it. The combination *Jesus Christ* is used by Matthew only once before, in the title to his *Genealogy*, in the first verse of his Gospel: *Genealogy of Jesus Christ, David's son, Abraham's son*; and only once after this passage in 16:21; *From that time Jesus Christ began to show to his disciples that he must . . . . be killed and raised again;* while *Jesus* apart from *Christ* is used by *Matthew* 148 times; and *Christ* apart from *Jesus* is used by him 14 times (2 sevens). The nature of the context readily explains the use in these two place of the full title *Jesus Christ*. In the one passage is recorded his one birth; in the other (so to speak), another birth. With his first declaration that He must lay down his life and take it up again, he began to be "declared Son of God by resurrection from the dead." No such reason for the use of the full name in *1:18* is as easily discernible.

Accordingly, the Bible of fully half of Christendom, that of the Roman communion, omits the disputed word. Moreover, the preceding verse ends with the words "Mary of whom was born Jesus, he who is called Christ." How natural that the evangelist should go on, "Now of the Christ (the one I have just been speaking of) the birth was thus:" But here, as oft elsewhere, the most plausible human reasoning proves vain before a single fact. The *omission of Jesus* reduces the number of forms in this passage to 104, and the number of words to 160, and the total numeric value of the passage becomes 92,714.

None of these numbers are multiples of seven, and the elaborate design of sevens disappears. The omission of either of the two other words about which *Westcott & Hort* are uncertain, or of all three, would have the same effect of destroying a clearly displayed design of sevens, except in the case of ό, with its numeric value of 70: this number being a multiple of seven the omission of ό would destroy the design in only two of the three items mentioned above. In like manner the change of ν into μ of *Μαριαν* would reduce the total value of the passage by ten, and that number again ceases to be a multiple of seven.

The numeric structure of this passage is thus a kind of automatic register of its accuracy. By its means is not only certainty given where even *Westcott & Hort* are uncertain, even the slightest departure from accuracy can be at once detected.

Thus in this very passage these editors have Δαυειδ for Δαυιδ, the lengthening of ι into ει, and the shortening of ει into ι having become frequent with copyists. But the numerics order the intrucing letter off as having no right here.

Other examples and explanations are found in the Introduction in the forefront of the volume, *The Greek Numeric New Testament.* The Bible Numerics Method is also elaborated in the treatise, *The Last Twelve Verses of Mark—Their Genuineness Established.*

XII

Summary: The Scope of Bible Numerics

Panin has done a competent job of explaining himself. It has been clearly demonstrated that the phenomena of Numerics is too complex for him to have either made up or manipulated; it simply cannot be done in one—or even a dozen—lifetime(s). Time also has vindicated Panin; as scholarship has increased over the last century since he did his work, the accepted critical text has steadily crept nearer and nearer to the definitive Greek text he published in 1934.

It is pleasant to reflect that the man had endearing qualities. His integrity was unmarred by the seeking either of revenue or adulation. His only interest was to put the scriptures into the same prominence among men that they have to God. And he never went 'wacko' like most who deal with numerics; he calmly and steadily did his work for the work's (and his Lord's) sake. His wit was legendary and his comprehension of the task was crystal clear. He knew how to be a true friend, and he never lost his sense of humor. This is the kind of person to whom it will be said, "Well done, you good and faithful servant."

We must remember that all this work was done without a calculator, far less a computer. When we look over the vast library of figures he mastered, it is more than a little mind-numbing. Yet there is a wonderful opportunity here to brush away the dust on his still solid foundation and build on it. The resources available to us today are virtually limitless. We can do in an hour what it would have taken him the better part of a week. . . or longer. However, is not so much the resources which languish in the far reaches the virtual warehouses of reference material that are needful, but what sustained him through all those lonely nights: the cultivation of an excellent spirit and the determination—as

James so aptly tells us—to endure. Each of us has his own gift from God; in addition, Paul tells us to "desire earnestly the greater gifts." There is no upper limit to what is possible when we walk in hopeful expectation before God: *Things which eye saw not, and ear heard not, And entered not into heart of man, Whatever things the God prepared for them that love him.*

As we have had good opportunity in these pages to familiarize ourselves with Ivan Panin and his work, let us briefly summarize some of the approaches he used, that we might have a better idea of where to begin, should we wish to pass his work on, or even to build on it ourselves.

We note first of all that his method is based on the plain meaning of the the Scripture. Natural divisions where a person or angel has a discourse, natural changes of subject, and natural divisions of subject matter. There are no 'magical' or arbitrary breaks in his sectioning of material. All is as the normal reader would expect to find in the normal process of comprehension.

His analysis then begins with the obvious before moving on to the more subtle. He counts the words, he notes variations in spelling. Then he moves on to the syllables and to the forms. By forms we mean, for example, the difference between Θεόν (*Theon*) and Θεὸς (*Theos*), both meaning God but with differing forms depending on context. He notes the writer, the book, and the vocabulary whether it is unique or common, both within the passage and compared to the rest of the scriptures. He notes the number of nouns, verbs, proper names and their spellings.

Then he moves on to the number of letters, syllables, diphthongs (two vowels combining in one syllable, as in '*ua*' the end of *Joshua*). He takes note of symmetries and serial progressions. Then he moves on to the values of the letters, both the place value (first, second, third letter) and numerical value (as each letter also represents a number.) He compares these, takes note of the evident patterns, and analyzes the patterns with intelligent diligence to discover the nature of the arrangements.

He was obliged to write his own concordance for these purposes, as there were none qualified for the requisite level of detail. He was then obliged to write a second concordance just to delineate the *forms* of the Greek words. These works were comprehensive and massive; the first was of a thousand pages and had every occurrence of the 137,903 Greek words in the New Testament. The second with the forms was twice its size. Bear in mind that these were in *preparation* for the actual work. It is as if you were to build a house, and like David did before Solomon, spent decades just gathering the materials. Panin spent six strenuous years on his first concordance, and two more on his second *before he even started the work in earnest*. This is the mark of someone who understands the scope of a project.

Note that despite the enormous amount of research involved, all these actions were part of what was eminently a <u>normal</u> approach to the task. If you were to start a pharmacy, you would not just put a stool behind a counter and hope for the best. First there are the years of education, then the securing of a place of business as well as a viable business plan, then the stocking, marketing, and all the arrangements as to the daily schedule of running the business. Endeavors of this scale take education, daily hard work, and lasting endurance. Thus Ivan Panin treated his life task with all the dignity and preparation of a master builder; and despite the lack of recognition from those who could not be bothered to peruse even the smallest part of his discoveries, he continued on with an intensity that eventually overwhelmed him, so that he left us and moved on to meet his Master in person.

Again, it must be emphasized that this was a <u>normal</u> process, even if so few have had the constancy to share in it. If there are six miles of shafts in a gold mine, and only one miner working the entire mine, this does not in any way alter the fact that there are miles of untouched shafts available. When we ignore a subject, especially one carefully prepared by God, that is a reflection on ourselves, not the subject. Proverbs 25:2 states that *"It is the glory of God to conceal a thing; but the glory of kings is to search out a thing."* God purposefully conceals the brighter glories of his creation and his Word, that our process of discovery allows us to share with him the joy of initially forming it. And if, like Panin, we find ourselves alone on that path, we are in good company: Paul tells Timothy that *"Yes, and all that would live godly in Christ Jesus will be persecuted."*

Panin was offered a lucrative position at a university and turned it down. Logic would have suggested to one of us, *Take the position, for it will afford the time and finances to really push this Numerics project forward.* But that is not God's logic, and Panin was following God. When one has a Father who keeps count of the hairs of one's head and promises to provide one's daily bread, one does not need the extra boost from the world which so quickly flips the tables around and demands repayment for its provision, often in a manner that destroys one's ability to continue on in simplicity and sincerity. He kept himself, as James says, *"unspotted from the world."*

*   *   *

Now let us address a subject that was dear to Panin's heart, and a major part of the object of his work as well as a very necessary issue to return to in this particular age. This is the subject of demonstrable facts.

It is evident—and somewhat of a tragedy—that the manner in which the word 'faith' is used today is significantly removed from the way in which Scripture uses it, as well as rather changed from what the Bible writers meant when using it. When the Gospel broke forth over the mankind, it was carried by eyewitnesses and supported by signs. Everywhere it went, every time we read in

Acts or elsewhere of it being delivered, it consisted solely of <u>facts</u> which could be clearly demonstrated to be true. Faith indeed was required to accept these <u>facts,</u> but it was faith in God who had revealed himself by a physical human being, not faith in some ethereal belief system. Today this has eroded to the point that not only do few know the facts, few even consider them to be necessary. But that is precisely where we exit reality and create religions instead of solid godly lives.

It is a historical fact that a normal flesh-and-blood human lived. It is a fact that he healed and taught, had joy and sorrow, hungered and slept. It is a fact that no one could convict him of sin, even when he invited them to. It is a fact that he was given an illegal trial, tortured and killed for political security and religious jealousy. It is a fact that he actually died. It is a fact that he was entombed for three full days and nights. It is a fact that he was raised in his own body and given from God resurrection life. It is a fact that he was seen by hundreds of people who knew him and could verify precisely who he was. It is a fact that God produced voluminous demonstrations and signs to establish undeniably that this human being has personally been given authority to establish new race.

These are facts. And without facts, we have nothing but vague belief systems, and we are little more than "...*babes, tossed to and fro and carried about with every wind of teaching, by the sleight of men, in craftiness, unto the wiles of error.*" Doctrinal systems of belief cannot save us. Only an actual relationship with the physical man (*a spirit has not flesh and bones as you see me*) Jesus as our actual daily Lord whom we believe, obey, and follow can save us; and even that is entirely up to him, not us. The Gospel of this <u>fact</u> went out *based on* facts, *teaching* facts, and proclaimed by eye-witnesses and as John says, "...*what we have heard, what we have seen with our eyes, what we beheld, and our hands handled.*" It is instructive to look at Paul's rendition of the Gospel in its entirety in First Corinthians 15:1-8:

"Now I make known to you, brethren, the gospel which I preached to you, which also you received, in which also you stand, by which also you are being saved, if you hold fast the word which I preached to you, except you believed to no purpose.

For I delivered to you among the first things what also I received: that Christ died for our sins according to the scriptures; and that he was buried; and that he has been raised on the third day according to the scriptures; and that he was seen of Cephas, then of the twelve; after this was seen of above five hundred brethren at once, of whom the more remain until now, but some are fallen asleep; after this was seen of James; then of all the apostles; and last of all, as of the untimely birth, he was seen of me also."

Note that there are *three* items in the Gospel that concern Christ's death, burial, and resurrection; and *five* items that concern who saw him afterwards. The greater part of the Gospel involves itself with the proofs of the facts given about the Christ. Now ask yourself: where are these 'proofs' today? Or for that matter, where is the interest in searching out and delivering these proofs? For without proof, we are merely asking people to believe, without verification, whatever we happen to want the Bible to say.

And we have proof. There is no historical event from Napoleon back to Nero that has more solid evidence than the resurrection of Jesus. We have more proof that Jesus was raised from the dead than we have that Nero even existed. These are facts, and we seem to have lost the impetus to ground ourselves and our children in them. Many of us are on such shaky ground in our souls that we suspect if we were to check into the facts, we would find them to be unsubstantiated. The we-were-once-monkeys camp is so widespread and brash that few can resist it—despite the fact that there is not a single verifiable fact in their entire arsenal of theories.

The books are out there and available. The detractors are many.

Yet the proof is undeniable. It is not our object here to write a defense of Christianity, but to point out that to relegate such important matters to a vaguely-defined idea of 'faith' (which is not faith, but blind adherence to man's religion) is to miss the Gospel altogether, and live a life of wavering doubt rather than calm confidence.

Panin saw this problem clearly, and it weighed heavily on him. When he discovered the Numeric patterns in the Scriptures, he found a way to present facts—and Numerics is but one set of facts among dozens that could be chosen—which he could personally work on and set in order for the demonstration of God's reality. With this motivation, he set himself to the task in an orderly and systematic fashion, and delivered to us the fruits of his labor.

For the reader, let us reiterate: if you do not have the time to explore Panin's Numerics, you *do* have access to some most excellent resources, not the least is his ***Numeric English New Testament***, which is quite simply the most accurate English translation available. In addition, it is based on his work, ***The New Testament in the Original Greek***, which—even if one were to completely disregard the Numerics—is still the most accurately researched and well-considered Greek critical text available. Panin did not *just* do Numerics; he hold his own with the best textual critics and editors the field has to offer.

And as far as the Numerics? The writer of this chapter has personally applied them to the Scriptures for two decades and *they work*. Consistently and always amazingly, the value of what Panin unearthed has been demonstrated. The age of the computer gives us virtually unlimited access to Numerics, yet be warned: at no point can we simply fasten on a 'method' (such as ELS; see Appendix III) and expect it to do the work for us. Scripture is living just as we are; if you were strapped down to a table with a tray of surgical instruments beside you and asked to sing an opera, you might not be fully willing. The scriptures do not subject themselves to cold dissection; we must be living and appreciating the scriptures to find its treasures. For example, on the second page of Chapter IV we pointed out:

> "*The Son of Man*" from Matthew 13:37 has the value of **37** x 80. This value of 2,960 is the total of the three figures in the previous example: *Godhead* 592 + *Jesus* 888 + *Christ* 1,480 = *the Son of Man* 2,960.

Now where did we get that? A computer could not discover these kinds of things by itself; someone must guide it to specific subjects.

These types of discoveries are made by dint of the fact that having read the Bible and appreciated it, we get a *sense* of where to look. If we are reading about figs and decide to explore their numerical phenomena, it would be only natural to check out olives at the same time. Thus discoveries, appreciation, and experience all go hand in hand.

On this somewhat positive and open-ended point, let us for now close this book, and commit reader and writer alike to the care and fellowship of an Eternal God and his Christ, who has seen fit to gift us with his Scriptures, as well as abundant demonstration of their value.

Bibliography

Verbal Inspiration of the Bible Scientifically Demonstrated, Ivan Panin, 1928

Aphorisms, Ivan Panin, 1903

The New Testament from the Greek Text as Established by Bible Numerics, Ivan Panin, 1914

New Testament in the Original Greek, Ivan Panin, 1934

The Pattern and the Prophecy, James Harrison, 1973

Mathematics Proves Holy Scriptures, Karl Sabiers, 1941

Genesis Literal, Iapetus Ducq, 2014

The Second Coming of the Antichrist, Les Mather, 1984

The Secret of the Universe, Nathan Wood, 1936

The Inspiration of the Scriptures Scientifically Demonstrated (Letter to the *N. Y. Sun*), Ivan Panin, 1899

The Hebraic Tongue Restored, Fabre d'Olivet, 1815

The Jonas Genre, Paul Kenneth Hubbard, 2009

A Holy Challenge for Today, Ivan Panin

An English Guide to the Various Readings of the Greek New Testament, Michael D. Marlowe, 2000

Novum Testamentum Graece, 28th Edition, Nestle-Aland, 2012

Novum Testamentum Graece, 27th Edition, Nestle-Aland, 1993

The New Testament in the Original Greek, Westcott & Hort, 1881

The Interlinear Bible, Jay P. Green, Sr., 1986

Appendix I

Letter	Name	Final Form?	Numeric Value	Place Value	English Sound
א	Aleph		1	1	<u>a</u> as in '<u>as</u>'
ב	Beth		2	2	b, bh
ג	Ghimel		3	3	g, gh
ד	Daleth		4	4	d, dh
ה	Hé		5	5	<u>h</u>, hé as in '<u>h</u>ospitalize'
ו	Vav		6	6	o, u, <u>v</u>, w, f as in '<u>v</u>ow'
ז	Zayin		7	7	z
ח	Chet		8	8	h, hé, ch see note
ט	Tet		9	9	t
י	Yod		10	10	i, ai, soft j, y
כ	Kaf	ך	20	11	c, ch, k see note
ל	Lamed		30	12	l
מ	Mem	ם	40	13	m
נ	Nun	ן	50	14	n
ס	Samekh		60	15	s, x
ע	Ayin		70	16	h, wh
פ	Pe	ף	80	17	p
צ	Zadi	ץ	90	18	<u>tz</u> as in 'klu<u>tz</u>'
ק	Qof		100	19	k, qu see note
ר	Resh		200	20	r
ש	Shin		300	21	sh
ת	Tav		400	22	th, t

The previous page shows the **Hebrew** letters with both their Numeric Value in Hebrew counting and their Place Value, that is, order in the alphabet. There are five "final forms", meaning that if that letter is the last letter in a word, the final form is used instead. The total of this Hebrew chart is 1495.

Note: On the pronunciations, there is a progression of soft to hard in the letters Hé, Chet, and Qof (ה, ח, ק) that ranges from a soft 'h' to a hard 'k'. And there is some overlap of sound between these three (and likewise Ayin (ע)).

The "final forms", when used in the numbering system, have the following values:

Letter	Name	Numeric Value	Place Value
ך	Kaf	500	23
ם	Mem	600	24
ן	Nun	700	25
ף	Pe	800	26
ץ	Zadi	900	27

This rounds the chart out nicely to include all requisite numbers from 1 to 900. It also makes the letters into a perfect cube, as 27 is 3^3, they can be arranged into a construct like a Rubik's Cube. This is important, because numbers that can be represented in three-dimensional form turn out to be very useful. The total of this chart comes out to 4995, which turns out to be a significant number in Bible Numerics. Here are two examples of verses whose values add up to 4995:

Even to them will I give in my house; and within my walls a place and a name better than of sons and of daughters: I will give them

158

an everlasting name, that will not be cut off. **Isaiah 56:5**

Wherefore comfort one another with these words.
First Thessalonians 4:18

The next page shows the values for the 24 letters of **Greek.**

Note that Stigma (ϛ), Koppa (C), and Sampsi (ϡ) with the respective values of 6, 90, and 900 had fallen out of usage as letters of the alphabet by the time the New Testament was written, but were retained for the numbering system. Thus they are not included in 'place values' but have a numerical equivalent. The only difference that their inclusion makes is that it give the whole numbering system a total value of 4995, just as the addition of the five "final forms" do for the Hebrew. None of these three 'extra' letters occur in the New Testament.

So to give an example of gematria, 'Logos' (Λογος) means 'Word' and is where we get our English word 'logic' from. Looking at the chart, Λ=30, o=70 (twice), γ=3, and ς=200. Adding those up gives us a value of **373** (which is a prime number) for the **numeric value** of word Logos.

Looking in the column that has its **place value**, we see that Λ=11, o=15 (twice), γ=3, and ς=18. Adding those up gives us a value of **62**.

We could add the article ('the') which in this case is Omicron (o=70) again. This brings the **numeric value** up to 443 (also prime) and the **place value** to **77,** or **7 x 11.**

So we can see the immense range in totals with Greek words. In Mark 14:36 we have Αββα (dad), which has a total numeric value of **6**. In 14:46 we have αυτω (him), which has a total numeric value of **1501**. Each word has only four letters, yet the range between **6** and **1501** is immense.

Letter		Name	Final Form?	Numeric Value	Place Value	English Sound
A	α	Alpha		1	1	<u>a</u> as in 'f<u>a</u>ther'
B	β	Beta		2	2	b
Γ	γ	Gamma		3	3	g
Δ	δ	Delta		4	4	d
E	ε	Epsilon		5	5	<u>e</u> as in '<u>e</u>ndure'
ϛ		Stigma		6		Not a letter
Z	ζ	Zeta		7	6	z
H	η	Eta		8	7	<u>ê</u> as in 'h<u>ey</u>'
Θ	θ	Theta		9	8	<u>th</u> as in '<u>th</u>rust'
I	ι	Iota		10	9	<u>i</u> as in '<u>i</u>terate'
K	κ	Kappa		20	10	k
Λ	λ	Lambda		30	11	l
M	μ	Mu		40	12	m
N	ν	Nu		50	13	n
Ξ	ξ	Xi		60	14	<u>ks</u> as in 'appendi<u>x</u>'
O	o	Omicron		70	15	<u>o</u> as in '<u>o</u>ften'
Π	π	Pi		80	16	p
Ϙ		Koppa		90		Not a letter
P	ρ	Rho		100	17	p
Σ	σ	Sigma	ς	200	18	s
T	τ	Tau		300	19	t
Y	υ	Upsilon		400	20	<u>u</u> as in 'p<u>u</u>t'
Φ	φ	Phi		500	21	f
X	χ	Chi		600	22	<u>ch</u> as in 'bellya<u>ch</u>e'
Ψ	ψ	Psi		700	23	ps
Ω	ω	Omega		800	24	<u>ô</u> as in 'escr<u>ow</u>'
ϡ		Sampsi		900		Not a letter

Appendix II

The Meanings of the First 50 Numbers

The following chart gives the meanings of each number from one to fifty. This is distilled from a much larger chart (22" x 34" in small print) that shows the relationships between the meanings and how they are derived.

1	Unity/Being	18	Rest/ Interrelationship	35	Perfected Ability: Accomplishment
2	Substance/Nature	19	Ability to Accomplish: Executabilty	36	Peace
3	Mechanics/ Workings	20	Recognition/ Honor	37	Artistic Capability
4	Action/Universality	21	Fulfillment	38	Solving
5	Ability/Fruit	22	Answering	39	Harvest
6	Allowance/ Freedom	23	Full Action in Every Capacity	40	Proving/ Testing
7	Perfection/ Completion	24	Ripening	41	Enjoying
8	That which is Completed	25	Satisfaction	42	Pleasure / Awareness
9	Interaction/ Full Mechanics/ Judgment	26	Multiplying/ Affecting	43	Stewardship Returned
10	Responsibility	27	Self-Knowledge/ Knowing	44	Answered/ Done
11	Response	28	Blessing	45	Indoctrination/ Belief
12	Full System/ Organization	29	Holding (In Understanding)	46	Accomplishing Everywhere
13	Accountability	30	Communication/ Giving	47	Settlement
14	Results	31	Self-Building	48	(Perfect) Potential
15	Possession	32	Effecting	49	Fulfillment of Blessing
16	Working	33	A Running System	50	Return
17	Creation	34	Unfurling		

A Casual Stroll through the
Meanings of the Numbers

As we start this journey, let us bear in mind that <u>meaning</u> is not <u>amount</u>. As we get higher and higher in numbers, they can seem more complicated, more powerful, but that is a reflection of their <u>amounts</u> <u>only</u>. As to their meanings, they are getting more *fragmented* and *smaller* in significance. **The lower a number is, the more powerful and far-reaching its meaning** until we get down to ONE, which is the ultimate symbol of power.

Let us also note a few elements regarding the character of numbers. <u>Prime</u> <u>Numbers</u> always produce a <u>new</u> <u>idea</u>. Scripture uses them as markers, and they are incredibly useful in the type of investigation done by Ivan Panin. They are also useful in seeing the 'character' of a word. '**Israel**', the name given to the lone man who stayed behind and fought with the angel totals **541**, and is <u>prime</u>. 'Abram' and 'Abraham', the father of a multitude, total **803** and **808** respectively. The first is **11** x **73** and the second is 2^3 x **101**. [That is using the 27-system which includes the 'final forms'. In the 22-system the numbers are **243** (3^5) and **248** (**23** x **31**) respectively].

Next of importance to note is that <u>numbers</u> <u>are</u> <u>not</u> <u>moral</u>. There are no 'good' and 'bad' numbers, not even 666 or 13. These numbers can seem bad or unlucky to us *because of the way we apply them*. For example, **13** means 'accountability'. For one who has been diligent in his work, it would be an utter delight to have a day of accountability, a day of review. The trouble is, most of us are less than diligent in our work, thus we are apprehensive of the day of reckoning, thus **13** becomes 'unlucky'.

Finally, let us look at mathematical operations. What does it mean to add two numbers, as opposed to multiplying them? Here are the guidelines to adding, subtracting, multiplying, dividing, and exponentials. Please bear in mind that one has to become accustomed to working with the **concepts** behind the numbers, not merely applying 'labels' of meaning.

- When **adding** numbers, do it two at a time (if you have a long string), and use the word '**of**', '**from**' or a similar word. Thus **10** (responsibility) **plus 18** (rest and interrelationship) **equals 28** (blessing). So we would phrase it, "*The rest from responsibility is blessing.*" This works for all addition operations on numbers and their meanings.

- When **multiplying** numbers, make one **possessive**. Thus **4** (action) **times 11** (response) **equals 44** (answered, done). So we would phrase it, "*Action's response is to answer and be done.*" This works for all multiplying operations on numbers and their meanings.

- When **subtracting** numbers, make the larger one possessive, and use the phrase, "*is derived from*". Thus **7** (perfection) **minus 2** (substance) **equals 5** (fruit). So we would phrase it, "*Perfection's substance is derived from its fruit,*" i.e., one can tell if something is perfect by looking at the fruit it produces, as Jesus mentions in Matthew 7. This works for all subtracting operations on numbers and their meanings.

- When **dividing** numbers, ask *how it relates*, or *how we can see it*. Thus **12** (organization) **divided by 3** (mechanics) **equals 4** (action). So we would phrase it, "***How do we see*** *the mechanics of an organization? By its actions.*" This works for all division operations on numbers and their meanings.

- To **power** numbers using an exponential (X^2), make the power a verb, and say "is defined as", or "is known as". Thus $2^5=32$; **2** (nature) **to the power of 5** (accomplishment) **equals 32** (effecting). So we would phrase it, "***Nature accomplishing is known as effecting.***" This works for all exponential operations on numbers and their meanings.

- To take **Square Root** of a number, say *"The foundation of. . ."* or *"The basic requirement for. . ."* Thus the **square root of 25** (satisfaction) is **5** (fruit). So we would phrase it, *"**The basic requirement for** satisfaction is fruit."* In other words, we are not going to achieve satisfaction unless have accomplished something. This works for all roots with numbers and their meanings.

This will help us sort through the many claims that are made regarding numbers. Numbers are designed to make sense, and their language, like every language, has very specific protocols. Before we get to the numbers themselves, let us look at the three elements that contribute to each meaning.

1. **Cyclic.** Meaning in nature, numbers, and scripture occurs in regular cycles. Sometimes these cycles are **regular**, such as every **third** number having something in common, and that having to do with the meaning of **three**. Sometimes these cycles are **progressive**, such as the Fibonacci series, which would follow the steps of 1, 2, 3, 5, 8, 13, 21, 34, 55, 81, etc., each number being a combination of the previous two. *The cyclic nature of numbers is one of the most valuable and least known tools of investigation into numerics.*

2. **Ordinal.** In Genesis 1, days 2 through 7 are called the second, third, fourth, fifth, sixth, and seventh days respectively. Not so day one. It is not called the *first* day, but day *one*. Hebrew has a word for *first*, but it does not use it there. This is an example of **ordinal** being used for days 2-7 and **cardinal** being used for day 1. The charts in Appendix 1 list both the Numeric Value and the Place Value. The first is **cardinal**, the second is **ordinal**. Ordinal simply means in what place the number is found with its companion numbers.

3. **Cardinal.** This is what most people think about when they think of what a number is. Cardinal is quite simply the *amount* that the number represents. The number **12** in

164

cyclic would mean that it is either noon or midnight on a clock. **12** in **ordinal** would mean you got picked **12ᵗʰ** for the team, which would mean you got picked last if there were 24 players available, and each team got 12. **12** in **cardinal** means that there are a dozen apples, team members, or doughnuts.

These three aspect of numbers are most valuable when all three are working together. It is useful to have the distinctions between them clearly in mind, for in Numerics, the fact that something is **6ᵗʰ** (ordinal) does not mean that there are **six** (cardinal) of that item. We see this in Appendix I on the chart of the Greek alphabet, where the <u>value</u> of the 24 letters are missing **6**, **90**, and **900**. Thus 'Theta' (**Θ**) has a **cardinal value** of **9**, but an **ordinal value** of **8**. And its **cyclic value** depends entirely on the scale of the cycle; if we are going in a three-cycle (1, 2, 3... 1, 2, 3... 1, 2, 3...) it would land on **2**. If we are going in a four-cycle (1. 2. 3. 4... 1. 2. 3. 4...) it would land on **4**.

Now. Let us embark on our journey through the first 50 numbers.

1

One is the most powerful and thus the most difficult number to understand. We are accustomed to thinking of all numbers containing it, yet it contains all numbers. Numerically, One is <u>unity through perfect balance</u>. When we balance something, say a bicycle wheel, we make sure every spoke weighs the same. One is the perfect balance of *diverse* <u>parts</u>, that is, all other numbers—each different from the rest—balance within the structure of One. It is as if we took the bicycle wheel and made every spoke a different weight, yet still balanced it. **One** is <u>unity</u>, <u>power</u>, <u>existence</u>, <u>wholeness</u>. It is also *loneliness, unapproachable light, singularity,* and *lack of need* respectively. God is One. The human was split into male and female, and thus was

---

designed to find Oneness in relationship rather than 'being'—this being fortunate since the nature of his 'being' was somewhat damaged by what happened in the Garden. The things in scripture that are described as being One are rare and fascinating. . . and because God is One, anything that partakes of Oneness must necessarily deal with him. This is why relationships are so emphasized by Scripture; it is a major part of Mankind's approach to God.

2

Two sets up the great Entity/Relationship pattern. *Even* numbers tend to be Entities (identifiable things) and *odd* numbers tend to be Relationships. We are generally more comfortable with Entities, because they can be labeled and described, unlike Relationships which depend entirely on what that they are relating. Two responds (to 1), fills out, effects, substantiates, and characterizes. Two is the *nature* of something, its *substance*, its *acceptance*. If One is light, Two is love.

When thinking of the **duality** involved with two, it is important to remember that numbers are not **moral**. That is to say, a true duality is not good versus bad, but inside versus outside, or ideal versus practical. Light and darkness are not a true duality; darkness is merely the absence of light, whereas light is certainly not the absence of darkness. Light and *love*, however, are a true duality, as are grace/truth or even particle/wave. . . and male/female.

Just as One is pure order, Two is pure *demonstration* of order. Two is the feminine foundation for all relationships.

3

One is **that** God is, Two is **what** God is, and Three is **who**

166

God is. Three is the workings, the plannings, the structure of anything, thus it is used for Wisdom, Counsels, and Intelligence. Everything has three dimensions, and each dimension is completely different from its two companions with no overlap. It is not the Father's job to manifest God, it is the Son's. It is not the Son's job to teach us about himself (he teaches us about the Father) it is the Spirit's. The pattern of the roles of the Trinity are stamped on everything in creation.

Three is *capacity*, *dimensions*, and the ability to use them. One introduces God, Two introduces Creation, and Three introduces the *process* of Creating, and what that process in turn will mean to God. Three is all-inclusive and contains the secrets to the mechanics by which anything works.

4

Four is universality and action. There are four winds, four directions, four corners of the earth. The simplest, and thus first, shape in three dimensions is the tetrahedron; it has four corners and four faces. Thus four is the beginning of the formation, or **substantiating** (remember *substance* is two) of things. This formation occurs in all directions at once, and thus includes all requisite actions.

Three, being dimensions, has no reference to a center-point; Four always emanates from a center; all action has a source-point. The geometry of Four shares the same geometry of a Carbon atom; the four directions are always 109.5° apart... just as Job addresses his four friends (the three and Elihu) and said, "*Mark me, and be astonished, and lay the hand upon the mouth*"; this phrase has a value of 1095.

The four actions of a human soul are *being*, *believing*, *perceiving*, and *loving*. Physically, these are *breathing*, *eating*, *sensing*, and *giving* (or *doing*) respectively.

5

Five is simply an amazing number. It is the second proper Prime after **One** (2 and 3 only qualify as primes under a cardinal definition when one ignores ordinal and cyclic) and along with **9** is one of the two keys to our base-10 counting system. Five is **ability** and **fruit**. The hand with its five fingers is the ultimate symbol of ability. Ability does not stand alone, it *accomplishes*; and the result of *accomplishment* is called **fruit**. If we slice an apple sideways, we will see that the seeds are enclosed in a five-pointed star.

Five also points toward death, because true fruit always contains the Seed, and as Jesus said, unless the seed falls into the ground and dies, it abides alone. The man of ability in scripture is David, and his story is replete with fives, 8 times in Kings and twice in Chronicles for a total of **10** (2 x **5**); from the five stones he chose from the brook to the five giants killed by him and his men.

Since Five is accomplishment, it is the end of the process of **1.** Conceiving, **2.** Assessing, **3.** Planning, **4.** Doing, and **5.** Accomplishing. After this, what has been fully formed must be let go, which leads us directly into **6**.

6

Six is *releasing, allowance, freedom*. Once *accomplishing* (**5**) a project, say building a car, Six is letting your friend taking it for a spin, not knowing whether he will wreck it or not. Six is the extent to which you will let something go; thus with God, the number 666 is the extent to which he will allow evil without stepping in and stopping it.

168

In the **3-cycle** mentioned in the number **3**'s description, four is *that* God does (action), five is *what* God does (what he accomplishes; fruit) and six is *what God doesn't do* (what God allows). Because when God allows us to do things without stopping us, we do all sorts of ridiculous things, six is variously seen by people as failure, sin, weakness, and 'man's number'. Yet remember that numbers are not *moral*; Six is just as easily a wonderful thing as a gateway to failure; it depends on how well we are able to handle our freedom. Solomon received 666 talents of gold per year; right up to the limit of what God would allow.

7

Seven is <u>Perfection</u>, as our friend Ivan Panin likes to point out to us. It is 'finished-ness'; there are seven parts to every endeavor, every progression, every monument of activity. Each of the seven stages is distinct and unique. The rainbow separates itself into seven clearly defined bands; our pianos have seven clearly defined notes.

Seven is the third Prime, and as '**third**', the <u>ordinal</u> form of **3**, it gives the *mechanics of perfection* to any system. This is why Panin finds so many texts can be demonstrated to be part of scripture (or not part of scripture), because the **7**'s are always there to indicate the structure of a perfect system.

Seven is not all crystal and roses; to accomplish perfection in this world, suffering is necessary. Jesus said "*Go say to that fox, Lo, I cast out demons and accomplish healings today and tomorrow, and the third day I am <u>perfected</u>. Nevertheless, I must go on today and tomorrow and the day following: for it cannot be that a prophet perish out of Jerusalem.*" The numeric value for "**the cross**" is **777**, as well as to *kill*, a *rod*, to *give*, and to *prove*. Lamentations 3:52 says "*My enemies chased me sore, like a bird, without* *cause" ...*which has the value of **777**.

8

Eight is <u>that</u> <u>which</u> <u>is</u> <u>perfected</u>. Eight's perfection is distinct from **7**'s perfection in that it does not have *parts* like **7**; it is in and of itself a whole new part. It is *that which is new, that which is not part of the system, yet has used the entire system.* It is often used (correctly) as the number for new creation. **888** is the numeric value of 'Jesus'. Philippians 2:16 speaks of the hope of New Creation thus: *"Holding forth the word of life; that I may have of what to glory in <u>Christ's</u> <u>day</u>, that I did not run in vain neither toil in vain."* This passage has the value of **8888**. There are **88** words in scripture with the value of **88**; the last one is in First John 5:4 *"...because whatever is begotten of God overcomes the world; and this is the **victory** that has overcome the world: our faith."* And the first word in scripture with the value of **88** is **Noah**, who took eight souls to a **new** start for humanity.

Eight is two cubed (**2³**), and according to the directions above, we would phrase it *"Nature (2) is planning (3) for new creation (8)."* The natural world, as God set it up, actually is <u>working</u> <u>toward</u> and <u>longing</u> <u>for</u> **new creation** (Romans 8:19-23).

9

Nine is a somewhat intimidating number. It is the <u>interaction of a full system</u>, whether that system be numbers or teaching man to number his days (Psalm **90**, *"So teach us to number our days, that we may apply our hearts unto wisdom."* This verse's value is **693**, or **9** x **107**). Thus it is used for **judgment**. Revelation 2:16 says *"Repent therefore; else I come to you quickly, and I will war against* *them with the sword of my mouth*"; this verse has a value of **9999**.

The physical universe is composed of Space, Time, and Energy (or matter if you will). Space has height, width, and breadth, Time has past, present, and future, and Energy has modulation, volume, and intensity (or for Matter, proton, neutron, and electron). These add up to Nine, the full system of the universe. Likewise there are nine planets and a woman's pregnancy lasts nine months, each required for a full system.

Nine is **3³** and from the **3-cycle** that we have been looking at, **7** is *that* God perfects, **8** is *what* God perfects, and **9** is *what* God *doesn't* perfect, that is, what enters into judgment and gets burned up, as it says in Second Peter 3:10 (verse value: **11119**, prime). *Verily, Snare, evil,* and the *branch* not bearing fruit in John 15:22 all equal **99** in Greek, but so does *great, fountain,* and *draw.* The number **9** likes to be taken seriously.

10

Ten is responsibility; not so much what one *has* to do, but what we *have the ability to do.* Ten is **2 x 5**; five is *ability*, and five more is the *response to ability*, or responsibility. Five toes balance the foot; ten toes balance the walk itself.

The ten commandments have clued in many as to its meaning. Ten is a 'triangle number' (think of the setup of 10 bowling pins) such as 3, 6, 15, 21, 28, etc. In the *action* cycle (**4**) it is capability, in the *accomplishment* cycle (**5**) it is response, in the *freedom* cycle (**6**) it is communicating perfection outward, and in the *perfection* cycle (**7**) it is structuring using responsive ability.

As in chapter 4 we looked at **666**, **777**, and **888** (all having **37** as a factor) for their different characters, let us list here some of the Greek words with similar values relating to **ten**. Each list has a different character.

610: *sow, laborer, work, build, continue, judge, crooked.*

710: *warm, answer, help, confirm, counsel, good, faithful, watch, find, wash, baptize, mercy, power*

810: *brother, Lord, friend, comforter, endure, purifying.*

These show some of the *facets* of what is associated with responsibility when put into differing numerical contexts.

11

Eleven is the secret weapon of prime numbers. He pops up in the strangest places, and often permeates a passage even more than his well-known brother **7**. **Eleven** means response. **11** answers, responds, and uses its full capacity to fulfil expectations. A good response is rare; Proverbs 9:9 says *"Give instruction to a wise man, and he will be yet wiser: teach a just man, and he will increase in learning."* This is how God likes us to respond, and the value of that verse is **1331**, or 11^3 (**11** x **11** x **11**). The previous verse has a similar theme; *"Reprove not a scorner, lest he hate you: rebuke a wise man, and he will love you"* and has the value of **4257** (3^3 x **11** x 43).

Music presents her own version of response in that the number of vibrations per second for each musical note is in multiples of eleven. And the sunspots occur in eleven-year cycles, indicating that it is possible the sun is responding to the earth as much as vice-versa.

One of the wisest responses in the Old Testament was when Solomon was faced with the two harlots arguing over a child; *"And the king said, Bring me a sword. And they brought a sword before the king."* This has the value of **1221**, or **11** x **111**, as does Job's challenge for anyone to be able to respond to his words in 24:25; *"And if it be not so*

172

now, who will make me a liar, and make my speech nothing worth?"

12

Twelve is an <u>organization</u>, a <u>full</u> <u>system</u>. It is contrasted from **9** (*interaction of a full system*) by the fact that it tends to be organized by a higher power, often God. For this reason it is sometimes called *<u>administrative</u> <u>organization</u>*. It is the first number whose factors include both the **dimensions** (**3**) and the **directions** (**4**); as such, it has both the **capacity** and **activity** (respectively) to provide a full structure. In music, there are **12** notes when we include the halftones.

As there were **12** disciples, the word *preach* has the value of **1728**, which is **12³** (**12** x **12** x **12**). And the list of twelves is almost inexhaustible; 12 tribes, twelve signs of the zodiac, 12 springs of water in Elim in the wilderness, and the list goes on and on.

In the **3-cycle** that we have been looking at, **10** is *<u>that</u>* God expects, **11** is *<u>what</u>* God expects, and **12** is *<u>what</u>* God *doesn't* expect, that is, he himself sets it up rather than relegating that organizing to man. In the *freedom* cycle (**6**) it is *<u>usable</u> <u>perfection</u>; <u>response</u> <u>released</u>*, and in the *perfection* cycle (**7**) it is *a <u>made</u> <u>organization</u>*.

More in-depth, learning to understand the *twelve parts* of **12** provides a comprehensive grasp on whatever subject is at hand, though it involves taking the time for to thoroughly familiarize one's self with the subject. The **twelve** elements of **mathematics** are: *measure (cycle), scale, span, orientate, standardize, reflect, define, apply, identify, extrapolate, sanctify,* and *specify*. In **art** they are *idealizing, choreographing, substantiation ordering, responding, solving (intuitive), naming, dignifying, forming, adjusting* *(environmental), realizing, planning (projecting),* and *embodying.* And again, these two lists are duplicate sets (though not in the same order here) applied in two differing contexts, <u>math</u> and <u>art</u>.

13

Thirteen is <u>accountability</u>, and as mentioned in the intro this gives it somewhat of a bad rap. In scripture, however, it is a very powerful force as well as a vital aid in navigating the infinite numerics. In Hebrew it is both the value of the word *One* and *Love.* The force of being accountable does come through loud and clear in the verses characterized by it; 13^3 **(13 x 13 x 13) = 2197**, which is the value of **Exodus 34:14** *"For you shall worship no other God: for Jehovah— Jealous is his name—is a jealous God."* Likewise with **Proverbs 28:24** *"Whoever robs his father or his mother, and says, It is no transgression; the same is the companion of a destroyer."* That verse has the **22**-system value of **2197** (13^3) and the **27**-system value of **2847** **(3 x 13 x 73)**. Fortunately, **Psalm 86:5** gives us a little glimpse of how nice it is to have mercy in the day of accountability: *"For you, Lord, are good, and ready to forgive; and plenteous in mercy to all them that call on you."* ...with a value of **1313**.

14

Fourteen means <u>results</u>. If **5** represents *ability* using the *hand* with its five fingers as a model, **14** represents the <u>*results*</u> attainable using that ability with **14** phalanges, or <u>finger</u> <u>bones</u> (as well as **14** in each foot) . There are also **14** <u>facial</u> <u>bones</u> in the human skull. It might also be of interest that an owl, who can turn his head all the way around, has **14** vertebra in his neck.

The result of Jacob working for Laban for **14** years was two

174

wives; the result of Job's patience and double blessing was **14,000** sheep. The passover was held on the **fourteenth** day of the month, and there are three sets of **14** progenitors in Jesus' genealogy in Matthew. Paul waited **14** years before he went to Jerusalem to present his Gospel to the Apostles.

Fourteen begins the full system of three-dimensional shapes; the simplest being the tetrahedron with **6** edges, + **4** sides + **4** faces = **14**. Four (action toward formation) **plus 10** (responsibility) = form, the results of formation.

It is the nature (**2**) of perfection (**7**) to produce results (**14**).

15

Fifteen means possession. When God took repossession of the earth in the days of Noah, nearly every measurement of the ark as well as every length of time mentioned was a multiple of **15**; as Psalm 124:4 says, *"Then the waters had overwhelmed us, the stream had gone over our soul"*—this verse has the value of **1515**. And **225** (**15²**) is the Greek value of the words *his, child, holy, sincere,* and *divine*.

In Leviticus 7:25 the fat of the sacrifices was owned by God; *"For whoever eats the fat of the beast, of which men offer an offering made by fire to Jehovah, even the soul that eats it will be cut off from his people."* and when David obtained possession of the promise from God that his Seed would abide, he said to God in Second Samuel 7:28 *"And now, O Lord Jehovah, you are that God, and your words are true, and you have promised this goodness to your servant..."* Both these verses have the value of **3375**, or **15³** (**15 x 15 x 15**).

The earth rotates **15°** every hour, and in the **24-clock** of Greek letters (Appendix III), each letter is **15°** apart. The time between the new moon and the full moon is **15 days**.

In the **3-cycle** that we have been looking at, **13** is _that_ God gets, **14** is _what_ God gets, and **15** is _what_ God _doesn't_ get, that is, what he already possesses.

16

Sixteen means <u>working</u> with the added sense of <u>substantiating</u>. It can also be applied to the exhaustion that comes of working. **16** is both 2^4 and 4^2; it is the only reciprocal exponent. Add to this fact that **4** is both **2 + 2** and **2 x 2**, and we see that **sixteen** is a very active number. Of note among the cycles is the _freedom_ cycle (**6**) in which **16** means _assets in action_. Greek words that equal **256** (16^2) include _fishers, shepherd, care, arm,_ and _deed..._ all 'working' ideas.

16^3 (**16** x **16** x **16**) equals **4096**, (and is 2^{12}), which is the value of the following verses:
Zephaniah 3:5 _"The righteous Jehovah is in the midst of her; he does no wrong: every morning does he bring his judgment to light, he fails not; but the unrighteous knows no shame."_
Daniel 8:27 _"And I Daniel fainted, and was sick, days; then I rose up, and did the king's business; and I was astonished at the vision, but none understood."_
Jonah 2:7 _"When my soul fainted within me I remembered Jehovah: and my prayer came in unto you, into your holy temple."_

17

Seventeen is the number of <u>creation</u>. **289** (**17** x **17**) is the Greek value of the words _receive, new, shape,_ and _distribute_. The thought is not so much that of God creating the earth, but the manner in which one either overcomes by creating a new way of going forward in life in the face of great difficulty, or succumbs. Three examples from scripture, all of which have the value of **4913** (**17³**, or **17 x 17 x 17**):

Ruth 2:10 *"And he said, Blessed are you of Jehovah, my daughter: for you have shown more kindness in the latter end than at the beginning, inasmuch as you followed not young men, whether poor or rich."*

Judges 16:21 *"But the Philistines took him, and put out his eyes, and brought him down to Gaza, and bound him with fetters of brass; and he did grind in the prison house."*

James 4:17 *"To him therefore that knows to do good, and does it not, to him it is sin."*

18

Eighteen is <u>rest</u>, specifically the rest of interrelationship. It takes the *full interaction* of **9** and tempers it with *nature* (**2**), as **2 x 9 = 18**. In the **3-cycle** that we have been looking at, **16** is <u>that</u> God works (**work**), **17** is <u>what</u> God works (**creation**), and **18** is <u>what</u> God <u>doesn't</u> work, that is, **rest**. **Eighteen** is *freedom's counsels* (**6 x 3**), and the *counsels* bring in the idea of interrelating.

18³ (**18 x 18 x 18**) **= 5832**, and Second Chronicles 30:1 has both the idea of a interrelationship and a day of rest combined nicely: *"And Hezekiah sent to all Israel and Judah, and wrote letters also to Ephraim and Manasseh, that they should come to the house of Jehovah at Jerusalem, to keep the passover to Jehovah God of Israel."* And there is the classic verse in First Timothy 2:12 (also **5832**) that addresses it: *"But I permit not a wife to teach, nor to have dominion over a husband, but to be in quietness."*

Eighteen is a reflective number, a doubling up of thought and experience. It is the only number that is twice the sum of its digits, and **18 x 20** (*recognition/honor*) give us the

19

Nineteen is <u>*executability*</u>; the ability to <u>accomplish</u>. It is the **7th** prime, and as such plays a pivotal role in getting our bearings in Scripture. When Joshua stopped the sun in the sky, five of the kings he defeated hid in a cave. Joshua ordered them brought out in 10:23 "*. . .and they did so, and brought forth those five kings unto him out of the cave, the king of Jerusalem, the king of Hebron, the king of Jarmuth, the king of Lachish, and the king of Eglon.*" This verse has the value of **6859** which is **19³**, or **19 x 19 x 19**. When God finished all of his creation, it says in Genesis 2:1 "*Thus the heavens and the earth were finished, and all the host of them.*" This verse (in the **27**-system) has a value of **2888**, which is **19² x 2³**.

We saw in chapter 6 how important the **19**-penny hexagon was to both Genesis 1:1 and John 1:1. The fact is that if one is to make a 'magic hexagon' starting with one and numbering all the spaces so that each row equals the same (in this case 38), **19** is the <u>only</u> <u>size</u> of a 'magic hexagon' to which this can be done:

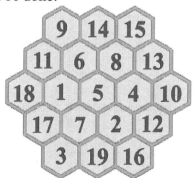

Nineteen, then, has a unique role among numbers, and is a vital clue to many of the relationships that are waiting to be searched out. When we go to the verses in First John which tell us what the Word did, we find **19** throughout: *"And the Word became flesh, and tabernacled among us, and we beheld his glory, glory as of an only begotten with a Father, full of grace and truth."*

In this verse, *"flesh"* is the key word, and is **19²** (**19 x 19**). The phrase "And the Word became flesh" is **1273** (**19 x 67**), "Tabernacled among us" is **1501** (**19 x 79**), *"we beheld his glory, glory as of an only begotten with a Father, full of grace and truth"* is **7068** (**19 x 372**), and *"as of an only begotten with a Father, full of grace"* is **4598** (**242 x 19**).

20

Twenty is <u>recognition</u>/<u>honor</u>; the idea is both a *display* of honor and recognition for having fulfilled responsibilities, especially in relationships. Job in 13:18 says *"Behold now, I have ordered my cause; I know that I will be justified."* ...and this verse has the value of **2020**. The number **20** also has the opposite aspect in which one does <u>not</u> get honor; as such, **20²** (**400**) is the value in Greek of *deceitfulness*, *transgression*, *defile*, and *lie* ...as well as *holy*. Leviticus 21:4 has both senses when it says *"But he shall not defile himself, being a chief man among his people, to profane himself,"* also **400**. And Second Chronicles 7:20 continues the theme of dishonor: *"Then will I pluck them up by the roots out of my land which I have given them; and this house, which I have sanctified for my name, will I cast out of my sight, and will make it to be a proverb and a byword among all nations."* That verse equals **8000**, which is **20³** (**20 x 20 x 20**).

Twenty is a <u>triangle</u> <u>pyramid</u> <u>number</u> as shown:

This means it relates directly to a 3-**dimensional** construct where the most intricate numerics are hidden.

21

Twenty-One is **3** x **7** and means <u>fulfillment</u> and <u>fullness</u>. In the **3-cycle** that we have been following, **19** is *that* God can finish (executability), **20** is *what* God can finish (honor), and **21** is *what* God *doesn't* finish, that is, it is already finished for him, as the honor that Christ gets for doing the work he was sent to do. Consequently, **21** is closely related to the <u>finished</u> <u>work</u> <u>of</u> <u>Christ</u>; his struggles being seen in a picture when Jacob wrestled with the Angel: *"And when he saw that he prevailed not against him, he touched the hollow of his thigh; and the hollow of Jacob's thigh was out of joint, as he wrestled with him."* ...which verse's value is **2121**.

A difficult yet important lesson that **twenty** teaches us is that we are to enter into God's rest as Hebrews 4 explains. Thus Matthew 5:37 says *"But let your word be, Yea, yea; Nay, nay: and whatever is more than these is of the evil one."* ...which has the value of **9261**, **21³** (**21** x **21** x **21**). For **21** x **73** = **777**, which is *the cross*, and Christ has already done that; we enter into his God's rest in the work. There are times when the glory of God is so taken up with his appreciation for his Son that we cannot approach, as

180

Exodus 40:35 says *"And Moses was not able to enter into the tent of the congregation, because the cloud abode on it, and the glory of Jehovah filled the tabernacle."* This verse is **2310** which is (**21** x **37**) + (**21** x **73**).

22

Twenty-Two is <u>answering</u>. It has the sense of *distributing service, returning thankfulness*, and *responding by initiating a creation*. It is like **11**, *response*, but takes it much farther; it is *how* one responds, and *to whom*. In the negative, it is Proverbs 15:12 "A scorner loves not one that reproves him: neither will he go unto the wise" (**22²**) and the force of the positive is shown in Isaiah 40:30 *"Who has directed the Spirit of Jehovah, or being his counselor has taught him?"* ...which has the value of **2200**.

23

Twenty-Three is another powerful prime; it means <u>full action</u> <u>in</u> <u>every</u> <u>capacity</u>. It has the sense of *awaking and acting* as well as *hyperactively accomplishing* and *using everything that you are*. On the intense side it it *the accountability of responsibility* (**13** + **10**) and on the energetic side it is the *fruit of rest* (**18** + **5**), as when one wakes in the morning and attacks a project.

There is a certain abandon to **23**, as Ecclesiastes 11:1 says *"Cast your bread upon the waters: for you will find it after many days"* (**1679**; **23** x **73**). The beauty of this energy can be seen in Song of Solomon 1:19 "I have compared you, O my love, to a company of horses in Pharaoh's chariots" (which verse value is **2323**) and the negative of this energy can be seen in Job 12:25 *"They grope in the dark without light, and he makes them to stagger like a drunken man."* ...whose value is **2300**.

24

Twenty-Four is the <u>perfection</u> of <u>fruit</u>; **ripening**. It has the sense of just beginning to enter into rest, and of making room for maturing to occur. The end of the fourth day in Genesis 1:19 and the seeing that the beasts that the earth brought forth were good in 25, both contain **24** as a factor. 24^2 (**576**) is the value of *Spirit, honor, overshadow, kindle,* and *finish* in Greek. A good example is found in Daniel 1:19 *"And the king communed with them; and among them all was found none like Daniel, Hananiah, Mishael, and Azariah: therefore stood they before the king"* which has a value of **2424**.

And **24** x **37** is **888** (*Jesus*), while **24** x **73** is **1752**, which is Proverbs 8:23 *"I was set up from everlasting, from the beginning, or ever the earth was"* ...Wisdom speaking.

25

Twenty-Five is <u>Satisfaction</u>, particularly the satisfaction that comes of one's own accomplishments. Song of Solomon 8:2 has *"I would lead you, and bring you into my mother's house, who would instruct me: I would cause you to drink of spiced wine of the juice of my pomegranate"* which has the value of **2525**.

25 is both the **5th** square and **5** x **5**. It is also the sum of two squares; $3^2 + 4^2 = 9 + 16 = 25$, thus it is often used as an example of the Pythagorean Theorem ($A^2 + B^2 = C^2$) which allows us to easily calculate the third leg of a triangle.

One can see Jacob's great satisfaction in his son Judah when he blesses him: *"Judah, you are he whom your brothers will praise: your hand will be in the neck of your enemies; your father's children will bow down before you"* which has a value of **1825**, or **25** x **73**).

182

26

Twenty-Six is <u>multiplying</u> and <u>affecting</u>. It is the number of *influence, what others can count on*, and one's *ability to have a full effect*. As **2** x **13**, it is the *nature* (**2**) of *accountability* (**13**) meaning that when one has successfully given an account, one can then move on and use that dignity to influence what happens next. **26²** (**676**) is the value of the Greek words *doer* (from James) and *new*. When the idea is negated, one has no ability to affect, thus **676** is the value of the first verse in First Kings "*Now king David was old and stricken in years; and they covered him with clothes, but he got no heat.*" The flip side for David is First Samuel 29:5 "*Is not this David, of whom they sang one to another in dances, saying, Saul slew his thousands, and David his ten thousands?*" which has the value of **2626**, as does Ezekiel 37:2, "*And caused me to pass by them round about: and, behold, there were very many in the open valley; and, lo, they were very dry*" in which God did some rather remarkable <u>multiplying</u> and <u>affecting</u>.

27

Twenty-Seven is <u>self</u> <u>knowing</u>. It has the sense of *self searching, self examination*, and *reexamination*. The Old Testament uses the expression "*And Adam <u>knew</u> his wife*", meaning that they made love. This is very much a part of **27**, for a man's wife is part of himself, and the marriage process is that of getting to one's <u>self</u>, that is, one's <u>wife</u>. Thus **27** is part of the mystery of Oneness.

Twenty-Seven is **3³**, and as such is central to inner counsels and workings. Both verses in Genesis 1 (26 & 27) which speak of God creating male and female and telling them to multiply and have dominion have **27** as a factor; **27** x **208** and **27** x **431** respectively. **Twenty-Seven** also has an application to knowing God, as Daniel 11:32 shows; "*And such as do wickedly against the covenant shall he corrupt by flatteries: but the people that <u>do</u> <u>know</u> their God shall be strong, and do.*" This verse has the value of **2727**.

And there is a warning against knowing one's self (or one's wife) so well that we do damage; both Exodus 20:13 and Deuteronomy 5:17 say "*Thou shalt no kill*" which in both instances has the value of **729**, or **27²**.

Twenty Seven is the number of Hebrew letters including the final forms. It is a most vital number to understanding how to put the letters into <u>three dimensions</u>. In two dimensions, as we saw in chapter 6, the numbers **37** and **73** are in prominence. But in three dimensions, **27** is primary. So is there a relationship between **27** and **37 & 73**? Let us shade in the **27 cube of Hebrew letters** as it sits within the **64 cube,** 'Truth', from page 40:

If we *remove* the **27 Hebrew letter cube**, we end up with this:

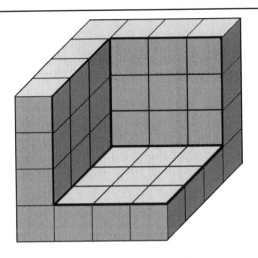

And how many cube are left? **Thirty-Seven**. But in using **64** and **27**, we used the **3rd** and **4th** cubes, skipping the first (1^3) and second (2^3). So let's slip all the cubes back in.

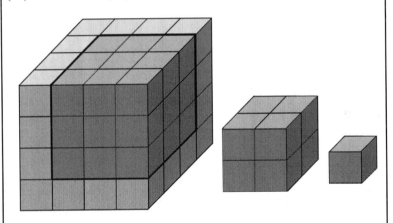

Much better; now all the cubed numbers up to **64** are accounted for. And total number cubes here? <u>73</u>.

This is one way to show that while different numbers are prominent in differing scenarios, they are always intricately related.

28

Twenty-Eight is the 7th Triangle Number (a triangle of pennies with each side 7 pennies long) and means <u>blessing</u>. It has the sense of '*Amen!*' It is the <u>accountability</u> of <u>possessions</u> and <u>overseeing</u>, especially your own business or family. In the negative it can mean destroying your possessions instead of blessing them, as Zephaniah 1:2 "*I will utterly consume all things from off the land, says Jehovah*" which has the value of **784**, or **28²** (**28** x **28**). But even this has God's mercy involved, for Job 33:28 says "*He will deliver his soul from going into the pit, and his life shall see the light.*" And the woman is well blessed in Song of Solomon 6:5 "*Turn away your eyes from me, for they have overcome me: your hair is as a flock of goats that appear from Gilead.*" These two verses have the values of **2800** and **2828** respectively.

Each time in Genesis 1 that it says "*and God blessed them*", the value is **765**, or (**28** x **24**) + **7**. The value of Genesis 2:3 "*And God blessed the seventh day, and sanctified it: because that in it he had rested from all his work which God created and made*" is **4928**, or **28** x **176**. And interestingly, the only Greek word with the value of **28** is <u>heal</u>.

29

Twenty-Nine is <u>holding</u>/<u>understanding</u>. It is what one holds within one's self so as to understand what to do. It means having possession of the results of your experience. As the 9th prime, it has a powerful application to inner strength. Ecclesiastes 7:10 has some advice about considering one's experience: "*Say not, How is it that the former days were better than these? for you do not inquire wisely concerning this.*" This verse has a value of **2929**. When

Nebuchadnezzar wrote his letter to the whole world after his restoration, in his new understanding he says *"I thought it good to show the signs and wonders that the High God has wrought toward me"* and this verse is **2030**, which is **29** x **70**.

30

Thirty means communication/giving. It is *understanding available to be used.* In the negative we see the lack of communication or giving in Job 19:14 *"My kinsfolk have failed, and my familiar friends have forgotten me"* which has a value of **30²**, or **900**. Psalms 36:8 gives the positive *"They will be abundantly satisfied with the fatness of your house; and you wilt make them drink of the river of your pleasures."* That verse has the value of **30** x **73**.

30 is the **4ᵗʰ** Square Pyramid Number after **1**, **5**, and **14**, meaning that if you stack ping-pong balls in a square pyramid, it will take **30** of them to make four levels high. The next level would take **55** balls, which is also the number of pennies in one of the two overlapping triangles on page 43 of the **73/37** star.

When God gave the lights in the expanse of the heavens (Genesis 1:16) to communicate signs, seasons, days, and years, the verse has a value of **5820** which is **30** x **193**.

31

Thirty-One is the **10ᵗʰ** prime, and means self-building. It is also the number for **naming**; the sense is *actively working on one's self or one's possessions* as in Deuteronomy 3:7 *"But all the cattle, and the spoil of the cities, we took for a prey to ourselves"* which has the value of **961**, or **31²**. When Adam named the animals, the word *name* equals **301**.

The negative side of not being able to build one's self up can be quite harsh, as we see in Esau in Genesis 27:34 *"And when Esau heard the words of his father, he cried with a great and exceeding bitter cry, and said unto his father, Bless me, even me also, O my father."* That verse has the value of **3100**. But the inclusion of God in the process is nice, as we see in Psalm 139:24 *"And see if there be any wicked way in me, and lead me in the way everlasting."*, which has the value of **31 x 73**.

32

Thirty-Two is 2^6 and means <u>working</u> <u>out</u>; **effecting**. Genesis 2:3 says *"And God blessed the seventh day, and sanctified it: because that in it he had rested from all his work which God created to make"*, and has the value of **4928 (32 x 11 x 7)**. Judges 20:1 shows the effectiveness of working together; *"Then all the children of Israel went out, and the congregation was gathered together as one man, from Dan even to Beer-sheba, with the land of Gilead, unto Jehovah in Mizpeh."* This verse has the value of **3200**. Likewise with Exodus 7:17 *"Thus says Jehovah, In this you will know that I am Jehovah: behold, I will smite with the rod that is in my hand upon the waters which are in the river, and they will be turned to blood"*, which has the value of **3232**.

33

Thirty-Three is a <u>running</u> <u>system</u>, a *full operation*. Ironically, the only Greek word that equals **33** is *hades*. This harkens to Luke 12:5 *"But I will forewarn you whom you shall fear: Fear him, which after he has killed has power to cast into hell; yea, I say unto you, Fear him!"* which has the value of **11,979**, which is **33³/3**.

There are **33** vertebrae in the human spine. David reigned for **33** years over all of Israel and had **33** mighty men. Jesus lived to **33**. An example of a full operation is in Numbers 41:38 "*And the officers which were over thousands of the host, the captains of thousands, and captains of hundreds, came near unto Moses*" which has the value of **3333**.

34

Thirty-Four means <u>unfurling</u>. In the *accomplishment cycle* it has the sense of <u>unfolding</u>; in the *perfecting cycle* it has the sense of <u>unleashing</u>. The unfolding of the seas and the dry land (Genesis 1:10) has the value of **2074** which is **34 x 61**. Isaiah 43:6 says "*I will say to the north, Give up; and to the south, Keep not back: bring my sons from far, and my daughters from the ends of the earth*" which verse has the value of **3434**. Eber was **34** when he had Peleg, in whose days the earth was divided; we are not told what forces were unleashed, only that they were.

It also has the sense of <u>unfurling</u> a <u>flag</u> for battle, as in Psalm 45:3 "*Gird your sword upon your thigh, O most mighty, with your glory and your majesty*" . . .this verse has the value of **1258**, which is **34 x 37**.

35

Thirty-Five is <u>perfected</u> <u>ability</u> or <u>accomplishment</u>. It is the *honor* of *possessions* and *creation's rest*. It is the value of the Greek words *glass* and *amethyst*, as well as *child* and *translate*. Psalm 98 greatly praises the accomplishments of God, and verse 7 says "*Let the sea roar, and the fullness of it; the world, and they that dwell in it*" and has the value of **1225** which is 35^2.

In Genesis 11:4, mankind had <u>perfected</u> his <u>ability</u> and wanted to make the ultimate <u>accomplishment</u>; "*And they said, Give help! Let us build us a city and a tower, and its top in the heavens; and we make for us a Name, lest we are scattering over the face of the whole earth.*" This verse has the value of **3535**. Joel 3:10 says "*Beat your plowshares into swords, and your pruning hooks into spears: let the weak say, I am strong*" which has the value of **3500**.

35 is the sum of the first five Triangular Numbers, making it a <u>Triangular Pyramid Number</u> as follows:

This construct has **35** spheres. The last time we saw this was with number **20**, this time with an additional level. The next will be **56**.

36

Thirty-Six is <u>peace</u>. It has the sense of *outspreading* and *leading toward awareness*. It is 6^2, the **6th** square number and also the product of two squares: $2^2 \times 3^2$. It is also the 8th Triangle Number and the only triangular number whose square root (**6**) is also a triangular number. The sum of the numbers from **1** to **36** is **666**. Here is what we mean by both a square number and a triangular number (both have 36 pennies):

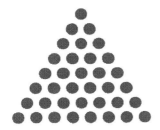

There was a sense of outspreading peace from the moon and the sun when *"God set them in the expanse of the heavens, to give light on the earth"* in Genesis 1:17, and the value of this verse is **36 x 67**.

One of the most beautiful passages about peace is the first half of John 14:27: *"I leave you peace; my peace I give to you: not as the world gives, give I to you."* The value of this verse is **36** x **244**, and even **244** is **2² x 61** . . .**sixty-one** being a most mysterious number that is the <u>primary numeric key</u> to **Psalm 119**. The first half of this phrase *"I leave you peace; my peace I give to you"* has the value of **3360**, which is **36** x **33.33333**. . .

John 18:9 says *"That the word be fulfilled, which he said, Of those whom you have given me, I lost not one"*, which has the value of **7776**, which is **36³ / 6**.

37

Thirty-Seven has had more said about it in this book than perhaps any other number. Here we mention a few things that have not been said.

37 means <u>artistic capability</u> and *solving*. It is closely connected with *creating* and the process of *translating* from one realm to another, including from this life to the next. Jeremiah 52:31 states that *"in the <u>thirty-seventh</u> year of the captivity of Jehoiachin king of Judah, in the twelfth month,* *on the twenty-fifth of the month, that Evil-Merodach king of Babylon, in the year that he began to reign, lifted up the head of <u>Jehoiachin</u> king of Judah, and brought him forth out of prison.*" Jehoiachin has the value of **111** which is **3** x **37**. Ishmael, Levi, and Amram lived to **137** (Sarah lived to **127** and Jacob to **147**).

Isaiah 52:15 has the value of **3737** and says "*...so will he astonish many nations; kings will shut their mouths at him; for what had not been told them will they see, and what they had not heard will they consider.*" Habakkuk 1:12 also has the value of **3737** and says "*Are you not from everlasting, Jehovah my God, my Holy One? We will not die. Jehovah, you have ordained Him for judgment; and you, O Rock, have appointed him for correction.*"

38

Thirty-Eight means <u>solving</u>, primarily through *planning* and *organizing*. In Deuteronomy 2:14 it states that it took **38** years for the generation of the men of war to be consumed from the midst of the camp. In John 5:5 a man had been infirm for **38** years by the pool called Bethzatha whom Jesus healed and told to sin no more lest something worse befall him—promptly went and tattled on Jesus to the Pharisees. Yet Jesus was using that very situation to organize the first of many discussions with the religious leaders that continue through the rest of the book; he was laying down the gauntlet, so to speak, having planned out and organized his approach to the severe attitudes against God of the day.

One form of the word *heal* (ιαθηι) in Greek has the value of **38**. There is then the question of who has the ability to size up a situation and solve it, as it says in Jeremiah 9:12 "*Who is the wise man, that may understand this? and who is he to whom the mouth of Jehovah has spoken, that he may* *declare it, for what the land perishes and is burned up like a wilderness, that none passes through"* . . .with the value of **3838**. And God is not interested in false solutions, as he says in Amos 5:22 *"Though you offer me burnt offerings and your meat offerings, I will not accept them: neither will I regard the peace offerings of your fat beasts"* which has a value of **2774**, which is **38** x **73**.

Psalm 111:2 says *"The works of Jehovah are great, <u>sought out</u> of all them that have pleasure in them"* which has the value of **1406** which is **38** x **37**. . . as does Proverbs 17:3 *"The fining pot for silver, and the furnace for gold: but Jehovah tries the hearts."*

39

Thirty-Nine is <u>harvest</u>; *fulfillment of rest.* Jeremiah 50:34 talks of this *"Their Redeemer is strong; Jehovah of hosts is his name: he will thoroughly plead their cause, that he may give rest to the land, and disquiet the inhabitants of Babylon."* The value of this verse is **3939**. And after everything that the woman goes through in Song of Solomon, her final way of phrasing what she says in so many forms is *"I am my beloved's, and his desire is toward me"* with a value of **1443** (**39** x **37**). Sharing that value, Psalm 128:6 says *"Yea, you wilt see your children's children, and peace upon Israel."*

Contrasted with a negative harvest, such as Zephaniah 1:15 *"That day is a day of wrath, a day of trouble and distress, a day of ruin and desolation, a day of darkness and gloominess, a day of clouds and thick darkness"* . . .is the positive of Jeremiah 33:12 *"Thus says Jehovah of hosts; Again in this place, which is desolate without man and without beast, and in all the cities thereof, shall be a habitation of shepherds causing their flocks to lie down"* and Deuteronomy 16:13 *"You shall observe the feast of tabernacles seven days, after that you have gathered in your corn and your wine".* All three of these verses have the value of **2847**, which is **39** x **73**.

40

Forty is well-known as <u>proving</u> and <u>testing</u>. Scripture is replete with **40**'s; days and **40** nights of rain in the flood, **40** days between when the ark rested and Noah opened the windows, the age of Isaac when he took Rebecca as wife, the age of his son Esau when he took two Canaanite wives, **40** days of embalming Jacob, **40** years of the Israelites eating manna, twice Moses on the mountain for **40** days and **40** nights, **40** silver bases under the boards on both the north and south sides of the tabernacle, **40** days of the spies searching out the land, **40** years of wandering in the wilderness (that do <u>not</u> exactly correspond to the **40** years of eating manna; they are offset by two years), maximum amount of stripes allowed when punishing someone under law, Moses' life of **120** was divided into **3** sets of **40**: Egypt, Jethro, and Israel; **40** years the land rest after Othniel, then Deborah, then Gideon; **40** sons of Gideon, **40** years under the rule of the Philistines until God raised up Sampson, **40** years Eli judged Israel, **40** days that Goliath defied Israel, the age of Ishbosheth Saul's son when he became king, the number of years David reigned, the age of Absalom when he tried to usurp the kingdom, . . .and we are not even halfway through the occurrences.

One of the lesson we can see in this pattern of **40**'s is that they all—without exception—require God's involvement. The following two verse give this idea clearly, both of which have the value of **1600**, or **40²**; Psalm 107:28 says *"Then they cry unto Jehovah in their trouble, and he brings them out of their distresses"* and Psalm 65:2 says *"O you that hear prayer, unto you will all flesh come."*

In Judges 6:4 we have Gideon testing Jehovah *"And God did so that night: for it was dry upon the fleece only, and there was dew on all the ground"* and in Job 36:9 Elihu explains how God proves people: *"Then he shows them their work, and their transgressions because they have increased."* Both these verses have the value of **1480**, or **40 x 37**. . . the same numerical value as **Christ**.

And we'll finish with this example of the ultimate test of life or death: *"Then the king held out the golden scepter toward Esther. So Esther arose, and stood before the king"*, Esther 8:4. This verse has the value of **4040**.

41

Forty-One means <u>enjoying</u>, <u>using</u>, and <u>appreciating</u>. The only Greek word with the value of **41** is *salt*, which allows us to appreciate food. Certain kings enjoyed the fruits of labor provided by those who came before them; Rehoboam was **41** when he began to reign; his grandson Asa reigned **41** years as did Jeroboam over Israel. Psalm 78:5 describes the use and appreciation of the law; *"For he established a testimony in Jacob, and appointed a law in Israel, which he commanded our fathers, that they should make them known to their children"*, this verse has the value of **4100**. On the negative side, here are some who did *not* appreciate the prophet Elisha in Second Kings 2:23: *"And he went up from there unto Bethel: and as he was going up by the way, there came forth little children out of the city, and mocked him, and said unto him, Go up, you bald head; go up, you bald head"* . . .which verse also has the value of **4100**. Note that the two she-bears that came out of the wood tore **42** of them; leading to the next number with a corresponding meaning to <u>enjoying/using</u>.

But Psalm 69:34 brings us back to enjoying; *"Let the heaven and earth praise him, the seas, and every thing that*

> *moves in it"* with a value of **1517 (41 x 37)**.

42

Forty-Two is <u>pleasure</u> and <u>awareness</u>, connected with *fulfillment substantiated*. It is different from the enjoying of **41** in that it is an outward sharing of pleasure rather than an inward <u>using</u> for one's self. **41** and **42** are a good example of a **meaning pair** in which two numbers occur beside each other which have the <u>male</u> and <u>female</u> meaning of the same idea. This is one reason why Ivan Panin's idea of <u>neighbor</u> numbers works.

The negation of **42** can be seen in the **42** months that the nations tread under foot the outer court of the temple, the **42** months that the Beast pursues his career, and the **42** royal persons from Judah that Jehu killed when establishing his kingdom—and breaking the truce between Israel and Judah. For the positive we have the **42** cities that were set aside for the Levites which would double as Cities of Refuge.

And the positive side is meant to be *outward*; to others or to God as Numbers 29:6 *"Beside the burnt offering of the month, and his meat offering, and the daily burnt offering, and his meat offering, and their drink offerings, according unto their manner, for a <u>sweet savor</u>, a sacrifice made by fire unto Jehovah"*, this verse has the value of **1746**, which is **42²**.

43

Forty-Three is <u>stewardship</u> <u>returned</u>. It is the *recognition* **(20)** that one has *acted fully in every capacity* + **(23)**. It is the one good thing that Jehu did in Second Kings 10:19 when he was given stewardship of the kingdom by Elisha's servant: he extricated Baal from Israel by slaying all his prophets: *"Now therefore call unto me all the prophets of Baal, all his servants, and all his priests; let none be wanting: for I have a great sacrifice to do to Baal; whoever will be wanting, he will not live. But Jehu did it in subtlety, to the intent that he might destroy the worshippers of Baal."* This verse has the value of **4343**. *Judge* (κρινομαι) and *deed* (πραξιν) in Greek both have the value of **301**, which is **43** x **7**.

And the comment regarding the woman in Song of Solomon 3:6 when she returns to her beloved with the stewardship of his love: *"Who is this that comes out of the wilderness like pillars of smoke, perfumed with myrrh and frankincense, with all powders of the merchant?"* This verse also has the value of **4343**. The Greek work *espouse* (μεμνηστευμενηι) has the value of **1161**, which is **43** x **37**.

Of course, God can *demand* an accounting of stewardship as he did to Job in 38:3, *"Gird up now your loins like a man; for I will demand of you, and answer you me"* and in Jeremiah 13:20, *"Lift up your eyes, and behold them that come from the north: where is the flock that was given you, your beautiful flock?"* These two verses are **1161** (**43** x **37**) and **3139** (**43** x **73**) respectively.

44

Forty-Four is answered/done, making another **meaning pair** with **43**. It also has the sense of being in *readiness for what is next*. In John 4:49 "The nobleman says unto him, Sir, come down before my little child die. (50) Jesus says to him, Go, your son lives." Verse 49 there in which the request was already answered and done, has the value of **4444**.

In First Samuel 1:27, Hannah presents Samuel to Eli and

says *"For this child I prayed; and Jehovah has given me my petition which I asked of him."* This verse has the value of **4400**. Eli had told her when he saw her last that Jehovah would grant her petition; answered and done. And in Genesis 24:65 *"And she is saying to the servant, What man is this that walks in the field to meet us? And the servant is saying, It is my master: and she is taking a veil, and she is covering herself."* This verse also has the value of **4400**, and has double the meaning; she was already considered married (*done* and *in readiness for what is next*) and now that Isaac was married, the servant's new master was Isaac, not Abraham as previously.

Because God knows our requests before we even make them, and because prophecy from God is as sure as if the event had already happened, both pray (προσευχομενη) and prophecy (προφητευομεν) in Greek have the value of **1628**, which is **44 x 37**. These are the only two Greek words with this value.

45

Forty-Five means indoctrination and belief. The idea is to saturate a problem with the solution; to be wholly occupied with something, as Paul says to Timothy in 4:15, "Meditate upon these things; give yourself wholly to them; that your profiting may appear to all", which has the value of **5200** (**45 x 115**) + **5²**.

Levi (through Phinehas) completely immersed himself in Jehovah's word in Deuteronomy 33:9, *"Who said unto his father and to his mother, I have not seen him; neither did he acknowledge his brethren, nor knew his own children: for they have observed your word, and kept your covenant."* Likewise in Numbers 24:1, Balaam finally realized that it was *Jehovah's* word, not some other entity *"And when Balaam saw that it pleased the LORD to bless Israel, he went not, as at other times, to seek for enchantments, but he set his face toward the wilderness.*" Both these verses have the value of **4545**.

Habakkuk 1:13 gives a good example: "*You art of purer eyes than to behold evil, and cannot look on iniquity: for which reason look you upon them that deal treacherously, and keep silent when the wicked swallows up a man more righteous than he.*" And Second Timothy 2:12 gives us the difference between truly believing and not: "*If we endure, we will also reign together: if we will deny him, he also will deny us.*" Both these verses have the value of **4500**.

And as to the character of doctrine, it is something we need to *get*, and get from a place where it is held. The four Greek words with the value of **1665** (45 x 37) are *have* (κυριευουσιν), *have* (εχωσιν), *obtain* (τετευχεν), and *synagogue* (συναγωγης).

45 is also a triangular number, as well as the sum of the digits 1, 2, 3, 4, 5, 6, 7, 8, and 9.

46

Forty-Six is accomplishing everywhere. It is as if one is in overdrive. It is also the number of human chromosomes. Accomplishing everywhere at once can be seen in Habakkuk 2:14, "*For the earth shall be filled with the knowledge of the glory of Jehovah, as the waters cover the sea.*" And the excitement is almost palpable in Genesis 29:12 "*And Jacob told Rachel that he was her father's brother, and that he was Rebekah's son: and she ran and told her father.*" Both of these verses have the value of **2116**, which is **46²**.

And we have the romantic side in Ruth 4:13: "*So Boaz took Ruth, and she was his wife: and when he went in unto her,*

Jehovah gave her conception, and she bare a son" which has the value of **3358**, which is **46** x **73**.

Then we have the beginning of the last paragraph of the Old Testament; Malachi 4:4, which says *"Remember you the law of Moses my servant, which I commanded unto him in Horeb for all Israel, with the statutes and judgments.,"* with the value of **4646**.

47

Forty-Seven is <u>settlement</u>, as the fulfillment of multiplying. Note that the planet Mars settles back into the same place every **47** years. The only Greek word with its value is *herd* (αγελη).

In Second Chronicles 7:2 the glory settled on the house of God *"And the priests could not enter into the house of Jehovah, because the glory of Jehovah had filled Jehovah's house."* This verse has the value of **1739**, or **47** x **37**. Its negation—the opposite of being settled—is in Job 18:18; *"He is driven from light into darkness, and chased out of the world."* This has the value of **1269**, or **47** x **27**.

And we have the romance of settlement in Proverbs 5:19, *"Let her be as the loving hind and pleasant roe; let her breasts satisfy you at all times; and be you ravished always with her love."* Then with God we have the settlement of events past, present and future in Isaiah 44:7: *"And who, as I, will call, and will declare it, and set it in order for me, since I appointed the ancient people? and the things that are coming, and shall come, let them declare unto them."* As well as the immovability of the settled heavens in Job 38:31; *"Can you bind the sweet influences of Pleiades, or loose the bands of Orion?"* These three verses have the value of **3431**, or **47** x **73**.

48

Forty-Eight is <u>perfection</u> <u>of</u> <u>potential</u>. It is what is achieved when the maturing process is healthy. **48** cities were given to the Levites in the land, including the **42** that were used as cities of refuge. **48** is most often seen in setting up a peaceful and stable scenario that has take an enduring consistent effort to produce. We see this in Genesis 47:12, *"And Joseph nourished his father, and his brethren, and all his father's household with bread, according to their families"* and First Chronicles 16:2 *"And when David had made an end of offering the burnt offerings and the peace offerings, he blessed the people in the name of Jehovah."* Both of these verses have the value of **2304** (**48²**), as well as the negation, one of which is found in Proverbs 25:28, *"He that has no rule over his own spirit is like a city that is broken down, and without walls."*

In Isaiah 50:4 we have *"The Lord Jehovah has given me the tongue of the learned, that I should know how to help by a word him that is instructed: he wakens morning by morning, he wakens my ear to hear as the instructed."* This verse has the value of **4800**.

49

Forty-Nine is **7²** and both its digits, **4** and **9** are squares. **49** means <u>fulfillment</u> <u>of</u> <u>blessing</u>, as it is mentioned in Leviticus 25:8 *"And you shall count seven sabbaths of years, seven times seven years; so that the days of the seven sabbaths of years be unto you <u>forty-nine</u> years."* And this verse even has the value of **7524**, or (**49 x 153**) + **3³**. And in First Samuel 16:3 God finally gets the king he wants *"And call Jesse to the sacrifice, and I will show you what you will do: and you will anoint unto me him whom I name unto you."* This verse has the value of **4949**.

In Joshua 21:43 we have *"And Jehovah gave unto Israel all the land which he swore to give unto their fathers; and they possessed it, and dwelt therein"* with a value of **4900**. And the negation is seen in Acts 13:40 when Paul is preaching, *"Beware therefore, lest that come upon you, which is spoken of in the prophets. . ."* also with a value of **4900**.

50

Fifty is return with the sense of *glory*; each **50** years in Israel was the Jubilee, in which all possessions returned to their original owners, from slaves to property, and all debts were erased. **50** is $1^2 + 7^2$ as well as $5^2 + 5^2$ as well as $3^2 + 4^2 + 5^2$. as well as $5^3 - 4^3 - 3^3 + 2^3 + 2^3$. The two Greek words with the value of **50** are *righteous* (δικαιε) and *I* (εμε).

First Corinthians 10:31 says *"Whether therefore you eat, or drink, or whatever you do, do all to the glory of God."* Likewise in Genesis 17:1 *"And when Abram was ninety years old and nine, Jehovah appeared to Abram, and said to him, I am the Almighty God; walk before me, and be you perfect."* Both these verses have the value of **5050**. And in Exodus 34:35 Moses returned with so much glory that they couldn't look at him: *"And the children of Israel saw the face of Moses, that the skin of Moses' face shone: and Moses put the veil upon his face again, until he went in to speak with him."* That verse has the value of **5000**.

And if something cannot return glory to God? Matthew 7:19: *"Every tree that brings not forth good fruit is hewn down, and cast into the fire."* This verse has the value of **3650**, or **50** x **73**.

Appendix III
Equidistant Letter Sequence, Acrostics, and Geometry

The debate regarding the ELS (**Equidistant Letter Sequence**) phenomena began in earnest in 1994 when Doron Witztum, Eliyahu Rips, and Yoav Rosenberg published an article in the journal *Statistical Science*. It was entitled *Equidistant Letter Sequences in the Book of Genesis*. This article describes an experiment which seems to show a remarkable proximity between names of rabbis and their dates of birth or death in the Book of Genesis. To this day there is a fierce debate over the validity of this experiment, the crux being whether the information sought for was determined *a priori* or not; that is, were the parameters set *before* the search was done, or were they adjusted concurrently.

Michael Drosnin's book *The Bible Code* demonstrates the potential power of ELS in scripture to address current events, such as the assassination of Israel's Prime Minister Yitzhak Rabin with which he begins his tale. Unfortunately, the book leans so far toward sensationalism and makes so many grammatical and spelling 'adjustments' that it fails to be taken seriously by most researchers. In spite of this, the subject has actually been studied for centuries, and the phenomena appears to be valid. For example, every 50th letter in both Genesis and Exodus spell out "Torah" starting with the first Tet, and the same ELS is found *backward* in Deuteronomy and Numbers.

One approach that has *not* been taken by many is a Dynamic Letter Sequence. We mentioned the Fibonacci Series near the end of chapter 3, which runs 0, 1, 1, 2, 3, 5, 8, 13, 21, 55, etc., each number being the sum of the previous two. This number is the pattern of much of nature, and is also found in geometric constructs like the 'golden spiral'. As a natural progression, it is an ideal sequence to test on scripture, and indeed produces its own results. For example, if one takes the Fibonacci Series as the skip interval and starts with the first letter, the following sentence emerges (remember Hebrew reads from right to left):

עַל	וּבִי	עוּ	שבּא	בּר
material form	desire for appearance	physical growth	to come or go	a son

"A son who comes to full growth and desired form..."

Likewise when one starts with the second letter (taking the 'zero' at the beginning of the Fibonacci Series as a signal to skip the first letter), the following emerges:

...ח	קיל	לים	רתו	ראי
	voice or sound	to the sea	his arresting/ stopping	you see

"You see his rebuking to the roaring of the sea..."

So it appears that there is fruit to be found in exploring this further.

*   *   *

There is a similar phenomena to ELS, and that is **Acrostics**. For example, Esther is the only book with no mention whatsoever of God in the text. However "YHWH" (יהוה) which most Christian Bibles translate "Jehovah" is found hidden in acrostics in the text. In 1:20, the phrase "...all the wives will give..." has "YHWH" as the first letter of each word . . .backwards. Moving to 5:4, the phrase "...let the king and Haman come this day..." has "YHWH" as the first letter of each word . . .forwards. Then in 5:13, the phrase "...yet all this avails me nothing..." has it as the *last* letter of each word . . .backwards. And lastly, in 7:7, the phrase "...that there was evil determined against him..." has "YHWH" as the *last* letter of each word . . .forwards. In addition, in 7:5, the phrase "...is he, and where is he..." spells "EHYHE" (אהוהא) using the *last* letter of each word. This reads the same forward and backwards, and is a direct quote of "I AM" from Exodus 3:14.

Another version of acrostics is the use of the alphabet, such as Psalms 119 in which there are 22 sections of eight verses each. In each section, all eight verses start with the same letter, starting with Aleph and moving right through in order to Tav, the final letter. Somewhat lesser known is the fact that the last chapter of Proverbs does the same thing with each verse. The book of Lamentations uses this device throughout. This is not meant to be 'hidden' but rather is a literary poetic device, somewhat akin to telling a complete story, as in the whole matter from A to Z.

Now the reader is likely more interested in the 'hidden' acrostics. Scripture is actually replete with them. For example, if we take the first letter of each patriarch from Adam to Terah and line them up, the following sentence in Hebrew is spelled out: *"I lift up those who rise against me. He pities; he bears those made from the year of dust."* And the acrostics continue similarly as the names go on. In Cain's line the first letter of each name from Adam to Jabal reads *"I take a people of them entirely for myself."* Now depending on how the words are divided up, the meaning can shift somewhat, but the messages are clearly there.

So the acrostics *are* there, but they take a great deal of time and wisdom to interpret. If the reader wishes to pursue these, please be very careful not to jump to conclusions, or fill in words and meanings that simply are not there, as a search on the internet will show is quite common. Scripture is not a crossword puzzle.

*   *   *

The **geometry** of numerics in scripture could fill several books. Here we will just touch on the subject to introduce the reader to the form of the subject.

Firstly there are geometries which are two-dimensional (flat) and geometries which are three-dimensional (solid). We saw in chapter six when we were examining the number 37 how that all the visible blocks in a 64-block cube at any one time yielded that number. The cube is probably the most straightforward of 3-D geometries, and the Rubik's Cube is a good model of the Hebrew alphabet or the Greek numbering system (which includes three symbols used for numbering but no longer being used as letters) . . .both having 27 pieces. The key to understanding it is to know which letters go where. We *could* just line them up in sequential order as follows:

But that is hardly symmetrical. Note the enormous disparity between the letter values of the top and bottom layers.

...The top layer adding up to 45, the middle layer to 450, and the bottom layer to 4,500. While this is nice and orderly in its own right, common sense would dictate that we arrange them in an order that leads to a more dynamic arrangement. For example, since we have spent so much time on the number **37**, let's look at the following 'magic square'. It has 36 squares numbered from 1 to 36 arranged as follows:

36 6	21↔16	29 3
31 1	15↔22	34 8
11 23	19 25	24 9
26 14	12 18	13 28
5 35	17↔20	4 30
2 32	27↔10	7 33

In this square, the total of every column, row, and diagonal is 111 (3 x **37**), each group of four totals 74 (2 x **37**), the perimeter totals 370 (10 x **37**), and each arrow pairs up two numbers that equal **37**. The reason this is being shown is to demonstrate that much more symmetry can be achieved by a careful arrangement of numbers (or letters).

Thus if we are going to arrange the letters of Greek or Hebrew into a three-dimensional shape, we need to consider carefully how to do it. If we were to take the 'magic square' above and draw a line from 1 to 2 to 3 and so on to 36, it would turn out looking like this:

208

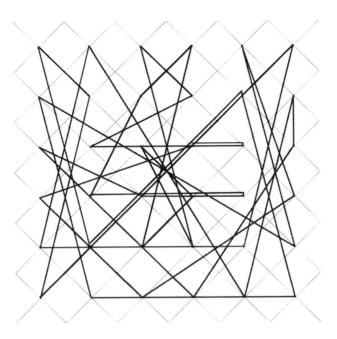

...which doesn't look very symmetrical at all. But let's look a bit closer and see what makes up this jumble of lines. First we shade in the obvious symmetries:

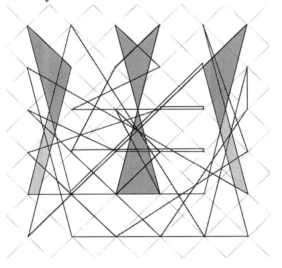

Then we remove all lines except those at 76°:

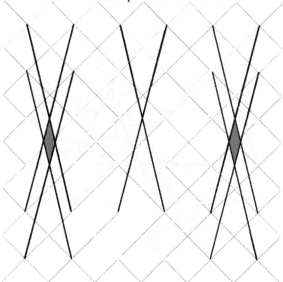

Or perhaps we take just the horizontal, vertical, and 45° lines:

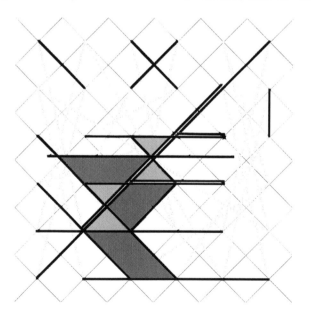

As you can see, we have a system of overlapping symmetries and compositions embedded in the square with many different patterns hidden in it:

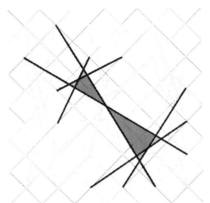

Furthermore, the patterns are working *with* the numbers. If we look at the number of the two ends of every 45° line, we find that each line counting from 1 is paired with a line equally distant counting backward from 36. So we have the line 2-3 paired with the line 34-35. Then 10-11 with 26-27, 15-16 with 21-22, and 18-19 taking up the middle.

The same goes for the horizontal lines: 4-5 is paired with 32-33, 12-13 with 24-25, and 13-14 with 23-24. All are equidistant from 1 and 36. The lines at 76° in the previous picture are an exception, yet their symmetry is found in *shape* whereas the *numerically* symmetrical horizontal, vertical and 45° lines make a non-symmetrical composition in shape, yet are symmetrical in *number.*

Now let us apply this to the Hebrew and Greek alphabets in three dimensions. We will go back to the cube with its blocks, and in this case use Hebrew because each letter, in addition to having a corresponding number like Greek, *also* has a unique meaning.

If we draw the alphabet as a path on a cube, the 'blocks' can be represented by the eight corners, twelve edges, six faces, and the center. This will give us our 27 places for letters. The two parameters we will use are (1) one unbroken line and (2) each of the six ancient letters (Aleph א , Hé ה , Vav ו , Het ח , Yod י , and Ayin ע) used as vowels before there were vowel points must land on one of the six faces. We will be using the five final forms (Kaf ך , Mem ם , Nun ן , Pe ף , and Tsadi ץ) to make the full 27. Here is the *only* way to make the path using our parameters:

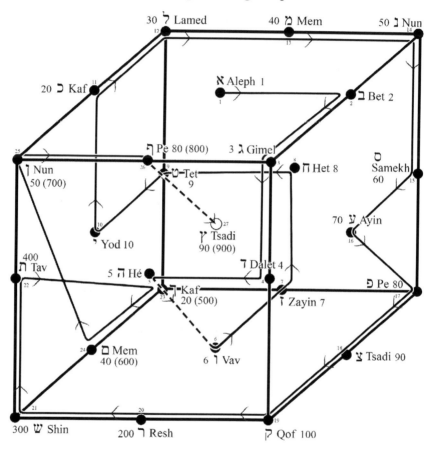

This arrangement turns out to have as many or more interesting features as the magic square we looked at. For one, the faces added together equal 100, and the faces with the center added together equal 1000. The corners with the center are 47×7^2, and the corners without the center are two primes, 43×41. The edges are completely opposite, being divisible by *all* of the following: 1, 2, 3, 4, 6, 8, 9, 12, 18, 24, 31, 36, 62, 72, 93, 124, 186, 248, 279, 372, 558, 744, and 1116. While the numbers are fascinating, let us move on to the actual meanings of each letter, and see what what this arrangement shows:

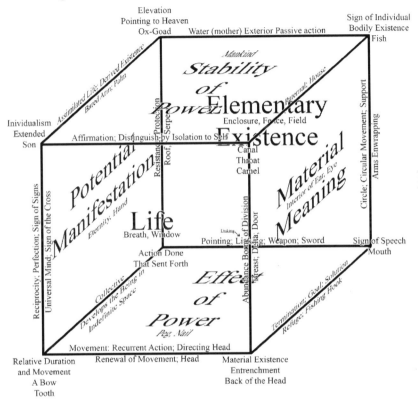

What we have done here is replace each letter with its meaning. Amazingly, the meanings line up with respect to one another. On one corner is *Material Existence, entrenchment* and on the opposite corner is *Elevation, pointing to heaven*. On the top face is *Stability of Power* and on the bottom face is *Effect of Power*. And so on. If we take the face on the right, *Material Meaning*, and look at the four edges and four corners surrounding it, they all relate to the idea of that which is material and physical. If we take the opposite face, *Potential Manifestation* and look at the corners

213

and edges surrounding it, they all relate to that which is ethereal. This is an example of a three-dimensional arrangement that works with the (1) geometry, (2) numerics, and (3) meanings.

So we have an introduction to the subject of geometry; it is vast. We might note before moving on that most flat charts and diagrams that yield good results are actually three-dimensional constructs that have been 'unfolded', or in some cases simply 'flattened' for the sake of being able to represent them in a drawing. The real value is when we find how to expand them back out into three dimensions, for it is there that the hidden relationships spring into life.

Now how does all this help us to understand the work of Panin? As far as we know, he did not draw shapes for his numerics, flat or otherwise. Yet there is a certain genius to his work because he *included every phenomena possible*. Thus he was covering the whole 'cube' by dint of excluding nothing. ELS or Acrostics can only take one so far; they are like one or two edges of the cube. Panin did not limit himself to one method; he explored them all. And as such, he was able to comprehensively get a sense of the Scriptures from a variety of vantage points. If the number of letters was in doubt, he would look at the forms of the words. If the forms of the words were in doubt, he would look at the dates. And so on.

There is a certain point as one immerses one's self into a subject when it becomes *internalized*. It is like learning a language; we struggle and struggle with the vocabulary and grammar . . .then one day it 'clicks'. We actually *enjoy* speaking the new language and learning more, and it is no longer a task. It even gets into our dreams. We become excited about it. The trouble is that our new-found joy is almost impossible to communicate with those who have never experienced the language. So what is one to do at this point?

214

What is useful at this point, and what Ivan Panin did, is to *translate* for the untaught something from the new language into theirs. Panin learned numerics so well that it was impossible for him to communicate even a small part of his discoveries. So what did he do? He diligently transcribed from Numerics into both the Greek of the New Testament and into an English version. We have those both today, and they are masterpieces of the highest caliber. His English version is not only accurate as far as which words belong and which ones do not, but it is also the most accurate word-for-word translation in English that we have. His experience as a Literary Critic, when turned from secular literature to Scripture, served to produce one of the finest English translations available for the last 100 years.

Appendix IV

The Secret Behind
Primes and Decimals

Decimal numbers can be confusing. They just go on and on and often seem random. Let's demystify them, then see how Scripture treats them.

Suppose you were measuring a board that was 16 feet long and needed to be divided evenly into seven pieces. So you figure out that 16 feet is 192 inches. You get your calculator out, divide 192 by seven, and it gives you 27.428571 428571 428571...

You notice that that remainder won't go away. Even when you add 428571 to itself, you get the following results:

$$.428571\ 428571\ 428571\ 428571...\ \text{plus itself equals:}$$
$$.8571\ 428571\ 428571\ 428571...\ \text{plus } .428571...\ \text{equals:}$$
$$1.28571\ 428571\ 428571\ 428571...\ \text{plus } .428571...\ \text{equals:}$$
$$1.71\ 428571\ 428571\ 428571\ 428571...\ \text{plus } .428571...\ \text{equals:}$$
$$2.1\ 428571\ 428571\ 428571\ 428571...\ \text{plus } .428571...\ \text{equals:}$$
$$2.571\ 428571\ 428571\ 428571\ 428571...\ \text{plus } .428571...\ \text{equals:}$$
$$3.0$$

...and so on, coming out to an even number every seventh step, which is what you would expect when adding $1/7$th's together. However, the continuity of the remainder is odd. **To make this point very simple, decimals are never random.** Furthermore, they are loaded with secrets.

Next step: find out if this is true for all numbers divided by seven. It is.

216

$$1/_7 = .1\ 428571\ 428571\ 428571...$$
$$2/_7 = .28571\ 428571\ 428571$$
$$3/_7 = .428571\ 428571\ 428571...$$
$$4/_7 = .571\ 428571\ 428571...$$
$$5/_7 = .71\ 428571\ 428571...$$
$$6/_7 = .8571\ 428571\ 428571...$$
$$7/_7 = 1$$
$$8/_7 = 1.1\ 428571\ 428571\ 428571...$$
$$9/_7 = 1.28571\ 428571\ 428571...$$
$$10/_7 = 1.\ 428571\ 428571\ 428571...$$
$$11/_7 = 1.571\ 428571\ 428571...$$

So we see that **7**, when put into a decimal expression. always breaks down using the same proportions; it maintains its identity no matter what. It even does strange things when we take any length of a string of numbers from the series and add all six of the possible starting points:

42	428	4285	42857	428571
28	285	2857	28571	285714
85	857	8571	85714	857142
57	571	5714	57142	571428
71	714	7142	71428	714285
14	142	1428	14285	142857
297	**2,997**	**29,997**	**299,997**	**2,999,997**

That last, **2,999,997** is **2079** x **1443**. Here are two sets of scriptures with these values; notice how their messages relate:

2079 My fruit is better than gold, yea, than fine gold; and my revenue than choice silver. **Proverbs 8:19**

1443 I am my beloved's, and his desire is toward me. **Song of Solomon 7:10**

2079 For he shall not much remember the days of his life; because God answers him with the joy of his heart. **Ecclesiastes 5:20**

<u>**1443**</u> Yea, you will see your children's children, and peace upon Israel. **Psalm 128:6**

If we would take the middle column that adds up to **29,997** and see what scriptures each of those six numbers equal, we would find that as above, each number has its own flavor. Here we will give one example: the top number, **4285** is about **vengeance**:

<u>**4285**</u> And Jehovah said to him, Therefore whoever slays Cain, vengeance shall be taken on him sevenfold. And Jehovah set a mark on Cain, lest any finding him should kill him. **Genesis 4:15**
<u>**4285**</u> And when Joseph's brothers saw that their father was dead, they said, Joseph will peradventure hate us, and will certainly requite us all the evil which we did to him. **Genesis 50:15**

Likewise each number has its own theme. But let us move on.

Next step, find out if this is true of any other numbers under 10. It isn't; they break down evenly (1,2,4,5,8) or indeterminably (3,6,9).

$$^{10}/_1 = 10$$
$$^{10}/_2 = 5$$
$$^{10}/_3 = 3.3333333...$$
$$^{10}/_4 = 2.5$$
$$^{10}/_5 = 2$$
$$^{10}/_6 = 1.6666666...$$
$$^{10}/_7 = 1.428571\ 428571\ 428571\ 428571...$$
$$^{10}/_8 = 1.25$$
$$^{10}/_9 = 1.1111111...$$

Next step, find any other numbers with the same characteristics as **7**, dividing this time into 100.

We find that **11** is strange; check it out on a calculator. Every two consecutive digits add up to nine. You can explore that one; let us move on to **13**:

218

$^{1}/_{13}$ = .076923 076923 076923 076923...
$^{2}/_{13}$ = .153846 153846 153846...
$^{3}/_{13}$ =   .23 076923 076923 076923...
$^{4}/_{13}$ =   3 076923 076923 076923...
$^{5}/_{13}$ =   3846 153846 153846...
$^{6}/_{13}$ =.   46 153846 153846...
$^{7}/_{13}$ = .53846 153846 153846...
$^{8}/_{13}$ =   .6 153846 153846...
$^{9}/_{13}$ =.   6923 076923 076923 076923...
$^{10}/_{13}$ = .76923 076923 076923 076923...
$^{11}/_{13}$ =   .846 153846 153846...
$^{12}/_{13}$ =   .923 076923 076923 076923...
$^{13}/_{13}$ = 1

13 uses a series of 6 repeating decimals, just like **7**, only it uses _two_ sets of them, and the way they are arranged is symmetrical (where the line is drawn) around the midpoint. Curious.

Taking 10/13 (**7692**) and 7/13 (**5384**) which are the second in each series, we find the following verses are all about the subject of hidden things:

5384 I have not <u>hid</u> your righteousness within my heart; I have declared your faithfulness and your salvation: I have not concealed your lovingkindness and your truth from the great congregation. **Psalm 40:10**

5384 And though they <u>hide</u> themselves in the top of Carmel, I will search and take them out thence; and though they be <u>hid</u> from my sight in the bottom of the sea, there will I command the serpent, and he shall bite them **Amos 9:3**

5384 But Jonathan Saul's son delighted much in David: and Jonathan told David, saying, Saul my father seeks to kill you: now therefore, I pray you, take heed to yourself until the morning, and abide in a secret place, and <u>hide yourself</u>. **First Samuel 19:2**

5384 But he that prophesies speaks to men to edification, and exhortation, and comfort. **First Corinthians 14:3** [Contrasted with the *hidden* things of the gift of tongues.]

7692 But if you had known what this means, I will have mercy, and not sacrifice, you would not have condemned the guiltless. **Matthew 12:7** [The meaning of the scriptures *hidden* from the Pharisees.]

7692 For as a snare shall it come on all them that dwell on the face of the whole earth. **Luke 21:35** [Time of the end *hidden* from those that dwell on the earth.]

That is one example of the many we could explore there. A this point we realize that only prime numbers have this characteristic, so let us go to **17**.

$1/17 =$ .0588235294117647	0588235294117647	058...	**First**
$2/17 =$ .117647	0588235294117647	058...	Eleventh
$3/17 =$ .17647	0588235294117647	058...	Twelfth
$4/17 =$ .235294117647	0588235294117647	058...	Fifth
$5/17 =$ .294117647	0588235294117647	058...	Eighth
$6/17 =$ .35294117647	0588235294117647	058...	Sixth
$7/17 =$ .4117647	0588235294117647	058...	Tenth
$8/17 =$ .47	0588235294117647	058...	Fifteenth
$9/17 =$ .5294117647	0588235294117647	058...	Seventh
$10/17 =$ .588235294117647	0588235294117647	058...	**Second**
$11/17 =$ .647	0588235294117647	058...	Fourteenth
$12/17 =$ .7	0588235294117647	058...	Sixteenth
$13/17 =$ .7647	0588235294117647	058...	Thirteenth
$14/17 =$ .8235294117647	0588235294117647	058...	Fourth
$15/17 =$ .88235294117647	0588235294117647	058...	**Third**
$16/17 =$ .94117647	0588235294117647	058...	Ninth
$17/17 = 1$			

...Giving us a string of **16** repeating decimals, unlike **7** or **13**, which both used a string of **6**. Note the order that is written out at the end of each line. If we were to fill in a 'magic square' in the exact order given (**First, Eleventh, Twelfth, Fifth,** etc. going down from the top) we would get the following:

1	11	12	5
8	6	10	15
7	2	14	16
13	4	3	9

...which is *almost* a magic square. The columns going across equal 29, 23, 39, 45. The rows going down equal 29, 39, 39, 29. Each diagonal equals 30. Now it is not difficult to make a magic square, so what is the hidden message in the number **17** here?

Combining the sums of the rows and columns, we have (1) **2923**, (2) **3945**, (3) **2939**, and (4) **3929**. The fact that it does not make a true 'magic square' gives us, instead of all the same number, four distinct numbers. Their respective meanings are (1) *Facing the task at hand*, (2) *Preparation for blessing*, (3) *Initiations and Presentations*, and (4) *Reflection*. Let's look at the verses whose values are the same as these four numbers.

Verses equaling **<u>2923</u>** *Facing the Task at Hand*
Six days shall you labor, and do all your work. **Exodus 20:9**
And the land will yield her fruit, and you will eat your fill, and dwell in it in safety. **Leviticus 25:19**
And they set them up images and groves in every high hill, and under every green tree. **Second Kings 17:10**
Jehovah will be terrible to them: for he will famish all the gods of the earth; and men will worship him, every one from his place, even all the isles of the heathen. **Zephaniah 2:11**
Surely the wrath of man will praise you: the remainder of wrath will you restrain. **Psalm 76:10**
And the princes of Succoth said, Are the hands of Zebah and Zalmunna now in your hand, that we should give bread to your army? **Judges 8:6**

Then came in the magicians, the astrologers, the Chaldeans, and the soothsayers: and I told the dream before them; but they did not make known to me the interpretation of it. **Daniel 4:9**

Verses equaling **<u>3945</u>** *Preparation for Blessing*
With your wisdom and with your understanding you hast gotten you riches, and have gotten gold and silver into your treasures. **Ezekiel 28:4**
You love righteousness, and hate wickedness: therefore God, your God, has anointed you with the oil of gladness above your fellows. **Psalm 45:7**
The oath which he swore to our father Abraham, **Luke 1:73**
And Esther answered, If it seem good to the king, let the king and Haman come this day to the banquet that I have prepared for him. **Esther 5:4**
So Moab was subdued that day under the hand of Israel. And the land had rest eighty years. **Judges 3:30**
And Jacob their father said unto them, Me have you bereaved: Joseph is not, and Simeon is not, and you will take Benjamin away: all these things are against me. **Genesis 42:36**

Verses equaling **<u>2939</u>** *Initiations and Presentations*
Come now therefore, and I will send you unto Pharaoh, that you may bring forth my people the children of Israel out of Egypt. **Exodus 3:10**
And set him before Eleazar the priest, and before all the congregation; and give him a charge in their sight. **Numbers 27:19**
Only he shall not go in unto the veil, nor come near unto the altar, because he has a blemish; that he profane not my sanctuaries: for I Jehovah do sanctify them. **Leviticus 21:23**
And Michal Saul's daughter loved David: and they told Saul, and the thing pleased him. **First Samuel 18:20**
And the angel of Jehovah went further, and stood in a narrow place, where was no way to turn either to the right hand or to the left. **Numbers 22:26**

And the man Micah had a house of gods, and made and ephod, and teraphim, and consecrated one of his sons, who became his priest. **Judges 17:5**

But I wrought for my name's sake, that it should not be polluted before the heathen, in whose sight I brought them out. **Ezekiel 20:14**

And it will come to pass in that day, says Jehovah, that there will be the noise of a cry from the fish gate, and a howling from the second, and a great crashing from the hills. **Zephaniah 1:10**

Verse equaling <u>**3929**</u> *Reflection*
A voice was heard upon the high places, weeping and supplications of the children of Israel: for they have perverted their way, and they have forgotten Jehovah their God. **Jeremiah 3:21**

So we find that scripture is consistent with decimal patterns. Let us continue our exploration and look at **19**.

$1/19 =$ .05263157894 736842105263157894 7368...
$2/19 =$ .105263157894 736842105263157894 7368...
$3/19 =$ .157894 736842105263157894 7368...
$4/19 =$ .2105263157894 736842105263157894 7368...
$5/19 =$ .263157894 736842105263157894 7368...
$6/19 =$ .3157894 736842105263157894 7368...
$7/19 =$ .36842105263157894 736842105263157894 7368...
$8/19 =$ .42105263157894 736842105263157894 7368...
$9/19 =$ .4 736842105263157894 7368...
$10/19 =$. 5263157894 736842105263157894 7368...
$11/19 =$ .57894 736842105263157894 7368...
$12/19 =$ .63157894 736842105263157894 7368...
$13/19 =$ .6842105263157894 736842105263157894 7368...
$14/19 =$ .736842105263157894 736842105263157894 7368...
$15/19 =$ .7894 736842105263157894 7368...
$16/19 =$ .842105263157894 736842105263157894 7368...
$17/19 =$ .894 736842105263157894 7368...

$^{18}/_{19} =$ .94 736842105263157894 7368...

$^{19}/_{19} = 1$

...Giving us a string of **18** repeating decimals, unlike **7** and **13** who use a string of **6**, but just like **17**, which uses a string of one less than itself (which possibly makes **7** part of the category of **17** and **19**, as it uses a string of 6, one less than itself.)

If we were to do **23** and **29** here, we would find that they both have repeating strings that are one less than themselves. However, **31** has a surprise for us:

$^{1}/_{31} =$ .032258064516129 0322580645..	1	
$^{2}/_{31} =$ .064516129 0322580645...	7	
$^{3}/_{31} =$ *.0 9677419354...*		*(15)*
$^{4}/_{31} =$ .129 0322580645....	13	
$^{5}/_{31} =$ .16129 0322580645...	11	
$^{6}/_{31} =$ *.1935483870 9677419354...*		*(6)*
$^{7}/_{31} =$ .2258064516129 0322580645...	3	
$^{8}/_{31} =$ .258064516129 0322580645...	4	
$^{9}/_{31} =$ .29 0322580645...	14	
$^{10}/_{31} =$ .32258064516129 0322580645...	2	
$^{11}/_{31} =$ *.35483870 9677419354...*		*(8)*
$^{12}/_{31} =$ *.3870 9677419354...*		*(12)*
$^{13}/_{31} =$ *.41935483870 9677419354...*		*(5)*
$^{14}/_{31} =$ .4516129 0322580645...	9	
$^{15}/_{31} =$ *.483870 9677419354...*		*(10)*
$^{16}/_{31} =$ .516129 0322580645...	10	
$^{17}/_{31} =$ *.5483870 9677419354...*		*(9)*
$^{18}/_{31} =$ .58064516129 0322580645...	5	
$^{19}/_{31} =$ .6129 0322580645...	12	
$^{20}/_{31} =$ .64516129 0322580645...	8	
$^{21}/_{31} =$ *.67741935483870 9677419354...*		*(2)*
$^{22}/_{31} =$ *.70 9677419354...*		*(14)*
$^{23}/_{31} =$ *.741935483870 9677419354...*		*(4)*
$^{24}/_{31} =$ *.7741935483870 9677419354...*		*(3)*

224

$^{25}/_{31} =$	.8064516129 0322580645...	6
$^{26}/_{31} =$	*.83870 9677419354...*	*(11)*
$^{27}/_{31} =$	*.870 9677419354...*	*(13)*
$^{28}/_{31} =$	.9 0322580645...	15
$^{29}/_{31} =$	*.935483870 9677419354...*	*(7)*
$^{30}/_{31} =$	*.967741935483870 9677419354...*	*(1)*
$^{31}/_{31} = 1$		

Again, just as the number **13**, there are *two* sets of repeating decimals; and these are in a symmetrical pattern around the center line. Curiouser and curiouser.

We are discovering that there is a symmetry in the decimal equivalents of prime numbers that is not there in other numbers. Now why would that be significant? And what happens when we continue to examine these with more primes? And why should **13** and **31** double up their decimal strings, while **17**, **23**, and **29** do not? And what is the relationship between the two strings in **29**? Or the two strings in **13**?

Well, let's add the strings from 31; **967741935483870** to **032258064516129**; we get **999999999999999**. And if we go back to the two strings for the number **13**, we find that any two symmetrical numbers folded around the center line equal **999999**. This also works for the folding line in 31. But like number folds with like with 13, and unlike folds with unlike on 31. Again, curious.

So let's look at the internal symmetry in **17**, **23**, and **29**. There is only one string to deal with, and we find that any two strings we add up that are symmetrical around the folding line add up to all 9's. This, of course, is no big deal; it is simply telling us that $^{11}/_{23}$rds plus $^{12}/_{23}$rds equal $^{23}/_{23}$rds. But what an odd order to put these into!

Consider this order; take the string 0588235294117647 from $^{1}/_{17}$.

225

Divide it into two parts, 05882352 and 94117647. Add them together and we get 99999999. Somewhat surprising. Here is the string from $1/23$... it is **0434782608695652173913**. This means cutting it neatly in half, and adding **04347826086** to **95652173913**. Sure enough, **99999999999**.

Do the double strings from **13** and **31** do this? $1/13 = $ **076923**. **076** + **923** = **999**. $2/13 = $ **153846**. . . **153** + **846** = **999**.

Does every string , no matter where it starts, equal all nines? Yes it does. For example, $5/17 = $ **2941176470588235**. Divvy it up into **29411764** and **70588235** and we've got all nines again

At this point, prime number decimals are looking a *lot* like a game of Sudoku. *Everything*, no matter how you add it, has to equal 9. All we have to do is figure out what order they are in, and we're home free.

Well, we know that the *length* of the decimal string will either be the prime number minus one, or half the prime number minus one. So the question is, what path is the order following?

When we *draw* the path, we see it's quite symmetrical. For the number **29**, make a clock with **29** numbers (yes, it's tricky; each number is 12° 24' 49.66" apart). Then take the far right number and line it up with the number on the far left. So we would start by putting the **1** on the clock inside the **1**. The **2** is at $10/29$, so you'd put the **2** inside the clock's **10**, and draw a line from **1** to **10** on the clock. The **3** is across from $13/29$, so we would put the **3** inside the clock's **13**, and draw a line from **10** to **13**. Once we have all the lines drawn, we can see that the shape the order makes is perfectly symmetrical, and more than a little strange. (**29**'s order is not listed above; look at **31** or **17** chart for examples of the order of where the decimal starts.)

This is a good way to get a visual of the prime numbers. But knowing they're symmetrical still doesn't tell us what exactly is going on. The **29-order** goes in the following sequence: **1, 12, 28, 23, 19, 11, 21, 6, 27, 2, 24, 22, 3, 4, 18, 17, 8, 10, 16, 13, 20, 7, 25, 5, 9, 14, 26, 15, 29,** and back to **1.** One of the 'symmetries' in the pattern has been shaded in.

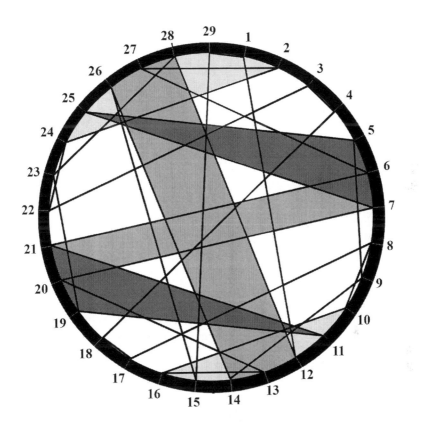

1. The 29 "Clock" of the Order of Decimal Places

The reason for seeing that there are visible patterns in prime number decimal sequences is that there are also patterns in Bible letter sequences. Suppose we made a **24-clock** with the **24 letters** of the Greek alphabet, and followed the sequence of letters in a verse similarly. It is a great deal easier to draw a **24-clock** than a

In this case, let us take the first verse of the Gospel of John. It says, *"Εν αρχη ην ὁ λογος, και ὁ λογος ην προς τον Θεον, και Θεος ην ὁ λογος. Οὑτος ην εν αρχη προς τον Θεον."* Following those letters in order produces the following 'clock':

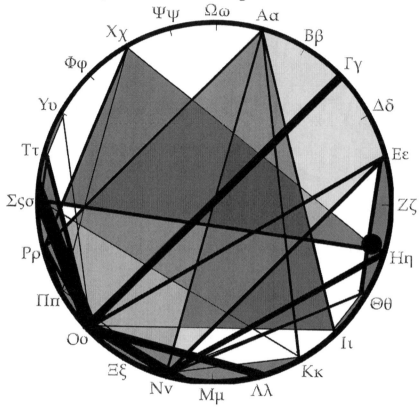

2. The 24 "Clock" of John 1:1-2

There are many symmetries here, and the overall structure is quite symmetrical even without analysis. The "clock" is made of the letters Alpha through Omega, and the progression of the text of John 1:1-2 traces the continuous line inside the circle. Where the line retraces itself, it is drawn beside the previous line to show the repetition. Note that there are only four lines (K-Σ, O-I, H-Π, and K-N) which are not doubled up. The first verse of Mark is quite different:

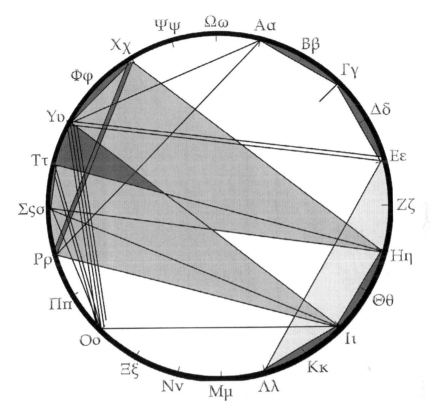

3. The 24 "Clock" of Mark 1:1

One of the symmetry configurations has been shaded in. Where there is a short line sticking out at Gamma (**Γγ**), it means the letter is doubled; in this case the word for "gospel".

As we can see, just as in Nature symmetries abound, and do so by geometry and mathematics, so also Numbers abound with their own patterns, as we have been seeing with the decimal patterns of prime numbers. In the same way, Scripture abounds with natural patterns. All four of these; **Nature**, **Numbers**, **Geometry**, and **Scripture** have patterns so complex and beautiful that it is evident that there is far more than the human mind involved.

Since we're on a roll here, let's look at Matthew:

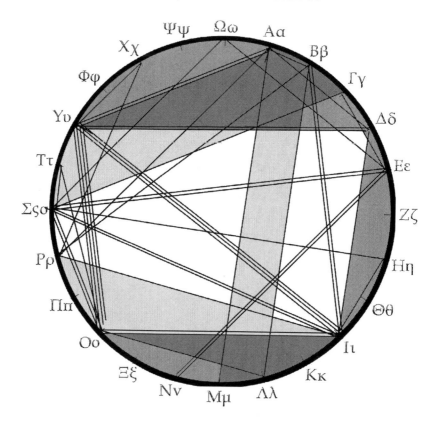

4. The 24 "Clock" of Matthew 1:1

Like the 'magic square' of Appendix III, initially it seems very confusing; not because there is no pattern but because there are *too many* patterns interweaving and interlocked. Like nature or mathematics, they must be carefully sifted through and analyzed. The shading on the above figure is merely one of dozens of ways to begin to see that there is an enormously intricate system of geometry laid out here. Altogether there are five sets of *two* parallel lines, one set of *three* parallel lines, and two sets of *four*. This makes **21 (3 x 7)** parallel lines altogether. In total, there are only ten lines in the entire construct that are not parallel with any other.

Now Luke has a comparatively lengthy introduction, and it can get somewhat involved. Here it is:

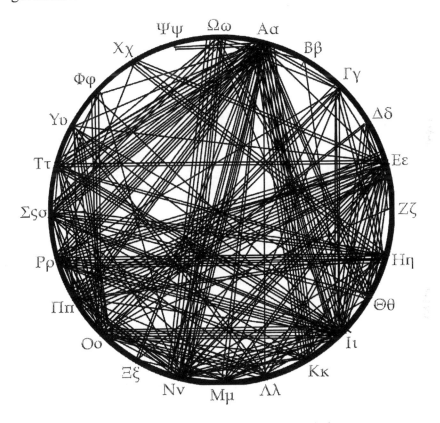

5. The 24 "Clock" of Luke 1:1-4

Because this one is so lengthy the method of using the same line and making it proportionally thicker is applied to it in the next picture. It is a way to see the *character* without getting bogged down in the geometry.

:

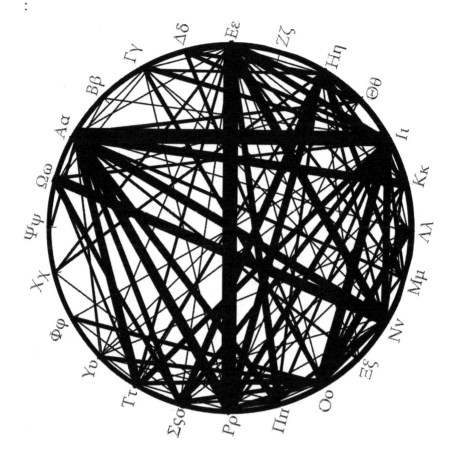

6. The 24 "Clock" of Luke 1:1-4

This one can be somewhat unsettling; it certainly is powerful. It has been turned 75° counterclockwise

This brings up an somewhat important point. If we were examining a Japanese garden, we could take a magnifying glass and a notebook, and carefully look over every detail and write down the name and parts of the plants. This is somewhat what we have been doing with Numeric analysis. But it is also nice to step back, take a breath, and look around at the whole panorama. This is what we mean by the character and flavor of a phenomena; and it helps enormously to have a visual. Here is the 'flavor' of First John 1:1...

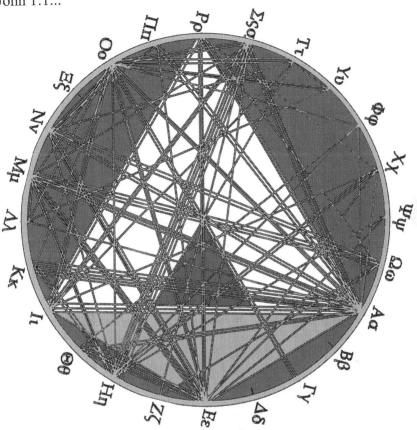

7. The 24 "Clock" of First John 1:1

Note how it is significantly different from the first verse of his Gospel, yet is still recognizable as having a distinct flavor from the other writers. It is like when one hears a piece of music for the first time, the composer or artist can still be identified. This is the beauty of Scripture; its depth and its delicacy.

Let's look at a few more from John. This next one is the last verse of his Second Epistle, "The children of your elect sister salute you." It is turned sideways to emphasize the particular symmetry that has been shaded in.

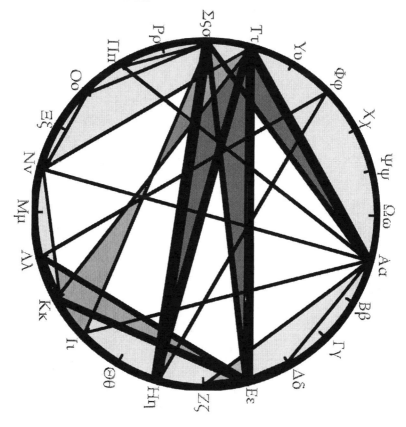

8. The 24 "Clock" of Second John 1:13

This one is loaded with beautiful symmetries; just one has been pointed out with the shading. John seems to fire away a salvo from select point, and then overlay as series of calming cross-lines. Matthew is very structured, and Mark has a flair for creativity.

Now before we go too much farther, just exactly what are we

looking for in these patterns? Anyone can color shapes into random lines; is this exercise actually demonstrating anything?

For example, if we take **John 1:4** and begin to shade in some of the symmetries, it quickly gets too complex; even with such a short verse, there are simply too many. So our first attempt. . .

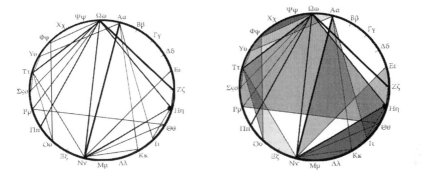

. . .comes out somewhat cluttered. So we slow down and begin to concentrate on one symmetry at a time.

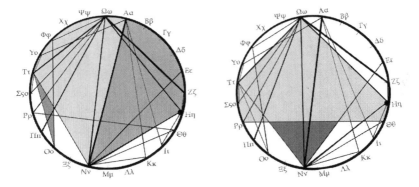

Okay, this is a bit easier to visualize. On the left we have triangles symmetrical *within* the clock, on the right we have a triangle that, while symmetrical, does not respect the borders. What else do we have?

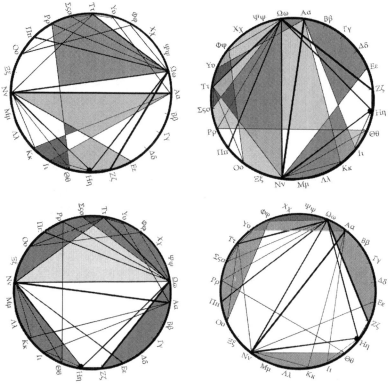

Even though these are merely showing a few symmetrical "X's", (and a triangle) on top, and borders on the bottom, they are already getting complex. All of these have been turned slightly.

What we are looking for are **symmetrical shapes, symmetrical compositions,** and **bands** (made by two parallel lines). This one has no bands; figures **1, 4,** and **12** have some good ones. Now there is no need to clutter up our pictures with mathematical formulas, yet all symmetries can be identified mathematically from the verses without having to actually draw them . . .even though drawing them is much more fun. So yes, we can sort through the scriptures and find **shapes, compositions, and bands** mathematically, all of which are evidence of intelligent design.

236

This next one will be First John. the last verse; "Little children, guard yourselves from the idols."

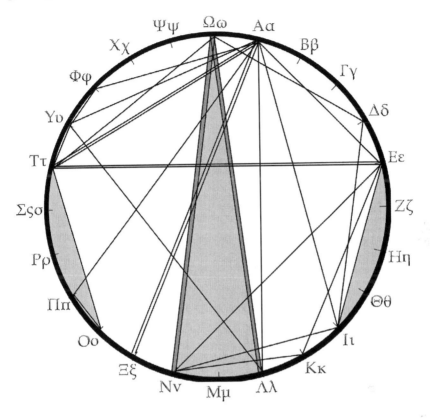

9. The 24 "Clock" of First John 5:21

Again, this one is loaded. And it is *definitely* John. Again, his 'flavor' is a few select points from which a burst of lines spread out, and an additional layer of compositionally calming lines that settle the picture's dynamics into a single powerful theme. It is useful and a relief to have Panin's Geek Text from which to work; many of the less thoroughly researched critical texts produce 'clocks' that are somewhat insufficient for visually appreciating the Word.

Here is the last verse of Matthew; "And lo, I am with you all the days till the consummation of the age." Matthew seems to come up with patterns that either feature a large trapezoids (figure **4**) or a mishmash of long sharp triangles.

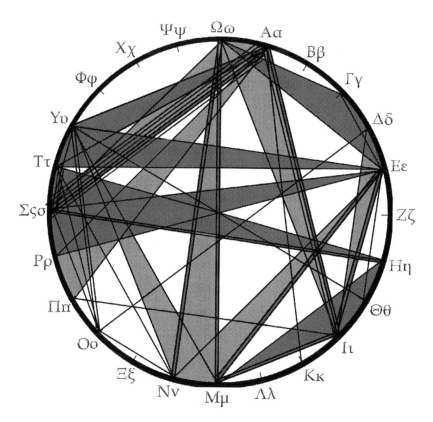

10. The 24 "Clock" of the Last Verse of Matthew

The dynamics are readily apparent. Now bear in mind as we go through these that they are *two-dimensional* representations of these verses. A three-dimensional depiction would be preferable, but somewhat difficult. We have seen in Appendix III how this might be approached; yet the 'Rubik's Cube' approach is not ideal for an alphabet that uses only 24 letters. There are 27 positions on the Cube, so three positions would always be empty. Three-dimensional geometries take time and patience to understand properly.

Let's look at two more from Matthew; a 'trapezoid' one, and a 'dynamic' one with his long sharp triangles. Here is Matthew 20:16 *"Thus the last shall be first, and the first last."*

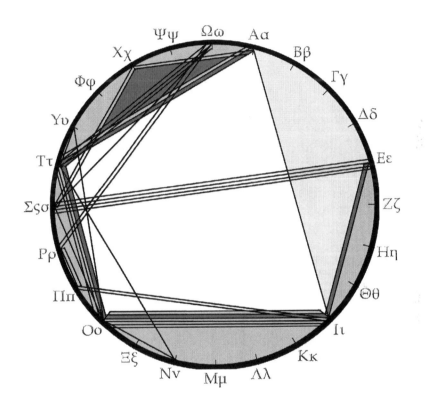

11. The 24 "Clock" of Matthew 20:16

And we see he has produced another Trapezoid. To finish up with Matthew, let's look at a verse from chapter 6 verse 27, *"And which of you by being anxious can add one cubit to his age?"*

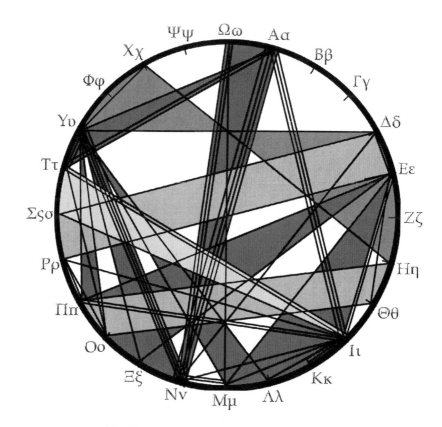

12. The 24 "Clock" of Matthew 6:27

The two on the following page round out **Mark**; they are:

Mark 13:37 *"And what I say to you I say to all, Watch."*

and

Mark 9:16 *"And he asked them, What question you with them?"*

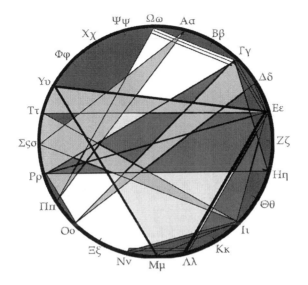

13. The 24 "Clock" of Mark 13:37

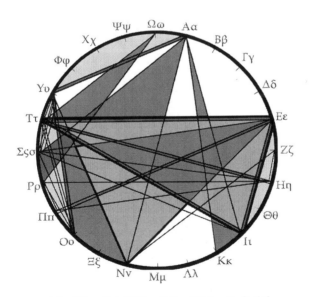

14. The 24 "Clock" of Mark 9:16

Moving on to Luke, here are two: **Luke 18:27** *"The things impossible with men are possible with God."* and **Luke 24:16** *"But their eyes were held that they should not know him."*

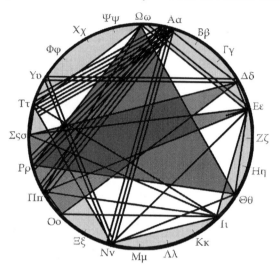

15. The 24 "Clock" of Luke 18:27

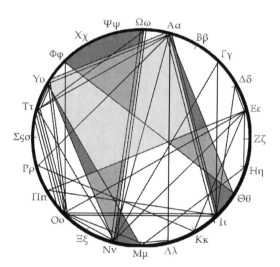

16. The 24 "Clock" of Luke 26:14

One of our last ones from John's writings; here is **Revelation 2:25** *"Nevertheless, what you have hold fast until I come."* Note that there are many symmetries there that have not been shaded. From this picture on, we have used proportionally thicker lines to show retraced paths rather than multiple lines as previously.

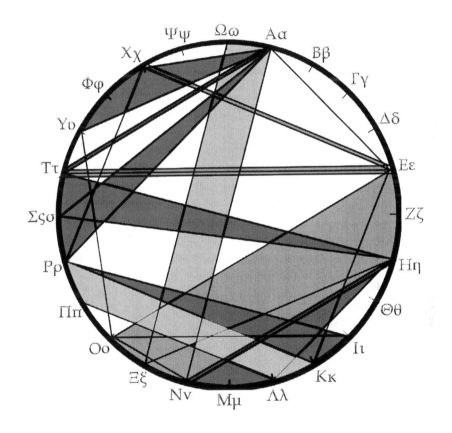

17. The 24 "Clock" of Revelation 2:25

And we might be remiss without including the last verse in the Bible, "The Grace of our Lord Jesus Christ be with the saints."

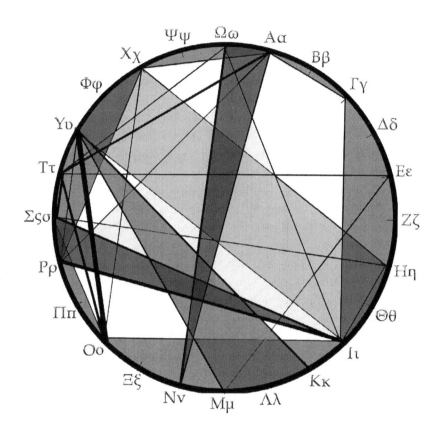

18. The 24 "Clock" of Revelation 22:21

Turning then to Paul's writings, we can see an entirely different 'flavor' of design produced. Paul was a prolific writer despite his weak eyes; here is the verse from **First Corinthians 15:21** that reads, *"For since by man is death, by man is also resurrection of the dead."*

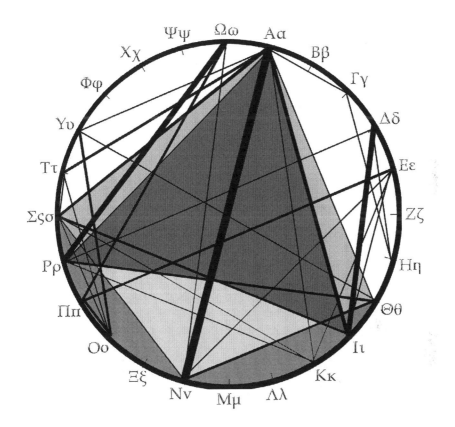

19. The 24 "Clock" of First Corinthians 15:21

Here is **Second Thessalonians 3:17** *"The Greeting of me Paul with my own hand."*

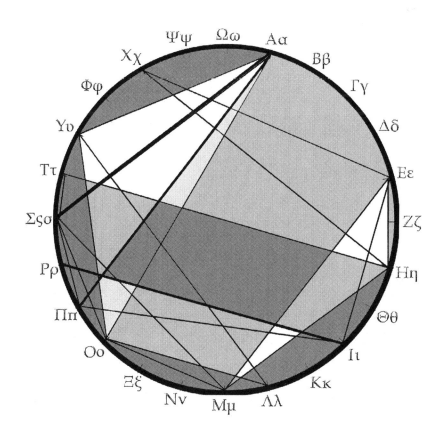

20. The 24 "Clock" of Second Thessalonians 3:17

And looking at **Jude**, here is **verse 2** of his one-chapter Epistle:
"Mercy to you and peace and love be multiplied."

It has been turned 15° clockwise for this pattern's clarity.

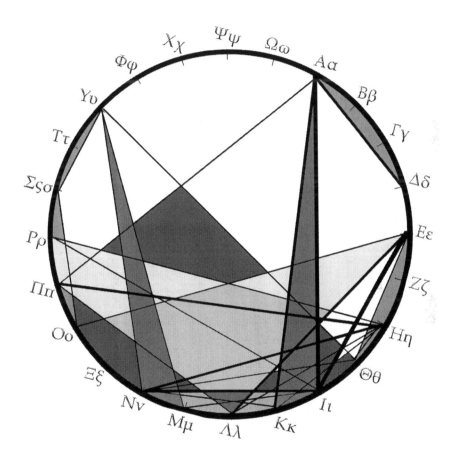

21. The 24 "Clock" of Jude 1:2

Moving on to **James**, for some reason his verses always come out looking rather picturesque. This first one is **James 5:7** *"Be patient therefore, brethren, until the presence of the Lord."*

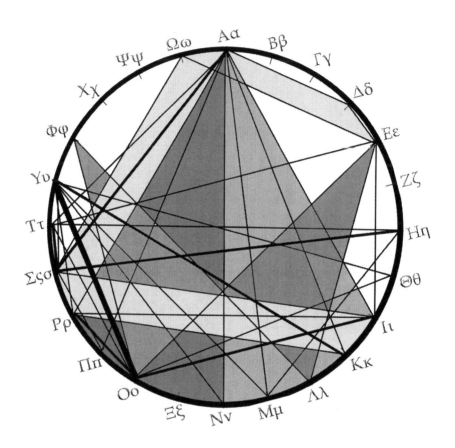

22. The 24 "Clock" of James 5:7

This one has been rotated 15° counterclockwise for this pattern's clarity. It is very unusual to get three sets of parallel lines, especially equally sized to the space between two companion letters.

This one is **James 2:19** "You believe that God is one; you do well: the demons also believe, and shudder."

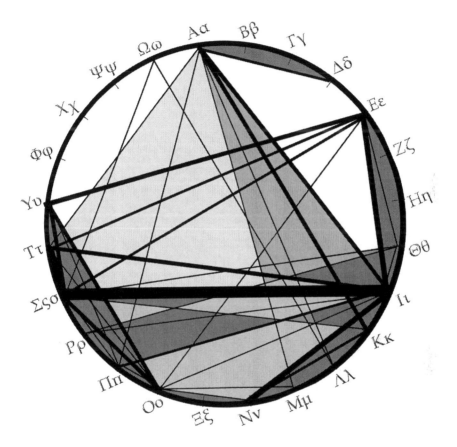

23. The 24 "Clock" of James 2:19

There are loads of patterns in this one; we couldn't resist the pyramid image. This has been rotated 22.5° counterclockwise.

Here is First Peter 1:8 *"Whom not seeing you love; on whom, though now you see him not..."*

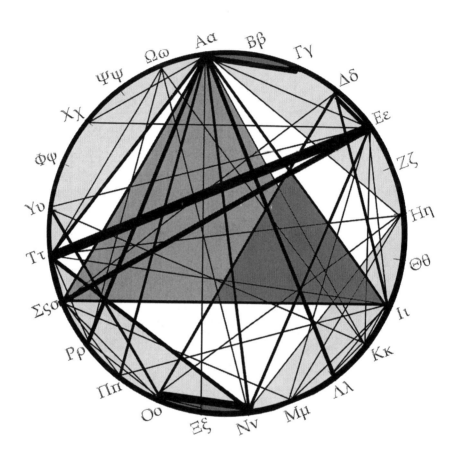

24. The 24 "Clock" of First Peter 1:8

Again, we have rotated the clock 22.5° counterclockwise. The great white square is most unusual.

250

And here is Second Peter 3:18 *"But grow in grace and knowledge of our Lord and Savior Jesus Christ."*

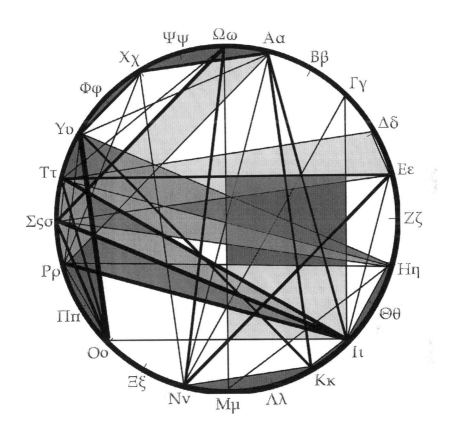

25. The 24 "Clock" of Second Peter 3:18

Of the New Testament writers, this leaves only the book of Hebrews, which was likely written by Timothy (see *The Jonas Genre* in the Bibliography; it's a good read and very thorough). At any rate, here is **Hebrews 12:29** *"For our God is indeed a consuming fire."*

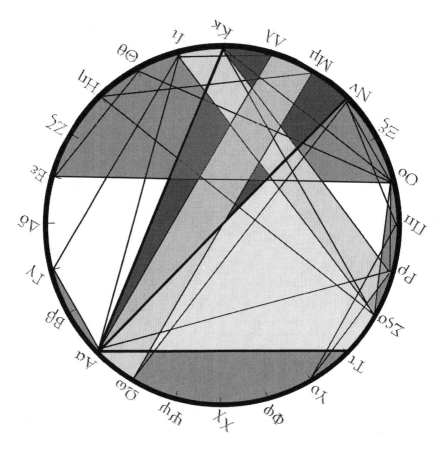

26. The 24 "Clock" of Hebrews 12:29

This image has been turned 150° counterclockwise.

252

This is **Hebrews 13:8** *"Jesus Christ the same yesterday and today, and to the ages."*

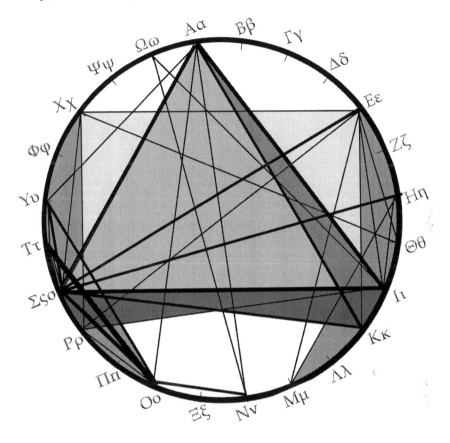

27. The 24 "Clock" of Hebrews 13:8

The image is turned 22.5° counterclockwise.

Now we started this exploration by noting that **Prime Number Decimals** occurred in a strange order, yet upon examination, they were found to have remarkable internal **symmetries**. For **figure 1** we made a 'clock' divided into **29** sections (12.414° each) and drew a line that depicted the order of decimal places. We then saw that Scripture is similarly set up; the sentences, when put into a **24 section clock**, produce rather remarkable designs. Now we turn from the Greek New Testament and look briefly at the Hebrew Old Testament. This is tricky because now we need a **27-section clock** *and* a **22-section clock**. The first is for the letters with the **5 final forms** and the second leaves them out. Both systems are used depending on the application and aptitude of the person investigating.

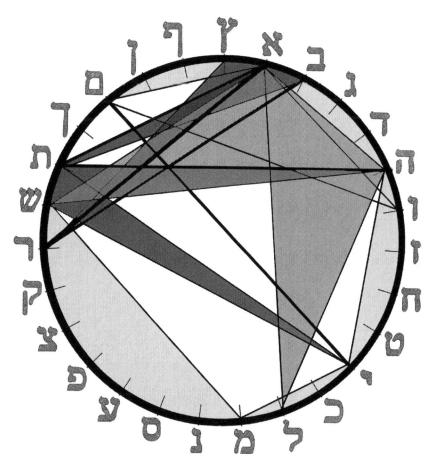

28. The 27 "Clock" of Genesis 1:1

254

Genesis 1:1 "In the beginning God creates the heaven and the earth" in the **27 section clock** facing, and below is **Genesis 1:1** using the **22 section clock** (leaving out the five final forms.)

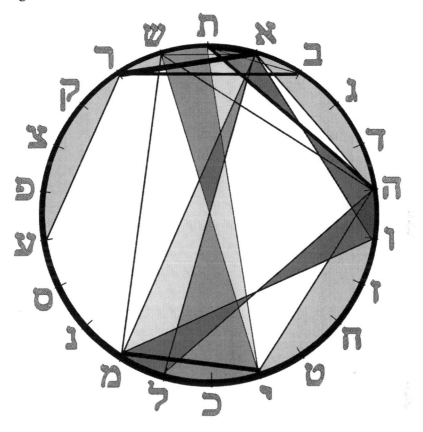

29. The <u>22</u> "Clock" of Genesis 1:1

This particular one is very unusual; the symmetries all consist of 'hourglass' figures, of which there are five major and multiple minor ones that are symmetrical.

Note that this is the **same exact verse** as the previous page. And next is part of **Genesis 1:2** "*...and the Spirit of God hovered over the fact of the waters.*" This is placed on the **27 clock** below:

255

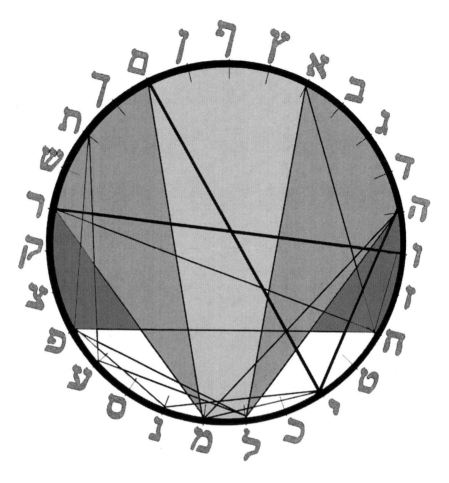

30. The <u>27</u> "Clock" of Genesis 1:2

This image has been turned 13.33° clockwise.

So yes, the symmetries are all there, but like the Prime Number sequences, they must be searched out. And we are merely introducing the subject with a wide variety of examples. This phenomena is quite ripe for exploration. Bear in mind that this is the *exact same letter sequence* as on the following page..

As a reminder, the five 'final forms' are simply a different way of writing a letter if it occurs at the <u>end</u> of a word. These five have a final form: ך replaces כ (Kaf, our **CH**) when it ends a word, ם replaces מ (Mem, our **M**), ן replaces נ (Nun, our **N**), ף replaces פ (Pe, our **P**), and ץ replaces צ (Zadi, pronounced **TZ**). Each one of these is the <u>same</u> <u>letter</u> yet with a different <u>numerical</u> <u>value</u>.

Here is **Genesis 1:2** "*...and the Spirit of God hovered over the fact of the waters.*" on the **22 clock**.

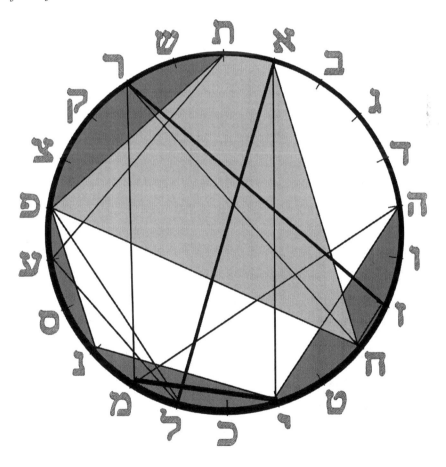

30. The <u>22</u> "Clock" of Genesis 1:2

Now that we have seen some connections between **Nature**, **Scripture**, **Geometry**, and **Mathematics**, let us return to our subject of decimals and end this chapter. We have two more items to look at: **13** and **73**.

We skipped a little problem with the number **13**. If you recall from thirty pages back, almost any way we added the sets of decimals, they came out to all **9**'s like a Sudoku puzzle. To catch us up, here is a copy of that section:

Again, just as the number **13**, there are *two* sets of repeating decimals; and these are in a symmetrical pattern around the center line. Curiouser and curiouser.

We are discovering that there is a symmetry in the decimal equivalents of prime numbers that is not there in other numbers. Now why would that be significant? And what happens when we continue to examine these with more primes? And why should **13** and **31** double up their decimal strings, while **17**, **23**, and **29** do not? And what is the relationship between the two strings in **31**? Or the two strings in **13**?

Well, let's add the strings from 31; **967741935483870** to **032258064516129**; we get **999999999999999**. And if we go back to the two strings for the number **13**, we find that any two symmetrical numbers folded around the center line equal **999999**. This also works for the folding line in 31. But like number folds with like with 13, and unlike folds with unlike on 31. Again, curious.

So... with **13**, unlike **31**, the two sets of decimals don't equal **9** nohow, frontward, backward, anyway you look at them... our Sudoku game is ruined. The two strings **13** uses are **076923** and **153846**. Added together, they equal **230769**. But wait a minute...

isn't **230769** located in ".0769**23 0769**23 076923" of $^1/_{13}$ below? In fact, it is exactly the value for $^3/_{13}$.

$^1/_{13} =$ **.076923 076923 076923...**
$^2/_{13} =$ .153846 153846 153846 153846...
$^3/_{13} =$ 　　**.23 076923 076923...**
$^4/_{13} =$ 　　**.3 076923 076923**
$^5/_{13} =$ 　.3846 153846 153846 153846...
$^6/_{13} =$ 　　.46 153846 153846 153846...
$^7/_{13} =$ .53846 153846 153846 153846...
$^8/_{13} =$ 　.6 153846 153846 153846...
$^9/_{13} =$ 　**.6923 076923 076923...**
$^{10}/_{13} =$ **.76923 076923 076923...**
$^{11}/_{13} =$ 　.846 153846 153846 153846...
$^{12}/_{13} =$ 　**.923 076923 076923...**

This is most peculiar. <u>For **13** only, the strings only equal 99999 if you split them and add them to themselves, but they equal each other when you add them together.</u>

Examples of adding them together:

.076923 **076923** 076923　　　.076923 076923 076923
+ .153846 153846 153846　　+ .076923 076923 076923
= 　　**.23 0769**　　　　　**.153846 153846 153846**

.153846 153846 153846
+ .153846 153846 153846
= 　　**.3 07692**

Examples of splitting the six digits in half and adding the halves:

	076	769	692	932	230	307		153	538	846	461	615
+	923	230	307	076	769	692		846	461	153	538	384
=	999	999	999	999	999	999		999	999	999	999	999

This is quite different from the other number, **31**, which also has two strings instead of one long one (.**967741935483870** and .**032258064516129**). But with **31**, the two strings add neatly to 999999999999999 instead of some part of the other string like **13**:

.032258064516129   .032258**064516129**
+ .967741935483870   **yet**   + .032258**064516129**
= .999999999999999   =   .**064516129**032258

            .967741**935483870**
and   + .967741**935483870**
       =   **1.93548387096774**

So exactly opposite to **13**, when you add one of the strings of **31** to itself, you get itself.

Likewise, splitting them as we did with **13** is impossible since we have 15 digits that repeat, and 15 does not divide evenly. So let's 'offset' the number to be added. The second number here will be the same string, but start at the **9th** digit of the decimal, where the **bold** starts:

    .032258064**516129** 032258064516129 0322580...
+   .**4516129** 032258064516129 032258064516129...
=   .483870 **967741935483870** 9677419354838709...

...So we find that when one of the two decimal strings is offset and added to itself, *it equals the other decimal string*. Since **13** is opposite to **31** in every way so far, what happens when we offset the *13* string and add it to itself? We can't offset them by 3 as that's the same as when we split them, and that adds up to all **9**'s. So let's offset them by 2.

    .076923   153846   .076923   .153846
+ .692307   **and**   384615   **and**   .230769   **and**   .461538
= .769230   **538461**   .**307692**   .**615384**

So again we find that opposite to **31**, **13** produces the same string when offset, instead of its other string.

Do all reciprocal number act as opposites like this? Are reciprocal gematria number in scripture important? What about 37 and 73, the only two factors of Genesis 1:1 (in the 22-Gematria system)? What about 71 and 17? How do primes that are their own reciprocal, like **101** act?

These questions are for all of us. Learning about how to tend a garden, understand the Bible, or using the tools of Numerics must be *investigated*. We can get our interest whetted by reading a book, but so much more can be discovered with diligence, research, and a love for discovery. The field is wide open and the little bit of information within this book is meant to pique our curiosity, not be the end-all of the process.

This chapter will conclude with a look at **73**. Recall that the gematria value of Genesis 1:1 is **2701**, which is **37** x **73**. Recall also that **37²** is **1369**, which is the value for *"And the Spirit of God hovered over the face of the waters."* So **73** and **37** are vital to scripture. Can their decimals contribute to our understanding of them?

And sure enough, we find that scripture is working with the natural progressions of the decimals in both **37** and **73**. The *first two* and the *last two* figures in **37**'s decimals series ($^1/_{37}$, $^2/_{32}$, and $^{35}/_{37}$, $^{36}/_{37}$; which are **.027**, **.054**, **.945**, and **.972**) are marked in bold in the **73** decimal progression below. The first and the last occur at positions **2**, **19**, **20**, **29**, **44**, **53,54**, and **71**. These sum to **292**, which is **4** x **73**. The second and the second-to-last occur at positions **4**, **15**, **33**, **35**, **38**, **40**, **58**, and **69**. These also sum to **292**. Their total is **584**, which is one less than **585**, the value of the first three words of Genesis.

But more importantly, the values of both the phrases "*God's Image*" and "*And the Spirit of God hovered over the face of the waters*" are **1369**. This figure occurs at positions **1, 10, 22, 27, 46, 51, 63** and **73**. These positions *also* sum to **292**. It is also **37²**, showing the relationship between **Scripture**, **37**, **73**, and **decimals**.

$^1/_{73}$ 0.0**1369**8630 **1369**8630 $^{30}/_{73}$ 0.41095890 41095890
$^2/_{73}$ 0.**027397260 27397260** $^{31}/_{73}$ 0.42465753 42465753
$^3/_{73}$ 0.041095890 41095890 $^{32}/_{73}$ 0.43835616 43835616
$^4/_{73}$ 0.**054794520 54794520** $^{33}/_{73}$ 0.**45205479 45205479**
$^5/_{73}$ 0.068493150 68493150 $^{34}/_{73}$ 0.46575342 46575342
$^6/_{73}$ 0.082191780 82191780 $^{35}/_{73}$ 0.**47945205 47945205**
$^7/_{73}$ 0.095890410 95890410 $^{36}/_{73}$ 0.49315068 49315068
$^8/_{73}$ 0.10958904 10958904 $^{37}/_{73}$ 0.50684931 50684931
$^9/_{73}$ 0.12328767 12328767 $^{38}/_{73}$ 0.**52054794 52054794**
$^{10}/_{73}$ 0.**1369**8630 **1369**8630 $^{39}/_{73}$ 0.53424657 53424657
$^{11}/_{73}$ 0.15068493 15068493 $^{40}/_{73}$ 0.**54794520 54794520**
$^{12}/_{73}$ 0.16438356 16438356 $^{41}/_{73}$ 0.56164383 56164383
$^{13}/_{73}$ 0.17808219 17808219 $^{42}/_{73}$ 0.57534246 57534246
$^{14}/_{73}$ 0.19178082 19178082 $^{43}/_{73}$ 0.58904109 58904109
$^{15}/_{73}$ 0.**20547945 20547945** $^{44}/_{73}$ 0.**60273972 60273972**
$^{16}/_{73}$ 0.21917808 21917808 $^{45}/_{73}$ 0.61643835 61643835
$^{17}/_{73}$ 0.23287671 23287671 $^{46}/_{73}$ 0.630**13698** 630**13698**
$^{18}/_{73}$ 0.24657534 24657534 $^{47}/_{73}$ 0.64383561 64383561
$^{19}/_{73}$ 0.**26027397 26027397** $^{48}/_{73}$ 0.65753424 65753424
$^{20}/_{73}$ 0.**27397260 27397260** $^{49}/_{73}$ 0.67123287 67123287
$^{21}/_{73}$ 0.28767123 28767123 $^{50}/_{73}$ 0.68493150 68493150
$^{22}/_{73}$ 0.30**136986** 30**136986** $^{51}/_{73}$ 0.**69863013 69863013**
$^{23}/_{73}$ 0.31506849 31506849 $^{52}/_{73}$ 0.71232876 71232876
$^{24}/_{73}$ 0.32876712 32876712 $^{53}/_{73}$ 0.**72602739 72602739**
$^{25}/_{73}$ 0.34246575 34246575 $^{54}/_{73}$ 0.**73972602 73972602**
$^{26}/_{73}$ 0.35616438 35616438 $^{55}/_{73}$ 0.75342465 75342465
$^{27}/_{73}$ 0.**36986301 36986301** $^{56}/_{73}$ 0.76712328 76712328
$^{28}/_{73}$ 0.38356164 38356164 $^{57}/_{73}$ 0.78082191 78082191
$^{29}/_{73}$ 0.**39726027** 39726027_ $^{58}/_{73}$ 0.79452**054** 79452**054**

$^{59}/_{73}$	0.80821917	80821917
$^{60}/_{73}$	0.82191780	82191780
$^{61}/_{73}$	0.83561643	83561643
$^{62}/_{73}$	0.84931506	84931506
$^{63}/_{73}$	0.8630**1369**	8630**1369**
$^{64}/_{73}$	0.87671232	87671232
$^{65}/_{73}$	0.89041095	89041095
$^{66}/_{73}$	0.90410958	90410958
$^{67}/_{73}$	0.91780821	91780821
$^{68}/_{73}$	0.93150684	93150684
$^{69}/_{73}$	0.945205**47**	945205**47**
$^{70}/_{73}$	0.95890410	95890410
$^{71}/_{73}$	0.**97260273**	**97260273**
$^{72}/_{73}$	0.98630136	98630**136**
$^{73}/_{73}$	1.0	
$^{74}/_{73}$	1.0**1369**863	0**1369**863
$^{75}/_{73}$	1.**02739726**	**02739726**

We can easily note that the first four numbers added to the next four in each set of eight add to **9999**.

As we saw earlier in this section with the two kinds of Hebrew "clocks", there is more than one way to do gematria. Many do not include the values of the Final Forms, which produces different results; yet fortunately, both system have been shown to work equally well; in fact the 22-alphabet and the 27-alphabet are mathematically and geometrically related; one was built from the other.

The figure of the first verse of Genesis being **37 x 73 (1369)** changes when we include the values of the five final forms: **1369** becomes **4631** which is **11 x 421**. In the expanded 27-letter system, for example, **Genesis 1:26**, "*And God said, Let us make Man in our image, after our likeness; and let them have dominion over the fish of the sea, and over the fowl of the heavens, and over the cattle, and over the whole earth, and over every creeping thing that creeps upon the earth*" equals **9433**, which is 2^7 x **73**.

And our **37** appears in verse 14 "And God said, Let there be lights in the expanse of the heavens, to divide between the day and the night; and let them be for signs, and for seasons, and for days and years," equals **7844** which is 2^2 x **37** x **53**.

In the 27 system, four out of the seven verses of the <u>first day</u> are

Prime Numbers; there are only two verses in the rest of the entire seven days that are prime. The section of verse 2 *without* the Spirit hovering is also prime, as well as verse 30 regarding the green herbs that the beasts will eat. Thus there are **7** prime verses in the **27**-system, and **1** (verse 5, calling the light day) in the **22**-system.

In chapter 6 we were constantly subtracting the section that says *"And the earth was waste and empty, and darkness was on the face of the deep"* which has a value of **2177** under the 22-system. In the 27-system it has a value of the prime number **4027**. We find that **4027** is equally useful; if we subtract it from the entire first day (**18,027**) we get **14,000** (2^4 x 5^2 x 7).

To demonstrate that the **22** and the **27** systems work together, we can look at verse 24 of Genesis 1 in which the earth brings forth all the animals that comprise Adam's rule, i.e., his <u>kingdom</u>. This verse has a **27**-system value of **6109**. Each one of the following verses (you can look them up) also has a value of **6109** *in the 22-system*, and each one is very specifically about setting up a <u>kingdom</u> (and one about setting up the priesthood):

Deuteronomy 17:15
Deuteronomy 11:22
First Kings 2:22
Nehemiah 9:22
Isaiah 45:1
Exodus 40:15

*   *   *

A FEW MORE EXAMPLES from the **27**-system will suffice to close out this Appendix.

The first two verses of Genesis have a value of **11,149**. These verses deal with both the creation of the heavens and earth, and the mention of the earth being waste and empty, which begs the issue of God's righteousness in creation. There are two New Testament verses which also have the value of **11,149**; they address both these issues.

Matthew 5:35 *"[Swear not at all; neither by the heaven, for it is God's throne;] nor by the earth, for it is the footstool of his feet; nor toward Jerusalem, for it is the great King's city."*

Romans 3:22 *"...even God's righteousness through faith in Jesus Christ unto all that believe; for there is no distinction."*

And just the first verse, **Genesis 1:1**, has a value of **4631**, the same as **Galatians 4:13** *"...but you know that because of infirmity of the flesh I preached the gospel to you the former time,"* thus we see that the Gospel starts even with the first verse of the Bible.

The second verse of the Bible has both the destruction of the earth and the hope of rebuilding (the Spirit hovering). Its value in the **27**-system is **6516**. The verses in the **22**-system that have the same value are all very specifically about building up or completely destroying:

Exodus 36:1
Deuteronomy 7:5
First Chronicles 21:15
Daniel 2:35

These are a few examples of instructive relationships within the scriptures that can be explored through Numerics. There is no limit to God's Word, and the age of the computer provides us with tools that put the entirety of the scriptures at our fingertips. This has been a long appendix, and the hope is that some of the intricacy and beauty of the holy text has been revealed.

Appendix V

Modern Scholarship and Panin

It is well known that Panin highly respected Westcott & Hort's work. He used it extensively and considered it head and shoulders above any other critical texts extant in his day.

Using his Numerics, however, allowed him to settle the marginal options as well as correct a great many doubtful readings. Of note among these was the reestablishment of many readings supposed by W & H to be "interpolations" (added sections) such as the last twelve verses of Mark and a section of John 8, as actually valid and part of the original scriptures.

Today, the Nestle-Aland *Novum Testamentum Graece* Edition 28 is considered among the top standards for contemporary textual scholarship. Thus to evaluate Panin's work we can take any improvements made by Nestle-Aland on Westcott & Hort's text, and compare them to Panin's Greek text to see just exactly where he stands in relationship to our better contemporary scholarship.

This is a list of the different readings between Nestle-Aland and Westcott & Hort. We will take these disagreements and look at how Panin—100 years ago, long before Nestle-Aland was even written—treated each of the same passages.

This list is in English so as to be intelligible to the common reader, thus the equivalent phrases in various translations will differ somewhat. The Greek texts of Nestle-Aland, Westcott & Hort, and Panin have been compared, as well as references variously to J. P. Green's Interlinear, the *Greek New Testament, Scriveners Textus Receptus* (1894), the *Transliterated Greek New Testament Scriveners Textus Receptus* (1894), and the *Concordant Greek Text Sublinear v1.6*. The reason for referring to the Textus

Receptus is that this was the primary text being corrected by Westcott & Hort, as well as Tregelles, Tischendorf, Alford, and Lachmann before them. Thus the corrections to the text (both N-A's and W&H's) are generally in reference to deviations from the Textus Receptus from which the King James Version was primarily translated, specifically here the readings of Stephens 1550 and of Elzevir 1624 which appeared in the Oxford Standard edition of 1769. Note that we said "primarily translated"; contrary to what many suppose, the KJV translators made use of many manuscripts outside the Textus Receptus.

There are thousands of variations. However, Nestle-Aland and Westcott & Hort agree on the vast majority of them. This list is composed of the small percentage of points (756 of them) upon which the two editorial teams—separated by over a century—differ. Even among the variations listed, the vast majority of them are not even found in the text proper, but in the 'marginal readings', which simply means a possible alternative reading that is supported by some of the manuscripts, though not the preferred reading. Each instance is noted and a full summary is included at the end of this chapter.

The abbreviations used will be:

Westcott & Hort	WH	
Nestle-Aland	NA	
Panin	P	
Marginal Reading	m[1]	(or bracketed within the text)
Extraneous	mm	(by which the editors indicate their opinion that the reading is extraneous, but of evident antiquity.)

Panin's text agrees with NA's version: **(PNA)**
Panin's text maintains W & H's version: **(PWH)**
Panin's text is different from either: **(U)** [for Unique]

---

1 Note that Westcott & Hort, unlike most others' collations, considered their marginal readings as of equal value to the text.

What is being investigated here is whether increased scholarship and discovery of additional manuscripts has moved the generally accepted text <u>closer</u> or <u>farther</u> from Panin's Greek text. This list does *not* include the passages in which Panin departs from the texts that N-A and W&H have left alone.

The Variations

Matthew

1:18. Omit "Jesus" before "Christ" and render "birth of the Christ". WHm (**PNA**)

1:18. Transpose "Jesus Christ" to "Christ Jesus". WHm (**PNA**)

2:13. Read "appeared" instead of "appears". WHm (**PNA**)

3:7. Omit "his" and render "the baptism." WH (**PNA**)

3:12. Add "his" before "the garner" and render "his garner". WHm (**PNA**)

3:14. Omit "John" and render "he forbade." WH (**PWH**) (**U**)

4:17. Omit "Repent, for" before "the kingdom". WHm (**PNA**)

5:1. Omit "unto him" after "came". WHm (**PNA**)

5:28. Omit "her" after "to lust after". WHm (**PNA**)

5:32. Omit "and whosoever shall marry her that is divorced commits adultery" at end of verse. WHm (**PNA**)

5:37. Read "your communication shall be" instead of "let your communication be". WHm (**PNA**)

5:46. Read "so" instead of "the same". WHm (**PNA**)

6:8. Add "God" before "your Father". WH (**PNA**)

6:21. Omit "also" after "heart be". WHm (**PNA**)

7:13. Omit "[is] the gate" and render "wide and broad is the way." WH (**PNA**)

7:14. Read "How" instead of "Because". NA (**PWH**)

7:24. Omit "these" and render "my sayings". WHm (**PNA**)

8:7. Omit "And" at the beginning of the verse. WH (**PWH**)

8:9. Add "placed" before "under authority". WH (**PWH**)

8:23. Add "the" before "a ship" and render "the ship". NA (**PWH**)

9:18. Read "entered" instead of "came". WHm (**PNA**)

9:18. Read "came to [him]" instead of "came". WH (**PNA**)

9:18. Omit "certain" before "ruler". WHm (**PNA**)

9:32. Omit "man" and render "[one] dumb". WH (**PWH**)

9:34. Omit "But the Pharisees said, He casts out devils through the prince of the devils" (the entire verse). WHm (**PNA**)

10:14. Add "from" after "dust" and render "from your feet". WHm (**PNA**)

10:16. Read "the serpent" instead of "serpents". WHm (**PNA**)

12:11. Omit "shall there be" before "among you". WHm (**PNA**)

12:22. Read "they brought" instead of "was brought". WH (**PWH**)

12:31. Add "to you" after "shall be forgiven" and render "unto you men". WHm (**PNA**)

12:32. Read "in no wise shall it be forgiven" instead of "it shall not be forgiven". WHm (**PNA**)

12:44. Add "and" after "empty". WH (**PWH**)

13:11. Omit "unto them" after "said". WH (**PWH**)

13:16. Omit "your" before "ears" and render "the ears". WHm (**PNA**)

13:28. Omit "servants" before "said unto him" and render "they". WH (**PWH**)

13:33. Omit "spoke he unto them" after "parable". WHm (**PNA**)

13:35. Add "Isaiah" after "prophet". WHm (**PNA**)

13:44. Omit "all" after "sells". WH (**PNA**)

13:45. Omit "man" after "merchant". WH (**PWH**)

14:15. Add "therefore" after "away". WHm (**PNA**)

14:16. Omit "Jesus" and render "he said". NAm (**PWH**)

14:22. Omit "immediately" before "Jesus constrained". WHm (**PNA**)

14:36. Omit "him" after "besought". WHm (**PNA**)

15:27. Omit "for" before "also the dogs". WHm (**PNA**)

15:31. Read "the dumb to hear" instead of "the dumb to speak". WHm (**PNA**)

15:31. Omit "the maimed to be whole" after "the dumb to speak". WH (**PWH**)

15:32. Omit "now" before "three days". WHm (**PNA**)

15:38. Add "about" before "four thousand". WHm (**PNA**)

15:38. Transpose "women and children" to "children and women". WHm (**PNA**)

16:1. Omit "The" before "Pharisees". WHm (**PNA**)

16:12. Omit "of bread" after "leaven". WHm (**PNA**)

16:20. Read "straitly charged" (or "rebuked") instead of "charged". WH (**PNA**)

16:21. Add "Christ" after "Jesus". WH (**PWH**)

16:22. Read "and rebuking [him], says to him" instead of "and began to rebuke him, saying". WHm (**PNA**)

17:15. Read "is ill" instead of "suffers grievously". WH (**PNA**)

17:23. Read "he shall rise again" instead of "he shall be raised up". WHm (**PNA**)

18:1. Add "But" at beginning of verse. WHm (**PNA**)

18:10. Omit "in heaven" after "their angels". WHm (**PNA**)

18:14. Read "my Father" instead of "your Father". WH (**PWH**)

18:21. Omit "to him". WHm (**PNA**)

18:27. Omit "that" and render "the servant". WHm (**PNA**)

19:3. Omit "for a man" after "lawful". WH (**PWH**)

19:9. Read "saving for the cause of fornication" instead of "except [it be] for fornication". WHm (**PNA**)

19:9. Read "causes her to suffer adultery" instead of "and shall marry another, commits adultery". WHm (**PNA**)

19:14. Add "unto them" after "said". WHm (**PNA**)

19:18. Omit "unto him" after "says". WHm (**PNA**)

19:29. Omit "houses, or" before "brethren". WHm (**PNA**)

19:29. Add "or houses" after "or lands". WHm (**PNA**)

19:29. Read "many times more" instead of "a hundredfold". WH (**PWH**)

20:8. Omit "them" after "give". WH (**PWH**)

20:15. Add "or" before "Is it not lawful". NA (**PWH**)

20:17. Read "Jesus being about to go up" instead of "Jesus going up". WH (**PWH**)

20:18. Omit "to death" after "condemn him". WHm (**PNA**)

20:21. Omit "your" and render "the right hand". WH (**PNA**)

20:26. Read "it is not" instead of "it shall not be". WH (**PWH**)

20:30. Omit "O Lord" after "have mercy on us". NAm (**PWH**)

20:30. Transpose "Have mercy on us, O Lord" to "Lord, have mercy on us". WH (**PWH**)

20:31. Transpose "Have mercy on us, O Lord" to "Lord, have mercy on us". WH (**PWH**)

21:24. Omit "and" at beginning of verse. WHm (**PNA**)

21:28. Omit "and" before "he came". WH (**PNA**)

21:29. Read "I [go], sir: and went not" instead of "I will not: but afterward he repented, and went". WH (**PNA**)

21:29. Omit "but" before "afterward". WH (**PNA**)

21:30. Read "other" instead of "second". NA (**PNA**)

21:30. Read "I will not: but afterward he repented, and went" instead of "I [go], sir: and went not". WH (**PNA**)

21:31. Read "The last" instead of "The first". WH (**PWH**)

22:10. Read "bride-chamber" instead of "wedding". WH (**PNA**)

22:20. Add "Jesus" before "he says" and render "Jesus says". WHm (**PNA**)

22:21. Omit "unto him" after "they say". WH (**PWH**)

22:35. Omit "[which was] a lawyer" after "one of them". NAm (**PNA**)

22:39. Omit "And" at beginning of verse. WH (**PNA**)

22:39. Read "likewise" instead of "like unto it". WH (**PNA**)

22:39. Re-accent "[is] like unto it" to "like [unto it] is this". WH (**PWH**)

23:21. Read "dwelt" instead of "dwells". WHm (**PNA**)

23:24. Omit "which" before "strain" and render "straining out a gnat, and swallowing". WH (**PWH**)

23:32. Read "You fill up" instead of "Fill you up". WHm (**PWH**)

23:37. Omit "her" before "chickens" and render "the chickens under the wings". WHm (**PNA**)

23:38. Omit "desolate" after "left unto you". WH (**PWH**)

24:24. Read "the very elect will be deceived" instead of "they will deceive the very elect". WH (**PNA**)

25:42. Add "and" before "I was thirsty". WH (**PWH**)

26:20. Add "disciples" after "twelve". WH (**PNA**)

26:39. Read "he went towards [them] a little" instead of "he went a little farther". WHm (**PNA**)

26:42. Omit "saying" after "prayed". WHm (**PNA**)

26:45. Add "for" before "behold". WHm (**PNA**)

26:56. Add "his" and render "his disciples". WHm (**PNA**)

27:4. Read "just" instead of "innocent". WH **(PWH)**

27:10. Read "I gave" instead of "(they) gave". WHm **(PNA)**

27:16. Add "Jesus" before "Barabbas". NA **(PWH)**

27:17. Add "Jesus" before "Barabbas". NA **(PWH)**

27:28. Read "clothed him" instead of "stripped him". WHm **(PNA)**

27:40. Add "and" before "come down" and render "save yourself, if you be the Son of God, and come down". NA **(PWH)**

27:41. Omit "also" before "the chief priests". WHm **(PNA)**

27:46. Read "eloi" (Aramaic) instead of "eli" (Hebrew). WH **(PWH)**

27:49. Add "but another took a spear and pierced his side, and there came forth water and blood" at end of verse. WH **(PNA)**

27:54. Read "were happening" instead of "were done". WH **(PNA)**

27:64. Omit "his" and render "the disciples". WH **(PWH)**

28:15. Read "is reported" instead of "is commonly reported". WHm **(U)**

28:19. Read "having baptized" instead of "baptizing". WHm **(PNA)**

Mark

1:4. Omit "and" and render "preaching". WH **(PNA) (U)**

1:7. Omit "me" after "after". WHm **(PNA)**

1:8. Omit "in" before "the Holy Spirit" and render "with the Holy Spirit". WH **(PWH) (U)**

1:9. Omit "And" at beginning of verse. WHm **(PWH)**

1:11. Omit "there came" before "a voice". WHm **(PNA)**

1:15. Omit "and saying" before "The time is fulfilled". WHm **(PNA)**

1:21. Omit "he entered into" and render "he taught in the synagogue". WHm **(PNA)**

1:24. Read "we know" instead of "I know". WHm **(PWH)**

1:25. Omit "saying" after "rebuked him". WHm **(PNA)**

1:29. Read "he was come out" instead of "they were come out". WHm **(PNA)**

1:29. Read "he entered" instead of "they entered". WHm (**PNA**)

1:34. Add "to be Christ" after "knew him". WH (**PWH**)

1:35. Omit "and departed" after "went out". WHm (**PNA**)

2:8. Omit "so" before "reasoned". WHm (**PNA**)

2:8. Omit "unto them" after "said". WHm (**PNA**)

2:9. Omit "and" after "Arise". WHm (**PNA**)

2:12. Omit "saying" after "glorified God". WHm (**PNA**)

2:18. Omit "disciples" after "your". WHm (**PNA**)

2:22. Omit "but new wine must be put into new bottles" at end of verse. WHm (**PNA**)

2:26. Omit "How" at beginning of verse. WHm (**PNA**)

3:1. Omit "the" before "synagogue" and render "a synagogue". WH (**PWH**)

3:7. Omit "followed" after "from Galilee". NAm (**PWH**)

3:8. Read "he is doing" instead of "he did". WH (**PNA**)

3:32. Add "and your sisters" after "brothers". NA (**PWH**)

3:35. Read "the things God wills" instead of "the will of God". WHm (**PNA**)

4:5. Add "and" after "stony ground". WH (**PWH**)

4:6. Read "they were scorched" instead of "it was scorched". WHm (**PNA**)

4:8. Read "unto thirty, and unto sixty, and unto an hundred" instead of "some thirty, and some sixty, and some an hundred". WHm (**U**)

4:16. Omit "likewise" before "which are sown". NA (**PNA**)

4:20. Re-accent "some thirtyfold, some sixty, and some an hundred" to "in thirtyfold, in sixty, and in an hundred". WH (**U**)

4:20. Omit "some" before "sixty" and before "a hundred". WHm (**U**)

4:21. Read "under a candlestick" instead of "on a candlestick". WHm (**PNA**)

5:2. Omit "immediately" before "there met him". WHm (**PNA**)

5:21. Omit "by ship" after "passed over again". NAm (**PWH**)

5:27. Add "the things" after "heard" and render "heard the things concerning Jesus". WH (**PWH**) (**U**)

6:2. Add "the" before "many". WH (**PWH**)

6:22. Add "and" before "the king". WH (**PWH**)

6:23. Add "much" (perhaps render "solemnly") after "swore unto her". NA (**PWH**)

6:44. Omit "of the loaves" after "eat". NAm (**PWH**)

7:4. Read "except they sprinkle themselves" instead of "except they wash" (literally "baptize themselves"). WH (**PWH**)

7:9. Read "establish" instead of "keep". NA (**PWH**)

7:28. Omit "Yes" before "Lord". NA (**PWH**)

7:37. Add "as" before "he makes". WHm (**PNA**)

8:2. Omit "with me" before "three days". WHm (**PNA**)

8:3. Read "are from afar" instead of "came from afar". WH (**PWH**)

8:12. Omit "unto you" after "I say". WH (**PWH**)

8:34. Read "follow" instead of "come". NA (**PWH**)

8:35. Omit "my" and "and" and render "for the gospel's sake". WHm (**PNA**)

9:8. Transpose "any more, save Jesus only with themselves" to "any more with themselves, save Jesus only". WH (**PWH**)

9:31. Omit "unto them" after "said". WHm (**PNA**)

10:1. Omit "by the" before "farther side" and render "beyond Jordan'. NAm (**PNA**)

10:2. Omit "the Pharisees came to him" and render "And they asked him". WHm (**PNA**)

10:6. Omit "them" after "made". WHm (**PNA**)

10:26. Read "saying unto him" instead of "saying among themselves". WH (**PWH**)

10:35. Add "two" before "sons". WH (**PWH**)

10:43. Read "let him be your minister" instead of "shall be your minister". WHm (**PNA**)

11:1. Omit "Bethphage" and render "even unto Bethany". WHm (**PNA**)

11:17. Omit "unto them" after "saying". WH (**PWH**)

12:17. Omit "unto them" after "said". WH (**PWH**)

12:28. Read "having perceived" instead of "perceiving". NA (**U**)

12:32. Omit "And" at beginning of verse. WH (**PWH**)

12:37. Omit "the" before "great crowd" and render "a great crowd heard". NAm (**PNA**)

13:32. Read "an angel" instead of "the angels". WHm (**PNA**)

14:7. Add "always" before "do them good". WH (**PWH**)

14:18. Read "which eat" (plural) instead of "which eats" (singular). WHm (**PNA**)

14:20. Add "one" before "dish". WH (**PWH**)

14:35. Read "he went towards [them]" instead of "he went forward". WHm (**PNA**)

14:39. Omit "and spake the same words" at end of verse. WHm (**PNA**)

14:49. Read "you were not taking me" instead of "you took me not". WHm (**PNA**)

14:60. Read "nothing that these" instead of "nothing? what [is it which] these". WHm (**PNA**)

14:69. Omit "again". WHm (**PNA**)

14:69. Read "said" instead of "began to say". WHm (**PNA**)

15:1. Read "prepared a consultation" instead of "held a consultation". WHm (**PNA**)

15:4. Omit "saying" after "asked him again". WHm (**PNA**)

15:10. Omit "the chief priests" and render "they had delivered". WHm (**PNA**)

15:12. Omit "whom ye call" before "the King of the Jews". NAm (**PWH**)

15:34. Read "lema" (Aramaic) instead of "lama" (Hebrew). NA (**PWH**)

15:34. Omit "my God" after "My God". WHm (**PNA**)

15:44. Read "was already dead" instead of "had been any while dead" at end of verse. WH (**PWH**)

16:4. Read "rolled back" instead of "rolled away". WH (**PWH**)

16:5. Read "coming to" instead of "entering into". A WHm (**PNA**)

16:14. Add "from the dead" after "risen". WH (**PWH**)

16:17. Omit "new" before "tongues". Tr WH (**PWH**)

Luke

1:17. Read "go near to in front of him" instead of "go before in

276

front of him". WHm (**PNA**)

2:13. Read "host of heaven" instead of "heavenly host". WHm (**PNA**)

3:9. Omit "good" before "fruit". WHm (**PNA**)

3:32. Read "Jobel" instead of "Obed". WH (**PNA**) (**U**)

3:33. Read "Admin" instead of "Aminadab". WH (**U**)

3:33. Read "Adam" instead of "Aminadab". WHm (**U**)

3:33. Add "which was [the son] of Admin" after "Aminadab". NA (**PWH**)

4:9. Omit "unto him" after "said". WHm (**PNA**)

4:17. Read "opened" instead of "unrolled". WH (**PWH**)

5:2. Read "boats" instead of "ships". WHm (**PWH**)

5:29. Read "with him" instead of "with them". WHm (**PNA**)

5:39. Omit "No man also having drunk old desires new: for he says, The old is good" (the entire verse). WHm (**PNA**)

6:35. Read "no man" instead of "nothing". WHm (**U**)

6:38. Omit "again" after "measured to you". WHm (**PNA**)

7:39. Add "the" before "prophet" and render "the prophet". WH (**PWH**)

8:13. Read "themselves have no root" instead of "these have no root". WHm (**PNA**)

8:28. Omit "God" and render 'Son of the Most High'. WHm (**PNA**)

8:29. Read "he was commanding" instead of "he commanded". WH (**PWH**)

9:18. Read "met with him" instead of "were with him". WHm (**PNA**)

9:22. Read "rise again" instead of "be raised". WHm (**PNA**)

9:25. Read "what does it advantage a man" instead of "what is a man advantaged". WHm (**PNA**)

10:27. Omit "your" before "God". WHm (**PNA**)

10:41. Omit "careful and" before "troubled" and omit "about many things" after "troubled". WHm (**PNA**)

10:42. Read "But few things are needful, or one" instead of "But one thing is needful". WH (**PWH**)

10:42. Omit "and" before "Mary". WHm (**PWH**)

11:25. Add "empty" before "swept". WH (**PWH**)

11:33. Omit "neither under a bushel" before "but on a candlestick". NAm (**PWH**)

12:11. Omit "or what thing" after "how". WHm (**PNA**)

12:19. Omit "laid up for many years; take your ease, eat, drink, [and]" after "much goods". WHm (**PNA**)

12:21. Omit "So [is] he that lays up treasure for himself, and is not rich toward God" (the entire verse). WHm (**PNA**)

12:22. Add "your" and render "your body". WH (**PWH**)

13:7. Add "therefore" before "cut it down". NA (**PWH**)

14:17. Read "bidden to come" instead of "bidden, Come". WHm (**PNA**)

14:32. Omit "conditions" and render "asks toward peace". WH (**PWH**)

15:21. Add "Make me as one of your hired servants" at end of verse. WH (**PWH**)

15:24. Read "is alive" instead of "is alive again". WHm (**U**)

16:12. Read "our own" instead of "your own". WH (**U**)

17:12. Read "rose up" instead of "stood". WH (**PNA**)

17:17. Omit "but" before "where". WHm (**PNA**)

17:23. Omit "go not after [them]" and render "do not follow". WHm (**U**)

17:34. Omit "one" before "bed" and render "a bed". WHm (**PNA**)

18:16. Omit "them" after "Jesus called". WHm (**U**)

19:9. Omit "is" before "a son". WHm (**PNA**)

19:13. Read "said to occupy them" instead of "said unto them, Occupy". WH (**PNA**)

19:38. Omit "that comes" after "King". WHm (**PNA**)

20:26. Read "the words" instead of "his words". WH (**PNA**)

20:33. Read "shall she be" instead of "is she". NAm (**PNA**)

21:6. Add "here" after "one stone". WH (**PNA**)

21:11. Transpose "famines, and pestilences" to "pestilences, and famines". WH (**PNA**)

21:19. Read "you will possess" instead of "possess you". WH (**U**)

21:24. Add "and they will be" at end of verse. WH (**PWH**)

22:11. Add "saying" before "The Master says". WHm (**PNA**)

22:19. Omit "which is given for you: this do in remembrance of me" at end of verse. WHmm (**PNA**)

22:20. Omit "Likewise also the cup after supper, saying, This cup is the new testament in my blood, which is shed for you" (the entire verse). WHmm (**PNA**)

22:30. Read "and you sit on thrones" instead of "and (may) sit on thrones". WH (**PNA**)

22:39. Omit "also" after "disciples". WHm (**PNA**)

22:62. Omit "And Peter went out, and wept bitterly" (the entire verse). WHm (**PNA**)

23:23. Read "[he] might crucify him" instead of "he might be crucified". WHm (**PNA**)

23:39. Omit "saying" after "railed on him". WH (**PNA**)

23:42. Read "in" instead of "into". WHm (**PWH**)

23:50. Add "and" before "[he was] a good man". NA (**PWH**)

24:3. Omit "of the Lord Jesus" after "the body". WHmm (**PNA**)

24:6. Omit "He is not here, but is risen" at beginning of verse. WHmm (**PNA**)

24:9. Omit "from the sepulchre" after "returned". WHm (**PNA**)

24:12. Omit "Then arose Peter, and ran unto the sepulchre; and stooping down, he beheld the linen clothes laid by themselves, and departed, wondering in himself at that which was come to pass" (the entire verse). WHmm (**PNA**)

24:24. Omit "even" before "so". WH (**PWH**)

24:36. Omit "and says unto them, Peace [be] unto you" at end of verse. WHmm (**PNA**)

24:40. Omit "And when he had thus spoken, he shewed them [his] hands and [his] feet" (the entire verse). WHmm (**PNA**)

24:49. Omit "behold" after "And". NAm (**PWH**)

24:49. Read "send out" instead of "send". WH (**PWH**)

John

1:26. Read "stands" instead of "has stood". WH (**PWH**)

1:27. Omit "he it is" and render "[even] he that comes after me". NA (**PNA**)

1:27. Omit "He it is, who" and render "[one] coming after me".

WH (**PNA**)

3:18. Omit "but" after "not condemned". WH (**PWH**)

3:27. Read "not even one thing" instead of "nothing". NA (**PWH**)

3:32. Omit "that" before "he testifies". WHm (**PNA**)

4:1. Read "Jesus" instead of "the Lord". NA (**PWH**)

4:1. Omit "than" before "John" and render "Jesus made more disciples and John baptized". WHm " (**PNA**)

4:9. Omit "for the Jews have no dealings with the Samaritans" at end of verse. WHm (**PNA**)

4:29. Read "that I did" instead of "that ever I did". WH (**PWH**)

5:2. Read "Bethsaida" instead of "Bethesda". WHm (**U**)

5:11. Read "who however answered" instead of "He answered". WH (**PNA**)

5:19. Omit "Jesus" and render "he answered". WHm (**PNA**)

5:29. Omit "and" before "they that have done evil". WH (**PWH**)

5:44. Omit "God" and render "honor that [comes] from the only [one]". WHm (**PNA**)

5:47. Read "how do ye believe" instead of "how shall ye believe". WHm (**PNA**)

6:10. Omit "the" before "men sat" and render "So they sat down, men [being] in number about five thousand". WHm (**PNA**)

6:14. Read "miracles" instead of "miracle". WH (**PWH**)

6:23. Re-accent "other" to "But" and render "But there came boats". WH (**PWH**)

6:32. Read "Moses gave you not" instead of "Moses has not given you". WH (**U**)

7:4. Read "he seeks it" instead of "he himself seeks". WHm (**PNA**)

7:10. Omit "as it were" before "in secret". NAm (**PWH**)

7:19. Read "Did not Moses give" instead of "Has not Moses given". WH (**PWH**)

7:47. Omit "them" after "answered". WHm (**PNA**)

8:2. Omit "and all the people came unto him; and he sat down, and taught them". WHm (**PNA**)

8:3. Read "sin" instead of "adultery". WHm (**PWH**)

8:5. Omit "us" after "commanded". WHm (**PNA**)

8:5. Add "concerning her" after "say you". WHm (**PNA**)

8:6. Omit "This they said, tempting him, that they might have to accuse him". WHm (**PNA**)

8:7. Omit "him" after "asking". WHm (**PNA**)

8:7. Omit "unto them" after "said". WHm (**PNA**)

8:8. Add "with his finger" before "wrote". WHm (**PNA**)

8:10. Read "he said unto the woman, Where" instead of "he said unto her, Woman, where". WHm (**PNA**)

8:16. Omit "the Father" and render "he that sent me". WHm (**PNA**)

8:34. Omit "of sin" and render "is a servant". WHm (**PNA**)

8:39. Read "do you" instead of "you would do". WH (**PWH**)

8:57. Read "has Abraham seen you" instead of "have you seen Abraham". WHm (**PNA**)

9:4. Read "as" instead of "while". WHm (**PNA**)

9:6. Read "put upon" instead of "anointed". WH (**PNA**)

9:27. Add "then" after "wherefore". WHm (**PNA**)

9:36. Omit "answered and" before "said". WHm (**PNA**)

9:36. Omit "and said" after "answered". WHm (**PNA**)

10:18. Read "No man took" instead of "No man takes". WH (**PWH**)

10:39. Omit "again" after "they sought". WHm (**PNA**)

11:45. Read "seen that which" instead of "seen the things which". WH (**PWH**)

12:4. Omit "Then" at beginning of verse. WHm (**PNA**)

12:18. Omit "also" after "For this cause the people". NAm (**PWH**)

12:29. Omit "therefore" after "The people". WHm (**PNA**)

13:2. Read "Judas, [son] of Simon Iscariot" instead of "Judas Iscariot, [son] of Simon". NA (**PWH**)

13:10. Omit "save" and "[his] feet" and render "needs not to wash, but is clean". WHm (**PNA**)

13:25. Omit "then" after "He" at beginning of verse. WH (**PWH**)

13:25. Read "therefore" instead of "then". NA (**PWH**)

13:26. Add "therefore" after "answered". WH (**PWH**)

13:37. Omit "Lord" before "why". WHm (**PNA**)

14:7. Read "If you have known" instead of "If you had known". NA (**PWH**)

14:7. Read "you will know" instead of "you should have known". NA (**PWH**)

14:7. Omit "and" before "from here on". WH (**PWH**)

14:7. Omit "him" after "and have seen". WH (**PNA**)

14:11. Read "his works' sake" instead of "the very works' sake". WHm (**PNA**)

14:14. Read "that will I do" instead of "I will do [it]". WH (**PWH**)

14:17. Read "is in you" instead of "will be in you". WH (**PWH**)

15:10. Omit "my" and render "the Father's". WH (**PNA**)

15:14. Read "the thing that I command" instead of "whatsoever I command". WH (**PNA**)

16:2. Omit "you" after "kills". WHm (**PNA**)

16:7. Read "in no wise should come" instead of "will not come". WH (**PNA**)

16:13. Read "he hears" instead of "he may hear". WH (**PWH**)

16:18. Omit "that he says" after "What is this". NAm (**PWH**)

16:18. Omit "what he says" at end of verse. WHm (**PNA**)

16:22. Read "will take" instead of "takes". WH (**PWH**)

16:27. Read "from the Father" instead of "from God". WH (**PNA**)

16:28. Read "out of the Father" instead of "from the Father". WH (**PNA**)

17:2. Read "he will give" instead of "he should give". WH (**PNA**)

17:7. Read "you gave" instead of "you have given". WH (**PNA**)

18:5. Read "he says unto them, I am Jesus" instead of "Jesus says unto them, I am [he]". WHm (**PWH**)

19:39. Read "roll" instead of "mixture". WH (**PWH**)

20:20. Add "both" after "showed". WH (**PNA**)

21:4. Read "morning was coming" instead of "morning was now come". WH (**PNA**)

21:12. Omit "And" before "none". WH (**PWH**)

21:17. Read "he says unto him, Lord" instead of "he said unto him, Lord". NA (**PWH**)

21:17. Omit "Jesus" and render "he says". NAm (**PWH**)

21:23. Omit "what [is that] to you" at end of verse. NAm (**PWH**)

21:24. Add "also" before "testifies". WHm (**PWH**)

Acts

1:7. Omit "And" at beginning of verse. WH (**PWH**)

1:19. Omit "proper" before "tongue". WH (**PWH**)

2:38. Add "says" after "unto them". NA (**PNA**)

2:38. Read "upon the name" instead of "in the name". NA (**PWH**)

2:44. Omit "were" before "together" and omit "and" after "together" and render "together had all things common". WH (**PWH**)

3:13. Add "God" before "of Isaac" and before "of Jacob". NA (**PWH**)

3:22. Omit "your" before "God" and render "the Lord God". WH (**PWH**)

3:26. Omit "your" before "iniquities". WHm (**PNA**)

4:1. Read "high priests" instead of "priests". WH (**PWH**)

4:4. Omit "about" before "five thousand". NAm (**PWH**)

5:32. Read "we in him are witnesses" instead of "we are his witnesses". WHm (**U**)

5:32. Omit "whom" after "the Holy Spirit" and render "And God hath given the Holy Spirit to them that obey him". WHm (**PNA**)

6:3. Read "Indeed" instead of "Wherefore" at beginning of verse. L WHm (**U**)

6:3. Omit "Wherefore" at beginning of verse. WHm (**U**)

7:15. Omit "into Egypt" after "Jacob went down". WHm (**PNA**)

7:34. Read "his groaning" instead of "their groaning". WH (**U**)

7:36. Omit "the land of" before "Egypt". L Tr WH (**PWH**)

7:38. Read "unto you" instead of "unto us". WH (**PWH**)

7:43. Read "Rompha" instead of "Remphan". WH (**PWH**)

7:43. Read "Raiphan" instead of "Remphan". NA (**U**)

7:46. Read "house of Jacob" instead of "God of Jacob". NA (**PWH**)

8:1. Omit "and" before "they were all scattered". WHm (**PNA**)

9:11. Read "Arise" instead of "Having risen". L WH (**PWH**)

9:21. Read "unto Jerusalem" instead of "in Jerusalem". NA (**PWH**)

10:19. Omit "three" before "men". WHm (**U**)

10:19. Read "two men" instead of "three men". WH (**PWH**)

10:45. Read "who came" instead of "as many as came". WH (**PWH**)

11:3. Read "he went in" instead of "You went in". WH (**PWH**)

11:3. Read "did eat" instead of "didst eat". WH (**PWH**)

11:23. Add "in" before "the Lord" and render "that they would cleave unto the purpose of their heart in the Lord". WH (**PNA**)

12:6. Read "brought him to [him]" instead of "brought him forth". WH (**PNA**)

12:17. Omit "unto them" after "declared". NAm (**PWH**)

12:24. Read "of the Lord" instead of "of God". WH (**PWH**)

13:19. Omit "And" at beginning of verse. WH (**PWH**)

13:22. Omit "a man" after "Jesse". WHm (**PNA**)

13:33. Read "unto our children" instead of "unto us their children". WH (**PWH**)

13:33. Omit "their" before "children" and render "unto us the children". NAm (**PWH**)

13:48. Read "word of God" instead of "word of the Lord". WH (**PWH**)

14:25. Read "unto Perga" instead of "in Perga". WHm (**PNA**)

16:11. Read "And" instead of "Therefore" at beginning of verse. NA (**PWH**)

16:12. Read "a city of the first district" instead of "the chief city of that part". NA (**PNA**)

16:26. Omit "immediately" before "all the doors". WHm (**PNA**)

16:32. Read "word of God" instead of "word of the Lord". WH (**PWH**)

17:3. Omit "the" before "Christ" and render "this is Christ Jesus, whom I preach unto you" or "this is Christ: Jesus whom I preach unto you".WHm (**PNA**)

17:28. Read "poets among us" instead of "poets among you". WHm (**PNA**)

17:30. Read "sends word to" instead of "commands". WH (**U**)

18:3. Read "they wrought" instead of "(he) wrought". WH (**PWH**)

18:7. Read "entered into" instead of "came into". NA (**PNA**)

18:26. Omit "of God" after "the way". NAm (**PWH**)

19:1. Add "down" after "came". NA (**PWH**)

19:24. Omit "silver" before "shrines". WHm (**PNA**)

19:34. Add "Great [is] Diana of the Ephesians" after "Great [is] Diana of the Ephesians". WHm (**PNA**)

20:5. Read "having gone thither" instead of "having gone before". WH (**U**)

20:10. Read "not to be troubled" instead of "Trouble not yourselves". WHm (**U**)

20:13. Read "we went thither" instead of "we went before". WHm (**PNA**)

20:15. Read "in the evening we arrived at Samos" instead of "the next [day] we arrived at Samos". WHm (**PNA**)

20:30. Omit "own selves" and render "Also of you shall". WHm (**PNA**)

20:32. Read "to the Lord" instead of "to God". WH (**PWH**)

21:25. Read "have sent" instead of "have written". WH (**PWH**)

22:11. Read "nothing" instead of "not". WHm (**PNA**)

22:11. Read "see" instead of "see clearly". WHm (**PWH**)

23:28. Omit "I brought him forth into their council" at end of verse. WHm (**PNA**)

24:26. Omit "him" after "given". WHm (**PNA**)

25:18. Add "evil" before "accusation". WHm (**U**)

26:21. Add "being" before "in the temple". NA (**PWH**)

26:26. Omit "also" before "I speak freely". WH (**PWH**)

27:27. Read "some country resounded to them" instead of "some country drew near to them" WHm (**PNA**)

27:37. Read "about threescore and sixteen" instead of "two hundred threescore and sixteen". WH (**PNA**)

27:39. Read "to save the ship" instead of "to thrust in the ship". WH (**U**)

28:1. Read "Melitene" instead of "Melita". WH (**PWH**)

28:9. Omit "also" after "others". WHm (**PNA**)

Romans
1:16. Omit "first" after "to the Jew". WHm (**PNA**)
1:27. Read "in them" instead of "in themselves". WH (**PNA**)
1:29. Transpose "wickedness, covetousness, maliciousness" to "wickedness, maliciousness, covetousness". WHm (**PNA**)
1:29. Transpose "wickedness, covetousness, maliciousness" to "maliciousness, wickedness, covetousness". WHm (**PNA**)
2:2. Read "For" instead of "But" at beginning of verse. WHm (**PWH**)
2:16. Read "in which God" instead of "when God". WH (**PNA**)
3:8. Omit "and" before "as some affirm". WHm (**PNA**)
3:22. Omit "Jesus" before "Christ". WHm (**PNA**)
4:1. Omit "has found" and render "What then shall we say of Abraham, our forefather according to the flesh?". WH (**PNA**)
5:1. Read "let us have" instead of "we have". WH (**PWH**)
5:3. Read "glorying" instead of "we glory". WHm (**U**)
5:6. Read "If indeed" instead of "For when". WH (**PNA**)
5:11. Omit "Christ" after "Jesus". WHm (**PNA**)
5:15. Omit "also" after "so". WHm (**PNA**)
5:17. Read "in one man's offense" instead of "by one man's offense". WHm (**PNA**)
5:17. Omit "of the gift" before "of righteousness". WHm (**PNA**)
5:17. Transpose "Jesus Christ" to "Christ Jesus". WHm (**PNA**)
6:3. Omit "Jesus" before "Christ". WHm (**PNA**)
6:11. Omit "to be" before "dead". NAm (**PWH**)
6:19. Omit "unto iniquity" after "and to iniquity". WHm (**PNA**)
8:11. Add "Jesus" after "Christ". WH (**PWH**)
8:11. Omit "also" before "quicken". WHm (**PNA**)
8:11. Read "because of his Spirit that dwells in you" instead of "by his Spirit, that dwells in you". WHm (**PNA**)
8:23. Omit "we" before "ourselves groan". WHm (**PNA**)
8:24. Omit "why" and read "await" instead of "hope for" and render "does he yet await?". WHm (**U**)
8:28. Add "God" and render "God works with all things for

good". WH (**PWH**)

8:34. Add "from the dead" after "risen". WH (**PWH**)

8:34. Omit "even" before "at the right hand". WH (**PWH**)

8:35. Read "God" instead of "Christ". WHm (**PNA**)

9:5. Re-punctuate "Christ [came], who is over all, God blessed forever" to "Christ [came], who is blessed God over all for ever". NA (**PWH**)

9:5. Re-punctuate "Christ [came], who is over all, God blessed forever" to "Christ [came]. He who is God over all [be] blessed forever". WHm (**U**)

9:13. Read "Even as" instead of "As" at beginning of verse. WH (**PWH**)

9:19. Add "then" after "Why". NA (**PWH**)

9:23. Omit "and" at beginning of verse. WH (**PWH**)

9:26. Omit "unto them" after "it was said". WHm (**PNA**)

10:5. Add "that" after "describes" and render "writes that". WH (**PWH**)

10:5. Omit "That" before "the man which does".WH (**PNA**)

10:9. Add "the word that" before "[the] Lord" and render "confess with thy mouth the word that Jesus [is] Lord". WH (**PWH**)

10:15. Read "even as" instead of "as". WH (**PWH**)

10:20. Add "among" after "manifest" and render "manifest among them". WHm (**PNA**)

11:8. Read "even as" instead of "according as". WH (**PNA**)

12:2. Read "and not to be conformed" instead of "And be not conformed". WHm (**PNA**)

12:2. Read "but to be transformed" instead of "but be you transformed". WHm (**PNA**)

13:13. Read "strifes and envyings" instead of "strife and envying". WHm (**PNA**)

13:14. Read "Christ Jesus" instead of "the Lord Jesus Christ". WHm (**PNA**)

14:13. Omit "or an occasion to fall" after "a stumbling block". WHm (**PNA**)

14:19. Read "We therefore follow after" instead of "Let us therefore follow after". WHm (**PNA**)

15:4. Add "all" before "written for our learning". WH (**PWH**)

15:4. Add "of the comfort" after "have hope". WHm (**PNA**)

15:5. Transpose "Christ Jesus" to "Jesus Christ". WHm (**PNA**)

15:8. Read "became a minister" (aorist) instead of "has become a minister". WHm (**PNA**)

15:18. Read "I do not dare" instead of "I will not dare". WHm (**PWH**)

15:19. Add "Holy" before "Spirit". WH (**PWH**)

16:21. Omit "my" before "workfellow" and render "the workfellow". WHm (**PNA**)

16:25. Omit the entire verse (with verses **25-27**). NAm (**PWH**)

16:26. Omit the entire verse (with verses **25-27**). NAm (**PWH**)

16:27. Omit the entire verse (with verses **25-27**). NAm (**PWH**)

First Corinthians

1:4. Omit "my" before "God always". WH (**PWH**)

2:4. Omit "words" and render "enticement of". NAm (**PWH**)

2:9. Read "whatsoever things" instead of "the things which". WH (**PNA**)

2:10. Read "For" instead of "But" at beginning of verse. WH (**PWH**)

2:13. Read "spiritually" instead of "with spiritual (things)". WHm (**PNA**)

3:2. Omit "yet" before "now". WHm (**PNA**)

3:12. Add "and" after "gold". WHm (**PNA**)

4:17. Add "very" after "this". WHm (**PNA**)

5:8. Read "not with the leaven of malice" instead of "neither with the leaven of malice". WHm (**PWH**)

5:13. Re-accent "judges" to "shall judge". NA (**PWH**)

6:7. Omit "therefore" after "Now" at beginning of verse. NAm (**U**)

6:11. Add "our" and render "our Lord". WH (**PWH**)

6:14. Read "also raised up us" instead of "will also raise up us". WHm (**PNA**)

6:16. Omit "Or" at beginning of verse. NAm (**PWH**)

7:5. Omit "your" before "incontinency". WHm (**PNA**)

7:13. Read "if any woman" instead of "the woman which". NA (**PWH**)

7:34. Omit "both" before "in body". WHm (**PNA**)

7:38. Read "shall do well" instead of "does well". WHm (**PNA**)

7:40. Read "for I think" instead of "and I think". WH (**PNA**)

8:6. Omit "but" at beginning of verse. WHm (**PNA**)

8:10. Omit "you" after "see" and render "see him that has". WHm (**PNA**)

9:7. Omit "or" before "who feeds a flock". WHm (**PNA**)

10:3. Omit "the same" before "spiritual meat". WHm (**PNA**)

10:20. Omit "they sacrifice" before "to devils". NAm (**PWH**)

11:15. Omit "her" after "given". NAm (**PWH**)

11:17. Read "Now this I charge [you], not praising [you], for" instead of "Now in this that I charge [you] I praise [you] not, that". WHm (**PNA**)

12:6. Read "and" instead of "but" before "it is the same God". WH (**PWH**)

12:21. Omit "And" at beginning of verse. WHm (**PNA**)

13:5. Read "seeks not what is not her own" instead of "seeks not her own". WHm (**PNA**)

13:8. Read "prophecy, it will fail" instead of "prophecies, they will fail". WHm (**PNA**)

14:6. Omit "by" before "doctrine". NAm (**U**)

14:15. Omit "and" after "sing with the spirit". WHm (**PNA**)

14:18. Read "a tongue" instead of "tongues". WHm (**PWH**)

15:14. Read "our faith" instead of "your faith". WH (**PWH**)

15:17. Add "is" before "vain". WH (**PWH**)

15:54. Omit "this corruptible shall have put on incorruption, and" before "this mortal". WH (**PWH**)

16:6. Omit "and" before "winter with you". WH (**U**)

16:10. Omit "also" after "as I". WH (**U**)

Second Corinthians

1:6. Omit "and salvation" after "afflicted, [it is] for your consolation". WHm (**PNA**)

1:6. Transpose "or whether we be comforted, [it is] for your consolation and salvation" to after "And our hope of you [is] steadfast" in verse **7**. WHm (**PNA**)

1:6. Read "for your consolation, which is effectual in the enduring of the same sufferings which we also suffer, (7) and our hope of you is steady; or whether we be comforted, [it is] for your consolation and salvation. Knowing". WHm (**PNA**)

1:12. Read "holiness" instead of "simplicity". WH (**PWH**)

1:15. Read "joy" instead of "benefit". WH (**PWH**)

1:19. Transpose "Jesus Christ" to "Christ Jesus". WH (**PNA**)

1:22. Omit "who" and render "and he has sealed us". WHm (**PNA**)

2:7. Omit "rather" before "to forgive". WH (**PNA**)

2:9. Read "in which [proof] ye are obedient" instead of "whether ye be obedient". WHm (**PNA**)

3:3. Add "and" before "written". WHm (**PWH**)

3:5. Read "as of them" instead of "as of ourselves". WH (**PNA**)

3:14. Re-punctuate to "the same veil at the reading of the old testament remains, not unveiled that [it] is done away in Christ". NA (**PNA**)

4:5. Read "through Jesus" instead of "for Jesus' sake". WHm (**PNA**)

4:14. Omit "the Lord" before "Jesus". WHm (**PNA**)

4:17. Omit "our" before "light affliction". WH (**PWH**)

5:3. Read "unclothed" instead of "clothed". NA (**PWH**)

7:12. Add "but" before "nor for his cause that suffered wrong". WH (**PWH**)

7:14. Omit "which [I made]" after "boasting". WH (**PWH**)

8:9. Omit "Christ" after "Jesus". WHm (**PNA**)

8:19. Read "in this grace" instead of "with this grace". WH (**PWH**)

9:4. Read "I say" instead of "we say". NA (**PWH**)

9:11. Read "thanksgiving of God" instead of "thanksgiving to God". WHm (**PNA**)

10:14. Omit "not" after "For we stretch" and render 'For do we stretch ourselves beyond [our measure], as though we reached not unto you?'. WHm (**PNA**)

11:30. Omit "my" before "infirmities". WHm (**PNA**)

12:1. Read "Now to glory is not expedient, but I will come" instead of "It is not expedient for me doubtless to glory. I will come". WHm (**U**)

12:3. Omit "I cannot tell" before "God knows". WHm (**PNA**)

12:9. Omit "my" before "infirmities". WH (**PWH**)

13:4. Read "weak with him" instead of "weak in him". WHm (**PNA**)

13:4. Omit "toward you" at end of verse. WHm (**PNA**)

13:5. Transpose "Jesus Christ" to "Christ Jesus". WHm (**PNA**)

13:14. Omit "Christ" after "Jesus". WHm (**PNA**)

Galatians

1:3. Omit "our" and render "the Lord". WHm (**PNA**)

1:6. Omit "of Christ" and render "into grace". NAm (**PWH**)

2:16. Transpose "faith of Jesus Christ" to "faith of Christ Jesus". WH (**PNA**)

3:21. Read "in the law" instead of "from the law". WH (**U**)

4:25. Omit "Agar" after "this". WHm (**PNA**)

5:6. Omit "Jesus" before "Christ". WHm (**PNA**)

6:4. Omit "every man" and render "let him prove". WHm (**PNA**)

6:10. Read "As we may have" instead of "As we have". WH (**PNA**)

6:12. Add "Jesus" after "Christ". WH (**PWH**)

6:13. Read "who have been circumcised" instead of "who are being circumcised". WHm (**U**)

6:18. Omit "our" and render "the Lord". WHm (**PNA**)

Ephesians

1:15. Omit "love" before "unto all the saints" and render "and which [faith ye shew] unto all the saints". WH (**PWH**)

2:5. Add "in" and render "together in Christ" instead of "together with Christ". WHm (**PNA**)

3:1. Omit "Jesus" before "Christ". NAm (**U**)

3:19. Read "that all the fulness of God might be filled up" instead of "that ye might be filled with all the fulness of God". WHm (**PNA**)

4:4. Omit "also" after "even as". WHm (**PNA**)

4:16. Read "member" instead of "part". WHm (**PNA**)

4:21. Re-accent "as the truth is in Jesus" to "as he is in truth, [even] in Jesus". WHm (**PNA**)

4:32. Read "forgiven us" instead of "forgiven you". WHm (**PNA**)

5:2. Read "given himself for you" instead of "given himself for us". WH (**PWH**)

5:32. Omit "concerning" before "the church". WHm (**U**)

6:12. Read "you wrestle" instead of "we wrestle". WHm (**PNA**)

6:19. Omit "of the gospel" after "the mystery". WHm (**PNA**)

Philippians

1:14. Add "of God" after "word". WH (**PWH**)

1:19. Read "But" instead of "For" at beginning of verse. WHm (**PNA**)

2:2. Read "of the same mind" instead of "of one mind" at end of verse. WHm (**PNA**)

2:12. Omit "as" before "in my presence". WHm (**PNA**)

2:21. Transpose "Jesus Christ's" to "Christ Jesus' ". WH (**PNA**)

2:26. Add "to see" before "you all" and render "longed to see you all". WH (**PWH**)

2:30. Read "of [the] Lord" instead of "of Christ". WH (**PNA**)

3:13. Read "not yet" instead of "not". WH (**PWH**)

Colossians

1:3. Omit "Christ" after "Jesus". WHm (**PNA**)

1:7. Read "for us a faithful minister" instead of "for you a faithful minister". WH (**PNA**)

1:12. Add "God" before "the Father". WHm (**PNA**)

1:14. Read "had redemption" instead of "have redemption". WHm (**PNA**)

1:22. Read "yet now were you reconciled" instead of "yet now has he reconciled". WHm (**PNA**)

3:12. Omit "and" before "beloved". WHm (**PNA**)

292

3:15. Omit "one" and render "the body". WHm (**PNA**)
3:16. Read "word of the Lord" instead of "word of Christ". WHm (**PNA**)

First Thessalonians
1:8. Add "in" before "Achaia". NA (**PWH**)
1:9. Read "show of you" instead of "show of us". WHm (**U**)
2:16. Read "has come" (perfect) instead of "came" (aorist). WHm (**PWH**)
3:2. Read "fellow laborer" instead of "minister of God". WHm (**PNA**)
3:13. Read "unblamably" instead of "unblamable". WHm (**PNA**)
4:1. Omit "then" after "Furthermore". WH (**PWH**)
5:3. Read "But" instead of "For" at beginning of verse. WHm (**PWH**)
5:4. Read "as thieves" instead of "as a thief". WH (**PWH**)
5:9. Omit "Christ" after "Jesus". WHm (**PNA**)

Second Thessalonians
1:4. Read "tribulations in which you are held" instead of "tribulations that you endure". WHm (**PNA**)
2:1. Omit "our" before "Lord" and render "the Lord". WHm (**PWH**)
2:14. Add "also" after "unto which". NA (**PWH**)
3:6. Read "you received" instead of "he received". WH (**PWH**)

First Timothy
1:12. Read "enables" instead of "enabled". WHm (**PNA**)
2:8. Read "doubtings" instead of "doubting". WH (**U**)
2:9. Read "adorn themselves modestly in apparel" instead of "adorn themselves in modest apparel". WHm (**PNA**)
3:14. Omit "unto you" after "to come". WHm (**PNA**)
4:6. Read "which you followed" instead of "which you have followed". WHm (**PNA**)
5:5. Read "the Lord" instead of "God". WHm (**PNA**)
5:20. Add "But" at beginning of verse. WH (**PWH**)

6:13. Omit "you" after "I give". NAm (**PWH**)

6:13. Transpose "Christ Jesus" to "Jesus Christ". WHm (**PWH**)

6:17. Read "mind not high things" instead of "be not highminded". WHm (**PNA**)

Second Timothy

1:2. Read "the Lord Jesus Christ our Lord" instead of "Christ Jesus our Lord". WHm (**PWH**)

2:22. Add "all" before "them that call". WHm (**PWH**)

4:2. Transpose "rebuke, exhort" to "exhort, rebuke". WHm (**PNA**)

4:21. Omit "all" before "the brethren". WHm (**PNA**)

Titus

1:1. Transpose "Jesus Christ" to "Christ Jesus". WHm (**PNA**)

1:1. Omit "Jesus" before "Christ". WHm (**PNA**)

2:10. Omit "fidelity" after "all good". WHm (**PNA**)

2:13. Transpose "Jesus Christ" to "Christ Jesus". WH (**PNA**)

3:9. Read "contention" instead of "contentions". WH (**PNA**)

Philemon

1:6. Omit "which is" after "every good thing". WHm (**PNA**)

Hebrews

1:8. Omit "and ever" after "for ever". WHm (**PNA**)

1:8. Read "his kingdom" instead of "your kingdom". WH (**PWH**)

4:3. Read "Therefore" instead of "For" at beginning of verse. WHm (**PWH**)

4:7. Read "as he has said before" instead of "as it is said". WHm (**PNA**)

6:2. Read "[even] the doctrine" (accusative case, referring back to "foundation") instead of "of the doctrine" (genitive, continuing the list). WH (**PWH**)

6:2. Omit "and" before "of resurrection". WH (**PNA**)

7:1. Read "who, having met" (broken construction) instead of "who met". WHm (**PNA**)

7:27. Read "offered himself" instead of "offered up himself". T WHm (**PNA**)

8:10. Read "heart" instead of "hearts". T WHm (**PWH**)

9:17. Read "it is not then of strength" instead of "it is of no strength at all". WH (**PWH**)

9:19. Omit "and of goats" after "calves". NAm (**PWH**)

10:1. Read "they can never" instead of "(it) can never". WH (**PWH**)

10:4. Transpose "bulls and of goats" to "goats and of bulls". WHm (**PNA**)

10:11. Read "high priest" instead of "priest". WHm (**PNA**)

11:11. Re-accent "Sara herself" to "by Sara herself" (instrumental dative) and render "Through faith, and by Sara herself, he received strength to establish seed when he was past age, because he judged". WHm (**U**)

11:11. Add "being barren" after "Sara herself" and render "Through faith, and Sara herself being barren, he received strength to establish seed when he was past age, because he judged". NA (**U**)

11:35. Read "They received women, their dead" instead of "Women received their dead". WHm (**PNA**)

11:37. Transpose "were sawn asunder, were tempted" to "were tempted, were sawn asunder". WH (**PWH**)

11:37. Omit "were tempted". NA (**PWH**)

12:3. Read "against themselves" instead of "against himself". WH (**PWH**)

12:9. Add "but" before "shall we not". NA (**PWH**)

12:11. Read "Indeed" instead of "Now" at beginning of verse. WH (**PNA**)

12:15. Add "the" before "many". WH (**PWH**)

12:19. Omit "not" and render "refused" instead of "entreated". WH (**PNA**)

12:21. Read "exceedingly quake" instead of "quake". WHm (**PWH**)

12:22. Re-punctuate "to an innumerable company of angels, (23) To the general assembly and church of the firstborn" to "to an innumerable company [in] the general assembly of angels, and to the church of the firstborn". WHm (**PNA**)

13:10. Omit "right" and render "they have not" instead of "they have no right". WHm (**PNA**)

13:21. Add "for himself" before "working". WHm (**PNA**)

13:21. Omit "and ever" after "for ever". NAm (**PWH**)

13:22. Read "to suffer the word" instead of "suffer (you) the word". WHm (**PNA**)

James

Title. Omit "The General Epistle" before "of James". WH (**PWH**)

2:3. Transpose "Stand you there, or sit" to "Stand you, or sit there". WH (**PNA**)

2:4. Omit "not" and render the verse as a statement. WHm (**PNA**)

2:26. Omit "For" at beginning of verse. WH (**PWH**)

4:14. Omit "what" before "[will be] on the morrow" and render "you know not what your life [will be] on the morrow". WH (**PWH**)

4:14. Omit "even" before "a vapor". L WHm (**PWH**)

5:4. Read "kept in arrears" instead of "kept back by fraud". WH (**U**)

5:14. Omit "of the Lord" after "name". WHm (**PNA**)

5:20. Read "Know you" instead of "Let him know". WH (**PNA**)

First Peter

2:1. Read "hypocrisy" instead of "hypocrisies". WH (**PWH**)

2:24. Read "your sins" instead of "our sins". WHm (**PNA**)

3:1. Omit "also" after "they". WH (**PWH**)

3:4. Transpose "meek and quiet" to "quiet and meek". WH (**PWH**)

3:7. Read "you in your prayers" instead of "your prayers". WHm (**PNA**)

3:18. Read "died for sins" instead of "suffered for sins". WH (**PWH**)

4:1. Read "unto sins" instead of "from sin". WH (**PWH**)

4:18. Add "then" after "where". WH (**PWH**)

296

4:19. Omit "their" and render "the souls". WH (**U**)

5:2. Add "according to God" after "willingly". NA (**PWH**)

5:10. Omit "(may he) settle" at end of verse. WH (**U**)

Second Peter

2:4. Read "dens of darkness" instead of "chains of darkness". WH (**PWH**)

2:8. Omit "that" before "righteous [man]" and render "For he, [being] righteous, dwelling". WH (**U**)

2:11. Omit "before the Lord" after "against them". WHm (**U**)

2:11. Read "from the Lord" instead of "before the Lord". NA (**U**)

2:13. Read "in their love feasts" instead of "with their own deceivings". WHm (**PNA**)

2:14. Read "insatiable for sin" instead of "that cannot cease from sin". WH (**PNA**)

2:15. Read "Beor" instead of "Bosor". WH (**PWH**)

2:15. Read "they loved" instead of "who loved". WHm (**PNA**)

3:5. Read "things put together by the word of God were the heavens of old and the earth" instead of "by the word of God the heavens were of old, and the earth put together". WHm (**PNA**)

First John

2:14. Omit "of God" after "word". WHm (**PNA**)

2:17. Omit "of it" after "lust". WHm (**PNA**)

2:20. Omit "and" before "you know". WH (**PWH**)

2:24. Omit "in" before "the Father". WHm (**PNA**)

3:13. Add "And" at beginning of verse. NA (**PWH**)

3:23. Read "we believe" instead of "we should believe". WHm (**PNA**)

4:3. Read "annuls" instead of "confesses not". WHm (**PNA**)

4:15. Add "Christ" after "Jesus". WH (**PWH**)

5:10. Read "in him" instead of "in himself". WH (**PNA**)

5:20. Read "we know him" instead of "we may know him". WH (**PNA**)

Second John

1:12. Read "your joy" instead of "our joy". WH (**PWH**)

Third John
1:4. Read "grace" (or 'thankfulness') instead of "joy". WH (**PWH**)

Jude
1:5. Read "ye know all things, how that the Lord, having once saved" instead of "ye once knew this, how that the Lord, having saved". NA (**PNA**)

1:5. Read "Jesus" instead of "the Lord". WHm (**PNA**)

1:15. Read "convince every soul" instead of "convince all that are ungodly". NA (**PWH**)

1:23. Read "and others save, pulling [them] out of the fire; and others pity with fear" instead of "and others save with fear, pulling [them] out of the fire". NA (**PNA**)

1:23. Read "Save [them], pulling [them] out of the fire; and others pity with fear". WH (**PNA**)

Revelation
1:5. Omit "our" before "sins". WHm (**PNA**)

1:6. Read "made for us" instead of "made us". WHm (**PNA**)

2:1. Read "[the] church, who" instead of "the church". WH (**PNA**)

2:7. Add "my" before "God". WHm (**PNA**)

2:8. Read "[the] church, who" instead of "the church". WH (**PNA**)

2:10. Read "not" instead of "not at all". WH (**PWH**)

2:10. Read "and may have tribulation" instead of "and you will have tribulation". WH (**U**)

2:14. Omit "because" before "you have". WHm (**PNA**)

2:18. Read "[the] church, who" instead of "the church". WH (**PNA**)

2:18. Omit "his" before "eyes". WHm (**PNA**)

2:20. Add "your" before "that woman" and render "your wife". WHm (**PNA**)

3:2. Read "have not found works of yours" instead of "have not found your works". WH (**PNA**)

3:7. Transpose "he that is holy, he that is true" to "he that is true, he that is holy". WHm (**PNA**)

3:17. Add "the" before "miserable". WHm (**PNA**)

5:10. Read "they will reign" instead of "we will reign". NA (**PWH**)

5:11. Add "as it were" after "I heard". WHm (**PNA**)

6:4. Omit "from" before "the earth" and render "take the peace of the earth". WHm (**PNA**)

6:11. Read "should have fulfilled [their course]" instead of "should be fulfilled". WHm (**U**)

7:3. Read "and the sea" instead of "neither the sea". WHm (**PNA**)

8:2. Read "was given" instead of "were given". WHm (**PNA**)

8:5. Transpose "voices and thunderings and lightnings" to "thunderings and lightnings and voices". WHm (**U**)

9:20. Omit "yet" before "repented not". WH (**PWH**)

11:17. Add "and" before "because". WHm (**PNA**)

12:6. Read "they feed" instead of "they should feed". WHm (**PNA**)

13:2. Read "of lions" instead of "of a lion". WHm (**PNA**)

13:7. Omit "And it was given unto him to make war with the saints, and to overcome them" at beginning of verse. WHm (**PNA**)

13:10. Read "[is] to be killed" instead of "kills". NA (**PWH**)

13:10. Omit "must" and render 'shall be killed'. NA (**PWH**)

13:15. Read "he will cause" instead of "(he should) cause" and render "that even the image of the beast should speak; and he shall cause". WHm (**PNA**)

13:16. Read "that he shall give them a mark" instead of "that he should give them a mark". WHm (**U**)

13:17. Omit "and" at beginning of verse. WHm (**PNA**)

14:3. Omit "as it were" before "a new song". NAm (**PWH**)

14:4. Omit "These are" at beginning of verse. WHm (**PNA**)

14:8. Omit "angel" after "another". WHm (**PNA**)

14:10. Omit "holy" before "angels". WHm (**PNA**)

15:3. Read "ages" instead of "saints". WH (**PWH**)

15:6. Read "stone" instead of "linen". WH (**PWH**)

16:5. Read "holy" instead of "and shalt be". WHm (**PWH**)

18:3. Read "have fallen by" instead of "have drunk of". WH (**PWH**)

18:3. Omit "the wine of" before "the wrath". WHm (**PNA**)

18:8. Omit "the Lord" before "God". WHm (**PNA**)

18:22. Omit "of whatsoever craft [he be]" after "craftsman". WHm (**PNA**)

18:23. Read "merchants of yours were" instead of "your merchants were". WHm (**PNA**)

19:7. Read "and we will give" instead of "and (let us) give". WH (**PWH**)

19:13. Read "sprinkled with" instead of "dipped in". WH (**PWH**)

19:14. Omit "which were" after "armies". NAm (**PWH**)

19:20. Add "the" before "with him" and render "and the one with him, the". WHm (**PNA**)

20:5. Read "And" instead of "But" at beginning of verse. WHm (**U**)

21:3. Read "his people" instead of "his peoples". WHm (**PNA**)

21:12. Add "the names" after "which are". NA (**PWH**)

22:16. Read "in the churches" instead of "over the churches" (KJV 'in the churches'). WHm (**PNA**)

22:21. Read "with the saints" instead of "with you all". WH (**PWH**)

22:21. Read "with all" instead of "with you all". NA (**PWH**)

The Evidence of the Editors' Collations

Here we look at the plain evidence of the last few hundreds of years of Textual Criticism. The above examples are listed to provide the reader with the requisite demonstration.

First let us note that comparatively little has been accomplished since Westcott & Hort produced their Greek Critical Text—this despite the fact that they largely ignored the overwhelming evidence of the Minority Texts; that is, all the little scraps of the Bible found (more than 5000 cataloged) which tend to agree with each other far more than the Majority Texts from which W&H worked. But that aside—to examine the subject in its proper context and detail is far outside the scope of this Appendix—we simply wish to view the selected evidence from the previous section here for our own purposes.

It is somewhat refreshing to see that often when there are several changes within one verse, Panin will agree with W&H on one, and with N-A on the other. There appears to be no 'slant' to his work; it is straightforward and thorough.

Note first of all that W & H made 665 changes that currently disagree with N-A. Subsequently, our contemporary N-A team has made a mere 91 changes that disagree with W&H, despite all the additional manuscripts that have been discovered since 1881. This is somewhat remarkable, and attests to both the thoroughness of W&H's scholarship and the consistency of the manuscripts themselves.

Of the 665 corrections with differences from N-A made by W & H, 400 are marginal readings, and 265 are in the text itself. However, unlike most editors, W&H considered their marginal readings to be nearly, if not equally, significant as the selected textual reading. Thus these get weighted somewhat more than, say, the marginal readings of N-A.

Of the 91 corrections with differences from W&H made by N-A, 24 are marginal readings, and 67 are in the text itself. (The information in the list is from the 27th edition.)

<u>Of all of W&H's changes found in the **margin**</u>, Panin disagrees with **372** and only agrees with **21**. Additionally, Panin has **26** readings in this category which agree with neither W&H nor N-A; they are unique to his collation.

<u>Of all of W&H's changes found in the **text**</u>, Panin disagrees in **102** places and agrees in **163**. Of these **102** disagreements, **22** of Panin's readings agree with neither W&H nor N-A; they are unique to his collation.

<u>Of all of N-A's changes found in the **margin**</u>, Panin disagrees with **21** and only agrees with **3**. <u>Of all of N-A's changes found in the **text**</u>, Panin disagrees with **58** and agrees with a mere **9**. Included in these **58** disagreements are **7** instances in which Panin departs from both W&H and N-A; they are unique to his collation.

This tells us several remarkable things.

First, and probably most significantly, of the **474** instances in which Panin disagrees with W&H, **426** <u>are fully supported by subsequent scholarship, as shown by the fact that N-A agree with Panin</u>. **This means that <u>90%</u> of Panin's differences with W&H, where they disagree with N-A, have been vindicated by modern scholarship.**

If we ignore the marginal readings of W&H and look *only* at the text itself, of the **265** instance in which Panin disagrees with W&H, **80** <u>are fully supported by subsequent scholarship, as shown by the fact that N-A agrees with Panin</u>. This means that

30% of text changes made by Panin—more than half a century before N-A 27 even existed—have been vindicated by modern scholarship. And these corrections were made to the **best example available** in Panin's day of textual criticism.

We can with confidence note that history is vindicating Panin's Numerical approach to the scriptures. The generally accepted text is moving closer and closer to what Panin put down a century ago. We note also that Panin (post mortem) is not impressed with our current methods of textual criticism, or at least is not impressed with that being done by N-A. Of the **91** corrections they make that disagree with W&H, Panin agrees with a mere **12**. The current methodology, or *critical apparatus* as it's called, can fall short; our departed friend is not the only critic of approaching the Scriptures without belief that they are the very Word of God. It is is wise to remove the sandals in some endeavors.

What we can observe here is not so much that Panin is close to Nestle-Aland 28, but that *Nestle-Aland is slowly but surely getting closer to Panin.*

This is a clear testimony to two things:
1. Panin's scholastic judgment was excellent with or without Numerics.
2. Numerics work.

It is that simple.

It might be useful for the reader to see the actual texts side-by-side. In the following sections, the first four chapters of John are presented in the Greek texts of Nestle-Aland (28th Edition) on the left, and Panin on the right. Note how very few differences exist in a text section of **2,933** words separated by a century. There are:
- Seven places of a spelling difference of *John*; 1:6, 15, 19, 26, 35, 40, 42, and 3:23.
- The spelling of *Isaiah* in 1:21, 25.

303

- The spelling of *I said* in 1:15.
- Whether *And I* is split into two words in 1:31, 33.
- The spelling of *stood* in 1:35.
- Whether *the* is included or not in 1:35, 46, 47, and 4:5.
- Whether *and* is included or not in 2:4 and 4:54.
- Whether *any-thing* is one word or two in 2:5.
- Whether it is *his brothers* or just *brothers* in 2:12.
- The spelling of the money changers' tables in 2:15.
- The spelling of *Rabbi* in 3:2, 4:26, and 4:31.
- The spelling of *to you* in 3:5.
- How John phrased that he was not the Christ in 3:28.
- Whether *is above all* belongs in 3:31.
- The spelling of *Samaritan* in 4:5, 7, 9, 39, and 40
- Whether *the woman* belongs in 4:11.
- Placement of *of you* in 4:16.
- Phrasing of *your speech* in 4:42.

As you can see, there are no earth-shattering changes here at all. Scholars are generally very honest and diligent people who are trained to take in every possible consideration to arrive at an accurate reading, and the consistency of the text demonstrates this.

Following the comparison with the Greek of Nestle-Aland, there will be a corresponding section having Panin on the *left* and Westcott & Hort's text on the *right* (right and left being reversed from the previous.) Again, there are no earth-shattering changes. We might note that there are a total of **40** variations between Panin and N-A, and **40** variations between Panin and W&H. The evidence is invariably pointing out the excellence of the Critical Text of Panin.

The Greek texts of John chapters one through four follow; textual variations are in **bold**.

1 Ἐν ἀρχῇ ἦν ὁ λόγος, καὶ ὁ λόγος ἦν πρὸς τὸν θεόν, καὶ θεὸς ἦν ὁ λόγος. 2 οὗτος ἦν ἐν ἀρχῇ πρὸς τὸν θεόν. 3 πάντα δι᾽ αὐτοῦ ἐγένετο, καὶ χωρὶς αὐτοῦ ἐγένετο οὐδὲ ἕν. ὃ γέγονεν 4 ἐν αὐτῷ ζωὴ ἦν, καὶ ἡ ζωὴ ἦν τὸ φῶς τῶν ἀνθρώπων· 5 καὶ τὸ φῶς ἐν τῇ σκοτίᾳ φαίνει, καὶ ἡ σκοτία αὐτὸ οὐ κατέλαβεν. 6 Ἐγένετο ἄνθρωπος, ἀπεσταλμένος παρὰ θεοῦ, ὄνομα αὐτῷ Ἰωάννης· 7 οὗτος ἦλθεν εἰς μαρτυρίαν ἵνα μαρτυρήσῃ περὶ τοῦ φωτός, ἵνα πάντες πιστεύσωσιν δι᾽ αὐτοῦ. 8 οὐκ ἦν ἐκεῖνος τὸ φῶς, ἀλλ᾽ ἵνα μαρτυρήσῃ περὶ τοῦ φωτός. 9 Ἦν τὸ φῶς τὸ ἀληθινόν, ὃ φωτίζει πάντα ἄνθρωπον, ἐρχόμενον εἰς τὸν κόσμον. 10 ἐν τῷ κόσμῳ ἦν, καὶ ὁ κόσμος δι᾽ αὐτοῦ ἐγένετο, καὶ ὁ κόσμος αὐτὸν οὐκ ἔγνω. 11 εἰς τὰ ἴδια ἦλθεν, καὶ οἱ ἴδιοι αὐτὸν οὐ παρέλαβον. 12 ὅσοι δὲ ἔλαβον αὐτόν, ἔδωκεν αὐτοῖς ἐξουσίαν τέκνα θεοῦ γενέσθαι, τοῖς πιστεύουσιν εἰς τὸ ὄνομα αὐτοῦ, 13 οἳ οὐκ ἐξ αἱμάτων οὐδὲ ἐκ θελήματος σαρκὸς οὐδὲ ἐκ θελήματος ἀνδρὸς ἀλλ᾽ ἐκ θεοῦ ἐγεννήθησαν. 14 Καὶ ὁ λόγος σὰρξ ἐγένετο καὶ ἐσκήνωσεν ἐν ἡμῖν, καὶ ἐθεασάμεθα τὴν δόξαν αὐτοῦ, δόξαν ὡς μονογενοῦς παρὰ πατρός, πλήρης χάριτος καὶ ἀληθείας. 15 Ἰωάννης μαρτυρεῖ περὶ αὐτοῦ καὶ κέκραγεν λέγων· οὗτος ἦν **ὃν εἶπον·** ὁ ὀπίσω μου ἐρχόμενος ἔμπροσθέν μου γέγονεν, ὅτι πρῶτός μου ἦν. 16 ὅτι ἐκ τοῦ πληρώματος αὐτοῦ ἡμεῖς πάντες ἐλάβομεν καὶ χάριν ἀντὶ χάριτος· 17 ὅτι ὁ νόμος διὰ Μωϋσέως ἐδόθη, ἡ χάρις καὶ ἡ ἀλήθεια διὰ Ἰησοῦ Χριστοῦ ἐγένετο. 18 Θεὸν οὐδεὶς ἑώρακεν πώποτε·

1 Εν αρχη ην ο λογος, και ο λογος ην προς τον Θεον, και Θεος ην ο λογος. 2 Ούτος ην εν αρχη προς τον Θεον. 3 παντα δι᾽ αυτου εγενετο, και χωρις αυτου εγενετο ουδε έν ὁ γεγονεν. 4 εν αυτω ζωη ην, και ή ζωη ην το φως των ανθρωπων. 5 και το φως εν τη σκοτια φαινει, και η σκοτια αυτο ου κατελαβεν. 6 εγενετο ανθρωπος απεσταλμενος παρα Θεου, ονομα αυτω **Ιωανης.** 7 ουτος ηλθεν εις μαρτυριαν, ίνα μαρτυρηση περι του φωτος, ίνα παντες πιστευσωσιν δι᾽ αυτου. 8 ουκ ην εκεινος το φως, αλλ᾽ ίνα μαρτυρηση περι του φωτος. 9 Ην το φως το αληθινον ό φωτιζει παντα ανθρωπον ερχομενον εις τον κοσμον. 10 εν τω κοσμω ην και ο κοσμος δι᾽ αυτου εγενετο, και ο κοσμος αυτον ουκ εγνω. 11 εις τα ιδια ηλθεν, και οἱ ιδιοι αυτον ου παρελαβον. 12 όσοι δε ελαβον αυτον, εδωκεν αυτοις εξουσιαν τεκνα Θεου γενεσθαι, τοις πιστευουσιν εις το ονομα αυτου, 13 οἱ ουκ εξ αἱματων ουδε εκ θεληματος σαρκος ουδε εκ θελματος ανδρος αλλ᾽ εκ Θεου εγεννηθησαν. 14 Και ο λογος σαρξ εγενετο και εσκηνωσεν εν ἡμιν, και εθεασαμεθα την δοξαν αυτου, δοξαν ὡς μονογενους παρα πατρος, πληρης χαριτος και αληθειας. 15 (**Ιωανης** μαρτυρει περι αυτου και κεκραγεν λεγων - ούτος ην **ὁ ειπων** - Ὁ οπισω μου ερχομενος εμπροσθεν μου γεγονεν, ότι πρωτος μου ην.) 16 ότι εκ του πληρωματος αυτου ἡμεις παντες ελαβομεν, και χαριν αντι χαριτος· 17 ότι ο νομος δια Μωυσεως εδοθη, ἡ χαρις και ἡ αληθεια δια Ιησου Χριστου εγενετο. 18 Θεον ουδεις ἑωρακεν πωποτε·

μονογενὴς θεὸς ὁ ὢν εἰς τὸν κόλπον τοῦ πατρὸς ἐκεῖνος ἐξηγήσατο. 19 Καὶ αὕτη ἐστὶν ἡ μαρτυρία τοῦ **Ἰωάννου**, ὅτε ἀπέστειλαν [πρὸς αὐτὸν] οἱ Ἰουδαῖοι ἐξ Ἱεροσολύμων ἱερεῖς καὶ Λευίτας ἵνα ἐρωτήσωσιν αὐτόν σὺ τίς εἶ; 20 καὶ ὡμολόγησεν καὶ οὐκ ἠρνήσατο, καὶ ὡμολόγησεν ὅτι ἐγὼ οὐκ εἰμὶ ὁ χριστός. 21 καὶ ἠρώτησαν αὐτόν· τί οὖν; σὺ **Ἠλίας** εἶ; καὶ λέγει· οὐκ εἰμί. ὁ προφήτης εἶ σύ; καὶ ἀπεκρίθη· οὔ. 22 εἶπαν οὖν αὐτῷ· τίς εἶ; ἵνα ἀπόκρισιν δῶμεν τοῖς πέμψασιν ἡμᾶς· τί λέγεις περὶ σεαυτοῦ; 23 ἔφη ἐγὼ *φωνὴ βοῶντος ἐν τῇ ἐρήμῳ εὐθύνατε τὴν ὁδὸν κυρίου,* καθὼς εἶπεν Ἠσαΐας ὁ προφήτης. 24 Καὶ ἀπεσταλμένοι ἦσαν ἐκ τῶν Φαρισαίων. 25 καὶ ἠρώτησαν αὐτὸν καὶ εἶπαν αὐτῷ· τί οὖν βαπτίζεις εἰ σὺ οὐκ εἶ ὁ χριστὸς οὐδὲ **Ἠλίας** οὐδὲ ὁ προφήτης; 26 ἀπεκρίθη αὐτοῖς ὁ **Ἰωάννης** λέγων ἐγὼ βαπτίζω ἐν ὕδατι· μέσος ὑμῶν ἔστηκεν ὃν ὑμεῖς οὐκ οἴδατε, 27 ὁ ὀπίσω μου ἐρχόμενος, οὗ οὐκ εἰμὶ [ἐγὼ] ἄξιος ἵνα λύσω αὐτοῦ τὸν ἱμάντα τοῦ ὑποδήματος. 28 ταῦτα ἐν Βηθανίᾳ ἐγένετο πέραν τοῦ Ἰορδάνου, ὅπου ἦν ὁ Ἰωάννης βαπτίζων. 29 Τῇ ἐπαύριον βλέπει τὸν Ἰησοῦν ἐρχόμενον πρὸς αὐτὸν καὶ λέγει· ἴδε ὁ ἀμνὸς τοῦ θεοῦ ὁ αἴρων τὴν ἁμαρτίαν τοῦ κόσμου. 30οὗτός ἐστιν ὑπὲρ οὗ ἐγὼ εἶπον ὀπίσω μου ἔρχεται ἀνὴρ ὃς ἔμπροσθέν μου γέγονεν, ὅτι πρῶτός μου ἦν. 31 **κἀγὼ** οὐκ ᾔδειν αὐτόν, ἀλλ' ἵνα φανερωθῇ τῷ Ἰσραὴλ διὰ τοῦτο ἦλθον ἐγὼ ἐν ὕδατι βαπτίζων. 32 Καὶ ἐμαρτύρησεν Ἰωάννης

μονογενης Θεος ὁ ων εις τον κολπον του πατρος εκεινος εξηγησατο. 19 Και αὐτη εστιν ἡ μαρτυρια του **Ιωανου**, ὅτε απεστειλαν προς αυτον οἱ Ιουδαιοι εξ Ἱεροσολυμων ιερεις και Λευειτας ινα ερωτησωσιν αυτον Συ τις ει; 20 και ὡμολογησεν και ουκ ηρνησατο, και ὡμολογησεν ὁτι Εγω ουκ ειμι ὁ Χριστος. 21 και ηρωτησαν αυτον Τι συ ουν; **Ηλειας** ει; και λεγει Ουκ ειμι. Ὁ προφητης ει συ; και απεκριθη Ου. 22 ειπαν ουν αυτω Τις ει; ινα αποκρισιν δωμεν τοις πεμψασιν ἡμας. τι λεγεις περι σεαυτου; 23 εφη Εγω φωνη βοωντος εν τη ερημω Ευθυνατε την οδον Κυριου, καθως ειπεν Ησαιας ὁ προφητης. 24 και απεσταλμενοι ησαν εκ των Φαρισαιων. 25 και ηρωτησαν αυτον και ειπαν αυτω Τι ουν βαπτιζεις ει συ ουκ ει ὁ Χριστος ουδε **Ηλειας** ουδε ὁ προφητης; 26 απεκριθη αυτοις ὁ **Ιωανης** λεγων Εγω βαπτιζω εν υδατι· μεσος υμων στηκει ὁν υμεις ουκ οιδατε, 27 οπισω μου ερχομενος, ου ουκ ειμι εγω αξιος ινα λυσω αυτου τον ιμαντα του υποδηματος. 28 ταυτα εν Βηθανια εγενετο περαν του Ιορδανου οπου ην ὁ Ιωανης βαπτιζων. 29 Τη επαυριον βλεπει τον Ιησουν ερχομενον προς αυτον, και λεγει Ιδε ὁ αμνος του Θεου ὁ αιρων την ἁμαρτιαν του κοσμου. 30 ουτος εστιν υπερ ου εγω ειπον Οπισω μου ερχεται ανηρ, ὁς εμπροσθεν μου γεγονεν, ὁτι πρωτος μου ην. 31 κα' 'γω ουκ ηδειν αυτον, αλλ' ινα φανερωθη τω Ισραηλ, δια τουτο ηλθον εγω εν υδατι βαπτιζων. 32 Και εμαρτυρησεν Ιωανης λέγων ὅτι τεθέαμαι τὸ πνεῦμα καταβαῖνον ὡς περιστερὰν ἐξ οὐρανοῦ καὶ ἔμεινεν ἐπ᾽ αὐτόν. 33 **κἀγὼ** οὐκ ᾔδειν αὐτόν, ἀλλ᾽ ὁ πέμψας με βαπτίζειν ἐν ὕδατι ἐκεῖνός μοι εἶπεν· ἐφ᾽ ὃν ἂν ἴδῃς τὸ πνεῦμα καταβαῖνον καὶ μένον ἐπ᾽ αὐτόν, οὗτός ἐστιν ὁ βαπτίζων ἐν πνεύματι ἁγίῳ. 34 **κἀγὼ** ἑώρακα καὶ μεμαρτύρηκα ὅτι οὗτός ἐστιν ὁ υἱὸς τοῦ θεοῦ. 35 Τῇ ἐπαύριον πάλιν **εἱστήκει ὁ Ἰωάννης** καὶ ἐκ τῶν μαθητῶν αὐτοῦ δύο 36 καὶ ἐμβλέψας τῷ Ἰησοῦ περιπατοῦντι λέγει· ἴδε ὁ ἀμνὸς τοῦ θεοῦ. 37 καὶ ἤκουσαν οἱ δύο μαθηταὶ αὐτοῦ λαλοῦντος καὶ ἠκολούθησαν τῷ Ἰησοῦ. 38 στραφεὶς δὲ ὁ Ἰησοῦς καὶ θεασάμενος αὐτοὺς ἀκολουθοῦντας λέγει αὐτοῖς· τί ζητεῖτε; οἱ δὲ εἶπαν αὐτῷ· **ῥαββί**, ὃ λέγεται μεθερμηνευόμενον διδάσκαλε, ποῦ μένεις; 39 λέγει αὐτοῖς· ἔρχεσθε καὶ ὄψεσθε. ἦλθαν οὖν καὶ εἶδαν ποῦ μένει καὶ παρ᾽ αὐτῷ ἔμειναν τὴν ἡμέραν ἐκείνην· ὥρα ἦν ὡς δεκάτη. 40 Ἦν Ἀνδρέας ὁ ἀδελφὸς Σίμωνος Πέτρου εἷς ἐκ τῶν δύο τῶν ἀκουσάντων παρὰ **Ἰωάννου** καὶ ἀκολουθησάντων αὐτῷ 41 εὑρίσκει οὗτος πρῶτον τὸν ἀδελφὸν τὸν ἴδιον Σίμωνα καὶ λέγει αὐτῷ· εὑρήκαμεν τὸν Μεσσίαν, ὅ ἐστιν μεθερμηνευόμενον χριστός. 42 ἤγαγεν αὐτὸν πρὸς τὸν Ἰησοῦν. ἐμβλέψας αὐτῷ ὁ Ἰησοῦς εἶπεν· σὺ εἶ Σίμων ὁ υἱὸς **Ἰωάννου**, σὺ κληθήσῃ Κηφᾶς, ὃ ἑρμηνεύεται Πέτρος. 43 Τῇ ἐπαύριον ἠθέλησεν ἐξελθεῖν εἰς τὴν Γαλιλαίαν καὶ εὑρίσκει Φίλιππον. καὶ λέγει αὐτῷ ὁ Ἰησοῦς· ἀκολούθει μοι. 44 ἦν δὲ ὁ Φίλιππος ἀπὸ Βηθσαϊδά, ἐκ τῆς

λεγων ὅτι Τεθεαμαι το Πνευμα καταβαινον ὡς περιστεραν εξ ουρανου, και εμεινεν επ᾽ αυτον. 33 **κα᾽ 'γω** ουκ ηδειν αυτον, αλλ᾽ ὁ πεμψας με βαπτιζειν εν υδατι εκεινος μοι ειπεν Εφ᾽ όν αν ιδης το Πνευμα καταβαινον και μενον επ᾽ αυτον, ουτος εστιν ὁ βαπτιζων εν Πνευματι Άγιω. 34 **κα᾽ 'γω** εωρακα, και μεμαρτυρηκα ὅτι ουτος εστιν ὁ υιος του Θεου. 35 Τη επαυριον παλιν **ιστηκει Ιωανης** και εκ των μαθητων αυτου δυο, 36 και εμβλεψας τω Ιησου περιπατουντι λεγει Ιδε, ὁ αμνος του Θεου. 37 και ηκουσαν οἱ δυο μαθηται αυτου λαλουντος και ηκολουθησαν τω Ιησου. 38 στραφεις δε ὁ Ιησους και θεασαμενος αυτους ακολουθουντας λεγει αυτοις Τι ζητειτε; οἱ δε ειπαν αυτω **Ῥαββει**, (ὁ λεγεται μεθερμηνευομενον Διδασκαλε,) που μενεις; 39 λεγει αυτοις Ερχεσθε και οψεσθε. ηλθαν ουν και ειδαν που μενει, και παρ᾽ αυτω εμειναν την ημεραν εκεινην· ωρα ην ὡς δεκατη. 40 ην Ανδρεας ὁ αδελφος Σιμωνος Πετρου εις εκ των δυο των ακουσαντων παρα **Ιωανου** και ακολουθησαντων αυτω 41 ευρισκει ουτος πρωτον τον αδελφον τον ιδιον Σιμωνα, και λεγει αυτω Ευρηκαμεν τον Μεσσιαν, (ὁ εστιν μεθερμηνευομενον Χριστος). 42 ηγαγεν αυτον προς τον Ιησουν. εμβλεψας αυτω ὁ Ιησους ειπεν Συ ει Σιμων ὁ υιος **Ιωανου**· συ κληθηση Κηφας, (ὁ ερμηνευεται Πετρος). 43 Τη επαυριον ηθελησεν εξελθειν εις την Γαλιλαιαν, και ευρισκει Φιλιππον και λεγει αυτω ὁ Ιησους Ακολουθει μοι. 44 ην δε ὁ Φιλιππος απο Βηθσαιδα, εκ της πόλεως Ἀνδρέου καὶ Πέτρου. 45 εὑρίσκει Φίλιππος τὸν Ναθαναὴλ καὶ λέγει αὐτῷ· ὃν ἔγραψεν Μωϋσῆς ἐν τῷ νόμῳ καὶ οἱ προφῆται εὑρήκαμεν, Ἰησοῦν υἱὸν τοῦ Ἰωσὴφ τὸν ἀπὸ Ναζαρέτ. 46 καὶ εἶπεν αὐτῷ Ναθαναήλ· ἐκ Ναζαρὲτ δύναταί τι ἀγαθὸν εἶναι; λέγει αὐτῷ [ὁ] Φίλιππος ἔρχου καὶ ἴδε. 47 Εἶδεν ὁ Ἰησοῦς τὸν Ναθαναὴλ ἐρχόμενον πρὸς αὐτὸν καὶ λέγει περὶ αὐτοῦ· ἴδε ἀληθῶς Ἰσραηλίτης ἐν ᾧ δόλος οὐκ ἔστιν. 48 λέγει αὐτῷ Ναθαναήλ· πόθεν με γινώσκεις; ἀπεκρίθη Ἰησοῦς καὶ εἶπεν αὐτῷ· πρὸ τοῦ σε Φίλιππον φωνῆσαι ὄντα ὑπὸ τὴν συκῆν εἶδόν σε. 49 ἀπεκρίθη αὐτῷ Ναθαναήλ· ῥαββί, σὺ εἶ ὁ υἱὸς τοῦ θεοῦ, σὺ βασιλεὺς εἶ τοῦ Ἰσραήλ. 50 ἀπεκρίθη Ἰησοῦς καὶ εἶπεν αὐτῷ· ὅτι εἶπόν σοι ὅτι εἶδόν σε ὑποκάτω τῆς συκῆς, πιστεύεις; μείζω τούτων ὄψῃ. 51 καὶ λέγει αὐτῷ· ἀμὴν ἀμὴν λέγω ὑμῖν, ὄψεσθε τὸν οὐρανὸν ἀνεῳγότα καὶ τοὺς ἀγγέλους τοῦ θεοῦ ἀναβαίνοντας καὶ καταβαίνοντας ἐπὶ τὸν υἱὸν τοῦ ἀνθρώπου.

2 Καὶ τῇ ἡμέρᾳ τῇ τρίτῃ γάμος ἐγένετο ἐν Κανὰ τῆς Γαλιλαίας, καὶ ἦν ἡ μήτηρ τοῦ Ἰησοῦ ἐκεῖ· 2 ἐκλήθη δὲ καὶ ὁ Ἰησοῦς καὶ οἱ μαθηταὶ αὐτοῦ εἰς τὸν γάμον. 3 καὶ ὑστερήσαντος οἴνου λέγει ἡ μήτηρ τοῦ Ἰησοῦ πρὸς αὐτόν· οἶνον οὐκ ἔχουσιν. 4 [καὶ] λέγει αὐτῇ ὁ Ἰησοῦς τί ἐμοὶ καὶ σοί, γύναι; οὔπω ἥκει ἡ ὥρα μου. 5 λέγει ἡ μήτηρ αὐτοῦ τοῖς διακόνοις· ὅ τι ἂν λέγῃ ὑμῖν ποιήσατε. 6 ἦσαν δὲ ἐκεῖ λίθιναι ὑδρίαι ἓξ κατὰ τὸν καθαρισμὸν τῶν Ἰουδαίων κείμεναι, χωροῦσαι ἀνὰ μετρητὰς

πολεως Ανδρεου και Πετρου. 45 ευρισκει Φιλιππος τον Ναθαναηλ, και λεγει αυτω Ὁν εγραψεν Μωυσης εν τω νομω και οἱ προφηται εὑρηκαμεν, Ιησουν υἱον του Ιωσηφ τον απο Ναζαρετ. 46 και ειπεν αυτω Ναθαναηλ Εκ Ναζαρετ δυναται τι αγαθον ειναι; λεγει αυτω ὁ Φιλιππος Ερχου και ιδε. 47 ειδεν Ιησους τον Ναθαναηλ ερχομενον προς αυτον και λεγει περι αυτου Ιδε αληθως Ισραηλειτης εν ᾧ δολος ουκ εστιν. 48 λεγει αυτω Ναθαναηλ Ποθεν με γινωσκεις; απεκριθη Ιησους και ειπεν αυτω, Προ του σε Φιλιππον φωνησαι, οντα ὑπο την συκην ειδον σε. 49 απεκριθη αυτω Ναθαναηλ Ῥαββει, συ ει ὁ υἱος του Θεου, συ βασιλευς ει του Ισραηλ. 50 απεκριθη Ιησους και ειπεν αυτω Ὁτι ειπον σοι ὁτι ειδον σε ὑποκατω της συκης πιστευεις; μειζω τουτων οψη. 51 και λεγει αυτω Αμην αμην λεγω ὑμιν, οψεσθε τον ουρανον ανεωγοτα και τους αγγελους του Θεου αναβαινοντας και καταβαινοντας επι τον υἱον του ανθρωπου.

2 Και τη ἡμερα τη τριτη γαμος εγενετο εν Κανα της Γαλιλαιας, και ην ἡ μητηρ του Ιησου εκει· 2 εκληθη δε και ὁ Ιησους και οἱ μαθηται αυτου εις τον γαμον. 3 και ὑστερησαντος οινου λεγει ἡ μητηρ του Ιησου προς αυτον Οινον ουκ εχουσιν. 4 και λεγει αυτη ὁ Ιησους Τι εμοι και σοι, γυναι; ουπω ηκει ἡ ωρα μου. 5 λεγει ἡ μητηρ αυτου τοις διακονοις Ὁτι αν λεγη ὑμιν, ποιησατε. 6 ησαν δε εκει λιθιναι ὑδριαι ἑξ κατα τον καθαρισμον των Ιουδαιων κειμεναι, χωρουσαι ανα μετρητας

δύο ἢ τρεῖς. 7 λέγει αὐτοῖς ὁ Ἰησοῦς· γεμίσατε τὰς ὑδρίας ὕδατος. καὶ ἐγέμισαν αὐτὰς ἕως ἄνω. 8 καὶ λέγει αὐτοῖς· ἀντλήσατε νῦν καὶ φέρετε τῷ ἀρχιτρικλίνῳ· οἱ δὲ ἤνεγκαν. 9 ὡς δὲ ἐγεύσατο ὁ ἀρχιτρίκλινος τὸ ὕδωρ οἶνον γεγενημένον καὶ οὐκ ᾔδει πόθεν ἐστίν, οἱ δὲ διάκονοι ᾔδεισαν οἱ ἠντληκότες τὸ ὕδωρ, φωνεῖ τὸν νυμφίον ὁ ἀρχιτρίκλινος 10 καὶ λέγει αὐτῷ· πᾶς ἄνθρωπος πρῶτον τὸν καλὸν οἶνον τίθησιν καὶ ὅταν μεθυσθῶσιν τὸν ἐλάσσω· σὺ τετήρηκας τὸν καλὸν οἶνον ἕως ἄρτι. 11 Ταύτην ἐποίησεν ἀρχὴν τῶν σημείων ὁ Ἰησοῦς ἐν Κανὰ τῆς Γαλιλαίας καὶ ἐφανέρωσεν τὴν δόξαν αὐτοῦ, καὶ ἐπίστευσαν εἰς αὐτὸν οἱ μαθηταὶ αὐτοῦ.

12 Μετὰ τοῦτο κατέβη εἰς Καφαρναοὺμ αὐτὸς καὶ ἡ μήτηρ αὐτοῦ καὶ οἱ ἀδελφοὶ [αὐτοῦ] καὶ οἱ μαθηταὶ αὐτοῦ καὶ ἐκεῖ ἔμειναν οὐ πολλὰς ἡμέρας.
13 Καὶ ἐγγὺς ἦν τὸ πάσχα τῶν Ἰουδαίων, καὶ ἀνέβη εἰς Ἱεροσόλυμα ὁ Ἰησοῦς. 14 Καὶ εὗρεν ἐν τῷ ἱερῷ τοὺς πωλοῦντας βόας καὶ πρόβατα καὶ περιστερὰς καὶ τοὺς κερματιστὰς καθημένους, 15 καὶ ποιήσας φραγέλλιον ἐκ σχοινίων πάντας ἐξέβαλεν ἐκ τοῦ ἱεροῦ τά τε πρόβατα καὶ τοὺς βόας, καὶ τῶν κολλυβιστῶν ἐξέχεεν τὸ **κέρμα** καὶ τὰς τραπέζας ἀνέτρεψεν, 16 καὶ τοῖς τὰς περιστερὰς πωλοῦσιν εἶπεν· ἄρατε ταῦτα ἐντεῦθεν, μὴ ποιεῖτε τὸν οἶκον τοῦ πατρός μου οἶκον ἐμπορίου. 17 ἐμνήσθησαν οἱ μαθηταὶ αὐτοῦ ὅτι γεγραμμένον ἐστίν· *ὁ ζῆλος τοῦ οἴκου σου*

δυο η τρεις. 7 λεγει αυτοις ὁ Ιησους Γεμισατε τας ὑδριας ὑδατος. και εγεμισαν αυτας ἑως ανω. 8 και λεγει αυτοις Αντλησατε νυν και φερετε τω αρχιτρικλινω. οἱ δε ηνεγκαν. 9 ὡς δε εγευσατο ὁ αρχιτρικλινος το ὑδωρ οινον γεγενημενον, και ουκ ῃδει ποθεν εστιν, οἱ δε διακονοι ῃδεισαν οἱ ηντληκοτες το ὑδωρ, φωνει τον νυμφιον ὁ αρχιτρικλινος 10 και λεγει αυτω Πας ανθρωπος πρωτον τον καλον οινον τιθησιν, και ὁταν μεθυσθωσιν τον ελασσω· συ τετηρηκας τον καλον οινον ἑως αρτι. 11 ταυτην εποιησεν αρχην των σημειων ὁ Ιησους εν Κανα της Γαλιλαιας, και εφανερωσεν την δοξαν αυτου, και επιστευσαν εις αυτον οἱ μαθηται αυτου.

12 Μετα τουτο κατεβη εις Καφαρναουμ, αυτος και ἡ μητηρ αυτου και οἱ αδελφοι και οἱ μαθηται αυτου· και εκει εμειναν ου πολλας ἡμερας.
13 Και εγγυς ην το πασχα των Ιουδαιων, και ανεβη εις Ιεροσολυμα ὁ Ιησους. 14 και εὑρεν εν τω ἱερω τους πωλουντας βοας και προβατα και περιστερας και τους κερματιστας καθημενους, 15 και ποιησας φραγελλιον εκ σχοινιων παντας εξεβαλεν εκ του ἱερου τα τε προβατα και τους βοας, και των κολλυβιστων εξεχεεν το **κερματα** και τας τραπεζας ανετρεψεν, 16 και τοις τας περιστερας πωλουσιν ειπεν Αρατε ταυτα εντευθεν, μη ποιειτε τον οικον του πατρος μου οικον εμποριου. 17 Εμνησθησαν οἱ μαθηται αυτου, ὁτι γεγραμμενον εστιν Ὁ ζηλος του οικου σου

καταφάγεταί με. 18 Ἀπεκρίθησαν οὖν οἱ Ἰουδαῖοι καὶ εἶπαν αὐτῷ· τί σημεῖον δεικνύεις ἡμῖν ὅτι ταῦτα ποιεῖς; 19 ἀπεκρίθη Ἰησοῦς καὶ εἶπεν αὐτοῖς· λύσατε τὸν ναὸν τοῦτον καὶ ἐν τρισὶν ἡμέραις ἐγερῶ αὐτόν. 20 εἶπαν οὖν οἱ Ἰουδαῖοι· τεσσεράκοντα καὶ ἓξ ἔτεσιν οἰκοδομήθη ὁ ναὸς οὗτος, καὶ σὺ ἐν τρισὶν ἡμέραις ἐγερεῖς αὐτόν; 21 ἐκεῖνος δὲ ἔλεγεν περὶ τοῦ ναοῦ τοῦ σώματος αὐτοῦ. 22 ὅτε οὖν ἠγέρθη ἐκ νεκρῶν, ἐμνήσθησαν οἱ μαθηταὶ αὐτοῦ ὅτι τοῦτο ἔλεγεν, καὶ ἐπίστευσαν τῇ γραφῇ καὶ τῷ λόγῳ ὃν εἶπεν ὁ Ἰησοῦς.
23 Ὡς δὲ ἦν ἐν τοῖς Ἱεροσολύμοις ἐν τῷ πάσχα ἐν τῇ ἑορτῇ, πολλοὶ ἐπίστευσαν εἰς τὸ ὄνομα αὐτοῦ θεωροῦντες αὐτοῦ τὰ σημεῖα ἃ ἐποίει· 24 αὐτὸς δὲ Ἰησοῦς οὐκ ἐπίστευεν αὐτὸν αὐτοῖς διὰ τὸ αὐτὸν γινώσκειν πάντας 25 καὶ ὅτι οὐ χρείαν εἶχεν ἵνα τις μαρτυρήσῃ περὶ τοῦ ἀνθρώπου· αὐτὸς γὰρ ἐγίνωσκεν τί ἦν ἐν τῷ ἀνθρώπῳ.
3 Ἦν δὲ ἄνθρωπος ἐκ τῶν Φαρισαίων, Νικόδημος ὄνομα αὐτῷ, ἄρχων τῶν Ἰουδαίων·2 οὗτος ἦλθεν πρὸς αὐτὸν νυκτὸς καὶ εἶπεν αὐτῷ ῥαββί, οἴδαμεν ὅτι ἀπὸ θεοῦ ἐλήλυθας διδάσκαλος· οὐδεὶς γὰρ δύναται ταῦτα τὰ σημεῖα ποιεῖν ἃ σὺ ποιεῖς, ἐὰν μὴ ᾖ ὁ θεὸς μετ᾽ αὐτοῦ. 3 ἀπεκρίθη Ἰησοῦς καὶ εἶπεν αὐτῷ· ἀμὴν ἀμὴν λέγω σοι, ἐὰν μή τις γεννηθῇ ἄνωθεν, οὐ δύναται ἰδεῖν τὴν βασιλείαν τοῦ θεοῦ. 4 Λέγει πρὸς αὐτὸν [ὁ] Νικόδημος· πῶς δύναται ἄνθρωπος γεννηθῆναι γέρων ὤν; μὴ δύναται εἰς τὴν κοιλίαν τῆς μητρὸς αὐτοῦ δεύτερον εἰσελθεῖν καὶ γεννηθῆναι; 5 ἀπεκρίθη Ἰησοῦς· ἀμὴν ἀμὴν λέγ ωσοι, ἐὰν

καταφαγεται με. 18 απεκριθησαν ουν οἱ Ιουδαιοι και ειπαν αυτω Τι σημειον δεικνυεις ἡμιν, ὅτι ταυτα ποιεις; 19 απεκριθη Ιησους και ειπεν αυτοις Λυσατε τον ναον τουτον και εν τρισιν ἡμεραις εγερω αυτον. 20 ειπαν ουν οἱ Ιουδαιοι Τεσσερακοντα και ἑξ ετεσιν οικοδομηθη ὁ ναος ουτος, και συ εν τρισιν ἡμεραις εγερεις αυτον; 21 εκεινος δε ελεγεν περι του ναου του σωματος αυτου. 22 ότε ουν ηγερθη εκ νεκρων, εμνησθησαν οἱ μαθηται αυτου ότι τουτο ελεγεν, και επιστευσαν τη γραφη και τω λογω όν ειπεν ὁ Ιησους.
23 Ὡς δε ην εν τοις Ἱεροσολυμοις εν τω πασχα εν τη ἑορτη, πολλοι επιστευσαν εις το ονομα αυτου, θεωρουντες αυτου τα σημεια ά εποιει. 24 αυτος δε ὁ Ιησους ουκ επιστευεν αυτον αυτοις δια το αυτον γινωσκειν παντας 25 και ότι ου χρειαν ειχεν ινα τις μαρτυρηση περι του ανθρωπου, αυτος γαρ εγινωσκεν τι ην εν τω ανθρωπω.
3 Ην δε ανθρωπος εκ των Φαρισαιων, Νικοδημος ονομα αυτω, αρχων των Ιουδαιων·2 ουτος ηλθεν προς αυτον νυκτος και ειπεν αυτω Ῥαββει, οιδαμεν ότι απο Θεου εληλυθας διδασκαλος· ουδεις γαρ δυναται ταυτα τα σημεια ποιειν ά συ ποιεις, εαν μη η ὁ Θεος μετ᾽ αυτου. 3 απεκριθη Ιησους και ειπεν αυτω Αμην αμην λεγω σοι, εαν μη τις γεννηθη ανωθεν, ου δυναται ιδειν την βασιλειαν του Θεου. 4 λεγει προς αυτον ὁ Νικοδημος Πως δυναται ανθρωπος γεννηθηναι γερων ων; μη δυναται εις την κοιλιαν της μητρος αυτου δευτερον εισελθειν και γεννηθηναι; 5 απεκριθη ὁ Ιησους Αμην αμην λεγω σοι, εαν

μή τις γεννηθῇ ἐξ ὕδατος καὶ πνεύματος, οὐ δύναται εἰσελθεῖν εἰς τὴν βασιλείαν τοῦ θεοῦ. 6 τὸ γεγεννημένον ἐκ τῆς σαρκὸς σάρξ ἐστιν, καὶ τὸ γεγεννημένον ἐκ τοῦ πνεύματος πνεῦμά ἐστιν. 7 μὴ θαυμάσῃς ὅτι εἶπόν σοι· δεῖ ὑμᾶς γεννηθῆναι ἄνωθεν. 8 τὸ πνεῦμα ὅπου θέλει πνεῖ καὶ τὴν φωνὴν αὐτοῦ ἀκούεις, ἀλλ᾽ οὐκ οἶδας πόθεν ἔρχεται καὶ ποῦ ὑπάγει· οὕτως ἐστὶν πᾶς ὁ γεγεννημένος ἐκ τοῦ πνεύματος. 9 Ἀπεκρίθη Νικόδημος καὶ εἶπεν αὐτῷ· πῶς δύναται ταῦτα γενέσθαι; 10 ἀπεκρίθη Ἰησοῦς καὶ εἶπεν αὐτῷ· σὺ εἶ ὁ διδάσκαλος τοῦ Ἰσραὴλ καὶ ταῦτα οὐ γινώσκεις; 11 ἀμὴν ἀμὴν λέγω σοι ὅτι ὃ οἴδαμεν λαλοῦμεν καὶ ὃ ἑωράκαμεν μαρτυροῦμεν, καὶ τὴν μαρτυρίαν ἡμῶν οὐ λαμβάνετε. 12 εἰ τὰ ἐπίγεια εἶπον ὑμῖν καὶ οὐ πιστεύετε, πῶς ἐὰν εἴπω ὑμῖν τὰ ἐπουράνια πιστεύσετε; 13 καὶ οὐδεὶς ἀναβέβηκεν εἰς τὸν οὐρανὸν εἰ μὴ ὁ ἐκ τοῦ οὐρανοῦ καταβάς, ὁ υἱὸς τοῦ ἀνθρώπου. 14 Καὶ καθὼς Μωϋσῆς ὕψωσεν τὸν ὄφιν ἐν τῇ ἐρήμῳ, οὕτως ὑψωθῆναι δεῖ τὸν υἱὸν τοῦ ἀνθρώπου, 15 ἵνα πᾶς ὁ πιστεύων ἐν αὐτῷ ἔχῃ ζωὴν αἰώνιον.

16 οὕτως γὰρ ἠγάπησεν ὁ θεὸς τὸν κόσμον, ὥστε τὸν υἱὸν τὸν μονογενῆ ἔδωκεν, ἵνα πᾶς ὁ πιστεύων εἰς αὐτὸν μὴ ἀπόληται ἀλλ᾽ ἔχῃ ζωὴν αἰώνιον. 17 οὐ γὰρ ἀπέστειλεν ὁ θεὸς τὸν υἱὸν εἰς τὸν κόσμον ἵνα κρίνῃ τὸν κόσμον, ἀλλ᾽ ἵνα σωθῇ ὁ κόσμος δι᾽ αὐτοῦ. 18 ὁ πιστεύων εἰς αὐτὸν οὐ κρίνεται· ὁ δὲ μὴ πιστεύων ἤδη κέκριται, ὅτι μὴ πεπίστευκεν εἰς τὸ ὄνομα τοῦ μονογενοῦς υἱοῦ τοῦ θεοῦ. 19 αὕτη

μη τις γεννηθη εξ ύδατος και Πνευματος, ου δυναται εισελθειν εις την βασιλειαν του Θεου. 6 το γεγεννημενον εκ της σαρκος σαρξ εστιν, και το γεγεννημενον εκ του Πνευματος πνευμα εστιν. 7 μη θαυμασης ότι ειπον σοι Δει ύμας γεννηθηναι ανωθεν. 8 το πνευμα όπου θελει πνει, και την φωνην αυτου ακουεις, αλλ᾽ ουκ οιδας ποθεν ερχεται και που ὑπαγει· ουτως εστιν πας ὁ γεγεννημενος εκ του Πνευματος. 9 απεκριθη Νικοδημος και ειπεν αυτω Πως δυναται ταυτα γενεσθαι; 10 απεκριθη Ιησους και ειπεν αυτω Συ ει ὁ διδασκαλος του Ισραηλ, και ταυτα ου γινωσκεις; 11 αμην αμην λεγω σοι ότι ὁ οιδαμεν λαλουμεν, και ὁ ἑωρακαμεν μαρτυρουμεν, και την μαρτυριαν ήμων ου λαμβανετε. 12 ει τα επιγεια ειπον ὑμιν και ου πιστευετε, πως εαν ειπω ύμιν τα επουρανια πιστευσετε; 13 και ουδεις αναβεβηκεν εις τον ουρανον ει μη ὁ εκ του ουρανου καταβας, ὁ υἱος του ανθρωπου. 14 και καθως Μωυσης ύψωσεν τον οφιν εν τη ερημω, ουτως ύψωθηναι δει τον υἱον του ανθρωπου, 15 ίνα πας ὁ πιστευων εν αυτω εχη ζωην αιωνιον.

16 ¶Ουτως γαρ ηγαπησεν ὁ Θεος τον κοσμον ώστε τον υἱον τον μονογενη εδωκεν, ίνα πας ὁ πιστευων εις αυτον μη αποληται αλλ᾽ εχη ζωην αιωνιον. 17 ου γαρ απεστειλεν ὁ Θεος τον υἱον εις τον κοσμον ίνα κρινη τον κοσμον, αλλ᾽ ίνα σωθη ὁ κοσμος δι᾽ αυτου. 18 ὁ πιστευων εις αυτον ου κρινεται· ὁ μη πιστευων ηδη κεκριται, ότι μη πεπιστευκεν εις το ονομα του μονογενους υἱου του Θεου. 19 αύτη

δέ ἐστιν ἡ κρίσις ὅτι τὸ φῶς ἐλήλυθεν εἰς τὸν κόσμον καὶ ἠγάπησαν οἱ ἄνθρωποι μᾶλλον τὸ σκότος ἢ τὸ φῶς· ἦν γὰρ αὐτῶν πονηρὰ τὰ ἔργα. 20 πᾶς γὰρ ὁ φαῦλα πράσσων μισεῖ τὸ φῶς καὶ οὐκ ἔρχεται πρὸς τὸ φῶς, ἵνα μὴ ἐλεγχθῇ τὰ ἔργα αὐτοῦ· 21 ὁ δὲ ποιῶν τὴν ἀλήθειαν ἔρχεται πρὸς τὸ φῶς, ἵνα φανερωθῇ αὐτοῦ τὰ ἔργα ὅτι ἐν θεῷ ἐστιν εἰργασμένα.

22 Μετὰ ταῦτα ἦλθεν ὁ Ἰησοῦς καὶ οἱ μαθηταὶ αὐτοῦ εἰς τὴν Ἰουδαίαν γῆν καὶ ἐκεῖ διέτριβεν μετ’ αὐτῶν καὶ ἐβάπτιζεν. 23 Ἦν δὲ καὶ ὁ **Ἰωάννης** βαπτίζων ἐν Αἰνὼν ἐγγὺς τοῦ Σαλείμ, ὅτι ὕδατα πολλὰ ἦν ἐκεῖ, καὶ παρεγίνοντο καὶ ἐβαπτίζοντο· 24 οὔπω γὰρ ἦν βεβλημένος εἰς τὴν φυλακὴν ὁ Ἰωάννης. 25 Ἐγένετο οὖν ζήτησις ἐκ τῶν μαθητῶν Ἰωάννου μετὰ Ἰουδαίου περὶ καθαρισμοῦ. 26 καὶ ἦλθον πρὸς τὸν Ἰωάννην καὶ εἶπαν αὐτῷ· **ῥαββί**, ὃς ἦν μετὰ σοῦ πέραν τοῦ Ἰορδάνου, ᾧ σὺ μεμαρτύρηκας, ἴδε οὗτος βαπτίζει καὶ πάντες ἔρχονται πρὸς αὐτόν. 27 Ἀπεκρίθη Ἰωάννης καὶ εἶπεν· οὐ δύναται ἄνθρωπος λαμβάνειν οὐδὲ **ἓν** ἐὰν μὴ ᾖ δεδομένον αὐτῷ ἐκ τοῦ οὐρανοῦ. 28 αὐτοὶ ὑμεῖς μοι μαρτυρεῖτε ὅτι εἶπον **[ὅτι]** οὐκ εἰμὶ ἐγὼ ὁ χριστός, ἀλλ’ ὅτι ἀπεσταλμένος εἰμὶ ἔμπροσθεν ἐκείνου. 29 ὁ ἔχων τὴν νύμφην νυμφίος ἐστίν· ὁ δὲ φίλος τοῦ νυμφίου ὁ ἑστηκὼς καὶ ἀκούων αὐτοῦ χαρᾷ χαίρει διὰ τὴν φωνὴν τοῦ νυμφίου. αὕτη οὖν ἡ χαρὰ ἡ ἐμὴ πεπλήρωται. 30 ἐκεῖνον δεῖ αὐξάνειν, ἐμὲ δὲ ἐλαττοῦσθαι. 31 Ὁ ἄνωθεν ἐρχόμενος ἐπάνω

δε εστιν ἡ κρισις ὁτι το φως εληλυθεν εις τον κοσμον και ηγαπησαν οἱ ανθρωποι μαλλον το σκοτος η το φως· ην γαρ αυτων πονηρα τα εργα. 20 πας γαρ ὁ φαυλα πρασσων μισει το φως και ουκ ερχεται προς το φως, ινα μη ελεγχθη τα εργα αυτου· 21 ὁ δε ποιων την αληθειαν ερχεται προς το φως, ινα φανερωθη αυτου τα εργα ὁτι εν θεω εστιν ειργασμενα.

22 Μετα ταυτα ηλθεν ὁ Ιησους και οἱ μαθηται αυτου εις την Ιουδαιαν γην, και εκει διετριβεν μετ’ αυτων, και εβαπτιζεν. 23 ην δε και ὁ **Ιωανης** βαπτιζων εν Αινων εγγυς του Σαλειμ, ὁτι ὑδατα πολλα ην εκει, και παρεγινοντο και εβαπτιζοντο· 24 ουπω γαρ ην βεβλημενος εις την φυλακην Ιωανης. 25 Εγενετο ουν ζητησις εκ των μαθητων Ιωανου μετα Ιουδαιου περι καθαρισμου. 26 και ηλθαν προς τον Ιωανην και ειπαν αυτω **Ραββει**, ὁς ην μετα σου περαν του Ιορδανου, ᾧ συ μεμαρτυρηκας, ιδε οὑτος βαπτιζει και παντες ερχονται προς αυτον. 27 απεκριθη Ιωανης και ειπεν Ου δυναται ανθρωπος λαμβανειν ουδε, εαν μη η δεδομενον αυτω εκ του ουρανου. 28 αυτοι ὑμεις μοι μαρτυρειτε ὁτι ειπον **εγω** Ουκ ειμι εγω ὁ Χριστος, αλλ’ ὁτι Απεσταλμενος ειμι εμπροσθεν εκεινου. 29 ὁ εχων την νυμφην νυμφιος εστιν· ὁ δε φιλος του νυμφιου, ὁ ἑστηκως και ακουων αυτου, χαρα χαιρει δια την φωνην του νυμφιου· αυτη ουν ἡ χαρα ἡ εμη πεπληρωται. 30 εκεινον δει αυξανειν, εμε δε ελαττουσθαι. 31 Ὁ ανωθεν ερχομενος επανω

πάντων ἐστίν· ὁ ὢν ἐκ τῆς γῆς ἐκ τῆς γῆς ἐστιν καὶ ἐκ τῆς γῆς λαλεῖ. ὁ ἐκ τοῦ οὐρανοῦ ἐρχόμενος [ἐπάνω πάντων ἐστίν]· 32 ὃ ἑώρακεν καὶ ἤκουσεν τοῦτο μαρτυρεῖ, καὶ τὴν μαρτυρίαν αὐτοῦ οὐδεὶς λαμβάνει. 33 ὁ λαβὼν αὐτοῦ τὴν μαρτυρίαν ἐσφράγισεν ὅτι ὁ θεὸς ἀληθής ἐστιν. 34 ὃν γὰρ ἀπέστειλεν ὁ θεὸς τὰ ῥήματα τοῦ θεοῦ λαλεῖ, οὐ γὰρ ἐκ μέτρου δίδωσιν τὸ πνεῦμα. 35 ὁ πατὴρ ἀγαπᾷ τὸν υἱὸν καὶ πάντα δέδωκεν ἐν τῇ χειρὶ αὐτοῦ. 36 ὁ πιστεύων εἰς τὸν υἱὸν ἔχει ζωὴν αἰώνιον· ὁ δὲ ἀπειθῶν τῷ υἱῷ οὐκ ὄψεται ζωήν, ἀλλ᾽ ἡ ὀργὴ τοῦ θεοῦ μένει ἐπ᾽ αὐτόν.

4 Ὡς οὖν ἔγνω ὁ Ἰησοῦς ὅτι ἤκουσαν οἱ Φαρισαῖοι ὅτι Ἰησοῦς πλείονας μαθητὰς ποιεῖ καὶ βαπτίζει ἢ Ἰωάννης 2—καίτοιγε Ἰησοῦς αὐτὸς οὐκ ἐβάπτιζεν ἀλλ᾽ οἱ μαθηταὶ αὐτοῦ —3 ἀφῆκεν τὴν Ἰουδαίαν καὶ ἀπῆλθεν πάλιν εἰς τὴν Γαλιλαίαν. 4 Ἔδει δὲ αὐτὸν διέρχεσθαι διὰ τῆς **Σαμαρείας.** 5 Ἔρχεται οὖν εἰς πόλιν τῆς **Σαμαρείας** λεγομένην Συχὰρ πλησίον τοῦ χωρίου ὃ ἔδωκεν Ἰακὼβ [τῷ] Ἰωσὴφ τῷ υἱῷ αὐτοῦ· 6 ἦν δὲ ἐκεῖ πηγὴ τοῦ Ἰακώβ. ὁ οὖν Ἰησοῦς κεκοπιακὼς ἐκ τῆς ὁδοιπορίας ἐκαθέζετο οὕτως ἐπὶ τῇ πηγῇ· ὥρα ἦν ὡς ἕκτη. 7 Ἔρχεται γυνὴ ἐκ τῆς **Σαμαρείας** ἀντλῆσαι ὕδωρ. λέγει αὐτῇ ὁ Ἰησοῦς· δός μοι πεῖν· 8 οἱ γὰρ μαθηταὶ αὐτοῦ ἀπελήλυθεισαν εἰς τὴν πόλιν ἵνα τροφὰς ἀγοράσωσιν. 9 λέγει οὖν αὐτῷ ἡ γυνὴ ἡ **Σαμαρῖτις·** πῶς σὺ Ἰουδαῖος ὢν παρ᾽ ἐμοῦ πεῖν αἰτεῖς γυναικὸς **Σαμαρίτιδος** οὔσης; οὐ γὰρ συγχρῶνται Ἰουδαῖοι **Σαμαρίταις.** 10 ἀπεκρίθη Ἰησοῦς

παντων εστιν· ὁ ων εκ της γης εκ της γης εστιν και εκ της γης λαλει· ὁ εκ του ουρανου ερχομενος **επανω παντων εστιν.** 32 ὁ ἑωρακεν και ηκουσεν τουτο μαρτυρει, και την μαρτυριαν αυτου ουδεις λαμβανει. 33 ὁ λαβων αυτου την μαρτυριαν εσφραγισεν ὁτι ὁ Θεος αληθης εστιν. 34 ὁν γαρ απεστειλεν ὁ Θεος τα ρηματα του Θεου λαλει· ου γαρ εκ μετρου διδωσιν το Πνευμα. 35 ὁ πατηρ αγαπα τον υιον, και παντα δεδωκεν εν τη χειρι αυτου. 36 ὁ πιστευων εις τον υιον εχει ζωην αιωνιον· ὁ δε απειθων τω υιω ουκ οψεται ζωην, αλλ᾽ ἡ οργη του Θεου μενει επ᾽ αυτον.

4 Ὡς ουν εγνω ὁ Κυριος ὁτι ηκουσαν οἱ Φαρισαιοι ὁτι Ιησους πλειονας μαθητας ποιει και βαπτιζει η Ιωαννης 2—καιτοιγε Ιησους αυτος ουκ εβαπτιζεν αλλ᾽ οἱ μαθηται αυτου —3 αφηκεν την Ιουδαιαν και απηλθεν παλιν εις την Γαλιλαιαν. 4 εδει δε αυτον διερχεσθαι δια της **Σαμαριας.** 5 ερχεται ουν εις πολιν της **Σαμαριας** λεγομενην Συχαρ πλησιον του χωριου ὁ εδωκεν Ιακωβ **τω** Ιωσηφ τω υιω αυτου· 6 ην δε εκει πηγη του Ιακωβ. ὁ ουν Ιησους κεκοπιακως εκ της οδοιποριας εκαθεζετο ουτως επι τη πηγη. ωρα ην ως εκτη. 7 ερχεται γυνη εκ της **Σαμαριας** αντλησαι ὑδωρ. λεγει αυτη ὁ Ιησους Δος μοι πειν· 8 οἱ γαρ μαθηται αυτου απεληλυθεισαν εις την πολιν, ινα τροφας αγορασωσιν. 9 λεγει ουν αυτω ἡ γυνη ἡ **Σαμαρειτις** Πως συ Ιουδαιος ων παρ᾽ εμου πειν αιτεις γυναικος **Σαμαρειτιδος** ουσης; ου γαρ συνχρωνται Ιουδαιοι **Σαμαρειταις.** 10 απεκριθη Ιησους καὶ εἶπεν αὐτῇ· εἰ ᾔδεις τὴν δωρεὰν τοῦ θεοῦ καὶ τίς ἐστιν ὁ λέγων σοι· δός μοι πεῖν, σὺ ἂν ᾔτησας αὐτὸν καὶ ἔδωκεν ἄν σοι ὕδωρ ζῶν. 11 Λέγει αὐτῷ [ἡ γυνή]· κύριε, οὔτε ἄντλημα ἔχεις καὶ τὸ φρέαρ ἐστὶν βαθύ· πόθεν οὖν ἔχεις τὸ ὕδωρ τὸ ζῶν; 12 μὴ σὺ μείζων εἶ τοῦ πατρὸς ἡμῶν Ἰακώβ, ὃς ἔδωκεν ἡμῖν τὸ φρέαρ καὶ αὐτὸς ἐξ αὐτοῦ ἔπιεν καὶ οἱ υἱοὶ αὐτοῦ καὶ τὰ θρέμματα αὐτοῦ; 13 ἀπεκρίθη Ἰησοῦς καὶ εἶπεν αὐτῇ· πᾶς ὁ πίνων ἐκ τοῦ ὕδατος τούτου διψήσει πάλιν· 14 ὃς δ᾽ ἂν πίῃ ἐκ τοῦ ὕδατος οὗ ἐγὼ δώσω αὐτῷ, οὐ μὴ διψήσει εἰς τὸν αἰῶνα, ἀλλὰ τὸ ὕδωρ ὃ δώσω αὐτῷ γενήσεται ἐν αὐτῷ πηγὴ ὕδατος ἁλλομένου εἰς ζωὴν αἰώνιον. 15 Λέγει πρὸς αὐτὸν ἡ γυνή· κύριε, δός μοι τοῦτο τὸ ὕδωρ, ἵνα μὴ διψῶ μηδὲ διέρχωμαι ἐνθάδε ἀντλεῖν. 16 λέγει αὐτῇ· ὕπαγε φώνησον τὸν ἄνδρα **σου** καὶ ἐλθὲ ἐνθάδε. 17 ἀπεκρίθη ἡ γυνὴ καὶ εἶπεν αὐτῷ· οὐκ ἔχω ἄνδρα. λέγει αὐτῇ ὁ Ἰησοῦς· καλῶς εἶπας ὅτι ἄνδρα οὐκ ἔχω· 18 πέντε γὰρ ἄνδρας ἔσχες καὶ νῦν ὃν ἔχεις οὐκ ἔστιν σου ἀνήρ· τοῦτο ἀληθὲς εἴρηκας. 19 Λέγει αὐτῷ ἡ γυνή· κύριε, θεωρῶ ὅτι προφήτης εἶ σύ. 20 οἱ πατέρες ἡμῶν ἐν τῷ ὄρει τούτῳ προσεκύνησαν· καὶ ὑμεῖς λέγετε ὅτι ἐν Ἰεροσολύμοις ἐστὶν ὁ τόπος ὅπου προσκυνεῖν δεῖ. 21 λέγει αὐτῇ ὁ Ἰησοῦς· πίστευέ μοι, γύναι, ὅτι ἔρχεται ὥρα ὅτε οὔτε ἐν τῷ ὄρει τούτῳ οὔτε ἐν Ἰεροσολύμοις προσκυνήσετε τῷ πατρί. 22 ὑμεῖς προσκυνεῖτε ὃ οὐκ οἴδατε· ἡμεῖς προσκυνοῦμεν ὃ οἴδαμεν, ὅτι ἡ σωτηρία ἐκ τῶν Ἰουδαίων ἐστίν. 23 ἀλλ᾽ ἔρχεται ὥρα καὶ νῦν ἐστιν,

και ειπεν αυτη Ει ηδεις την δωρεαν του Θεου και τις εστιν ὁ λεγων σοι Δος μοι πειν, συ αν ητησας αυτον και εδωκεν αν σοι ύδωρ ζων. 11 λεγει αυτω Κυριε, ουτε αντλημα εχεις και το φρεαρ εστιν βαθυ· ποθεν ουν εχεις το ύδωρ το ζων; 12 μη συ μειζων ει του πατρος ημων Ιακωβ, ὁς εδωκεν ήμιν το φρεαρ και αυτος εξ αυτου επιεν και οἱ υιοι αυτου και τα θρεμματα αυτου; 13 απεκριθη Ιησους και ειπεν αυτη Πας ὁ πινων εκ του ύδατος τουτου διψησει παλιν· 14 ὁς δ᾽ αν πιη εκ του ύδατος ου εγω δωσω αυτω, ου μη διψησει εις τον αιωνα, αλλα το ύδωρ ὁ δωσω αυτω γενησεται εν αυτω πηγη ύδατος αλλομενου εις ζωην αιωνιον. 15 λεγει προς αυτον ή γυνη Κυριε, δος μοι τουτο το ύδωρ, ινα μη διψω μηδε διερχωμαι ενθαδε αντλειν. 16 λεγει αυτη Ύπαγε, φωνησον **σου** τον ανδρα, και ελθε ενθαδε. 17 απεκριθη ή γυνη και ειπεν αυτω Ουκ εχω ανδρα. λεγει αυτη ὁ Ιησους Καλως ειπας ὅτι Ανδρα ουκ εχω 18 πεντε γαρ ανδρας εσχες, και νυν ὁν εχεις ουκ εστιν σου ανηρ· τουτο αληθες ειρηκας. 19 λεγει αυτω ή γυνη Κυριε, θεωρω ὅτι προφητης ει συ. 20 οἱ πατερες ήμων εν τω ορει τουτω προσεκυνησαν· και ὑμεις λεγετε ὅτι εν Ἰεροσολυμοις εστιν ὁ τοπος ὅπου προσκυνειν δει. 21 λεγει αυτη ὁ Ιησους Πιστευε μοι, γυναι, ὅτι ερχεται ώρα ὅτε ουτε εν τω ορει τουτω ουτε εν Ἰεροσολυμοις προσκυνησετε τω πατρι. 22 ὑμεις προσκυνειτε ὁ ουκ οιδατε· ημεις προσκυνουμεν ὁ οιδαμεν, ὅτι ή σωτηρια εκ των Ιουδαιων εστιν. 23 αλλα ερχεται ώρα και νυν εστιν, ὅτε οἱ ἀληθινοὶ προσκυνηταὶ προσκυνήσουσιν τῷ πατρὶ ἐν πνεύματι καὶ ἀληθείᾳ· καὶ γὰρ ὁ πατὴρ τοιούτους ζητεῖ τοὺς προσκυνοῦντας αὐτόν. 24 πνεῦμα ὁ θεός, καὶ τοὺς προσκυνοῦντας αὐτὸν ἐν πνεύματι καὶ ἀληθείᾳ δεῖ προσκυνεῖν. 25 Λέγει αὐτῷ ἡ γυνή· οἶδα ὅτι Μεσσίας ἔρχεται ὁ λεγόμενος χριστός· ὅταν ἔλθῃ ἐκεῖνος, ἀναγγελεῖ ἡμῖν ἅπαντα. 26 λέγει αὐτῇ ὁ Ἰησοῦς· ἐγώ εἰμι, ὁ λαλῶν σοι.

27 Καὶ ἐπὶ τούτῳ ἦλθαν οἱ μαθηταὶ αὐτοῦ καὶ ἐθαύμαζον ὅτι μετὰ γυναικὸς ἐλάλει οὐδεὶς μέντοι εἶπεν· τί ζητεῖς ἢ τί λαλεῖς μετ' αὐτῆς; 28 ἀφῆκεν οὖν τὴν ὑδρίαν αὐτῆς ἡ γυνὴ καὶ ἀπῆλθεν εἰς τὴν πόλιν καὶ λέγει τοῖς ἀνθρώποις· 29 δεῦτε ἴδετε ἄνθρωπον ὃς εἶπέν μοι πάντα **ὅσα** ἐποίησα, μήτι οὗτός ἐστιν ὁ χριστός; 30 ἐξῆλθον ἐκ τῆς πόλεως καὶ ἤρχοντο πρὸς αὐτόν. 31 Ἐν τῷ μεταξὺ ἠρώτων αὐτὸν οἱ μαθηταὶ λέγοντες· **ῥαββί,** φάγε. 32 ὁ δὲ εἶπεν αὐτοῖς· ἐγὼ βρῶσιν ἔχω φαγεῖν ἣν ὑμεῖς οὐκ οἴδατε. 33 ἔλεγον οὖν οἱ μαθηταὶ πρὸς ἀλλήλους· μή τις ἤνεγκεν αὐτῷ φαγεῖν; 34 λέγει αὐτοῖς ὁ Ἰησοῦς· ἐμὸν βρῶμά ἐστιν ἵνα ποιήσω τὸ θέλημα τοῦ πέμψαντός με καὶ τελειώσω αὐτοῦ τὸ ἔργον. 35 οὐχ ὑμεῖς λέγετε ὅτι ἔτι τετράμηνός ἐστιν καὶ ὁ θερισμὸς ἔρχεται; ἰδοὺ λέγω ὑμῖν, ἐπάρατε τοὺς ὀφθαλμοὺς ὑμῶν καὶ θεάσασθε τὰς χώρας ὅτι λευκαί εἰσιν πρὸς θερισμόν. ἤδη 36 ὁ θερίζων μισθὸν λαμβάνει καὶ συνάγει καρπὸν εἰς ζωὴν αἰώνιον, ἵνα ὁ σπείρων ὁμοῦ χαίρῃ καὶ ὁ θερίζων. 37 ἐν γὰρ τούτῳ ὁ λόγος ἐστὶν ἀληθινὸς ὅτι

ὅτε οἱ αληθινοι προσκυνηται προσκυνησουσιν τω πατρι εν πνευματι και αληθεια, και γαρ ὁ πατηρ τοιουτους ζητει τους προσκυνουντας αυτον. 24 πνευμα ὁ Θεος, και τους προσκυνουντας αυτον εν πνευματι και αληθεια δει προσκυνειν. 25 λεγει αυτω ἡ γυνη Οιδα ὁτι Μεσσιας ερχεται, ὁ λεγομενος Χριστος· ὁταν ελθη εκεινος, αναγγελει ἡμιν ἁπαντα. 26 λεγει αυτη ὁ Ιησους Εγω ειμι, ὁ λαλων σοι.

27 Και επι τουτω ηλθαν οἱ μαθηται αυτου· και εθαυμαζον ὁτι μετα γυναικος ελαλει· ουδεις μεντοι ειπεν Τι ζητεις; η Τι λαλεις μετ' αυτης; 28 αφηκεν ουν την ὑδριαν αυτης ἡ γυνη και απηλθεν εις την πολιν και λεγει τοις ανθρωποις 29 Δευτε ιδετε ανθρωπον ὁς ειπεν μοι παντα **ἁ** εποιησα· μητι ουτος εστιν ὁ Χριστος; 30 εξηλθον εκ της πολεως, και ηρχοντο προς αυτον. 31 Εν τω μεταξυ ηρωτων αυτον οἱ μαθηται λεγοντες **Ῥαββει,** φαγε. 32 ὁ δε ειπεν αυτοις Εγω βρωσιν εχω φαγειν ἣν ὑμεις ουκ οιδατε. 33 ελεγον ουν οἱ μαθηται προς αλληλους Μη τις ηνεγκεν αυτω φαγειν; 34 λεγει αυτοις ὁ Ιησους Εμον βρωμα εστιν ἱνα ποιησω το θελημα του πεμψαντος με και τελειωσω αυτου το εργον. 35 ουχ ὑμεις λεγετε ὁτι Ετι τετραμηνος εστιν και ὁ θερισμος ερχεται; ιδου λεγω ὑμιν, επαρατε τους οφθαλμους ὑμων και θεασασθε τας χωρας ὁτι λευκαι εισιν προς θερισμον· ηδη 36 ὁ θεριζων μισθον λαμβανει και συναγει καρπον εις ζωην αιωνιον, ἱνα ὁ σπειρων ὁμου χαιρη και ὁ θεριζων. 37 εν γαρ τουτω ὁ λογος εστιν αληθινος ὁτι

ἄλλος ἐστὶν ὁ σπείρων καὶ ἄλλος ὁ θερίζων. 38 ἐγὼ ἀπέστειλα ὑμᾶς θερίζειν ὃ οὐχ ὑμεῖς κεκοπιάκατε· ἄλλοι κεκοπιάκασιν καὶ ὑμεῖς εἰς τὸν κόπον αὐτῶν εἰσεληλύθατε.

39 Ἐκ δὲ τῆς πόλεως ἐκείνης πολλοὶ ἐπίστευσαν εἰς αὐτὸν τῶν **Σαμαριτῶν** διὰ τὸν λόγον τῆς γυναικὸς μαρτυρούσης ὅτι εἶπέν μοι πάντα ἃ ἐποίησα. 40 ὡς οὖν ἦλθον πρὸς αὐτὸν οἱ **Σαμαρῖται**, ἠρώτων αὐτὸν μεῖναι παρ᾽ αὐτοῖς· καὶ ἔμεινεν ἐκεῖ δύο ἡμέρας. 41 καὶ πολλῷ πλείους ἐπίστευσαν διὰ τὸν λόγον αὐτοῦ, 42 τῇ τε γυναικὶ ἔλεγον ὅτι οὐκέτι διὰ τὴν **σὴν** λαλιὰν πιστεύομεν, αὐτοὶ γὰρ ἀκηκόαμεν καὶ οἴδαμεν ὅτι οὗτός ἐστιν ἀληθῶς ὁ σωτὴρ τοῦ κόσμου.

43 Μετὰ δὲ τὰς δύο ἡμέρας ἐξῆλθεν ἐκεῖθεν εἰς τὴν Γαλιλαίαν· 44 αὐτὸς γὰρ Ἰησοῦς ἐμαρτύρησεν ὅτι προφήτης ἐν τῇ ἰδίᾳ πατρίδι τιμὴν οὐκ ἔχει. 45 ὅτε οὖν ἦλθεν εἰς τὴν Γαλιλαίαν, ἐδέξαντο αὐτὸν οἱ Γαλιλαῖοι πάντα ἑωρακότες ὅσα ἐποίησεν ἐν Ἱεροσολύμοις ἐν τῇ ἑορτῇ, καὶ αὐτοὶ γὰρ ἦλθον εἰς τὴν ἑορτήν.

46 Ἦλθεν οὖν πάλιν εἰς τὴν Κανὰ τῆς Γαλιλαίας, ὅπου ἐποίησεν τὸ ὕδωρ οἶνον. Καὶ ἦν τις βασιλικὸς οὗ ὁ υἱὸς ἠσθένει ἐν Καφαρναούμ. 47 οὗτος ἀκούσας ὅτι Ἰησοῦς ἥκει ἐκ τῆς Ἰουδαίας εἰς τὴν Γαλιλαίαν ἀπῆλθεν πρὸς αὐτὸν καὶ ἠρώτα ἵνα καταβῇ καὶ ἰάσηται αὐτοῦ τὸν υἱόν, ἤμελλεν γὰρ ἀποθνήσκειν. 48 εἶπεν οὖν ὁ Ἰησοῦς πρὸς αὐτόν· ἐὰν μὴ σημεῖα καὶ τέρατα ἴδητε, οὐ μὴ πιστεύσητε.

49 λέγει πρὸς αὐτὸν ὁ βασιλικός· κύριε, κατάβηθι πρὶν ἀποθανεῖν τὸ

αλλος εστιν ὁ σπειρων και αλλος ὁ θεριζων. 38 εγω απεστειλα υμας θεριζειν ὁ ουχ ὑμεις κεκοπιακατε· αλλοι κεκοπιακασιν, και ὑμεις εις τον κοπον αυτων εισεληλυθατε.

39 Εκ δε της πολεως εκεινης πολλοι επιστευσαν εις αυτον των **Σαμαρειτων** δια τον λογον της γυναικος μαρτυρουσης ότι Ειπεν μοι παντα ά εποιησα. 40 ὡς ουν ηλθον προς αυτον οἱ **Σαμαρειται**, ηρωτων αυτον μειναι παρ᾽ αυτοις· και εμεινεν εκει δυο ήμερας. 41 και πολλω πλειους επιστευσαν δια τον λογον αυτου, 42 τη τε γυναικι ελεγον ότι Ουκετι δια την λαλιαν **σου** πιστευομεν· αυτοι γαρ ακηκοαμεν, και οιδαμεν ότι ουτος εστιν αληθως ὁ σωτηρ του κοσμου.

43 Μετα δε τας δυο ήμερας εξηλθεν εκειθεν εις την Γαλιλαιαν. 44 αυτος γαρ Ιησους εμαρτυρησεν ότι προφητης εν τη ιδια πατριδι τιμην ουκ εχει. 45 ότε ουν ηλθεν εις την Γαλιλαιαν, εδεξαντο αυτον οἱ Γαλιλαιοι, παντα εωρακοτες όσα εποιησεν εν Ἱεροσολυμοις εν τη εορτη, και αυτοι γαρ ηλθον εις την εορτην.

46 Ηλθεν ουν παλιν εις την Κανα της Γαλιλαιας, όπου εποιησεν το ύδωρ οινον. και ην τις βασιλικος ου ὁ υἱος ησθενει εν Καφαρναουμ. 47 ουτος, ακουσας ότι Ιησους ήκει εκ της Ιουδαιας εις την Γαλιλαιαν, απηλθεν προς αυτον και ηρωτα ινα καταβη και ιασηται αυτου τον υἱον, ημελλεν γαρ αποθνησκειν. 48 ειπεν ουν ὁ Ιησους προς αυτον Εαν μη σημεια και τερατα ιδητε, ου μη πιστευσητε.

49 λεγει προς αυτον ὁ βασιλικος Κυριε, καταβηθι πριν αποθανειν το

παιδίον μου. 50 λέγει αὐτῷ ὁ Ἰησοῦς· πορεύου, ὁ υἱός σου ζῇ. Ἐπίστευσεν ὁ ἄνθρωπος τῷ λόγῳ ὃν εἶπεν αὐτῷ ὁ Ἰησοῦς καὶ ἐπορεύετο. 51 ἤδη δὲ αὐτοῦ καταβαίνοντος οἱ δοῦλοι αὐτοῦ ὑπήντησαν αὐτῷ λέγοντες ὅτι ὁ παῖς αὐτοῦ ζῇ. 52 ἐπύθετο οὖν τὴν ὥραν παρ' αὐτῶν ἐν ᾗ κομψότερον ἔσχεν· εἶπαν οὖν αὐτῷ ὅτι ἐχθὲς ὥραν ἑβδόμην ἀφῆκεν αὐτὸν ὁ πυρετός. 53 ἔγνω οὖν ὁ πατὴρ ὅτι [ἐν] ἐκείνῃ τῇ ὥρᾳ ἐν ᾗ εἶπεν αὐτῷ ὁ Ἰησοῦς· ὁ υἱός σου ζῇ, καὶ ἐπίστευσεν αὐτὸς καὶ ἡ οἰκία αὐτοῦ ὅλη. 54 Τοῦτο [δὲ] πάλιν δεύτερον σημεῖον ἐποίησεν ὁ Ἰησοῦς ἐλθὼν ἐκ τῆς Ἰουδαίας εἰς τὴν Γαλιλαίαν.

παιδιον μου. 50 λεγει αυτω ὁ Ιησους Πορευου· ὁ υἱος σου ζῃ. επιστευσεν ὁ ανθρωπος τω λογω ὁν ειπεν αυτω ὁ Ιησους και επορευετο. 51 ηδη δε αυτου καταβαινοντος οἱ δουλοι αυτου ὑπηντησαν αυτω λεγοντες ὁτι ὁ παις αυτου ζῃ. 52 επυθετο ουν την ὡραν παρ' αυτων εν η· κομψοτερον εσχεν· ειπαν ουν αυτω ὁτι Εχθες ὡραν εβδομην αφηκεν αυτον ὁ πυρετος. 53 εγνω ουν ὁ πατηρ ὁτι εκεινη τη ὡρα εν η· ειπεν αυτω ὁ Ιησους Ὁ υἱος σου ζῃ, και επιστευσεν αυτος και ἡ οικια αυτου ὁλη. 54 τουτο δε παλιν δευτερον σημειον εποιησεν ὁ Ιησους ελθων εκ της Ιουδαιας εις την Γαλιλαιαν.

| Panin | Westcott & Hort |

Panin

1 Εν αρχη ην ὁ λογος, και ὁ λογος ην προς τον Θεον, και Θεος ην ὁ λογος. 2 Ούτος ην εν αρχη προς τον Θεον. 3 παντα δι' αυτου εγενετο, και χωρις αυτου εγενετο ουδε ἑν ὁ γεγονεν. 4 εν αυτω ζωη ην, και ἡ ζωη ην το φως των ανθρωπων. 5 και το φως εν τη σκοτια φαινει, και ἡ σκοτια αυτο ου κατελαβεν. 6 εγενετο ανθρωπος απεσταλμενος παρα Θεου, ονομα αυτω **Ιωανης**. 7 ούτος ηλθεν εις μαρτυριαν, ίνα μαρτυρηση περι του φωτος, ίνα παντες πιστευσωσιν δι' αυτου. 8 ουκ ην εκεινος το φως, αλλ' ίνα μαρτυρηση περι του φωτος. 9 Ην το φως το αληθινον ὁ φωτιζει παντα ανθρωπον ερχομενον εις τον κοσμον. 10 εν τω κοσμω ην και ὁ κοσμος δι' αυτου εγενετο, και ὁ κοσμος αυτον ουκ εγνω. 11 εις τα ιδια ηλθεν, και οἱ ιδιοι αυτον ου παρελαβον. 12 όσοι δε ελαβον αυτον, εδωκεν αυτοις εξουσιαν τεκνα Θεου γενεσθαι, τοις πιστευουσιν εις το ονομα αυτου, 13 οἱ ουκ εξ αἱματων ουδε εκ θεληματος σαρκος ουδε εκ θεληματος ανδρος αλλ' εκ Θεου εγεννηθησαν. 14 Και ὁ λογος σαρξ εγενετο και εσκηνωσεν εν ἡμιν, και εθεασαμεθα την δοξαν αυτου, δοξαν ὡς μονογενους παρα πατρος, πληρης χαριτος και αληθειας. 15 (**Ιωανης** μαρτυρει περι αυτου και κεκραγεν λεγων - ούτος ην ὁ ειπων - Ὁ οπισω μου ερχομενος εμπροσθεν μου γεγονεν, ὁτι πρωτος μου ην.) 16 ότι εκ του πληρωματος αυτου ἡμεις παντες ελαβομεν, και χαριν αντι χαριτος 17 ότι ὁ νομος δια Μωυσεως εδοθη, ἡ χαρις και ἡ αληθεια δια Ιησου Χριστου εγενετο. 18 Θεον ουδεις ἑωρακεν

Westcott & Hort

1 εν αρχη ην ο λογος και ο λογος ην προς τον θεον και θεος ην ο λογος 2 ουτος ην εν αρχη προς τον θεον 3 παντα δι αυτου εγενετο και χωρις αυτου εγενετο ουδε εν ο γεγονεν 4 εν αυτω ζωη ην και η ζωη ην το φως των ανθρωπων 5 και το φως εν τη σκοτια φαινει και η σκοτια αυτο ου κατελαβεν 6 εγενετο ανθρωπος απεσταλμενος παρα θεου ονομα αυτω **ιωαννης** 7 ουτος ηλθεν εις μαρτυριαν ινα μαρτυρηση περι του φωτος ινα παντες πιστευσωσιν δι αυτου 8 ουκ ην εκεινος το φως αλλ ινα μαρτυρηση περι του φωτος 9 ην το φως το αληθινον ο φωτιζει παντα ανθρωπον ερχομενον εις τον κοσμον 10 εν τω κοσμω ην και ο κοσμος δι αυτου εγενετο και ο κοσμος αυτον ουκ εγνω 11 εις τα ιδια ηλθεν και οι ιδιοι αυτον ου παρελαβον 12 οσοι δε ελαβον αυτον εδωκεν αυτοις εξουσιαν τεκνα θεου γενεσθαι τοις πιστευουσιν εις το ονομα αυτου 13 οι ουκ εξ αιματων ουδε εκ θεληματος σαρκος ουδε εκ θεληματος ανδρος αλλ εκ θεου εγεννηθησαν 14 και ο λογος σαρξ εγενετο και εσκηνωσεν εν ημιν και εθεασαμεθα την δοξαν αυτου δοξαν ως μονογενους παρα πατρος πληρης χαριτος και αληθειας 15 **ιωαννης** μαρτυρει περι αυτου και κεκραγεν λεγων ουτος ην ο ειπων ο οπισω μου ερχομενος εμπροσθεν μου γεγονεν οτι πρωτος μου ην 16 οτι εκ του πληρωματος αυτου ημεις παντες ελαβομεν και χαριν αντι χαριτος 17 οτι ο νομος δια μωυσεως εδοθη η χαρις και η αληθει δια ιησου χριστου εγενετο 18 θεον ουδεις εωρακεν

πωποτε· μονογενης Θεος ὁ ων εις τον κολπον του πατρος εκεινος εξηγησατο.

19 Και αύτη εστιν ἡ μαρτυρια του **Ιωανου**, ότε απεστειλαν προς αυτον οἱ Ιουδαιοι εξ Ἱεροσολυμων ἱερεις και Λευειτας ἱνα ερωτησωσιν αυτον Συ τις ει; 20 και ὡμολογησεν και ουκ ηρνησατο, και ὡμολογησεν ὁτι Εγω ουκ ειμι ὁ Χριστος. 21 και ηρωτησαν αυτον Τι **συ ουν**; **Ηλειας** ει; και λεγει Ουκ ειμι. Ὁ προφητης ει συ; και απεκριθη Ου. 22 ειπαν ουν αυτω Τις ει; ἱνα αποκρισιν δωμεν τοις πεμψασιν ἡμας. τι λεγεις περι σεαυτου; 23 εφη Εγω φωνη βοωντος εν τη ερημῳ Ευθυνατε την ὁδον Κυριου, καθως ειπεν Ησαιας ὁ προφητης. 24 και απεσταλμενοι ησαν εκ των Φαρισαιων. 25 και ηρωτησαν αυτον και ειπαν αυτω Τι ουν βαπτιζεις ει συ ουκ ει ὁ Χριστος ουδε **Ηλειας** ουδε ὁ προφητης; 26 απεκριθη αυτοις ὁ **Ιωανης** λεγων Εγω βαπτιζω εν ὑδατι· μεσος ὑμων στηκει ὁν ὑμεις ουκ οιδατε, 27 οπισω μου ερχομενος, οὐ ουκ ειμι **εγω** αξιος ἱνα λυσω αυτου τον ἱμαντα του ὑποδηματος. 28 ταυτα εν Βηθανιᾳ εγενετο περαν του Ιορδανου ὁπου ην ὁ Ιωανης βαπτιζων.

29 Τη επαυριον βλεπει τον Ιησουν ερχομενον προς αυτον, και λεγει Ιδε ὁ αμνος του Θεου ὁ αιρων την ἁμαρτιαν του κοσμου. 30 ούτος εστιν ὑπερ οὗ εγω ειπον Οπισω μου ερχεται ανηρ, ὁς εμπροσθεν μου γεγονεν, ὁτι πρωτος μου ην. 31 **κα'** 'γω ουκ ηδειν αυτον, αλλ' ἱνα φανερωθη τῳ Ισραηλ, δια τουτο ηλθον εγω εν ὑδατι βαπτιζων

32 Και εμαρτυρησεν Ιωανης

πωποτε μονογενης θεος ο ων εις τον κολπον του πατρος εκεινος εξηγησατο

19 και αυτη εστιν η μαρτυρια του **ιωαννου** οτε απεστειλαν προς αυτον οι ιουδαιοι εξ ιεροσολυμων ιερεις και λευιτας ινα ερωτησωσιν αυτον συ τις ει 20 και ωμολογησεν και ουκ ηρνησατο και ωμολογησεν οτι εγω ουκ ειμι ο χριστος 21 και ηρωτησαν αυτον τι **ουν [συ]** ηλιας ει και λεγει ουκ ειμι ο προφητης ει συ και απεκριθη ου 22 ειπαν ουν αυτω τις ει ινα αποκρισιν δωμεν τοις πεμψασιν ημας τι λεγεις περι σεαυτου 23 εφη εγω φωνη βοωντος εν τη ερημω ευθυνατε την οδον κυριου καθως ειπεν ησαιας ο προφητης 24 και απεσταλμενοι ησαν εκ των φαρισαιων 25 και ηρωτησαν αυτον και ειπαν αυτω τι ουν βαπτιζεις ει συ ουκ ει ο χριστος ουδε **ηλιας** ουδε ο προφητης 26 απεκριθη αυτοις ο **ιωαννης** λεγων εγω βαπτιζω εν υδατι μεσος υμων στηκει ον υμεις ουκ οιδατε 27 οπισω μου ερχομενος ου ουκ ειμι **[εγω]** αξιος ινα λυσω αυτου τον ιμαντα του υποδηματος 28 ταυτα εν βηθανια εγενετο περαν του ιορδανου οπου ην ο ιωαννης βαπτιζων

29 τη επαυριον βλεπει τον ιησουν ερχομενον προς αυτον και λεγει ιδε ο αμνος του θεου ο αιρων την αμαρτιαν του κοσμου 30 ουτος εστιν υπερ ου εγω ειπον οπισω μου ερχεται ανηρ ος εμπροσθεν μου γεγονεν οτι πρωτος μου ην 31 **καγω** ουκ ηδειν αυτον αλλ ινα φανερωθη τω ισραηλ δια τουτο ηλθον εγω εν υδατι βαπτιζων

32 και εμαρτυρησεν ιωαννης

λεγων ότι Τεθεαμαι το Πνευμα
καταβαινον ώς περιστεραν εξ
ουρανου, και εμεινεν επ᾽ αυτον.
33 **κα᾽ ᾽γω** ουκ ηδειν αυτον, αλλ᾽ ό
πεμψας με βαπτιζειν εν ύδατι εκεινος
μοι ειπεν Εφ᾽ όν αν ιδῃς το Πνευμα
καταβαινον και μενον επ᾽ αυτον,
ούτος εστιν ό βαπτιζων εν Πνευματι
Ἁγιῳ. 34 κα᾽ ᾽γω έωρακα, και
μεμαρτυρηκα ότι ούτος εστιν ό υίος
του Θεου. 35 Τῃ επαυριον παλιν
ἱστηκει **Ιωανης** και εκ των
μαθητων αυτου δυο, 36 και εμβλεψας
τῳ Ιησου περιπατουντι λεγει Ιδε, ό
αμνος του Θεου. 37 και ηκουσαν οί
δυο μαθηται αυτου λαλουντος και
ηκολουθησαν τῳ Ιησου. 38 στραφεις
δε ό Ιησους και θεασαμενος αυτους
ακολουθουντας λεγει αυτοις Τι
ζητειτε; οί δε ειπαν αυτῳ **Ῥαββει**, (ό
λεγεται μεθερμηνευομενον
Διδασκαλε,) που μενεις; 39 λεγει
αυτοις Ερχεσθε και οψεσθε. ηλθαν
ουν και ειδαν που μενει, και παρ᾽
αυτῳ εμειναν την ἡμεραν εκεινην·
ὡρα ην ὡς δεκατη. 40 ην Ανδρεας ό
αδελφος Σιμωνος Πετρου είς εκ των
δυο των ακουσαντων παρα **Ιωανου**
και ακολουθησαντων αυτῳ
41 εὑρισκει ούτος πρωτον τον
αδελφον τον ιδιον Σιμωνα, και λεγει
αυτῳ Εὑρηκαμεν τον Μεσσιαν, (ό
εστιν μεθερμηνευομενον Χριστος).
42 ηγαγεν αυτον προς τον Ιησουν.
εμβλεψας αυτῳ ό Ιησους ειπεν Συ ει
Σιμων ό υίος **Ιωανου**· συ κληθησῃ
Κηφας, (ό ἑρμηνευεται Πετρος).

43 Τῃ επαυριον ηθελησεν εξελθειν
εις την Γαλιλαιαν, και εὑρισκει
Φιλιππον και λεγει αυτῳ ό Ιησους
Ακολουθει μοι. 44 ην δε ό
Φιλιππος απο Βηθσαιδα, εκ της

λεγων οτι τεθεαμαι το πνευμα
καταβαινον ως περιστεραν εξ
ουρανου και εμεινεν επ αυτον
33 **καγω** ουκ ηδειν αυτον αλλ ο
πεμψας με βαπτιζειν εν υδατι εκεινος
μοι ειπεν εφ ον αν ιδης το πνευμα
καταβαινον και μενον επ αυτον
ουτος εστιν ο βαπτιζων εν πνευματι
αγιω 34 καγω εωρακα και
μεμαρτυρηκα οτι ουτος εστιν ο υιος
του θεου 35 τη επαυριον παλιν
ειστηκει **ιωαννης** και εκ των
μαθητων αυτου δυο 36 και εμβλεψας
τω ιησου περιπατουντι λεγει ιδε ο
αμνος του θεου 37 και ηκουσαν οι
δυο μαθηται αυτου λαλουντος και
ηκολουθησαν τω ιησου 38 στραφεις
δε ο ιησους και θεασαμενος αυτους
ακολουθουντας λεγει αυτοις τι
ζητειτε οι δε ειπαν αυτω **ραββι** ο
λεγεται μεθερμηνευομενον
διδασκαλε που μενεις 39 λεγει
αυτοις ερχεσθε και οψεσθε ηλθαν
ουν και ειδαν που μενει και παρ
αυτω εμειναν την ημεραν εκεινην
ωρα ην ως δεκατη 40 ην ανδρεας ο
αδελφος σιμωνος πετρου εις εκ των
δυο των ακουσαντων παρα **ιωαννου**
και ακολουθησαντων αυτω
41 ευρισκει ουτος πρωτον τον
αδελφον τον ιδιον σιμωνα και λεγει
αυτω ευρηκαμεν τον μεσσιαν ο
εστιν μεθερμηνευομενον χριστος
42 ηγαγεν αυτον προς τον ιησουν
εμβλεψας αυτω ο ιησους ειπεν συ ει
σιμων ο υιος **ιωαννου** συ κληθηση
κηφας ο ερμηνευεται πετρος

43 τη επαυριον ηθελησεν εξελθειν
εις την γαλιλαιαν και ευρισκει
φιλιππον και λεγει αυτω ο ιησους
ακολουθει μοι 44 ην δε ο
φιλιππος απο βηθσαιδα εκ της

πολεως Ανδρεου και Πετρου.
45 ευρισκει Φιλιππος τον Ναθαναηλ, και λεγει αυτω Όν εγραψεν Μωυσης εν τω νομω και οἱ προφηται εὑρηκαμεν, Ιησουν υἱον του Ιωσηφ τον απο Ναζαρετ. 46 και ειπεν αυτω Ναθαναηλ Εκ Ναζαρετ δυναται τι αγαθον ειναι; λεγει αυτω ὁ Φιλιππος Ερχου και ιδε. 47 ειδεν Ιησους τον Ναθαναηλ ερχομενον προς αυτον και λεγει περι αυτου Ιδε αληθως Ισραηλειτης εν ᾧ δολος ουκ εστιν. 48 λεγει αυτω Ναθαναηλ Ποθεν με γινωσκεις; απεκριθη Ιησους και ειπεν αυτω, Προ του σε Φιλιππον φωνησαι, οντα ὑπο την συκην ειδον σε. 49 απεκριθη αυτω Ναθαναηλ **Ῥαββει**, συ ει ὁ υἱος του Θεου, συ βασιλευς ει του Ισραηλ. 50 απεκριθη Ιησους και ειπεν αυτω Ότι ειπον σοι οτι ειδον σε ὑποκατω της συκης πιστευεις; μειζω τουτων οψῃ. 51 και λεγει αυτω Αμην αμην λεγω ὑμιν, οψεσθε τον ουρανον ανεῳγοτα και τους αγγελους του Θεου αναβαινοντας και καταβαινοντας επι τον υἱον του ανθρωπου.

2 Και τῃ ἡμερᾳ τῃ τριτῃ γαμος εγενετο εν Κανα της Γαλιλαιας, και ην ἡ μητηρ του Ιησου εκει 2 εκληθη δε και ὁ Ιησους και οἱ μαθηται αυτου εις τον γαμον. 3 και ὑστερησαντος οινου λεγει ἡ μητηρ του Ιησου προς αυτον Οινον ουκ εχουσιν. 4 και λεγει αυτῃ ὁ Ιησους Τι εμοι και σοι, γυναι; ουπω ἡκει ἡ ὡρα μου. 5 λεγει ἡ μητηρ αυτου τοις διακονοις Ότι αν λεγῃ ὑμιν, ποιησατε. 6 ησαν δε εκει λιθιναι ὑδριαι ἑξ κατα τον καθαρισμον των Ιουδαιων κειμεναι, χωρουσαι ανα μετρητας δυο

πολεως ανδρεου και πετρου
45 ευρισκει φιλιππος τον ναθαναηλ και λεγει αυτω ον εγραψεν μωυσης εν τω νομω και οι προφηται ευρηκαμεν ιησουν υιον του ιωσηφ τον απο ναζαρετ 46 και ειπεν αυτω ναθαναηλ εκ ναζαρετ δυναται τι αγαθον ειναι λεγει αυτω ο φιλιππος ερχου και ιδε 47 ειδεν ιησους τον ναθαναηλ ερχομενον προς αυτον και λεγει περι αυτου ιδε αληθως ισραηλιτης εν ω δολος ουκ εστιν 48 λεγει αυτω ναθαναηλ ποθεν με γινωσκεις απεκριθη ιησους και ειπεν αυτω προ του σε φιλιππον φωνησαι οντα υπο την συκην ειδον σε 49 απεκριθη αυτω ναθαναηλ **ραββι** συ ει ο υιος του θεου συ βασιλευς ει του ισραηλ 50 απεκριθη ιησους και ειπεν αυτω οτι ειπον σοι οτι ειδον σε υποκατω της συκης πιστευεις μειζω τουτων οψῃ 51 και λεγει αυτω αμην αμην λεγω υμιν οψεσθε τον ουρανον ανεῳγοτα και τους αγγελους του θεου αναβαινοντας και καταβαινοντας επι τον υιον του ανθρωπου

2 και τη ημερα τη τριτη γαμος εγενετο εν κανα της γαλιλαιας και ην η μητηρ του ιησου εκει 2 εκληθη δε και ο ιησους και οι μαθηται αυτου εις τον γαμον 3 και υστερησαντος οινου λεγει η μητηρ του ιησου προς αυτον οινον ουκ εχουσιν 4 και λεγει αυτη ο ιησους τι εμοι και σοι γυναι ουπω ηκει η ωρα μου 5 λεγει η μητηρ αυτου τοις διακονοις **ο τι** αν λεγη υμιν ποιησατε 6 ησαν δε εκει λιθιναι υδριαι εξ κατα τον καθαρισμον των ιουδαιων κειμεναι χωρουσαι ανα μετρητας δυο

η τρεις. 7 λεγει αυτοις ὁ Ιησους Γεμισατε τας ὑδριας ὑδατος. και εγεμισαν αυτας ἕως ανω. 8 και λεγει αυτοις Αντλησατε νυν και φερετε τω αρχιτρικλινω. οἱ δε ηνεγκαν. 9 ὡς δε εγευσατο ὁ αρχιτρικλινος το ὕδωρ οινον γεγενημενον, και ουκ ῃδει ποθεν εστιν, οἱ δε διακονοι ῃδεισαν οἱ ηντληκοτες το ὕδωρ, φωνει τον νυμφιον ὁ αρχιτρικλινος 10 και λεγει αυτω Πας ανθρωπος πρωτον τον καλον οινον τιθησιν, και ὁταν μεθυσθωσιν τον ελασσω· συ τετηρηκας τον καλον οινον ἕως αρτι. 11 ταυτην εποιησεν αρχην των σημειων ὁ Ιησους εν Κανα της Γαλιλαιας, και εφανερωσεν την δοξαν αυτου, και επιστευσαν εις αυτον οἱ μαθηται αυτου.

12 Μετα τουτο κατεβη εις Καφαρναουμ, αυτος και ἡ μητηρ αυτου και οἱ αδελφοι και οἱ μαθηται αυτου· και εκει εμειναν ου πολλας ἡμερας. 13 Και εγγυς ην το πασχα των Ιουδαιων, και ανεβη εις Ιεροσολυμα ὁ Ιησους. 14 και εὑρεν εν τῳ ἱερῳ τους πωλουντας βοας και προβατα και περιστερας και τους κερματιστας καθημενους, 15 και ποιησας φραγελλιον εκ σχοινιων παντας εξεβαλεν εκ του ἱερου τα τε προβατα και τους βοας, και των κολλυβιστων εξεχεεν το κερματα και τας τραπεζας ανετρεψεν, 16 και τοις τας περιστερας πωλουσιν ειπεν Αρατε ταυτα εντευθεν, μη ποιειτε τον οικον του πατρος μου οικον εμποριου. 17 Εμνησθησαν οἱ μαθηται αυτου, ὁτι γεγραμμενον εστιν Ὁ ζηλος του οικου σου

η τρεις 7 λεγει αυτοις ο ιησους γεμισατε τας υδριας υδατος και εγεμισαν αυτας εως ανω 8 και λεγει αυτοις αντλησατε νυν και φερετε τω αρχιτρικλινω οι δε ηνεγκαν 9 ως δε εγευσατο ο αρχιτρικλινος το υδωρ οινον γεγενημενον και ουκ ηδει ποθεν εστιν οι δε διακονοι ηδεισαν οι ηντληκοτες το υδωρ φωνει τον νυμφιον ο αρχιτρικλινος 10 και λεγει αυτω πας ανθρωπος πρωτον τον καλον οινον τιθησιν και οταν μεθυσθωσιν τον ελασσω συ τετηρηκας τον καλον οινον εως αρτι 11 ταυτην εποιησεν αρχην των σημειων ο ιησους εν κανα της γαλιλαιας και εφανερωσεν την δοξαν αυτου και επιστευσαν εις αυτον οι μαθηται αυτου

12 μετα τουτο κατεβη εις καφαρναουμ αυτος και η μητηρ αυτου και οι αδελφοι και οι μαθηται αυτου και εκει εμειναν ου πολλας ημερας 13 και εγγυς ην το πασχα των ιουδαιων και ανεβη εις ιεροσολυμα ο ιησους 14 και ευρεν εν τω ιερω τους πωλουντας βοας και προβατα και περιστερας και τους κερματιστας καθημενους 15 και ποιησας φραγελλιον εκ σχοινιων παντας εξεβαλεν εκ του ιερου τα τε προβατα και τους βοας και των κολλυβιστων εξεχεεν τα κερματα και τας τραπεζας ανετρεψεν 16 και τοις τας περιστερας πωλουσιν ειπεν αρατε ταυτα εντευθεν μη ποιειτε τον οικον του πατρος μου οικον εμποριου 17 εμνησθησαν οι μαθηται αυτου οτι γεγραμμενον εστιν ο ζηλος του οικου σου

καταφαγεται με. 18 απεκριθησαν ουν
οἱ Ιουδαιοι και ειπαν αυτω Τι
σημειον δεικνυεις ἡμιν, ὁτι ταυτα
ποιεις; 19 απεκριθη Ιησους και ειπεν
αυτοις Λυσατε τον ναον τουτον και
εν τρισιν ἡμεραις εγερω αυτον.
20 ειπαν ουν οἱ Ιουδαιοι
Τεσσερακοντα και ἑξ ετεσιν
οικοδομηθη ὁ ναος ουτος, και συ εν
τρισιν ἡμεραις εγερεις αυτον;
21 εκεινος δε ελεγεν περι του ναου
του σωματος αυτου. 22 ὁτε ουν
ηγερθη εκ νεκρων, εμνησθησαν οἱ
μαθηται αυτου ὁτι τουτο ελεγεν, και
επιστευσαν τη γραφη και τω λογω ὁν
ειπεν ὁ Ιησους.
23 Ὡς δε ην εν τοις Ἱεροσολυμοις
εν τω πασχα εν τη ἑορτη, πολλοι
επιστευσαν εις το ονομα αυτου,
θεωρουντες αυτου τα σημεια ἁ
εποιει. 24 αυτος δε ὁ Ιησους ουκ
επιστευεν αυτον αυτοις δια το αυτον
γινωσκειν παντας 25 και ὁτι ου
χρειαν ειχεν ἱνα μαρτυρηση περι
του ανθρωπου, αυτος γαρ εγινωσκεν
τι ην εν τω ανθρωπω.
3 Ην δε ανθρωπος εκ των
Φαρισαιων, Νικοδημος ονομα αυτω,
αρχων των Ιουδαιων 2 ουτος ηλθεν
προς αυτον νυκτος και ειπεν αυτω
Ῥαββει, οιδαμεν ὁτι απο Θεου
εληλυθας διδασκαλος· ουδεις γαρ
δυναται ταυτα τα σημεια ποιειν ἁ συ
ποιεις, εαν μη η ὁ Θεος μετ᾽ αυτου.
3 απεκριθη Ιησους και ειπεν αυτω
Αμην αμην λεγω σοι, εαν μη τις
γεννηθη ανωθεν, ου δυναται ιδειν την
βασιλειαν του Θεου. 4 λεγει προς
αυτον **ὁ** Νικοδημος Πως δυναται
ανθρωπος γεννηθηναι γερων ων; μη
δυναται εις την κοιλιαν της μητρος
αυτου δευτερον εισελθειν και
γεννηθηναι; 5 απεκριθη **ὁ** Ιησους
Αμην αμην λεγω σοι, εαν

καταφαγεται με 18 απεκριθησαν ουν
οι ιουδαιοι και ειπαν αυτω τι
σημειον δεικνυεις ημιν οτι ταυτα
ποιεις 19 απεκριθη ιησους και ειπεν
αυτοις λυσατε τον ναον τουτον και
[εν] τρισιν ημεραις εγερω αυτον
20 ειπαν ουν οι ιουδαιοι
τεσσερακοντα και εξ ετεσιν
οικοδομηθη ο ναος ουτος και συ εν
τρισιν ημεραις εγερεις αυτον
21 εκεινος δε ελεγεν περι του ναου
του σωματος αυτου 22 οτε ουν
ηγερθη εκ νεκρων εμνησθησαν οι
μαθηται αυτου οτι τουτο ελεγεν και
επιστευσαν τη γραφη και τω λογω ον
ειπεν ο ιησους
23 ως δε ην εν τοις ιεροσολυμοις
εν τω πασχα εν τη εορτη πολλοι
επιστευσαν εις το ονομα αυτου
θεωρουντες αυτου τα σημεια α
εποιει 24 αυτος δε ιησους ουκ
επιστευεν αυτον αυτοις δια το αυτον
γινωσκειν παντας 25 και οτι ου
χρειαν ειχεν ινα τις μαρτυρηση περι
του ανθρωπου αυτος γαρ εγινωσκεν
τι ην εν τω ανθρωπω
3 ην δε ανθρωπος εκ των
φαρισαιων νικοδημος ονομα αυτω
αρχων των ιουδαιων 2 ουτος ηλθεν
προς αυτον νυκτος και ειπεν αυτω
ραββι οιδαμεν οτι απο θεου
εληλυθας διδασκαλος ουδεις γαρ
δυναται ταυτα τα σημεια ποιειν α συ
ποιεις εαν μη η ο θεος μετ αυτου
3 απεκριθη ιησους και ειπεν αυτω
αμην αμην λεγω σοι εαν μη τις
γεννηθη ανωθεν ου δυναται ιδειν την
βασιλειαν του θεου 4 λεγει προς
αυτον [ο] νικοδημος πως δυναται
ανθρωπος γεννηθηναι γερων ων μη
δυναται εις την κοιλιαν της μητρος
αυτου δευτερον εισελθειν και
γεννηθηναι 5 απεκριθη [ο] ιησους
αμην αμην λεγω σοι εαν

μη τις γεννηθη εξ ύδατος και
Πνευματος, ου δυναται εισελθειν εις
την βασιλειαν του Θεου. 6 το
γεγεννημενον εκ της σαρκος σαρξ
εστιν, και το γεγεννημενον εκ του
Πνευματος πνευμα εστιν. 7 μη
θαυμασης ότι ειπον σοι Δει ύμας
γεννηθηναι ανωθεν. 8 το πνευμα
όπου θελει πνει, και την φωνην
αυτου ακουεις, αλλ' ουκ οιδας ποθεν
ερχεται και που ύπαγει· ούτως εστιν
πας ό γεγεννημενος εκ του
Πνευματος. 9 απεκριθη Νικοδημος
και ειπεν αυτω Πως δυναται ταυτα
γενεσθαι; 10 απεκριθη Ιησους και
ειπεν αυτω Συ ει ό διδασκαλος του
Ισραηλ, και ταυτα ου γινωσκεις;
11 αμην αμην λεγω σοι ότι ό
οιδαμεν λαλουμεν, και ό έωρακαμεν
μαρτυρουμεν, και την μαρτυριαν
ήμων ου λαμβανετε. 12 ει τα επιγεια
ειπον ύμιν και ου πιστευετε, πως εαν
ειπω ύμιν τα επουρανια πιστευσετε;
13 και ουδεις αναβεβηκεν εις τον
ουρανον ει μη ό εκ του ουρανου
καταβας, ό υίος του ανθρωπου.
14 και καθως Μωυσης ύψωσεν τον
οφιν εν τη ερημω, ούτως ύψωθηναι
δει τον υίον του ανθρωπου, 15 ίνα
πας ό πιστευων εν αυτω εχη ζωην
αιωνιον.

16 Ούτως γαρ ηγαπησεν ό Θεος
τον κοσμον ώστε τον υίον τον
μονογενη εδωκεν, ίνα πας ό
πιστευων εις αυτον μη αποληται
αλλ' εχη ζωην αιωνιον. 17 ου γαρ
απεστειλεν ό Θεος τον υίον εις τον
κοσμον ίνα κρινη τον κοσμον, αλλ'
ίνα σωθη ό κοσμος δι' αυτου. 18 ό
πιστευων εις αυτον ου κρινεται· ό
μη πιστευων ηδη κεκριται, ότι μη
πεπιστευκεν εις το ονομα του
μονογενους υίου του Θεου. 19 αύτη

μη τις γεννηθη εξ υδατος και
πνευματος ου δυναται εισελθειν εις
την βασιλειαν του θεου 6 το
γεγεννημενον εκ της σαρκος σαρξ
εστιν και το γεγεννημενον εκ του
πνευματος πνευμα εστιν 7 μη
θαυμασης οτι ειπον σοι δει υμας
γεννηθηναι ανωθεν 8 το πνευμα
οπου θελει πνει και την φωνην
αυτου ακουεις αλλ ουκ οιδας ποθεν
ερχεται και που υπαγει ουτως εστιν
πας ο γεγεννημενος εκ του
πνευματος 9 απεκριθη νικοδημος και
ειπεν αυτω πως δυναται ταυτα
γενεσθαι 10 απεκριθη ιησους και
ειπεν αυτω συ ει ο διδασκαλος του
ισραηλ και ταυτα ου γινωσκεις
11 αμην αμην λεγω σοι οτι ο
οιδαμεν λαλουμεν και ο εωρακαμεν
μαρτυρουμεν και την μαρτυριαν
ημων ου λαμβανετε 12 ει τα επιγεια
ειπον υμιν και ου πιστευετε πως εαν
ειπω υμιν τα επουρανια πιστευσετε
13 και ουδεις αναβεβηκεν εις τον
ουρανον ει μη ο εκ του ουρανου
καταβας ο υιος του ανθρωπου
14 και καθως μωυσης υψωσεν τον
οφιν εν τη ερημω ουτως υψωθηναι
δει τον υιον του ανθρωπου 15 ινα
πας ο πιστευων εν αυτω εχη ζωην
αιωνιον

16 ουτως γαρ ηγαπησεν ο θεος
τον κοσμον ωστε τον υιον τον
μονογενη εδωκεν ινα πας ο
πιστευων εις αυτον μη αποληται
αλλ εχη ζωην αιωνιον 17 ου γαρ
απεστειλεν ο θεος τον υιον εις τον
κοσμον ινα κρινη τον κοσμον αλλ
ινα σωθη ο κοσμος δι αυτου 18 ο
πιστευων εις αυτον ου κρινεται ο
μη πιστευων ηδη κεκριται οτι μη
πεπιστευκεν εις το ονομα του
μονογενους υιου του θεου 19 αυτη

δε εστιν ἡ κρισις ὅτι το φως ελήλυθεν εις τον κοσμον και ηγαπησαν οἱ ανθρωποι μαλλον το σκοτος η το φως· ην γαρ αυτων πονηρα τα εργα. 20 πας γαρ ὁ φαυλα πρασσων μισει το φως και ουκ ερχεται προς το φως, ἱνα μη ελεγχθη τα εργα αυτου· 21 ὁ δε ποιων την αληθειαν ερχεται προς το φως, ἱνα φανερωθη αυτου τα εργα ὅτι εν θεω εστιν ειργασμενα.

22 Μετα ταυτα ηλθεν ὁ Ιησους και οἱ μαθηται αυτου εις την Ιουδαιαν γην, και εκει διετριβεν μετ᾽ αυτων, και εβαπτιζεν. 23 ην δε και ὁ **Ιωανης** βαπτιζων εν Αινων εγγυς του Σαλειμ, ὅτι ὑδατα πολλα ην εκει, και παρεγινοντο και εβαπτιζοντο· 24 ουπω γαρ ην βεβλημενος εις την φυλακην Ιωανης. 25 Εγενετο ουν ζητησις εκ των μαθητων Ιωανου μετα Ιουδαιου περι καθαρισμου. 26 και ηλθαν προς τον Ιωανην και ειπαν αυτω Ῥαββει, ὅς ην μετα σου περαν του Ιορδανου, ᾧ συ μεμαρτυρηκας, ιδε οὑτος βαπτιζει και παντες ερχονται προς αυτον. 27 απεκριθη Ιωανης και ειπεν Ου δυναται ανθρωπος λαμβανειν **ουδε**, εαν μη ᾗ δεδομενον αυτῳ εκ του ουρανου. 28 αυτοι ὑμεις μοι μαρτυρειτε ὅτι ειπον **εγω** Ουκ ειμι εγω ὁ Χριστος, αλλ᾽ ὅτι Απεσταλμενος ειμι εμπροσθεν εκεινου. 29 ὁ εχων την νυμφην νυμφιος εστιν· ὁ δε φιλος του νυμφιου, ὁ ἑστηκως και ακουων αυτου, χαρα χαιρει δια την φωνην του νυμφιου· αὑτη ουν ἡ χαρα ἡ εμη πεπληρωται. 30 εκεινον δει αυξανειν, εμε δε ελαττουσθαι. 31 Ὁ ανωθεν ερχομενος επανω

δε εστιν η κρισις οτι το φως ελήλυθεν εις τον κοσμον και ηγαπησαν οι ανθρωποι μαλλον το σκοτος η το φως ην γαρ αυτων πονηρα τα εργα 20 πας γαρ ο φαυλα πρασσων μισει το φως και ουκ ερχεται προς το φως ινα μη ελεγχθη τα εργα αυτου 21 ο δε ποιων την αληθειαν ερχεται προς το φως ινα φανερωθη αυτου τα εργα οτι εν θεω εστιν ειργασμενα

22 μετα ταυτα ηλθεν ο ιησους και οι μαθηται αυτου εις την ιουδαιαν γην και εκει διετριβεν μετ αυτων και εβαπτιζεν 23 ην δε και [ο] **ιωαννης** βαπτιζων εν αινων εγγυς του σαλειμ οτι υδατα πολλα ην εκει και παρεγινοντο και εβαπτιζοντο 24 ουπω γαρ ην βεβλημενος εις την φυλακην ιωαννης 25 εγενετο ουν ζητησις εκ των μαθητων ιωαννου μετα ιουδαιου περι καθαρισμου 26 και ηλθον προς τον ιωαννην και ειπαν αυτω **ραββι** ος ην μετα σου περαν του ιορδανου ω συ μεμαρτυρηκας ιδε ουτος βαπτιζει και παντες ερχονται προς αυτον 27 απεκριθη ιωαννης και ειπεν ου δυναται ανθρωπος λαμβανειν **ουδεν** εαν μη η δεδομενον αυτω εκ του ουρανου 28 αυτοι υμεις μοι μαρτυρειτε οτι ειπον [εγω] ουκ ειμι εγω ο χριστος αλλ οτι απεσταλμενος ειμι εμπροσθεν εκεινου 29 ο εχων την νυμφην νυμφιος εστιν ο δε φιλος του νυμφιου ο εστηκως και ακουων αυτου χαρα χαιρει δια την φωνην του νυμφιου αυτη ουν η χαρα η εμη πεπληρωται 30 εκεινον δει αυξανειν εμε δε ελαττουσθαι 31 ο ανωθεν ερχομενος επανω

παντων εστιν· ὁ ων εκ της γης εκ της γης εστιν και εκ της γης λαλει· ὁ εκ του ουρανου ερχομενος επανω παντων εστιν. 32 ὁ ἑωρακεν και ηκουσεν τουτο μαρτυρει, και την μαρτυριαν αυτου ουδεις λαμβανει. 33 ὁ λαβων αυτου την μαρτυριαν εσφραγισεν ὁτι ὁ Θεος αληθης εστιν. 34 ὁν γαρ απεστειλεν ὁ Θεος τα ῥηματα του Θεου λαλει· ου γαρ εκ μετρου διδωσιν το Πνευμα. 35 ὁ πατηρ αγαπᾳ τον υἱον, και παντα δεδωκεν εν τῃ χειρι αυτου. 36 ὁ πιστευων εις τον υἱον εχει ζωην αιωνιον· ὁ δε απειθων τῳ υἱῳ ουκ οψεται ζωην, αλλ᾽ ἡ οργη του Θεου μενει επ᾽ αυτον.

4 Ὡς ουν εγνω ὁ Κυριος ὁτι ηκουσαν οἱ Φαρισαιοι ὁτι Ιησους πλειονας μαθητας ποιει και βαπτιζει **η** Ιωανης 2—καιτοιγε Ιησους αυτος ουκ εβαπτιζεν αλλ᾽ οἱ μαθηται αυτου —3 αφηκεν την Ιουδαιαν και απηλθεν παλιν εις την Γαλιλαιαν. 4 εδει δε αυτον διερχεσθαι δια της **Σαμαριας**. 5 ερχεται ουν εις πολιν της **Σαμαριας** λεγομενην Συχαρ πλησιον του χωριου ὁ εδωκεν Ιακωβ **τῳ** Ιωσηφ τῳ υἱῳ αυτου· 6 ην δε εκει πηγη του Ιακωβ. ὁ ουν Ιησους κεκοπιακως εκ της οδοιποριας εκαθεζετο οὑτως επι τῃ πηγῃ. ωρα ην ὡς ἑκτη. 7 ερχεται γυνη εκ της **Σαμαριας** αντλησαι ὑδωρ. λεγει αυτῃ ὁ Ιησους Δος μοι πειν· 8 οἱ γαρ μαθηται αυτου απεληλυθεισαν εις την πολιν, ἱνα τροφας αγορασωσιν. 9 λεγει ουν αυτῳ ἡ γυνη ἡ **Σαμαρειτις** Πως συ Ιουδαιος ων παρ᾽ εμου πειν αιτεις γυναικος **Σαμαρειτιδος** ουσης; **ου γαρ συνχρωνται Ιουδαιοι Σαμαρειταις.** 10 απεκριθη Ιησους

παντων εστιν ο ων εκ της γης εκ της γης εστιν και εκ της γης λαλει ο εκ του ουρανου ερχομενος επανω παντων εστιν 32 ο εωρακεν και ηκουσεν τουτο μαρτυρει και την μαρτυριαν αυτου ουδεις λαμβανει 33 ο λαβων αυτου την μαρτυριαν εσφραγισεν οτι ο θεος αληθης εστιν 34 ον γαρ απεστειλεν ο θεος τα ρηματα του θεου λαλει ου γαρ εκ μετρου διδωσιν το πνευμα 35 ο πατηρ αγαπα τον υιον και παντα δεδωκεν εν τη χειρι αυτου 36 ο πιστευων εις τον υιον εχει ζωην αιωνιον ο δε απειθων τω υιω ουκ οψεται ζωην αλλ η οργη του θεου μενει επ αυτον

4 ως ουν εγνω ο κυριος οτι ηκουσαν οι φαρισαιοι οτι ιησους πλειονας μαθητας ποιει και βαπτιζει **[η]** ιωαννης 2 καιτοιγε ιησους αυτος ουκ εβαπτιζεν αλλ οι μαθηται αυτου 3 αφηκεν την ιουδαιαν και απηλθεν παλιν εις την γαλιλαιαν 4 εδει δε αυτον διερχεσθαι δια της **σαμαρειας** 5 ερχεται ουν εις πολιν της **σαμαρειας** λεγομενην συχαρ πλησιον του χωριου ο εδωκεν ιακωβ **[τω]** ιωσηφ τω υιω αυτου 6 ην δε εκει πηγη του ιακωβ ο ουν ιησους κεκοπιακως εκ της οδοιποριας εκαθεζετο ουτως επι τη πηγη ωρα ην ως εκτη 7 ερχεται γυνη εκ της **σαμαρειας** αντλησαι υδωρ λεγει αυτη ο ιησους δος μοι πειν 8 οι γαρ μαθηται αυτου απεληλυθεισαν εις την πολιν ινα τροφας αγορασωσιν 9 λεγει ουν αυτω η γυνη η **σαμαριτις** πως συ ιουδαιος ων παρ εμου πειν αιτεις γυναικος **σαμαριτιδος** ουσης **[ου γαρ συγχρωνται ιουδαιοι σαμαριταις]** 10 απεκριθη ιησους και ειπεν αυτη Ει ηδεις την δωρεαν του Θεου και τις εστιν ὁ λεγων σοι Δος μοι πειν, συ αν ητησας αυτον και εδωκεν αν σοι ὑδωρ ζων. 11 λεγει αυτω Κυριε, ουτε αντλημα εχεις και το φρεαρ εστιν βαθυ· ποθεν ουν εχεις το ὑδωρ το ζων; 12 μη συ μειζων ει του πατρος ἡμων Ιακωβ, ὁς εδωκεν ἡμιν το φρεαρ και αυτος εξ αυτου επιεν και οἱ υἱοι αυτου και τα θρεμματα αυτου; 13 απεκριθη Ιησους και ειπεν αυτη Πας ὁ πινων εκ του ὑδατος τουτου διψησει παλιν· 14 ὁς δ᾽ αν πιη εκ του ὑδατος οὑ εγω δωσω αυτω, ου μη διψησει εις τον αιωνα, αλλα το ὑδωρ ὁ δωσω αυτω γενησεται εν αυτω πηγη ὑδατος ἁλλομενου εις ζωην αιωνιον. 15 λεγει προς αυτον ἡ γυνη Κυριε, δος μοι τουτο το ὑδωρ, ἱνα μη διψω μηδε διερχωμαι ενθαδε αντλειν. 16 λεγει αυτη Ὑπαγε, φωνησον σου τον ανδρα, και ελθε ενθαδε. 17 απεκριθη ἡ γυνη και ειπεν **αυτω** Ουκ εχω ανδρα. λεγει αυτη ὁ Ιησους Καλως ειπας ὁτι Ανδρα ουκ εχω 18 πεντε γαρ ανδρας εσχες, και νυν ὁν εχεις ουκ εστιν σου ανηρ· τουτο αληθες ειρηκας. 19 λεγει αυτω ἡ γυνη Κυριε, θεωρω ὁτι προφητης ει συ. 20 οἱ πατερες ἡμων εν τω ορει τουτω προσεκυνησαν· και ὑμεις λεγετε ὁτι εν Ιεροσολυμοις εστιν ὁ τοπος ὁπου προσκυνειν δει. 21 λεγει αυτη ὁ Ιησους Πιστευε μοι, γυναι, ὁτι ερχεται ωρα ὁτε ουτε εν τω ορει τουτω ουτε εν Ἱεροσολυμοις προσκυνησετε τω πατρι. 22 ὑμεις προσκυνειτε ὁ ουκ οιδατε· ἡμεις προσκυνουμεν ὁ οιδαμεν, ὁτι ἡ σωτηρια εκ των Ιουδαιων εστιν. 23 αλλα ερχεται ωρα και νυν εστιν,

και ειπεν αυτη ει ηδεις την δωρεαν του θεου και τις εστιν ο λεγων σοι δος μοι πειν συ αν ητησας αυτον και εδωκεν αν σοι υδωρ ζων 11 λεγει αυτω κυριε ουτε αντλημα εχεις και το φρεαρ εστιν βαθυ ποθεν ουν εχεις το υδωρ το ζων 12 μη συ μειζων ει του πατρος ημων ιακωβ ος εδωκεν ημιν το φρεαρ και αυτος εξ αυτου επιεν και οι υιοι αυτου και τα θρεμματα αυτου 13 απεκριθη ιησους και ειπεν αυτη πας ο πινων εκ του υδατος τουτου διψησει παλιν 14 ος δ αν πιη εκ του υδατος ου εγω δωσω αυτω ου μη διψησει εις τον αιωνα αλλα το υδωρ ο δωσω αυτω γενησεται εν αυτω πηγη υδατος αλλομενου εις ζωην αιωνιον 15 λεγει προς αυτον η γυνη κυριε δος μοι τουτο το υδωρ ινα μη διψω μηδε διερχωμαι ενθαδε αντλειν 16 λεγει αυτη υπαγε φωνησον σου τον ανδρα και ελθε ενθαδε 17 απεκριθη η γυνη και ειπεν [αυτω] ουκ εχω ανδρα λεγει αυτη ο ιησους καλως ειπας οτι ανδρα ουκ εχω 18 πεντε γαρ ανδρας εσχες και νυν ον εχεις ουκ εστιν σου ανηρ τουτο αληθες ειρηκας 19 λεγει αυτω η γυνη κυριε θεωρω οτι προφητης ει συ 20 οι πατερες ημων εν τω ορει τουτω προσεκυνησαν και υμεις λεγετε οτι εν ιεροσολυμοις εστιν ο τοπος οπου προσκυνειν δει 21 λεγει αυτη ο ιησους πιστευε μοι γυναι οτι ερχεται ωρα οτε ουτε εν τω ορει τουτω ουτε εν ιεροσολυμοις προσκυνησετε τω πατρι 22 υμεις προσκυνειτε ο ουκ οιδατε ημεις προσκυνουμεν ο οιδαμεν οτι η σωτηρια εκ των ιουδαιων εστιν 23 αλλα ερχεται ωρα και νυν εστιν ότε οἱ αληθινοι προσκυνηται προσκυνησουσιν τω πατρι εν πνευματι και αληθεια, και γαρ ὁ πατηρ τοιουτους ζητει τους προσκυνουντας αυτον. 24 πνευμα ὁ Θεος, και τους προσκυνουντας αυτον εν πνευματι και αληθεια δει προσκυνειν. 25 λεγει αυτω ἡ γυνη Οιδα ὁτι Μεσσιας ερχεται, ὁ λεγομενος Χριστος· ὁταν ελθη εκεινος, αναγγελει ἡμιν ἁπαντα. 26 λεγει αυτη ὁ Ιησους Εγω ειμι, ὁ λαλων σοι.

27 Και επι τουτῳ ηλθαν οἱ μαθηται αυτου· και εθαυμαζον ὁτι μετα γυναικος ελαλει· ουδεις μεντοι ειπεν Τι ζητεις; η Τι λαλεις μετ᾽ αυτης; 28 αφηκεν ουν την ὑδριαν αυτης ἡ γυνη και απηλθεν εις την πολιν και λεγει τοις ανθρωποις 29 Δευτε ιδετε ανθρωπον ὁς ειπεν μοι παντα ἁ εποιησα· μητι οὑτος εστιν ὁ Χριστος; 30 εξηλθον εκ της πολεως, και ηρχοντο προς αυτον. 31 Εν τῳ μεταξυ ηρωτων αυτον οἱ μαθηται λεγοντες Ῥαββι, φαγε. 32 ὁ δε ειπεν αυτοις Εγω βρωσιν εχω φαγειν ἡν ὑμεις ουκ οιδατε. 33 ελεγον ουν οἱ μαθηται προς αλληλους Μη τις ηνεγκεν αυτω φαγειν; 34 λεγει αυτοις ὁ Ιησους Εμον βρωμα εστιν ἱνα ποιησω το θελημα του πεμψαντος με και τελειωσω αυτου το εργον. 35 ουχ ὑμεις λεγετε ὁτι Ετι τετραμηνος εστιν και ὁ θερισμος ερχεται; ιδου λεγω ὑμιν, επαρατε τους οφθαλμους ὑμων και θεασασθε τας χωρας ὁτι λευκαι εισιν προς θερισμον· ηδη 36 ὁ θεριζων μισθον λαμβανει και συναγει καρπον εις ζωην αιωνιον, ἱνα ὁ σπειρων ὁμου χαιρη και ὁ θεριζων. 37 εν γαρ τουτῳ ὁ λογος εστιν αληθινος ὁτι

οτε οι αληθινοι προσκυνηται προσκυνησουσιν τω πατρι εν πνευματι και αληθεια και γαρ ο πατηρ τοιουτους ζητει τους προσκυνουντας αυτον 24 πνευμα ο θεος και τους προσκυνουντας αυτον εν πνευματι και αληθεια δει προσκυνειν 25 λεγει αυτω η γυνη οιδα οτι μεσσιας ερχεται ο λεγομενος χριστος οταν ελθη εκεινος αναγγελει ημιν απαντα 26 λεγει αυτη ο ιησους εγω ειμι ο λαλων σοι

27 και επι τουτω ηλθαν οι μαθηται αυτου και εθαυμαζον οτι μετα γυναικος ελαλει ουδεις μεντοι ειπεν τι ζητεις η τι λαλεις μετ αυτης 28 αφηκεν ουν την υδριαν αυτης η γυνη και απηλθεν εις την πολιν και λεγει τοις ανθρωποις 29 δευτε ιδετε ανθρωπον ος ειπεν μοι παντα α εποιησα μητι ουτος εστιν ο χριστος 30 εξηλθον εκ της πολεως και ηρχοντο προς αυτον 31 εν τω μεταξυ ηρωτων αυτον οι μαθηται λεγοντες **ραββι** φαγε 32 ο δε ειπεν αυτοις εγω βρωσιν εχω φαγειν ην υμεις ουκ οιδατε 33 ελεγον ουν οι μαθηται προς αλληλους μη τις ηνεγκεν αυτω φαγειν 34 λεγει αυτοις ο ιησους εμον βρωμα εστιν ινα ποιησω το θελημα του πεμψαντος με και τελειωσω αυτου το εργον 35 ουχ υμεις λεγετε οτι ετι τετραμηνος εστιν και ο θερισμος ερχεται ιδου λεγω υμιν επαρατε τους οφθαλμους υμων και θεασασθε τας χωρας οτι λευκαι εισιν προς θερισμον ηδη 36 ο θεριζων μισθον λαμβανει και συναγει καρπον εις ζωην αιωνιον ινα ο σπειρων ομου χαιρη και ο θεριζων 37 εν γαρ τουτω ο λογος εστιν αληθινος οτι

αλλος εστιν ὁ σπειρων και αλλος ὁ θεριζων. 38 εγω απεστειλα ὑμας θεριζειν ὁ ουχ ὑμεις κεκοπιακατε· αλλοι κεκοπιακασιν, και ὑμεις εις τον κοπον αυτων εισεληλυθατε.

39 Εκ δε της πολεως εκεινης πολλοι επιστευσαν εις αυτον των **Σαμαρειτων** δια τον λογον της γυναικος μαρτυρουσης ὁτι Ειπεν μοι παντα ἁ εποιησα. 40 ὡς ουν ηλθον προς αυτον οἱ **Σαμαρειται,** ηρωτων αυτον μειναι παρ᾽ αυτοις· και εμεινεν εκει δυο ἡμερας. 41 και πολλω πλειους επιστευσαν δια τον λογον αυτου, 42 τῃ τε γυναικι ελεγον **ὁτι** Ουκετι δια την **λαλιαν σου** πιστευομεν· αυτοι γαρ ακηκοαμεν, και οιδαμεν ὁτι οὑτος εστιν αληθως ὁ σωτηρ του κοσμου.

43 Μετα δε τας δυο ἡμερας εξηλθεν εκειθεν εις την Γαλιλαιαν. 44 αυτος γαρ Ιησους εμαρτυρησεν ὁτι προφητης εν τῃ ιδια πατριδι τιμην ουκ εχει. 45 ὁτε ουν ηλθεν εις την Γαλιλαιαν, εδεξαντο αυτον οἱ Γαλιλαιοι, παντα ἑωρακοτες ὁσα εποιησεν εν Ἱεροσολυμοις εν τῃ ἑορτῃ, και αυτοι γαρ ηλθον εις την ἑορτην.

46 Ηλθεν ουν παλιν εις την Κανα της Γαλιλαιας, ὁπου εποιησεν το ὑδωρ οινον. και ην τις βασιλικος οὑ ὁ υἱος ησθενει εν Καφαρναουμ. 47 οὑτος, ακουσας ὁτι Ιησους ἡκει εκ της Ιουδαιας εις την Γαλιλαιαν, απηλθεν προς αυτον και ηρωτα ἱνα καταβῃ και ιασηται αυτου τον υἱον, ημελλεν γαρ αποθνησκειν. 48 ειπεν ουν ὁ Ιησους προς αυτον Εαν μη σημεια και τερατα ιδητε, ου μη πιστευσητε.

49 λεγει προς αυτον ὁ βασιλικος Κυριε, καταβηθι πριν αποθανειν το

αλλος εστιν ο σπειρων και αλλος ο θεριζων 38 εγω απεστειλα υμας θεριζειν ο ουχ υμεις κεκοπιακατε αλλοι κεκοπιακασιν και υμεις εις τον κοπον αυτων εισεληλυθατε

39 εκ δε της πολεως εκεινης πολλοι επιστευσαν εις αυτον των **σαμαριτων** δια τον λογον της γυναικος μαρτυρουσης οτι ειπεν μοι παντα α εποιησα 40 ως ουν ηλθον προς αυτον οι **σαμαριται** ηρωτων αυτον μειναι παρ αυτοις και εμεινεν εκει δυο ημερας 41 και πολλω πλειους επιστευσαν δια τον λογον αυτου 42 τη τε γυναικι ελεγον [οτι] ουκετι δια την **σην λαλιαν** πιστευομεν αυτοι γαρ ακηκοαμεν και οιδαμεν οτι ουτος εστιν αληθως ο σωτηρ του κοσμου

43 μετα δε τας δυο ημερας εξηλθεν εκειθεν εις την γαλιλαιαν 44 αυτος γαρ ιησους εμαρτυρησεν οτι προφητης εν τη ιδια πατριδι τιμην ουκ εχει 45 οτε ουν ηλθεν εις την γαλιλαιαν εδεξαντο αυτον οι γαλιλαιοι παντα εωρακοτες οσα εποιησεν εν ιεροσολυμοις εν τη εορτη και αυτοι γαρ ηλθον εις την εορτην

46 ηλθεν ουν παλιν εις την κανα της γαλιλαιας οπου εποιησεν το υδωρ οινον και ην τις βασιλικος ου ο υιος ησθενει εν καφαρναουμ 47 ουτος ακουσας οτι ιησους ηκει εκ της ιουδαιας εις την γαλιλαιαν απηλθεν προς αυτον και ηρωτα ινα καταβη και ιασηται αυτου τον υιον ημελλεν γαρ αποθνησκειν 48 ειπεν ουν ο ιησους προς αυτον εαν μη σημεια και τερατα ιδητε ου μη πιστευσητε

49 λεγει προς αυτον ο βασιλικος κυριε καταβηθι πριν αποθανειν το

παιδιον μου. 50 λεγει αυτω ὁ Ιησους Πορευου· ὁ υίος σου ζῇ. επιστευσεν ὁ ανθρωπος τω λογω ὁν ειπεν αυτω ὁ Ιησους και επορευετο. 51 ηδη δε αυτου καταβαινοντος οἱ δουλοι αυτου ὑπηντησαν αυτω λεγοντες ὁτι ὁ παις αυτου ζῇ. 52 επυθετο ουν την ὡραν παρ' αυτων εν ἡ' κομψοτερον εσχεν· ειπαν ουν αυτω ὁτι Εχθες ὡραν ἑβδομην αφηκεν αυτον ὁ πυρετος. 53 εγνω ουν ὁ πατηρ ὁτι εκεινη τῃ ὡρᾳ εν ἡ' ειπεν αυτω ὁ Ιησους Ὁ υίος σου ζῇ, και επιστευσεν αυτος και ἡ οικια αυτου ὁλη. 54 τουτο **δε** παλιν δευτερον σημειον εποιησεν ὁ Ιησους ελθων εκ της Ιουδαιας εις την Γαλιλαιαν.

παιδιον μου 50 λεγει αυτω ο ιησους πορευου ο υιος σου ζη επιστευσεν ο ανθρωπος τω λογω ον ειπεν αυτω ο ιησους και επορευετο 51 ηδη δε αυτου καταβαινοντος οι δουλοι αυτου υπηντησαν αυτω λεγοντες οτι ο παις αυτου ζη 52 επυθετο ουν την ωραν παρ αυτων εν η κομψοτερον εσχεν ειπαν ουν αυτω οτι εχθες ωραν εβδομην αφηκεν αυτον ο πυρετος 53 εγνω ουν ο πατηρ οτι εκεινη τη ωρα εν η ειπεν αυτω ο ιησους ο υιος σου ζη και επιστευσεν αυτος και η οικια αυτου ολη 54 τουτο [δε] παλιν δευτερον σημειον εποιησεν ο ιησους ελθων εκ της ιουδαιας εις την γαλιλαιαν

Appendix VI

John 3:16 Numerical Analysis

This chapter is to show how Ivan Panin took the word and letter place values as well as the word and letter numeric values and factored the sums to reveal the numeric patterns in the Greek text. Using this technique, one can verify Panin's methods as well as explore for one's self the character of the numerical language in the text. While proof of the Divine origin of all of scripture is readily apparent, the actual exploration itself is quite as deep and complex as learning the nuances of the Greek or Hebrew language.

Thus, in the following example there are a multitude of numbers which do not seem to clearly connect. This is because the language is vast and detailed. For example, in the following page we might note that the last word of the second phrase has the Word Place Value of **61**, and the 1st and 9th words of the last phrase have the Word Totals of **61**. This is little other than a nice coincidence if we are unfamiliar with scriptural numerics at large, and remember that **61** is the base prime upon which the numerics of Psalm 119 are based, which is about *law*. Looking then at the three words involved in John 3:16, *He gives* has the Word Place Value of 61 as well as *"that"* and *"but"* in the last phrase—which qualify the two resulting conditions of His giving. This makes a statement as to the legal qualifications for such gifts. As such, not perishing and having eternal life are shown to be *legally unassailable* by the numeric markers.

This is not readily apparent to most of us who simply wish to see an amazing array of 7's. There *are* many amazing and easily identifiable numbers, and these have been pointed out. Yet the language of numerics is complex, and we have not cherry-picked in the following examples; *all* the numerics are laid out, whether fully understood yet or not.

86	**21**	**70**	**15**	**46**	←Word Place Values

15 20 19 24 18　3 1 17　　7 3 1　16 7 18　5 13　15　8　5 15 18　←Letter Place Values

Ο ὕ τ ω ς　γ ὰ ρ　ἠ γ ά π η σ ε ν　ὁ　Θ ε ὸ ς　←Text

70 400 300 800 200　3 1 100　8 3 1　80 8 200 5 50　70　9 5 70 200　←Letter Values

1770　　**104**　　　　**355**　　**70**　**284**　←Word Totals

Thus, *in this manner*　for　　　loves　　the　God　←Translation

47　　　**83**　　　　(**368**, 30 letters total)　(368 + 3453 + 34 = **3855**, next section)

9 15 13　10 15 18 12 15 13　　2⁴ x 23 and 361 (next section) + 7

τ ὸ ν　κ ό σ μ ο ν,　(**3453**, 7 words total)

300 70 50　20 70 200 40 70 50　3 x 1151 (first verse of Nahum = 1151)

420　　**450**

the　　world

66　　**47**　　**57**　　**47**　　　　**83**

24　18 19 5　19 15 13　20 9 15 13　19 15 13　12 15 13 15　3　5 13　7

ὥ σ τ ε　τ ὸ ν　υ ἱ ὸ ν　τ ὸ ν　μ ο ν ο γ ε ν ῆ

800 200 300 5　300 70 50　400 10 70 50　300 70 50　40 70 50 70 3　5 50 8

1305　　**420**　　**530**　　**420**　　　**296**

so also, *so that*　the　son　　the　only-born, *only begotten*

61　　(**361**, 28 letters total)　(361 + 3855 = **4216**)　(361 + 368 = 729 = 3⁶ = 9³)

5　4　24　10 5 13　19²　　　2³ x 17 x 31

ἔ δ ω κ ε ν,　(**3855**, 6 words total)

5　4 800 20 5 50　3 x 5 x 257 or 2⁸ x 15 + 1

884

he gives

23　　**35**　　**15**　　**124**　　**32**　　**68**

9 13 1　16 1 18　15　16 9　18 19 5 20 24 13　5　9 18　1　20 19 15 13

ἵ ν α　π ᾶ ς　ὁ　π ι σ τ ε ύ ω ν　ε ἰ ς　α ὐ τ ὸ ν

10 50 1　80 1 200　70　80 10 200 300 5 400 800 50　5 10 200　1 400 300 70 50

61　　**281**　　**70**　　**1845**　　**215**　　**821**

that　every　the　believing, *one believing*　into　him

23　　**79**　(**399**) ←/→ (**200**) 23　**43**　**50**

12　7　1　16 15 11　7　19 1　9 /　1　11 11　5 22　7 9　6 24　7 13

μ ὴ　ἀ π ό λ η τ α ι / ἀ λ λ’　ἔ χ η ι　ζ ω ὴ ν

40 8　1 80 70 30 8 300 1 10 / 1　30 30　5 600 8 10　7 800　8 50

48　　**500**　(3841)←/→(2540) 61　**623**　　**865**

no　should-be-being-destroyed　but　may-be-having　life

84　　(**599**, 51 (3 x 17) letters total) (**Whole Verse: 1328**, 109 letters total, 1 'elided' for 110)

1　9 24　13 9 15 13　[399 is 3 x 7 x 19 and 200 is 2³ x 5²]　　2⁴ x 83　　37 + 73

α ἰ ώ ν ι ο ν.　(**6381**, 12 words total) (**Whole Verse: 13,689**; 25 words total)

1　10 800 50 10 70 50　3² x 709　　　(7 + 37 + 73)² or 117²; 5²

991　　　　(**Whole Verse with Place Values Added = 15,000 + 17**)

eternal, *to the age*　15,017 + 25 words = 15,042 = 2 x 3 x 23 x 109　15,042 + 109 letters = **15,151** (109

x 139)　2³ x 3 x 5⁴

332

Again, we could merely search out a particular number (say, 7) and attempt to calculate the odds of it occurring with such frequency. On the other hand, *every* number has equal significance—yet differing in character as star differs from star in glory—and the casual reader, unfamiliar with the numeric world hidden behind the letters could be overwhelmed. Thus we will take our journey through this verse following the exact method by which it has been examined: the reader is invited to share the same process of discovery as the writer, with all its bumps, near-misses, and hopefully, its final unveiling.

First let us get the lay of the land. We would not look for a cactus flower in the Amazon jungle, nor expect to harvest coconuts in Nova Scotia. The Gospel of John has its own character, and we wish to have tools appropriate for the occasion. Note then, that just as a book has an introduction, John also has both an introduction and an epilogue. A large book would not suffice to examine all the material, so let us take a look at the first verse (Appendix I) and the last verse (Appendix II) to familiarize ourselves with the 'ground rules' and the numbers that are particularly prominent to John's Gospel.

Diving right in then, we note that the first verse of John has the value of 3^2 x **13** x **31**. These we take as primary, and note that it can be written as reversed numbers, similar to Genesis 1:1, as **39** x **93**. We will also want to keep a lookout for **37** and **73**, as Genesis 1:1 has the value of **2701** (**37** x **73**). Note that the appendixes use the *exact same method* of analysis for John 1:1-2, 3:16, and 21:25. This prevents us from the temptation to cherry-pick which numbers we like and ignore the others. The fact is that *every* number is important: out job is to figure out *how* they are important and *how* they relate, as well as *what* they are telling us. Because all Scripture relates to the rest of Scripture, and because our space and time is limited here, we will focus our journey on determining the answer to the following question: *What is the numeric message of John 3:16, and how does it fit within the* *greater context of John's Gospel?* We are beginning by finding the most prominent numbers that emerge, such as the fact that John's Gospel is replete with **3**'s.

In addition to **3, 13, 31, 37,** and **73** (all prime), we note that John 1:1 has **17** words of 52 letters (4 x **13**) spread into three phrases. Also, both the first and last (each with **5** words and **15** letters) of its three phrase divisions have **17** as a factor. The first two phrases' place values (**171** and 269) equal 440, which is (4 x **37**) + (4 x **73**). The second and third phrases' place values (269 and 163) equal 432, which is 3^3 x 4^3. The first and last phrases' place values equal 334, which is 100 + 100 + **67** + **67**. Are these **67**'s significant? Yes; the total place values of verse one is 603, which is 3^2 x **67**. In fact, if we go to the second verse, the total place values there are 335, which is 5 x **67**, and the total place values of the first two verses are 938, or 2 x **7** x **67**, having 77^{23} letters. If we add the word totals of each phrase, the 1st and 2nd equal 3 x 937, the 1st and 3rd equal **17** x 123, and the 2nd and 3rd equal 7^2 x 48. The digits of the prime number 7541 that represents both verses' values again equal **17**.

From there we can get into far more detail, such as adding the 'place values' to the 'word values' of verse two equals 13^2 x **19**, but let us move on to the last verse in John and pick out the prominent features there.

John 21:25 has 23 words whose values equal 8891 (**17** x 523 and sum of digits 2 x **13**) and 104 letters (2^3 x **13**) whose place values equal 1084 (2^2 x 271 and sum of digits **13**). The first half of the verse has 14 (**2** x **7**) words whose values equal 3691 (*prime*) and whose place values equal 539 (7^2 x **19** and sum of digits **17**). These 14 words have 56 (2^3 x **7**) letters. The second half of the verse has 9 (3^2) words of 48 (2^4 x **3**) letters. Their value is 5200 (2^4 x 5^2 x **13**) and their place value is 545 (5 x **109**).

---

23 Note that the 77th Star Number (Appendix III) 35113 equals **13** x **37** x **73**.

There are features throughout, such as the first two words of the first phrase having a place value of **73**, the first two words of the second phrase having a place value of 2^4 x **7** and a word value of **13** x 100, but let us move on again, taking with us the most prominent features. We currently have in our repertoire of 'John' numbers, **3, 7, 13, 17, 19, 31, 37, 67, 73,** and **109**. There are uses of **5, 23, 47, 137,** and **147**; but nowhere near as frequent. Note that by normal distribution (if this were not Scripture) we should also be seeing a corresponding frequency of the other primes **11, 29, 41, 43, 53,** etc., but we are not. In other passages **11** is very prominent; but we are in John now, and it is used sparingly.

Let us begin with what Panin would call the *features*. John 3:16 has 25 (5^2) words and **109** letters (one letter, the final α of ἀλλ' is 'elided', or left out like English does with contractions; if counted, there would be 110, which is **37 + 73**... but the text properly has **109**). These 25 words are in four groups, the first having **7** words. Their place values are 1328 (2^4 x 83) and their word values equal **13,698** (117^2, as well as $(7 + 37 + 73)^2$ and sum of digits 3^3). The place values added to the word values is **15,000 + 17**. Adding in the number of words gives us **15,042**, which is 2 x 3 x **23** x **109**. Adding in the number of letters gives us **15,151** which is **109** x 139, the sum of the digits of both 15,151 and 139 being **13**.

The first of the four phrases has **7** words of 30 letters whose place values equal 368 (2^4 x **23** and sum of digits **17**) which is also the second phrase's place values (361) + **7**. Its word total is 3453 (3 x 1151). The first word is the **triangular pyramid number 1771** (see Appendix III) minus one. and the last three words are 1224; **35^2** minus one. This theme of enormously difficult numbers to find, plus or minus one, actually turns out to be an indication of what is going on. When a number is within *one* of a very significant figure, the message is to note it and keep looking rather than stop there.

The second of the four phrases has 6 words and 28 (2^2 x **7**) letters whose place values equal 361 (**19^2**). Its word total is 3855 (3 x 5 x 257 or (2^8 + 1) x 15) and sum of its digits being **3** x **7**. The place values of 361 plus the word values of 3855 equal 4216 (2^3 x **17** x **31**) and sum of its digits being **13**. The first five words have the value of 2971, which is **54** x **54** + **54** + 1; 54 is 2 x 3^3. The last five words have the value of 2550, which is **50** x **50** + **50**. The two phrases *the Son* and *the only begotten* have the values of 950 and 716 respectively, which add up to 1666 (2 x 7^2 x **17**).

The first two phrases together have **13** words that have the place values of 729, which is 3^6 or 9^3, having 58 (2 x 29) letters. Their word value is 7308 (2^2 x 3^2 x **7** x **29**), and when added to their place values equals 8037 (**3** x **19** x **47**).

The third phrase has 8 (2^3) words that have the place values of **399** (3 x **7** x **19**) and 33 letters. The word value is 3841 (**23** x 167 or **61^2** + 120 which when added to the **33** letters equals 3872 (2 x **13** x 149). The first two words equal 342 (7^3 - 1) and the phrase *on him* equals 1036 (2^2 x **7** x **37**). Likewise the phrase *should not perish* equals 548 (2^2 x **137**) with sum of its digits being **17**.

The fourth phrase has 4 (2^2) words that have place values of **200** (2^3 x 5^2) and 18 letters. The word value is 2540 (2^2 x 5 x **127**), the last **3** words have the value of 2479 (**37** x **67**), and the last two words have the value of 1856 (2^6 x **29**).

The last two phrases together have 12 words that have the place values of 599 (*prime*) and **51** (3 x **17**) letters. The first and ninth words both have the value of **61**, which prime number is the main key to Psalm 119. They have the word value of 6381 (3^2 x 709).

The fourth phrase's value of 2470 (sum of digits **13**) is the **19**[th] square pyramid number, and 2470 + **17** = 2485 = (950 *the son* + 716 *the only-begotten* + 821 *him*) the **3** references to Jesus in the verse. The five verbs in the verse equal 377 (**13** x **29** and sum of digits **17**). The entire verse of John 3:16 (**13,689**) added to John 1:1 (**3627**) equals **17,316** (2^2 x 3^2 x **13** x **37**).

So having laid out these features, we can conclude that there is indeed something very significant going on in John 3:16, and we can also conclude that it has something to do with the book as a whole. The question now becomes, *What is it?*

For the answer to this, we look at what shape it makes. The verse has four sections and refers to salvation that goes out in all (four) directions for *whosoever believes in him.* If we were to construct a four-sided pyramid with spheres, it would look something like this:

This pyramid has five layers: the top has 1 sphere, the next layer down has 4, the next 9, the next 16, and the bottom 25. Altogether there are 55 spheres. Now we look over the data in our *features* and notice that the number **17** (meaning *Creation*) appears far more frequently than could be expected by happenstance alone. There are two aspects of what God is doing about his creation in John 3:16: God's is about loving the world and giving his Son, and ours is about believing in him and receiving life. These **2** aspects of **17** added together equal **34**. We note also that the verse's total of **13,689** is almost exactly the number of spheres in a square pyramid **13,685** which is **34** (2 x **17**) layers high. In fact, there are precisely **4** spheres left over, which suggests the following picture:

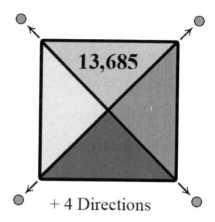

+ 4 Directions

And this square pyramid of **13,685** is equal to the **33ʳᵈ** (6545) and **34ᵗʰ** (7140) triangular pyramids added together. So the geometric message in John 3:16 would be that the gospel goes out in all directions from a structure that is precise down to the last letter.

The first and last verse also equal the **33ʳᵈ** square pyramid (12,529)+11, and when added to John 3:16 + **7**, equals the **34ᵗʰ** octahedral number (26,207); yet this is a good place to stop our journey for now. Note that we did not ignore the numbers we found that were not in the list of prominent ones. Each of these is a clue to another verse and a new idea... again, every scripture is connected to every other scripture, and the truths we find in the plain meaning of the passages parallel the numbers perfectly.

Appendix I

John 1 : 1—2

18	56	20	15	62	**(171**, 15 letters)
5 13	1 17 22 7 9	7 13	15	11 15 3 15 18	3^2 x 19

Ε ν α ρ χ η ι η ν ὁ λ ο γ ο ς, **(1275**, 5 words)

5 50	1 100 600 8 10	8 50	70	30 70 3 70 200	3 x 5^2 x 17
55	719	58	70	373	
in	origin, *beginning*	was	the	word	

20	15	62	20	64	47	41	**(269**, 22 letters)
10 1 9	15	11 15 3 15 18	7 13	16 17 15 18	19 15 13	8 5 15 13	*Prime*

κ α ι ὁ λ ο γ ο ς η ν π ρ ο ς τ ο ν Θ ε ο ν, **(1536**, 7 words)

20 1 10	70	30 70 3 70 200	8 50	80 100 70 200	300 70 50	9 5 70 50	2^9 x 3
31	70	373	58	450	420	134	
and	the	word	was	with	the	God	

20	46	20	15	62	**(163**, 15 letters total)
10 1 9	8 5 15 18	7 13	15	11 15 3 15 18	*Prime*

κ α ι Θ ε ο ς η ν ὁ λ ο γ ο ς. **(816**, 5 words)

20 1 10	9 5 70 200	8 50	70	30 70 3 70 200	2^4 x 3 x 17
31	284	58	70	373	
and	God	was	the	word	

(First Verse place values: **603**; 52 letters)
3^2 x 67; 4 x 13
(First Verse word values: **3,627**; 17 words)
3^2 x 13 x 31

87	20	18	56	66	47	41
15 20 19 15 18	7 13	5 13	1 17 22 7 9	16 17 15 18	19 15 13	8 5 15 13

Ο ὐ τ ο ς η ν ε ν α ρ χ η ι π ρ ο ς τ ο ν Θ ε ο ν

70 400 300 70 200	8 50	5 50	1 100 600 8 10	80 100 70 200	300 70 50	9 5 70 50
1040	58	55	719	450	420	134
This	was	in	original, *beginning*	with	the	God

(Second verse place values: **335** (5 x 67); 25 (5^2) letters)
(Second verse word values: **2876** (2^2 x 719); 6 words)

(First two verses place values: **938** (2 x 7 x 67); 77 (7 x 11) letters)
(First two verses word values: **6503** (7 x 929); 23 words)

(First Verse with Place Values Added = 4230 (2 x 3^2 x 5 x 47))
4230 + 17 words = **4247** (31 x 137)   **4247** + 52 letters = **4299** (3 x 1433)

(Second Verse with Place Values Added = 3211 (13^2 x 19))
3211 + 6 words = **3217** (*Prime*)   **3217** + 25 letters = **3242** (2 x 1621)

(Both Verses with Place Values Added = 7441 (7 x 1063))
7441 + 23 words = **7464** (2^3 x 3 x 311)   **7464** + 77 letters = **7541** (*Prime*)

Appendix II

John 21 : 25

64	9	20	24	54	1
5 18 19 9 13	4 5	10 1 9	1 11 11 1	16 15 11 11 1	1
Ε σ τ ι ν	δ ε	κ α ι	α λ λ α	π ο λ λ α	ἁ
5 200 300 10 50	4 5	20 1 10	1 30 30 1	80 70 30 30 1	1
565	**9**	**31**	**62**	**211**	**1**
is	yet	and	others	many	as

88	15	87	43	19
5 16 15 9 7 18 5 13	15	9 7 18 15 20 18	1 19 9 13 1	5 1 13
ε π ο ι η σ ε ν	ὁ	Ι η σ ο υ ς,	ἅ τ ι ν α	ε α ν
5 80 70 10 8 200 5 50	70	10 8 200 70 400 200	1 300 10 50 1	5 1 50
428	**70**	**888**	**362**	**56**
does	the	Jesus	which-any	if-ever

78	19	18	(First half place values: **539**, 56 letters total)
3 17 1 21 7 19 1 9	10 1 8	5 13	7^2 x 11, 2^3 x 7
γ ρ α φ η τ α ι	κ α θ᾽	ἓ ν,	(**First half** word values: **3691**, 14 words)
3 100 1 500 8 300 1 10	20 1 9	5 50	*Prime*, 2 x 7
923	**30**	**55**	
may be *be*ing written	according to	one	

44	68	46	47	83
15 20 4 5	1 20 19 15 13	15 9 12 1 9	19 15 13	10 15 18 12 15 13
ο υ δ ε	α υ τ ο ν	ο ι μ α ι	τ ο ν	κ ο σ μ ο ν
70 400 4 5	1 400 300 70 50	70 10 40 1 10	300 70 50	20 70 200 40 70 50
479	**821**	**131**	**420**	**450**
not yet, *not even*	same	I-am-surmising	the	world

115	20	88	34
22 24 17 7 18 5 9 13	19 1	3 17 1 21 15 12 5 13 1	2 9 2 11 9 1
χ ω ρ η σ ε ι ν	τ α	γ ρ α φ ο μ ε ν α	β ι β λ ι α.
600 800 100 8 200 5 10 50	300 1	3 100 1 500 70 40 5 50 1	2 10 2 30 10 1
1773	**301**	**770**	**55**
to-space, *contain*	the	*be*ing-written	books

(**Second half** place values: **545** (5 x 109);   48 letters)
(**Second half** word values: **5200** (2^4 x 5^2 x 13);   9 (3^2) words)

(**Whole verse** place values: **1084** (2^2 x 271);   104 (2^3 x 13) letters)
(**Whole verse** word values: **8891** (17 x 523);   23 words)
Whole Verse with Place Values Added = 1084 + 8891 = 9975 (3 x 5^2 x 7 x 19)
9975 + 23 words = **9998** (2 x 4999)   **9998** + 104 letters = **10,102** (2 x 5051)

First and Last Verses of John place values = **603 +1084 = 1687** (7 x 241); 156 letters
First and Last Verses of John word values = **3627 + 8891 = 12,518** (2 x 11 x 569)

First and Last Verses with Place Values Added = 14,205 (3 x 5 x 947)
14,205 + 40 words = **14,245** (5 x 7 x 11 x 37), **14,245** + 156 letters = **14,361** (3 x 4787)

Appendix III

2- and 3-Dimensional Numbers

These lists are a quick reference for those who wish to determine if a certain number has an obvious geometrical shape. There are many more lists that could be added, but these lay out the most significant two-dimensional and three-dimensional shapes and solids. Note that when a number is powered higher than **3**, it loses its dimensional characteristics and become geometrically meaningless. For example, the first two phrases of John 3:16 have the cumulative place values of **729**, which is 3^6. However, 3^6 cannot be visually represented, so we recalculate the number as 9^3, which can be represented as a cube with a side of 9 units and containing 729 units thusly:

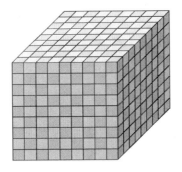

Often there is more than one way of representing the same number geometrically; the most straightforward is best. **729** could also be 27 separate Rubik's cubes, but that would be of little use in visualizing a single sum. The important thing to realize when dealing with Numerics is that <u>a visual representation organizes and clarifies even the most complex groups of numbers</u>. Furthermore, 2-dimensional (flat) geometries help *relate* different numbers, and 3-dimensional (solid) geometries help find the *conclusion* to a passage.

Note that while the lists below look huge, only **9.7%** of the numbers from 1 to 1000 are 2-dimensional shapes, and a mere **7%** are 3-dimensional solids... and most these are found under 100. Altogether, only **11%** of numbers from 100 to 1000 are geometrically significant. So when one fits, as in the case of John 3:16, definitely pay attention.

Square Numbers n x n or n²

1	4	9	16	25	36	49	64	81	100
121	144	169	196	225	256	289	324	361	400
441	484	529	576	625	676	729	784	841	900
961	1024	1089	**1156**	1225	1296	1369	1444	1521	1600
1681	1764	1849	1936	2025	2116	2209	2304	2401	2500
2601	2704	2809	2916	3025	3136	3249	3364	3481	3600
3721	3844	3969	4096	4225	4356	4489	4624	4761	4900
5041	5184	5329	5476	5625	5776	5929	6084	6241	6400
6561	6724	6889	7056	7225	7396	7569	7744	7921	8100
8281	8464	8649	8836	9025	9216	9409	9604	9801	10000
10201	10404	10609	10816	11025	11236	11449	11664	**11881**	12100
12321	12544	12769	12996	13225	13456	**13689**	13924	14161	14400
14641	14884	15129	15376	15625	15876	16129	16384	16641	16900
17161	17424	17689	17956	18225	18496	18769	19044	19321	19600
19881	20164	20449	20736	21025	21316	21609	21904	22201	22500
22801	23104	23409	23716	24025	24336	24649	24964	25281	25600
25921	26244	26569	26896	27225	27556	27889	28224	28561	28900
29241	29584	29929	30276	30625	30976	31329	31684	32041	32400
32761	33124	33489	33856	34225	34596	34969	35344	35721	36100
36481	36864	37249	37636	38025	38416	38809	39204	39601	40000
40401	40804	41209	41616	42025	42436	42849	43264	43681	44100
44521	44944	45369	45796	46225	46656	47089	47524	47961	48400
48841	49284	49729	50176	50625	51076	51529	51984	52441	52900
53361	53824	54289	54756	55225	55696	56169	56644	57121	57600
58081	58564	59049	59536	60025	60516	61009	61504	62001	62500
63001	63504	64009	64516	65025	65536	66049	66564	67081	67600

68121	68644	69169	69696	70225	70756	71289	71824	72361	72900
73441	73984	74529	75076	75625	76176	76729	77284	77841	78400
78961	79524	80089	80656	81225	81796	82369	82944	83521	84100
84681	85264	85849	86436	87025	87616	88209	88804	89401	90000
90601	91204	91809	92416	93025	93636	94249	94864	95481	96100
96721	97344	97969	98596	99225	99856	100489	101124	101761	102400
103041	103683	104329	104976	105625	106276	106929	107584	108241	108900
109561	110224	110889	111556	112225	112896	113569	114244	114921	115600
116281	116964	117649	118336	119025	119716	120409	121104	121801	122500
123201	123904	124609	125316	126025	126736	127449	128164	128881	129600
130321	131044	131769	132496	133225	133596	134689	135424	136161	136900
137641	138384	139129	139876	140625	141376	142129	142884	143641	144400
145161	145924	146689	147456	148225	148996	149769	150544	151321	152100
152881	153664	154449	155236	156025	156816	157609	158404	159201	160000
160801	161604	162409	163216	164025	164836	165649	166464	167281	168100
168921	169744	170569	171396	172225	173056	173889	174724	175561	176400
177241	178084	178929	179776	180625	181476	182329	183184	184041	184900
185761	186624	187489	188356	189225	190096	190969	191844	192721	193600
194481	195364	196249	197136	198025	198916	199809	200704	201601	202500
203401	204304	205209	206116	207025	207936	208849	209764	210681	211600
212521	213444	214369	215296	216225	217156	218089	219024	219961	220900
221841	222784	223729	224676	225625	226576	227529	228484	229441	230400
231361	232324	233289	234256	235225	236196	237169	238144	239121	240100
241081	242064	243049	244036	245025	246016	247009	248004	249001	250000
251001	252004	253009	254016	255025	256036	257049	258064	259081	260100
261121	262144	263169	264196	265225	266256	267289	268324	269361	270400
271441	272484	273529	274576	275625	276676	277729	278784	279841	280900
281961	283024	284089	285156	286225	287296	288369	289444	290521	291600
292681	293764	294849	295936	297025	298116	299209	300304	301401	302500
303601	304704	305809	306916	308025	309136	310249	311364	312481	313600
314721	315844	316969	318096	319225	320356	321489	322624	323761	324900
326041	327184	328329	329476	330625	331776	332929	334084	335241	336400
337561	338724	339889	341056	342225	343396	344569	345744	346921	348100
349281	350464	351649	352836	354025	355216	356409	357604	358801	360000

Triangle Numbers $\quad \dfrac{n\,(n+1)}{2}$

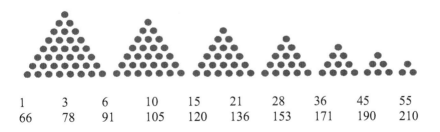

| 1 | 3 | 6 | 10 | 15 | 21 | 28 | 36 | 45 | 55 |
| 66 | 78 | 91 | 105 | 120 | 136 | 153 | 171 | 190 | 210 |

231	**253**	276	300	325	351	378	406	435	465
496	528	561	595	630	666	**703**	741	780	820
861	903	946	990	1035	1081	1128	1176	1225	1275
1326	1378	1431	1485	1540	1596	1653	1711	1770	1830
1891	1953	2016	2080	2145	2211	2278	2346	2415	2485
2556	2628	**2701**	2775	2850	2926	**3003**	3081	3160	3240
3321	3403	3486	3570	3655	3741	3828	3916	4005	4095
4186	4278	4371	4465	4560	4656	4753	4851	4950	5050
5151	5253	5356	5460	5565	5671	5778	5886	**5995**	6105
6216	6328	6441	6555	6670	6786	6903	7021	7140	7260
7381	7503	7626	7750	7875	8001	8128	8256	8385	8515
8646	8778	8911	9045	9180	9316	9453	9591	9730	9870
10011	10153	10296	10440	10585	10731	10878	11026	11175	11325
11476	11628	11781	11935	12090	12246	12403	12561	12720	12880
13041	13203	13366	13530	13695	13861	14028	14196	14365	14535
14706	14878	15051	15225	15400	15576	15753	15931	16110	16290
16471	16653	16836	17020	17205	17391	17578	17766	17955	18145
18336	18528	18721	18915	19110	19306	19503	19701	19900	20100
20301	20503	20706	20910	21115	21321	21528	21736	21945	22155
22366	22578	22791	23005	23220	23436	23653	23871	24090	24310
24531	24753	24976	25200	25425	25651	25878	26106	26335	26565
26796	27028	27261	27495	27730	27966	28203	28441	28680	28920
29161	29403	29646	29890	30135	30381	30628	30876	31125	31375
31626	31878	32131	32385	32640	32896	33153	33411	33670	33930
34191	34453	34716	34980	35245	35511	35778	36046	36315	36585
36856	37128	37401	37675	37950	38226	38503	38781	39060	39340
39621	39903	40186	40470	40755	41041	41328	41616	41905	42195
42486	42778	43071	43365	43660	43956	44253	44551	44850	45150
45451	45753	46056	46360	46665	46971	47278	47586	47895	48205
48516	48828	**49141**	49455	49770	50086	50403	50721	51040	51360
51681	52003	52326	52650	52975	53301	53628	53956	54285	54615
54946	55278	55611	55945	56280	56616	56953	57291	57630	57970
58311	58653	58996	59340	59685	60031	60378	60726	61075	61425
61776	62128	62481	62835	63190	63546	63903	64261	64620	64980
65341	65703	66066	66430	66795	67161	67528	67896	68265	68635
69006	69378	69751	70125	70500	70876	71253	71631	72010	72390
72771	73153	73536	73920	74305	74691	75078	75466	75855	76245
76636	77028	77421	77814	78210	78606	79003	79401	79800	80200
80601	81003	81406	81810	82215	82621	83028	83436	83845	84255
84666	85078	85491	85905	86320	86736	87153	87571	87990	88410
88831	89253	89676	90100	90525	90951	91378	91806	92235	92665
96096	93528	93961	94395	94830	95266	95703	96141	96580	97020
97461	97903	98346	98790	99235	99681	100128	100576	101025	101475
101926	102378	102831	103285	103740	104196	104653	105111	105570	106030

Hexagon Numbers   (3 x Side) (Side - 1) + 1

1	7	19	**37**	61	91	127	169	217	271
331	397	469	547	631	721	817	919	1027	1141
1261	1387	1519	1657	1801	1951	2107	2269	2437	2611
2791	2977	3169	3367	3571	3781	**3997**	4219	4447	4681
4921	5167	5419	5677	5941	6211	6487	6769	7057	7351
7651	7957	8269	8587	8911	9241	9577	9919	10267	10621
10981	11347	11719	12097	12481	12871	13267	13669	14077	14491
14911	15337	**15769**	16207	16651	17101	17557	18019	18487	18961
19441	19927	20419	20917	21421	21931	22447	22969	23497	24031
24571	25117	25669	26227	26791	27361	27937	28519	29107	29701
30301	30907	31519	32137	32761	33391	34027	34669	35317	35971
36631	37297	37969	38647	39331	40021	40717	41419	42127	42841
43561	44287	45019	45757	46501	47251	48007	48769	49537	50311
51091	51877	52669	53467	54271	55081	55897	56719	57547	58381
59221	60067	60919	61777	62641	63511	64387	65269	66157	67051
67951	68857	69769	70687	71611	72541	73477	74419	75367	76321
77281	78247	79219	80197	81181	82171	83167	84169	85177	86191
87211	88237	89269	90307	91351	92401	93457	94519	95587	96661
97741	98827	99919	101017	102121	103321	104347	105469	106597	107731
108827	110017	111169	112327	113491	114661	115837	117019	118207	119401
120601	121807	123019	124237	125461	126691	127927	129169	130417	131671
132931	134197	135469	136747	138031	139321	140617	141919	143227	144541
145861	147187	148519	149857	151201	152551	153907	155269	156637	158011
159391	160777	162169	163567	164971	166381	167797	169219	170647	172081
173521	174967	176419	177877	179341	180811	182287	183769	185257	186751
188251	189757	191269	192787	194311	195841	197377	198919	200467	202021
203581	205147	206719	208297	209881	211471	213067	214669	216277	217891
219511	221137	222769	224407	226051	227701	229357	231019	232687	234361
236041	237727	239419	241117	242821	244531	246247	247969	249697	251431
253171	254917	256669	258427	260191	261961	263737	265519	267307	269101
270901	272707	274519	276337	278161	279991	281827	283669	285517	287371
289231	291097	292969	294847	296731	298621	300517	302419	304327	306241
308161	310087	312019	313957	315901	317851	319807	321769	323737	325711
327691	329677	331669	333667	335671	337681	339697	341719	343747	345781
347821	349867	351919	353977	356041	358111	360187	362269	364357	366451

(**37** is the only Hexagon Number under 1000 that is also a Star Number.)

__Star Numbers__ (6 x Side of point including gully) x (Side - 1) + 1, or

$$6n(n-1)+1$$

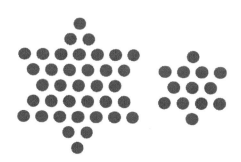

1	13	**37**	**73**	**121**	181	**253**	337	433	541
661	37793	937	1093	1261	1441	1633	1837	2053	2281
2521	2773	3037	3313	3601	3901	4213	4537	4873	5221
5581	5953	6337	6733	7141	7561	7993	8437	8893	9361
9841	10333	10837	11353	11881	12421	12973	13537	14113	14701
15301	15913	16537	17173	17821	18481	19153	19837	20533	21241
21961	22693	23437	24193	24961	25741	26533	27337	28153	28981
29821	30673	31537	32413	33301	34201	**35113**	36037	36973	37921
38881	39853	40837	41833	42841	43861	44893	45937	46993	48061
49141	50233	51337	52453	53581	54721	55873	57037	58213	59401
60601	61813	63037	64273	65521	66781	68053	69337	70633	71941
73261	74593	75937	77293	78661	80041	81443	82837	84253	85681
87121	88573	90037	91513	93001	94501	96013	97537	99073	100621
102181	103753	105337	106933	108541	110161	111793	113437	115093	116761
118441	120133	121837	123553	125281	127021	127773	130537	132313	134101
135901	137713	139537	141373	143221	145081	146953	148837	150733	152641
154561	156493	158437	160393	162361	164341	166333	168337	170353	172381
174421	176473	178537	180613	182701	184801	186913	189037	191173	193321
195481	197653	199837	202033	204241	206461	208693	210937	213193	215461
217741	220033	222337	224653	226981	229321	231673	234037	236413	238801
241201	243613	246037	248473	250921	253381	255853	258337	260833	263341
265861	268393	270937	273493	276061	278641	281233	283837	286453	289081
291721	294373	297037	299713	302401	305101	307813	310537	313273	316021
318781	321553	324337	327133	329941	332761	335593	338437	341293	344161
347041	249933	352837	355753	358681	361621	364573	367537	370513	373501

Hexahedral (Cube) Numbers   n x n x n   or   n³

1	8	27	64	125	216	343	512	729	1000
1331	1728	2197	2744	3375	4096	4913	5832	6859	8000
9261	10648	12167	13824	15625	17576	19683	21952	24389	27000
29791	32768	35937	39304	42875	46656	50653	54872	59319	64000
68921	74088	79507	85184	91125	97336	103823	110592	117649	125000
132651	140608	148877	157464	166375	175616	185193	195112	205379	216000
226981	238328	250047	262144	274625	287496	300763	314432	328509	343000
357911	373248	389017	405224	421875	438976	456533	474552	493039	512000

Triangle Pyramid (Tetrahedral) Numbers $\dfrac{n\,(n+1)\,(n+2)}{6}$

1	4	10	20	35	56	84	120	165	220
286	364	455	560	680	816	969	1140	1330	1540
1771	2024	2300	2600	2925	3276	3654	4060	4495	4960
5456	5984	**6545**	**7140**	7770	8436	9139	9880	10660	11480
12341	13244	14190	15180	16215	17296	18424	19600	20825	22100
23426	24804	26235	27720	29260	30856	32509	34220	35990	37820
39711	41664	43680	45760	47905	50116	52394	54740	57155	59640

62196	64824	67525	70300	73150	76076	79079	82160	85320	88560
91881	95284	98770	102340	105995	109736	113564	117480	121485	125580
129766	134044	138415	142880	147440	152096	156849	161700	166650	171700
176851	182104	187460	192920	198485	204156	209934	215820	221815	227920
234136	240464	246905	253460	260130	266916	273819	280840	287980	297660
302621	310124	317750	325500	333375	341376	349504	357760	366145	374660

Two consecutive Triangle Pyramid Numbers make a Square Pyramid Number.

Square Pyramid Numbers $\dfrac{n\,(n+1)\,(2n+1)}{6}$

1	5	14	30	55	91	140	204	285	385
506	650	819	1015	1240	1496	1785	2109	**2470**	2870
3311	3795	4324	4900	5525	6201	6930	7714	8555	9455
10416	11440	12529	**13685**	14910	16206	17575	19019	20540	22140
23821	25585	27434	29370	31395	33511	35720	38024	40425	42925
45526	48230	51039	53955	56980	60116	63365	66729	70210	73810
77531	81375	85344	89440	93665	98021	102510	107134	111895	116795
121836	127020	132349	137825	143450	149226	155155	161239	167480	173880
180441	187165	194054	201110	208335	215731	223300	231044	238965	247065
255346	263810	272459	281295	290320	299536	308945	318549	328350	338350
348551	358955	369564	380380	391405	402641	414090	425754	437635	449735

Octahedral Numbers $\dfrac{n(2n^2 + 1)}{3}$

1	6	19	44	85	146	231	344	489	670
891	1156	1469	1834	2255	2736	3281	3894	4579	5340
6181	7106	8119	9224	10425	11726	13131	14644	16269	18010
19871	21856	23969	26214	28595	31116	33781	36594	39559	42680
45961	49406	53019	56804	60765	64906	69231	73744	78449	83350
88451	93756	99269	104994	110935	117096	123481	130094	136939	144020
151341	158906	166719	174784	183105	191686	200531	209644	219029	228690
238631	248856	259369	270174	281275	292676	304381	316394	328719	341360
354321	367606	381219	395164	409445	424066	439031	454344	470009	486030

Centered Octahedral Numbers $\dfrac{(2n + 1)(2n^2 + 2n + 3)}{3}$

1	7	25	63	129	231	377	575	833	1159
1561	2047	2625	3303	4089	4991	6017	7175	8473	9919
11521	13287	15225	17343	19649	22151	24857	27775	30913	34279
37881	41727	45825	50183	54809	59711	64897	70375	76153	82239
88641	95367	102425	109823	117569	125671	134137	142975	152193	161799
171801	182207	193025	204263	215929	228031	240577	253575	267033	280959
295361	310247	325625	341503	357889	374791	392217	410175	428673	447719

Icosahedral Numbers

$$\frac{n(5n^2 - 5n + 2)}{2}$$

1	12	48	124	255	456	742	1128	1629	2260
3036	3972	5083	6384	7890	9616	11577	13788	16264	19020
22071	25432	29118	33144	37525	42276	47412	52948	58899	65280
72106	79392	87153	95404	104160	113436	123247	133608	144534	156040
168141	180852	194188	208164	222795	238096	254082	270768	288169	306300
325176	344812	365223	386424	408430	431256	454917	479428	504804	531060

Centered Icosahedral Numbers

$$\frac{(5n^2 + 5n + 3)}{3}$$

1	13	55	147	309	561	923	1415	2057	2869
3871	5083	6525	8217	10179	12431	14993	17885	21127	24739
28741	33153	37995	43287	49049	55301	62063	69355	77197	85609
94611	104223	114465	125357	136919	149171	162133	175825	190267	205479
221481	238293	255935	274427	293789	314041	335203	357295	380337	404349

350

Dodecahedral Numbers $\dfrac{n\,(3n-1)\,(3n-2)}{2}$

1	20	84	220	455	816	1330	2024	2925	4060
5456	7140	9139	11480	14190	17296	20825	24804	29260	34220
39711	45760	52394	59640	67525	76076	85320	95284	105995	117480
129766	142880	156849	171700	187460	204156	221815	240464	260130	280840
302621	325500	349504	374660	400995	428536	457310	487344	518665	551300

Centered Dodecahedral Numbers

$$(2n + 1)\,(5n^2 + 5n + 1)$$

1	33	155	427	909	1661	2743	4215	6137	8569
11571	15203	19525	24597	30479	37231	44913	53585	63307	74139
86141	99373	113895	129767	147049	165801	186083	207955	231477	256709
283711	312543	343265	375937	410619	447371				

All 2-Dimensional Numbers from 1 to 1000
(9.7% of numbers)

1	3	4	6	7	9	10	13	15	16
19	21	25	28	36	37	45	49	55	61
64	66	73	78	81	91	100	105	120	121
127	136	144	153	169	171	181	190	196	210
217	225	231	253	256	271	276	289	300	324
325	331	337	351	361	378	397	400	406	433
435	441	465	469	484	496	528	529	541	547
561	576	595	625	630	631	661	666	676	703
721	729	741	780	784	793	817	820	841	861
900	903	919	937	946	961	990			

All 3-Dimensional Numbers from 1 to 1000
(7% of numbers)

1	4	5	6	7	8	10	12	13	14
19	20	25	27	30	33	35	44	48	55
56	63	64	84	85	91	120	124	125	129
140	146	147	155	165	204	216	220	231	255
285	286	309	343	344	364	377	385	427	455
456	489	506	512	560	561	575	650	670	680
729	742	816	819	833	891	909	923	969	1000

45890447R10196

Made in the USA
Charleston, SC
05 September 2015